THE BOOK OF
UNUSUAL QUOTATIONS

THE BOOK OF
UNUSUAL QUOTATIONS

Selected and edited by

RUDOLF FLESCH

CASSELL · LONDON

CASSELL & COMPANY LTD
35 Red Lion Square, London, W.C.1
and at
210 Queen Street, Melbourne; 26/30 Clarence Street,
Sydney; 24 Wyndham Street, Auckland; 1068 Broad-
view Avenue, Toronto 6; P.O. Box 275, Cape Town;
P.O. Box 11190, Johannesburg; Haroon Chambers,
South Napier Road, Karachi; 13/14 Ajmeri Gate
Extension, New Delhi 1; 15 Graham Road, Ballard
Estate, Bombay 1; 17 Chittaranjan Avenue, Calcutta
13; P.O. Box 23, Colombo; Denmark House (3rd
Floor), 84 Ampang Road, Kuala Lumpur; Avenida 9
de Julho 1138 São Paulo; Galeria Güemes, Escritorio
454/59 Florida 165, Buenos Aires; Marne 5b, Mexico
5, D.F.; Sanshin Building, 6 Kanda Mitoschiro-cho,
Chiyodaku, Tokyo; 97 rue Monge, Paris 5e; 25 Ny
Strandvej, Espergaerde, Copenhagen; Beulingstraat
2, Amsterdam-C; Bederstrasse 51, Zürich 2

FIRST PUBLISHED 1959

PRINTED AND BOUND IN ENGLAND BY
HAZELL WATSON AND VINEY LTD
AYLESBURY AND SLOUGH
F.958

PREFACE

Everybody has a hobby. Mine has been, for many years, the extremely mild and innocuous one of collecting books I like to read and reread. This doesn't make me a book collector in any sense of the word; but it *has* filled quite a few shelves in our house with a decidedly odd collection of books— old and new, hardbound and paperback, illustrated or miserably printed. Among the items that have somehow accumulated are the notebooks of Friedrich Nietzsche, a dozen or so translations of Lao-tse, the conversations of William Hazlitt with James Northcote, the collected aphorisms of the Viennese writer Karl Kraus, the complete essays of Montaigne, the letters of Goethe's mother, practically all the essays of Chesterton, the speeches of Mark Twain, almost all the works of Robert Benchley, and a hopelessly incomplete set of the unabridged *Arabian Nights*.

What does all this add up to? Obviously nothing in particular, except the image of a magpie sort of omnivorous reader. Or so I thought—until I looked at my bookshelves one day and was hit by the thought that there was, after all, a common denominator; that this was, if it was anything, a collection of paradoxes and unusual ideas. Chesterton was a "prince of paradoxes"; so was Lao-tse; so was Montaigne; so was Hazlitt; so was Oscar Wilde; so was Samuel Butler; so was Karl Kraus; so was Nietzsche. Why not extract these paradoxes and striking ideas and make a book out of them?

And that, very simply, was the beginning of this book. Of course, after I got to work on it, I went beyond my own four walls and did a good deal of library reading and excerpting. But even then I didn't do anything that can properly be called research; rather, I proceeded by the methodless method of 'determined browsing'—rummaging among the kind of books that I might have added to my library if I had found them in a cheap edition in a secondhand bookshop.

In other words, any resemblance between this book and a standard collection of 'familiar' or 'famous' quotations is purely coincidental. Or rather this book is, properly speaking, the exact opposite of a standard collection of quotations. That sort of book is primarily an aid for the person who loves to quote—and to quote *right*. Nobody's memory is perfect, and nobody knows all the exact words and exact sources of all the verbal scraps that fill his mind. So there are Bartlett, and Stevenson, and the *Oxford Dictionary of Quotations*, and half a dozen others—and if misquotation is still a common failing, it certainly isn't the fault of the makers of reference books.

This book isn't meant to compete with those excellent reference tools. On the contrary, it begins, so to speak, where Bartlett leaves off. It is meant for the person whose mind *doesn't* deliver up a suitable, verifiable quotation whenever such things as *travel* or *solitude* or *school* or *family* are mentioned:

nothing comes to *his* mind but a few endlessly repeated old saws that he wouldn't think of quoting seriously in front of a modern audience. What he wants, and needs, is something different, something that will stimulate people's thinking—and perhaps stimulate his own thinking too, as he is preparing his article or speech.

That's what this book is trying to do. It gives you about six thousand 'unusual' quotations—quotations that will be unfamiliar to you, to your audience, to almost everybody. Of course, that doesn't mean that every single quotation in this book will be unfamiliar to every single reader or listener—but it does mean that hardly anything in this book will strike anyone as hackneyed or trite.

You will find three types of 'unusual' quotations in this book. First, there is the genuine paradox—the idea that is exactly the opposite of the accepted, 'normal' way of thinking. Possibly the best example, and the most paradoxical paradox in this book is Oscar Wilde's 'The imagination imitates; it is the critical spirit that creates.' At first glance, of course, this seems complete nonsense, and you may want to let it go at that. On the other hand, it may start you thinking about what Oscar Wilde could possibly have meant, and act as an enormously powerful mental stimulant.

Second, there is what might be called the semi-paradox—an old idea seen from a new angle, a striking reformulation of a well-known truth. Take, for example, this maxim by Henry S. Haskins, the wise old author of the anonymously published *Meditations in Wall Street*: 'The man who has a dogmatic creed has more time left for his business.' This isn't as perverse and upsetting as Oscar Wilde's dictum about the critical spirit, but it certainly is unusual too. It makes you think, and it will make the people think who read you or listen to you.

Third, there is the unusual quotation that fits neither of these two categories—the oddity, the striking witticism, the ordinary idea coming from an extraordinary source. For instance, there is 'A woman is always buying something' by—of all people—Ovid; or 'Every family has prize kin' by the sage of Topeka, Kansas, E. W. Howe; or 'As soon as Herr and Frau Mueller get to heaven, they'll ask for picture postcards' by the German poet Christian Morgenstern.

And then, there are *quite* unclassifiable items—Samuel Pepys on the best night's sleep he ever had, and Eugène Delacroix on why all pictures look grey, and Thomas G. Masaryk's definition of determinism, and Lin Yutang's catalogue of Chinese leisure-time activities. I have no excuse and no rationale to offer. These things struck me as quotable, and I expect other people will find them so too.

And now, after having confessed to the highly casual origins of this book, let me be businesslike and set down in four steps.

How to Use This Book:

1. To find a quotation on a given topic, look for that topic in the alphabetical arrangement of the book itself. For example, if you want something

on painting, you will find nine quotations listed under the heading *Painting*.

2. To find further quotations, use the cross-references at the bottom of the listed quotations. For example, after the quotations listed under *Painting*, you will find cross-references to *Art, Painter, Painting and Sculpture, Picture, Raphael*. These cross-references will lead you to many additional quotations that may suit your purpose.

3. You can find still more quotations by using the AUTHOR INDEX, beginning on page 329. For example, you will find a number of pertinent quotations on painting by looking up quotations from such painters as Constable, Leonardo, van Gogh, Renoir, Cézanne, etc.

4. Finally, the book will, paradoxically, become more useful to you the more you browse in it without any immediate purpose. Inevitably, some quotations will stick in your mind and, inevitably, you will vaguely remember them when you can use them. In this case, the book will function like any other book of quotations and, with the help of the AUTHOR INDEX and the other reference features, you will easily be able to verify the exact wording and source. For example, you might, in browsing through the book, have come upon A. P. Herbert's definition of a highbrow: 'A highbrow is the kind of person who looks at a sausage and thinks of Picasso.' Suppose that some time later you want to use this quotation in reference to modern painting. You will then be able to find it again instantly, even if you remember nothing but either the last name of the author or the word *highbrow*.

R. F.

ACKNOWLEDGEMENTS

Grateful acknowledgement is made to the following for permission to reprint selections included in this book:

George Allen & Unwin Ltd. for quotations from *Unpopular Essays* and *Portraits from Memory* by Bertrand Russell.

Jonathan Cape Ltd. for quotations from *Notebooks* by Samuel Butler.

Chatto and Windus Ltd. for quotations from various works by Aldous Huxley; and from various works by Aubrey Menen.

Miss D. E. Collins and Hodder & Stoughton, Ltd. for quotations from *What I Saw in America*; Miss D. E. Collins and Methuen & Co. Ltd. for quotations from *Tremendous Trifles* by G. K. Chesterton; Miss D. E. Collins for quotations from *What's Wrong with the World* by G. K. Chesterton.

Constable and Company Ltd. for quotations from *All Trivia* by Logan Pearsall Smith; and from various works by George Santayana.

Curtis Brown Ltd. for quotations from *The Importance of Living* and *My Country and My People* by Lin Yutang; and from various works by Joyce Carey.

Crane and Company, Inc. for quotations from *Country-Town Sayings* by E. W. Howe.

J. M. Dent & Sons Ltd. for quotations from the Everyman translation of the works of Balzac; from various works by Joseph Conrad; from various works by Robert Lynd; and from the Everyman translation of *Pensées* by Pascal.

Andre Deutsch Ltd. for quotations from *Conversations with Kafka* by Janouch.

E. P. Dutton & Co., Inc. for quotations from *Conversation* by André Maurois.

Dennis Dobson for quotations from various works by Robert Benchley.

The English Universities Press Ltd. for quotations from *The Art of Living* by André Maurois.

Victor Gollancz, Ltd. for quotations from *One Man's Meat* by E. B. White.

Hamish Hamilton Ltd. for quotations from various works by James Thurber; from various works by Angela Thirkell; and from *Second Tree from the Corner* by E. B. White.

Harcourt, Brace & Company, Inc. for quotations from *Lincoln Steffens Speaking*.

Harvard University Press for quotations from *The Holmes-Pollock Correspondence* and *The Holmes-Laski Letters*.

A. M. Heath & Co. Ltd. for quotations from *Maxims of Marcel Proust* translated by Justin O'Brien.

William Heinemann Ltd. for quotations from *The Face of a Nation* by Thomas Wolfe.

Fred C. Kelly for quotations from *Life and Times of Kin Hubbard* by Fred Kelly.

Alfred A. Knopf. Inc. for quotations from *The Prophet* and *Sand and Foam* by Kahlil Gibran.

John Lane The Bodley Head Ltd. for quotations from *The Dialogues of Alfred North Whitehead*; from various works by Stephen Leacock; from *Complete Short Stories* by Saki; from various works by Anatole France; and from *Heretics* by Gilbert K. Chesterton.

Meridian Books for quotations from *The Essence of Laughter* by Charles Baudelaire, edited by Peter Quennell.

Methuen & Co. Ltd. for quotations from various works by E. V. Lucas; and from various works by A. A. Milne.

William Morrow and Company, Inc. for quotations from *Meditations in Wall Street* by Henry S. Haskins. Copyright 1940 by William Morrow and Company, Inc.

John Murray, Ltd. for quotations from various works by Freya Stark.

John Murray, Ltd. and the Trustees of the Estate of Sir Arthur Conan Doyle for quotations from *The Sherlock Holmes Stories* by Conan Doyle.

Navajivan Trust for quotations from *Selected Writings* by Ghandi.

W. W. Norton & Company, Inc. for quotations from *Letters* by Rainer Maria Rilke, translated by Greene and Norton.

Oxford University Press for quotations from *The Thoughts of Marcus Aurelius Antoninus*, translated by John Jackson, and from *The Analects of Confucius*, translated by Soothill, both from The World Classics series.

Penguin Books Ltd. for quotations from *The Imitation of Christ* by Thomas à Kempis.

A. D. Peters for quotations from various works by J. B. Priestley; and from various works by Hilaire Belloc.

G. P. Putnam's Sons for quotations from *Gravity and Grace* by Simone Weil, Copyright 1952 by G. P. Putnam's Sons.

Routledge & Kegan Paul Ltd. for quotations from *Basic Verities* by Charles Péguy.

Martin Secker & Warburg Ltd. for quotations from *Journal* by Eugène Delacroix; from *Journals* by André Gide; from *The True Believer* and *The Passionate State of Mind* by Eric Hoffer; from *The Voices of Silence* by André Malraux; and from various works by George Orwell.

The Society of Authors for quotations from various works by George Bernard Shaw.

Simon and Schuster, Inc. for quotations from *The Business of Life* by William Feather.

The Vanguard Press for quotations from *As William James Said*, edited by Elizabeth Perkins Aldrich, copyright 1942 by Henry James.

ABROAD

Your idle people, that leave their native country, and go abroad for some reason or reasons which may be derived from one of these general causes:—
> Infirmity of body,
> Imbecility of mind, or
> Inevitable necessity.
> LAURENCE STERNE

See also **Foreign, Travel.**

ABSENT

Absence extinguishes small passions and increases great ones, as the wind will blow out a candle, and blow in a fire.
LA ROCHEFOUCAULD

Presents, I often say, endear absents. CHARLES LAMB

Absentee: A person with an income who has had the forethought to remove himself from the sphere of exaction. AMBROSE BIERCE

Woman's great strength lies in being late or absent. ALAIN

Such things as an absence, the refusal of an invitation, or an unintentional coldness accomplish more than all the cosmetics and fine clothes in the world.
MARCEL PROUST

ABSENT-MINDED

Lord Dudley was one of the most absent men I think I ever met in society. One day he met me in the street, and invited me to meet myself. 'Dine with me today; dine with me, and I will get Sydney Smith to meet you.' I admitted the temptation he held out to me, but said I was engaged to meet him elsewhere. SYDNEY SMITH

ABSORBED

It is a cursed evil to any man to become so absorbed in any subject as I am in mine. CHARLES DARWIN

See also **Interest.**

ABSTAIN

In doubt if an action be just, abstain. ZOROASTER

Total abstinence is easier for me than perfect moderation.
ST. AUGUSTINE

To be afflicted by colic and to be afflicted by abstaining from oysters are two evils in the place of one.
MONTAIGNE

Abstinence is as easy to me as temperance would be difficult.
SAMUEL JOHNSON

Zoroaster said, "When in doubt, abstain," but this does not always apply. At cards, when in doubt, take the trick. JOSH BILLINGS

See also **Asceticism, Self-Denial.**

ABSTRACT

An abstract style is always bad. Your sentences should be full of stones, metals, chairs, tables, animals, men, and women. ALAIN

ABSTRACTIONS

Perhaps the efforts of the true poets, founders, religious, literatures, all ages, have been, and ever will be, our time and times to come, essentially the same—to bring people back from their present strayings and sickly abstractions, to the costless, average, divine, original concrete. WALT WHITMAN

Enthusiasm for anything other than abstractions is a sign of weakness and sickness.
CHARLES BAUDELAIRE

The pursuit of truth is just a polite name for the intellectual's favourite pastime of substituting simple and therefore false abstractions for the living complexities of reality.

ALDOUS HUXLEY

See also **Generality.**

ABSURD

It is in human nature to think wisely and to act in an absurd fashion.

ANATOLE FRANCE

Why shouldn't things be largely absurd, futile, and transitory? They are so, and we are so, and they and we go very well together.

GEORGE SANTAYANA

ACCEPT

He who doesn't accept the conditions of life sells his soul.

CHARLES BAUDELAIRE

'I accept the universe,' is reported to have been a favourite utterance of our New England transcendentalist, Margaret Fuller; and when someone repeated this phrase to Thomas Carlyle, his sardonic comment is said to have been: 'Gad! she'd better!'   WILLIAM JAMES

The truest kinship with humanity would lie in doing as humanity has always done, accepting with sportsmanlike relish the estate to which we are called, the star of our happiness, and the fortunes of the land of our birth.   G. K. CHESTERTON

Almost any event will put on a new face when received with cheerful acceptance, and no questions asked.

HENRY S. HASKINS

See also **Contentment.**

ACCIDENT

There are no accidents so unfortunate from which skilful men will not draw some advantage, nor so fortunate that foolish men will not turn them to their hurt.

LA ROCHEFOUCAULD

Sometimes there are accidents in our life the skilful extraction from which demands a little folly.

LA ROCHEFOUCAULD

There is always some accident in the best things, whether thoughts or expressions or deeds. The memorable thought, the happy expression, the admirable deed are only partly ours.   HENRY DAVID THOREAU

Accident: An inevitable occurrence due to the action of immutable natural laws.   AMBROSE BIERCE

Accidents are accidents only to ignorance.   GEORGE SANTAYANA

Accidents exist only in our heads, in our limited perceptions. They are the reflections of the limit of our knowledge.   FRANZ KAFKA

See also **Chance, Happen.**

ACCOUNTS

Coming home tonight I did go to examine my wife's accounts, and finding things that seemed somewhat doubtful I was angry, though she did make it pretty plain; but confessed that when she do miss a sum she do add something to other things to make it, and upon my being very angry she do protest she will here lay up something for herself to buy her a necklace with, which madded me and do still trouble me, for I fear she will forget by degrees the way of living cheap and under sense of want.

SAMUEL PEPYS

Keeping accounts, sir, is of no use when a man is spending his own money, and has nobody to whom he is to account. You won't eat less beef today because you have written down what it cost yesterday.
SAMUEL JOHNSON

ACCURACY

In all pointed sentences, some degree of accuracy must be sacrificed to conciseness. SAMUEL JOHNSON

After having spent years in striving to be accurate, we must spend as many more in discovering when and how to be inaccurate.
SAMUEL BUTLER

See also **Inaccuracy.**

ACHIEVEMENT

Achievement: The death of endeavour and the birth of disgust.
AMBROSE BIERCE

About all some men accomplish in life is to send a son to Harvard.
E. W. HOWE

See also **Attain, Done, Success.**

ACQUAINTANCE

Acquaintance: A degree of friendship called slight when its object is poor and obscure, and intimate when he is rich and famous.
AMBROSE BIERCE

The wisest man I have ever known once said to me: 'Nine out of every ten people improve on acquaintance'; and I have found his words true. FRANK SWINNERTON

ACTION

He who acts, spoils; he who grasps, lets slip. LAO-TSE

Nobody can become perfect by merely ceasing to act.
BHAGAVAD-GITA

Tsze-Kung asked what constituted a superior man. The Master said, 'He acts before he speaks, and afterwards speaks according to his actions.' CONFUCIUS

I expect no other result from acting than to act, and look to no far-reaching consequences or projects.
MONTAIGNE

Action makes more fortunes than caution. VAUVENARGUES

We don't have enough time to premeditate all our actions.
VAUVENARGUES

Something inherently mean in action! Even the creation of the universe disturbs my idea of the Almighty's greatness.
SAMUEL TAYLOR COLERIDGE

Action is but coarsened thought— thought become concrete, obscure, and unconscious. FRÉDÉRIC AMIEL

A man who has to be convinced to act before he acts is *not* a man of action. It's as if a tennis player before returning the ball began to question himself as to the physical and moral value of tennis. You must act just as you breathe.
GEORGES CLÉMENCEAU

Life is action and passion; therefore, it is required of a man that he should share the passion and action of his time at peril of being judged not to have lived.
OLIVER WENDELL HOLMES, JR.

Our actions are not altogether our own; they depend less upon us than upon chance. They are given to us from every hand; we do not always deserve them. ANATOLE FRANCE

Men of thought should have nothing to do with action.
OSCAR WILDE

Action, indeed, is always easy, and when presented to us in its most aggravated, because more continuous, form, which I take to be that of real industry, becomes simply the refuge of people who have nothing whatever to do. OSCAR WILDE

The basis of action is lack of imagination. It is the last resource of those who know not how to dream. OSCAR WILDE

Performance must precede volition. ALAIN

The soul of all action is blindness. He who knows, cannot act any longer. Knowing means foregoing action and renouncing passion. EGON FRIEDELL

Successful action tends to become an end in itself. ERIC HOFFER

See also **Active, Activity, Doing, Passivity, Thought and Action.**

ACTIVE

The more perfection anything has, the more active and the less passive it is; and contrariwise, the more active it is, the more perfect it becomes. SPINOZA

ACTIVITY

For most men rest is stagnation and activity madness. EPICURUS

Activity is the only road to knowledge. GEORGE BERNARD SHAW

See also **Action, Doing.**

ADAGE

Adage: Boned wisdom for weak teeth. AMBROSE BIERCE

See also **Maxims.**

ADAM

What a good thing Adam had—when he said a good thing, he knew nobody had said it before. MARK TWAIN

ADAPT

Adapt yourself to the things among which your lot has been cast and love sincerely the fellow creatures with whom destiny has ordained that you shall live. MARCUS AURELIUS

Greatness of soul consists not so much in soaring high and in pressing forward, as in knowing how to adapt and limit oneself. MONTAIGNE

Perfection seems to be nothing more than a complete adaptation to the environment; but the environment is constantly changing, so perfection can never be more than transitory. W. SOMERSET MAUGHAM

The undisciplined mind is far better adapted to the confused world in which we live today than the streamlined mind. JAMES THURBER

ADJECTIVE

As to the adjective; when in doubt, strike it out. MARK TWAIN

ADMIRATION

We always like those who admire us. LA ROCHEFOUCAULD

Admiration, like love, wears out. VAUVENARGUES

It is only an auctioneer who can equally and inpartially admire all schools of art. OSCAR WILDE

ADOPTION

It takes more trouble and as much risk to adopt a son as to get one in the ordinary way. SAMUEL BUTLER

ADVANTAGE

Next to knowing when to seize an opportunity, the most important thing in life is to know when to forego an advantage.
BENJAMIN DISRAELI

It is the greatest of all advantages to enjoy no advantage at all.
HENRY DAVID THOREAU

ADVENTURE

What a large volume of adventures may be grasped within this little span of life, by him who interests his heart in everything, and who, having eyes to see what time and chance are perpetually holding out to him as he journeyeth on his way, misses nothing he can *fairly* lay his hands on!
LAURENCE STERNE

Without adventure civilization is in full decay.
ALFRED NORTH WHITEHEAD

ADVERSITY

Adversity has ever been considered as the state in which a man most easily becomes acquainted with himself, being free from flatterers.
SAMUEL JOHNSON

When fate is adverse, a wise man can always strive for happiness and sail against the wind to attain it.
ROUSSEAU

Adversity has the same effect on a man that severe training has on the pugilist—it reduces him to his fighting weight.
JOSH BILLINGS

By trying we can easily learn to endure adversity. Another man's, I mean.
MARK TWAIN

See also **Misfortune, Success and Failure.**

ADVERTISING

He who advertises his name loses it; he who does not increase [knowledge] diminishes it; he who refuses to learn, merits extinction; and he who puts his talent to selfish use, commits spiritual suicide.
TALMUD

Advertisements contain the only truths to be relied on in a newspaper.
THOMAS JEFFERSON

If man can make himself a real master of his art [of advertising], we may say that he has learnt his trade, whatever his trade may be. Let him know how to advertise, and the rest will follow.
ANTHONY TROLLOPE

You can tell the ideals of a nation by its advertisements.
NORMAN DOUGLAS

It used to be that a fellow went on the police force after everything else failed, but today he goes in the advertising game.
KIN HUBBARD

When I had looked at the lights of Broadway by night, I said to my American friends: 'What a glorious garden of wonders this would be, to any one who was lucky enough to be unable to read.'
G. K. CHESTERTON

The advertisement is one of the most interesting and difficult of modern literary forms.
ALDOUS HUXLEY

Merchandising reached its apogee in the Lux advertisement which portrayed two articles of lingerie discussing their wearers' effluvia, for all the world like rival stamp collectors.
S. J. PERELMAN

See also **Promote.**

ADVICE

Advice: The smallest current coin.
AMBROSE BIERCE

Just as I do not ask advice, I rarely give it. If my advice is not often called for, still less is it followed. I know of no public or private business which it has corrected or bettered. MONTAIGNE

We give advice, but we cannot give the wisdom to profit by it.
LA ROCHEFOUCAULD

If a man loves to give advice, it is a sure sign that he himself wants it.
LORD HALIFAX

I give myself sometimes admirable advice, but I am incapable of taking it.
LADY MARY WORTLEY MONTAGU

Advice is offensive, because it shows us that we are known to others, as well as to ourselves.
SAMUEL JOHNSON

The advice of old age gives light without heat, like the winter sun.
VAUVENARGUES

Advice is like snow; the softer it falls, the longer it dwells upon, and the deeper it sinks into, the mind.
SAMUEL TAYLOR COLERIDGE

There are exceptions to all rules, but it seldom answers to follow the advice of an opponent.
BENJAMIN DISRAELI

Advice is a drug in the market; the supply always exceeds the demand.
JOSH BILLINGS

Before giving advice we must have secured its acceptance, or rather, have made it desired.
FRÉDÉRIC AMIEL

She generally gave herself very good advice (though she very seldom followed it). LEWIS CARROLL

To profit from good advice requires more wisdom than to give it.
JOHN CHURTON COLLINS

When people seek advice, it is too often in the hope of finding the adviser side with their second familiar self instead of their awful first self of which they know so little.
GEORGE MACDONALD

The only thing to do with good advice is to pass it on. It is never of any use to oneself. OSCAR WILDE

A bad cold wouldn't be so annoying if it weren't for the advice of our friends. KIN HUBBARD

Unasked advice is a trespass on sacred privacy.
HENRY S. HASKINS

Advice is always a confession.
ANDRÉ MAUROIS

Give me all the other advice you like, but don't tell me how to: bring up my children; train my dog; fish for trout; scramble eggs; cast my vote; select the right books; read a newspaper; keep regular; watch a football game; buy meat; eat lobster; appreciate good music; improve my disposition; relax; or prepare myself for heaven.
WILLIAM FEATHER

See also **Consultation.**

AFFAIRS

[When he was elected mayor of Bordeaux:] I am willing to take your affairs in hand, but not into my liver and lungs. MONTAIGNE

See also **Business, Office.**

AFFECTATION

All affectation is a fault.
CERVANTES

It is the absence of all affectation or even of *consciousness*, that constitutes the perfection of nature or art.
JAMES NORTHCOTE

It is a form of affectation to emphasize the fact that you do not indulge in it.   LA ROCHEFOUCAULD

See also **Insincere, Pretension.**

AFFECTION
Opinion and affection extremely differ. . . . I love apples the best of any fruit, it does not follow that I must think apples to be the best of fruit.   JOHN SELDEN

In nine cases out of ten, a woman had better show more affection than she feels.   JANE AUSTEN

See also **Love.**

AFFIRMATION
Of all forms of monotony, the monotony of affirmation is the worst.
JOSEPH JOUBERT

Man lives by affirmation even more than he does by bread.
VICTOR HUGO

See also **Yes.**

AFRAID
'The trouble is, Sancho,' said Don Quixote, 'you are so afraid that you cannot see or hear properly; for one of the effects of fear is to disturb the senses and cause things to appear other than what they are.'
CERVANTES

He who is too much afraid of being duped has lost the power of being magnanimous.   FRÉDÉRIC AMIEL

See also **Fear, Terrified.**

AGE
One of the main things, at my age [57] is to avoid strain—'pushing forward' (as you do when you are in a taxi and are getting late for an appointment).   ARNOLD BENNETT

Age will not be defied.
FRANCIS BACON

As a man advances in life he gets what is better than admiration—judgment to estimate things at their own value.   SAMUEL JOHNSON

Many a man that can't direct you to a corner drugstore will get a respectful hearing when age has further impaired his mind.
FINLEY PETER DUNNE

See also **Eighty, Fifty, Forty, Forty-Five, Forty-Six, Growing Old, Middle-Aged, Old Age, One-Hundred-and-Ten, Seventy, Seventy-Five, Sixty, Thirty-Nine, Twenty-Seven, Young, Young and Old.**

AGNOSTIC
'Of course you are quite irreligious?' 'Oh, by no means. The fashion just now is a Roman Catholic frame of mind with an agnostic conscience: you get the medieval picturesqueness of the one with the modern conveniences of the other.'
SAKI

I was much cheered on my arrival [in prison] by the warder at the gate, who had to take particulars about me. He asked my religion, and I replied 'agnostic.' He asked how to spell it, and remarked with a sigh: 'Well, there are many religions, but I suppose they all worship the same God.'
BERTRAND RUSSELL

Agnosticism is no new thing; what is new is an agnostic culture.
ANDRÉ MALRAUX

See also **Atheism.**

AGREE
When you say that you agree to a thing in principle you mean that you have not the slightest intention of carrying it out in practice.
BISMARCK

Elinor agreed with it all, for she did not think he deserved the compliment of rational opposition.

JANE AUSTEN

When people agree with me I always feel that I must be wrong.

OSCAR WILDE

AGREEABLE

I have been formed by a vast number of scenes of the most different natures, and I question any uniform education could have produced a character so agreeable.

JAMES BOSWELL

The greatest mistake is the trying to be more agreeable than you can be.

WALTER BAGEHOT

Nobody can be as agreeable as an uninvited guest.   KIN HUBBARD

See also **Disagreeable, Pleasing.**

AIN'T

Maybe ain't ain't so correct, but I notice that lots of folk who ain't using ain't ain't eatin'.

WILL ROGERS

See also **Grammar.**

ALARM CLOCK

Of all the moral luxuries known to man, there is none to surpass that which can be got from winding an alarm clock and setting it for an hour when not even a housemaid or a milkman will be stirring.

ROBERT LYND

See also **Early Rising.**

ALCOHOL

The human intellect owes its superiority over that of the lower animals in great measure to the stimulus which alcohol has given to imagination—imagination being little else than another name for illusion.   SAMUEL BUTLER

Oh, he [my brother] occasionally takes an alcoholiday.

OSCAR WILDE

See also **Drinking.**

ALL-INCLUSIVENESS

The love of all-inclusiveness is as dangerous in philosophy as in art.

GEORGE SANTAYANA

ALMS

A man's giving in alms one piece of silver in his lifetime is better for him than giving one hundred when about to die.   MOHAMMED

See also **Benevolence, Charity, Philanthropy.**

ALONE

The strongest man upon earth is he who stands most alone.

HENRIK IBSEN

I wander about those great empty streets of Boston and I never see a living creature. I could not be more alone in the Sahara.   HENRY JAMES

See also **Loneliness, Solitude.**

ALPHABET

I often think how much easier life would have been for me and how much time I should have saved if I had known the alphabet. I can never tell where I and J stand without saying G, H to myself first. I don't know whether P comes before R or after, and where T comes in has to this day remained something that I have never been able to get into my head.   W. SOMERSET MAUGHAM

AMATEUR

A man must love a thing very much if he not only practises it without any hope of fame and money, but even practises it without any hope of doing it well.

G. K. CHESTERTON

See also **Professional.**

AMBITION

Keen ambition banishes pleasure, from youth onwards, and reigns alone. VAUVENARGUES

Ambition often puts men upon doing the meanest offices; so climbing is performed in the same posture with creeping. JONATHAN SWIFT

Put personal ambition away from you, and then you will find consolation in living or in dying, whatever may happen to you.

FRÉDÉRIC AMIEL

Ambition is the last refuge of the failure. OSCAR WILDE

See also **Aspirations.**

AMERICA

It was wonderful to find America, but it would have been more wonderful to miss it. MARK TWAIN

Perhaps, after all, America never has been discovered. I myself would say that it had merely been detected. OSCAR WILDE

Of course, America had often been discovered before, but it had always been hushed up. OSCAR WILDE

The youth of America is their oldest tradition. It has been going on now for three hundred years. To hear them talk we would imagine they were in their first childhood. As far as civilization goes they are in their second. OSCAR WILDE

America is a young country with an old mentality. GEORGE SANTAYANA

I would not hesitate to say that the United States is the finest society on a grand scale that the world has thus far produced.

ALFRED NORTH WHITEHEAD

It is a fabulous country, the only fabulous country; it is the only place where miracles not only happen, but where they happen all the time. THOMAS WOLFE

See also **American, England and America, Texas.**

AMERICAN

I am willing to love all mankind, except an American.

SAMUEL JOHNSON

A good scholar will find Aristophanes and Hafiz and Rabelais full of American history.

RALPH WALDO EMERSON

The actual God of many Americans, perhaps of most, is simply the current of American life, which is large and hopeful enough to employ all the idealism they have.

CHARLES HORTON COOLEY

Some American Delusions.
(1) That there is no class-consciousness in the country.
(2) That American coffee is good.
(3) That Americans are business-like.
(4) That Americans are highly-sexed and that redheads are more highly-sexed than others.

W. SOMERSET MAUGHAM

I sometimes think that the saving grace of America lies in the fact that the overwhelming majority of Americans are possessed of two great qualities—a sense of humour and a sense of proportion.

FRANKLIN DELANO ROOSEVELT

AMUSEMENT

Amusement is the happiness of those that cannot think.
ALEXANDER POPE

What a pity it is that we have no amusements in England but vice and religion! SYDNEY SMITH

Few of us can bear the theory of our amusements. It is essential to the pride of a man to believe that he is industrious. WALTER BAGEHOT

The only way to amuse some people is to slip and fall on an icy pavement, or on a banana skin. E. W. HOWE

Life would be tolerable but for its amusements.
GEORGE BERNARD SHAW

Life, it seems to me, is worth living, but only if we avoid the amusements of grown-up people. ROBERT LYND

See also **Fun, Pleasure.**

AMUSING

Once, when SYDNEY SMITH said grace, the young lady who sat next to him said, 'You always are so amusing.'

ANALOGY

All perception of truth is the perception of an analogy; we reason from our hands to our head.
HENRY DAVID THOREAU

ANALYSIS

Analysis kills spontaneity. The grain once ground into flour springs and germinates no more.
FRÉDÉRIC AMIEL

See also **Psychoanalysis.**

ANATOMY

Anatomy is to physiology as geography to history; it describes the theatre of events.
JEAN FRANÇOIS FERNEL

See also **Body.**

ANCESTOR

Genealogy: An account of one's descent from an ancestor who did not particularly care to trace his own. AMBROSE BIERCE

ANCIENT

What then is the widsom of the times called old? Is it the wisdom of grey hairs? No. It is the wisdom of the cradle. Sir THOMAS BROWNE

It is only by an effort of reason, to which fancy is averse, that I bring myself to believe that the sun shone as bright, that the sky was as blue and the earth as green, two thousand years ago as it is at present. How ridiculous this seems; yet so it is! WILLIAM HAZLITT

The systematic thought of ancient writers is now nearly worthless; but their detached insights are priceless.
ALFRED NORTH WHITEHEAD

ANECDOTES

Anecdotes are so rare that centuries pass them on. 'Don't tell me what the end is like,' was said in 1880 of the woman who was reading *The Life of Jesus*, in 1925 of the woman who attended the play *Saint Joan*.
ANDRÉ MAUROIS

See also **Joke, Story.**

ANGEL

Man is neither angel nor brute, and the unfortunate thing is that he who would act the angel acts the brute.
PASCAL

ANGER

Anger raises invention, but it overheats the oven. LORD HALIFAX

A man said to the prophet, 'Give me a command.' He said, 'Do not get angry.' The man repeated the question several times and he said, 'Do not get angry.'

SAYINGS OF MOHAMMED

I never work better than when I am inspired by anger; when I am angry, I can write, pray, and preach well, for then my whole temperament is quickened, my understanding sharpened, and all mundane vexations and temptations depart.

MARTIN LUTHER

If you strike a child, take care that you strike it in anger, even at the risk of maiming it for life. A blow in cold blood neither can nor should be forgiven.

GEORGE BERNARD SHAW

ANGLICAN CHURCH

The merit claimed for the Anglican Church is, that if you let it alone, it will let you alone.

RALPH WALDO EMERSON

ANIMALS

I think I could turn and live with animals, they are so placid and self-contain'd;
I stand and look at them long and long.
They do not sweat and whine about their condition;
They do not lie awake in the dark and weep for their sins;
They do not make me sick discussing their duty to God.

WALT WHITMAN

We believe today that man is a descendant of the animals. But couldn't it be that the animals are offshoots of mankind, retarded specimens of man—man in a stage of arrested development?

CHRISTIAN MORGENSTERN

See also **Bees, Bulldog, Camel, Cat, Dog, Fleas, Fly, Frogs, Insect, Kitten.**

ANSWER

A correct answer is like an affectionate kiss.   GOETHE

See also **Question, Repartee.**

ANTIPATHY

Violent antipathies betray a secret affinity.   WILLIAM HAZLITT

See also **Enmity, Hate.**

ANTIQUITY

Damn the age; I will write for antiquity.   CHARLES LAMB

ANXIETY

Do not push forward a wagon; you will only raise the dust about yourself. Do not think of all your anxieties; you will only make yourself ill.

SHIH KING

Nothing in life is more remarkable than the unnecessary anxiety which we endure, and generally occasion ourselves.   BENJAMIN DISRAELI

See also **Fear, Fret, Worry.**

APHORISM

I fancy mankind may come, in time, to write all aphoristically, except in narrative; grow weary of preparation, and connection, and illustration, and all those arts by which a big book is made.

SAMUEL JOHNSON

Aphorisms are salted and not sugared almonds at Reason's feast.

LOGAN PEARSALL SMITH

An aphorism is never exactly true; it is either a half-truth or one-and-a-half truths.   KARL KRAUS

See also **Epigram, Maxim, Paradox.**

APOLOGY

Apologies are seldom of any use.

SAMUEL JOHNSON

There are occasions on which all apology is rudeness.

SAMUEL JOHNSON

To apologize is to lay the foundation for a future offence.

AMBROSE BIERCE

APPEARANCE

It is only the shallow people who do not judge by appearances.

OSCAR WILDE

APPLE DUMPLINGS

Coleridge declares that a man cannot have a good conscience who refuses apple dumplings, and I confess that I am of the same opinion.

CHARLES LAMB

ARGUING

Anyone who conducts an argument by appealing to authority is not using his intelligence; he is just using his memory.

LEONARDO DA VINCI

Deep-seated perferences cannot be argued about—you cannot argue a man into liking a glass of beer.

OLIVER WENDELL HOLMES, JR.

A half truth in argument, like a half brick, carries better.

STEPHEN LEACOCK

The Chinese have a story based on three or four thousand years of civilization. Two Chinese coolies were arguing heatedly in the midst of a crowd. A stranger expressed surprise that no blows were being struck. His Chinese friend replied, 'The man who strikes first admits that his ideas have given out.'

FRANKLIN DELANO ROOSEVELT

Whoever still argues at forty has never loved truth. ANDRÉ MAUROIS

I have won every argument I ever had with myself.

WILLIAM FEATHER

See also **Argument, Controversy, Dispute, Quarrel.**

ARGUMENT

People are usually more convinced by reasons they discovered themselves than by those found by others. PASCAL

Sound instinct needs no argument; it supplies one. VAUVENARGUES

I dislike arguments of any kind. They are always vulgar, and often convincing. OSCAR WILDE

See also **Reason.**

ARISTOTLE

Aristotle invented science, but destroyed philosophy.

ALFRED NORTH WHITEHEAD

Aristotle discovered all the half-truths which were necessary to the creation of science.

ALFRED NORTH WHITEHEAD

Aristotle could have avoided the mistake of thinking that women have fewer teeth than men by the simple device of asking Mrs. Aristotle to open her mouth.

BERTRAND RUSSELL

Aristotle was famous for knowing everything. He taught that the brain exists merely to cool the blood and is not involved in the process of thinking. This is true only of certain persons. WILL CUPPY

ART (DEFINITIONS)

Art is man added to nature.

FRANCIS BACON

What is art? Prostitution.

CHARLES BAUDELAIRE

The business of art lies just in this—to make that understood and felt which, in the form of an argument, might be incomprehensible and inaccessible. LEO TOLSTOY

Art is the imposing of a pattern on experience, and our aesthetic enjoyment in recognition of the pattern. ALFRED NORTH WHITEHEAD

Art is the economy of feeling; it is emotion cultivating good form. HERBERT READ

All art is a revolt against man's fate. ANDRÉ MALRAUX

To the question 'What is art?' we answer: 'That whereby forms are transmuted into style.' ANDRÉ MALRAUX

ART

Art is consummate when it seems to be nature. LONGINUS

Art is the daughter of pleasure. J. J. WINCKELMANN

In art it's not thinking that does the job, but making. GOETHE

Every original talent shows the same phases in its development as art in general goes through in its various evolutions, to wit: timidity and dryness at the beginning. and breadth or negligence as to details at the end. EUGÉNE DELACROIX

The highest condition of art is artlessness. HENRY DAVID THOREAU

Almost all that our society considers to be art, good art, and the whole of art, far from being real and good art, and the whole of art, is not even art at all, but only a counterfeit of it. LEO TOLSTOY

All that is not pertinent in art is impertinent. SAMUEL BUTLER

All great art and literature is propaganda. GEORGE BERNARD SHAW

Nothing is really so poor and melancholy as art that is interested in itself and not in its subject. GEORGE SANTAYANA

It is proper to enjoy the cheaper grades of art, but they should not be formally endorsed. GEORGE ADE

Art, if it is to be reckoned as one of the great values of life, must teach men humility, tolerance, wisdom and magnanimity. The value of art is not beauty, but right action. W. SOMERSET MAUGHAM

Picasso only registers the deformities which have not yet penetrated our consciousness. Art is a mirror which goes 'fast' like a watch—sometimes. FRANZ KAFKA

The wisdom of art consists in concealing art. LIN YUTANG

. See also **Art (Definitions), Art and Science, Artificial, Arts, Creative, Literature, Masterpiece, Music, Painting, Painting and Sculpture, Work of Art.**

ART AND SCIENCE

Art is I; science is we. CLAUDE BERNARD

See also **Art, Science.**

ART OF LIVING

The art of living is more like that of wrestling than of dancing; the main thing is to stand firm and be ready for an unforeseen attack. MARCUS AURELIUS

When I am going out for an evening I arrange the fire in my stove so that I do not fail to find a good one when I return, though it would have engaged my frequent attention present. So that, when I know I am to be at home, I sometimes make believe that I may go out, to save trouble. And this is the art of living, too—to leave our life in a condition to go alone, and not to require a constant supervision. We will then sit down serenely to live, as by the side of a stove.

HENRY DAVID THOREAU

The art of life lies in a constant readjustment to our surroundings.

OKAKURA KAKUZO

See also **Life, Living, Rules of Life.**

ARTICHOKE

Within every artichoke is an acanthus leaf, and the acanthus is what man would have made of the artichoke, had God asked him his advice. ANDRÉ MALRAUX

ARTIFICIAL

All things are artificial, for nature is the art of God.

SIR THOMAS BROWNE

See also **Natural.**

ARTIST

I prefer to think how arms, legs, and head are attached to the body than whether I myself am or am not more or less an artist.

VINCENT VAN GOGH

No great artist ever sees things as they really are. If he did he would cease to be an artist. OSCAR WILDE

God made the world as an artist and that is why the world must learn from its artists.

GEORGE BERNARD SHAW

The notion of making money by popular work, and then retiring to do good work on the proceeds, is the most familiar of all the devil's traps for artists.

LOGAN PEARSALL SMITH

This is the reason that the artist lives and works and has his being: that from life's clay and his own nature, and from his father's common earth of toil and sweat and violence and error and bitter anguish, he may distil the beauty of an everlasting form, enslave and conquer man by his enchantment, cast his spell across the generations, beat death down upon his knees, kill death utterly, and fix eternity with the grappling-hooks of his own art. THOMAS WOLFE

See also **Genius.**

ARTS

There is no one who has cooked but has discovered that each particular dish depends for its rightness upon some little point which he is never told. It is not only so of cooking: it is so of splicing a rope; of painting a surface of wood; of mixing mortar; of almost anything you like to name among the immemorial human arts. HILAIRE BELLOC

ASCETICISM

As a grass-blade, if badly grasped, cuts the arm, badly-practiced asceticism leads to hell. DHAMMAPADA

See also **Abstain, Self-Denial.**

ASK

People always get what they ask for; the only trouble is that they never know, until they get it, what it actually is that they have asked for.

ALDOUS HUXLEY

See also **Pray, Prayer.**

ASPIRATIONS

The most absurd and reckless aspirations have sometimes led to extraordinary success.

VAUVENARGUES

When people come and talk to you of their aspirations, before they leave you you'd better count your spoons. LOGAN PEARSALL SMITH

See also **Ambition.**

ASTONISHED

It is a mark of genius not to astonish but to be astonished.

AUBREY MENEN

See also **Surprise.**

ASTROLOGY

Astrology fosters astronomy. Mankind *plays* its way up.

G. C. LICHTENBERG

ATHEISM

Atheism shows strength of mind, but only to a certain degree.

PASCAL

Atheism is the vice of a few intelligent people. VOLTAIRE

The complete atheist stands on the penultimate step to most perfect faith (he may or he may not take a further step), but the indifferent person has no faith whatever except a bad fear, and that but rarely, and only if he is sensitive.

FEODOR DOSTOEVSKI

In a way, the greatest praise of God is his denial by the atheist who thinks creation is so perfect it does not need a creator.

MARCEL PROUST

He who has faith is never alone. But the atheist is always alone, even if from morning to night he lives in crowded streets. IGNAZIO SILONE

See also **Agnostic.**

ATHENS

The Periclean Age in Athens was in every sense of the word an age in which any peaceful and prudent citizen of our times would refuse to live, in which he could not but be mortally unhappy.

JAKOB BURCKHARDT

ATOM

I will paint for man not only the visible universe, but all that he can conceive of nature's immensity in the womb of the atom. PASCAL

We shall never get people whose time is money to take much interest in atoms. SAMUEL BUTLER

The conception of the atom stems from the concepts of subject and substance: there has to be 'something' to account for any action. The atom is the last descendant of the concept of the soul.

FRIEDRICH NIETZSCHE

ATTAIN

The significance of a man is not in what he attains, but rather in what he longs to attain. KAHLIL GIBRAN

See also **Achievement, Success.**

ATTENTION

The true art of memory is the art of attention. SAMUEL JOHNSON

Absolutely unmixed attention is prayer. SIMONE WEIL

See also **Inattention, Overlook, Unnoticed.**

ATTILA

As a conqueror, Attila was only a flash in the pan. WILL CUPPY

AUCTION

Attend no auctions if thou hast no money. TALMUD

See also **Bargain, Buy.**

AUSTEN, JANE

To me, Poe's prose is unreadable—like Jane Austen's. No, there is a difference. I could read his prose on a salary, but not Jane's.
MARK TWAIN

AUTHOR

While an author is yet living, we estimate his powers by his worst performance; and when hs is dead, we rate them by his best.
SAMUEL JOHNSON

The man who is asked by an author what he thinks of his work, is put to the torture, and is not obliged to speak the truth. SAMUEL JOHNSON

The conversation of authors is not so good as might be imagined; but, such as it is, it is better than any other. WILLIAM HAZLITT

Authors in general are not good listeners. WILLIAM HAZLITT

It is a good thing when these authors die, for then one gets their works and is done with them.
LORD MELBOURNE

Nothing is more painful to me than the disdain with which people treat second-rate authors, as if there were room only for the first-raters.
CHARLES AUGUSTIN SAINTE-BEUVE

See also **Writer;** and **Jane Austen, Beerbohm, Byron, Chesterfield, Dickens, Emerson, Henry James, Milton, Montaigne, Pope, Rousseau. Scott, Shakespeare, Shaw, Tennyson, Tolstoy, Wordsworth.**

AUTOBIOGRAPHY

There is no description equal in difficulty to a description of oneself, and certainly none in profitableness. MONTAIGNE

See also **Biography, Memoirs.**

AVARICE

Avarice is more opposed to economy than to liberality.
LA ROCHEFOUCAULD

AVERAGE

To leave the mean is to abandon humanity. The greatness of the human soul consists in knowing how to preserve the mean. PASCAL

I have most of my life been miserably conscious that I am not the average Englishman. Let no one think I say this with self-satisfaction, for I think that there is nothing better than to be like everybody else. It is the only way to be happy, and it is with but a wry face that one tells oneself that happiness is not everything.
W. SOMERSET MAUGHAM

See also **Mediocre, Normal, Ordinary.**

B

BABIES

Families with babies and families without babies are sorry for each other. E. W. HOWE

BACKSLIDING

Lord, vouchsafe me always modest progress toward better things, and never to backslide.
MEISTER ECKHART

BAD

A bad man is the sort who weeps every time he speaks of a good woman. H. L. MENCKEN

A bad man is the sort of man who admires innocence, and a bad woman is the sort of woman a man never gets tired of.

OSCAR WILDE

Men become bad and guilty because they speak and act without foreseeing the results of their words and their deeds. FRANZ KAFKA

See also **Evil, Good, Good and Bad, Wicked.**

BALANCE

A state of balance is attractive only when one is on a tightrope; seated on the ground, there is nothing wonderful about it. ANDRÉ GIDE

BANKER

A banker is a fellow who lends his umbrella when the sun is shining and wants it back the minute it begins to rain. MARK TWAIN

See also **Lend.**

BARGAIN

When a man is discontented with himself, it has one advantage, however, that it puts him into an excellent frame of mind for making a bargain. LAURENCE STERNE

One of the difficult tasks in this world is to convince a woman that even a bargain costs money.

E. W. HOWE

See also **Buy.**

BARK

One dog barks at something; the rest bark at him.

CHINESE PROVERB

BASEBALL

Eighteen men play a game of baseball and eighteen thousand watch them, and yet those who play are the only ones who have any official direction in the matter of rules and regulations. The eighteen thousand are allowed to run wild.

ROBERT BENCHLEY

BASHFUL

Great bashfulness is oftener an effect of pride than of modesty.

LORD HALIFAX

No cause more frequently produces bashfulness than too high an opinion of our own importance.

SAMUEL JOHNSON

BATHING

Medicated baths can be no better than warm water: their only effect can be that of tepid moisture.

SAMUEL JOHNSON

If the father of our country, George Washington, was Tutankhamened tomorrow, and, after being aroused from his tomb, was told that the American people today spend two billion dollars yearly on bathing material, he would say, '*What got 'em so dirty?*' WILL ROGERS

See also **Washing.**

BATTLE

The fate of a battle is the result of a moment, of a thought: the hostile forces advance with various combinations, they attack each other and fight for a certain time, the critical moment arrives, a mental flash decides, and the least reserve accomplishes the object.

NAPOLEON I

Nothing except a battle lost can be half so melancholy as a battle won.

DUKE OF WELLINGTON

In the long run all battles are lost, and so are all wars.

H. L. MENCKEN

See also **War.**

BEAUTIFUL

Most works are most beautiful with out ornament. WALT WHITMAN

The most beautiful subjects? The simplest and the least clad.

ANATOLE FRANCE

The epithet beautiful is used by surgeons to describe operations which their patients describe as ghastly, by physicists to describe methods of measurement which leave sentimentalists cold, by lawyers to describe cases which ruin all the parties to them, and by lovers to describe the objects of their infatuation, however unattractive they may appear to the unaffected spectators. GEORGE BERNARD SHAW

The only beautiful things are the things that do not concern us.

OSCAR WILDE

Seldom is a Gothic head more beautiful than when broken.

ANDRÉ MALRAUX

See also **Beauty, Pretty.**

BEAUTY

There is no excellent beauty that has not some strangeness in the proportion. FRANCIS BACON

We are conscious of beauty when there is a harmonious relation between something in our nature and the quality of the object which delights us. PASCAL

Beauty is a manifestation of secret natural laws, which otherwise would have been hidden from us forever. GOETHE

The great use of female beauty, the great practical advantage of it is, that it naturally and unavoidably tends to keep the husband in good-humour with himself, to make him, to use the dealer's phrase, pleased with his bargain.

WILLIAM COBBETT

I derive no pleasure from talking with a young woman half an hour simply because she has regular features. HENRY DAVID THOREAU

Beauty is a finer utility whose end we do not see.

HENRY DAVID THOREAU

The world, which the Greeks called Beauty, has been made such by being gradually divested of every ornament which was not fitted to endure.

HENRY DAVID THOREAU

Beauty is not the starting point, but the point of arrival; a thing can only be beautiful if it is true. Truth itself is only a complete harmony, and harmony is finally only a bundle of utilities. RODIN

If I had to choose between beauty and truth, I should not hesitate; it is beauty that I should keep, feeling sure that it bears within it a truth loftier and more profound than truth itself. ANATOLE FRANCE

The ladies who try to keep their beauty are the ladies who lose it.

LOGAN PEARSALL SMITH

There is a beauty in mechanical fitness which no art can enhance.

NORMAN DOUGLAS

Youth is happy because it has the ability to see beauty. Anyone who keeps the ability to see beauty never grows old. FRANZ KAFKA

Beauty is only skin deep, but it's a valuable asset if you're poor and haven't any sense. KIN HUBBARD

See also **Beautiful.**

BED

Better to sit up all night, than to go to bed with a dragon.
JEREMY TAYLOR

Whoever thinks of going to bed before twelve o'clock is a scoundrel.
SAMUEL JOHNSON

The happiest part of a man's life is what he passes lying awake in bed in the morning. SAMUEL JOHNSON

My bedfellows are cough and cramp; we sleep three in a bed.
CHARLES LAMB

For recruiting the spirits there is nothing like lying a good while in bed. LORD MELBOURNE

Give me a bed and a book and I am happy. LOGAN PEARSALL SMITH

There is a proverb, 'As you have made your bed, so you must lie in it,' which is simply a lie. If I have made my bed uncomfortable, please God, I will make it again.
G. K. CHESTERTON

It is amazing how few people are conscious of the importance of the art of lying in bed.
LIN YUTANG

BEE

What is not good for the hive is not good for the bee.
MARCUS AURELIUS

BEERBOHM, MAX

The Gods bestowed on Max the gift of perpetual old age.
OSCAR WILDE

BEGGAR

He is not expected to become bail or surety for anyone. No man troubleth him with questioning his religion or politics. He is the only free man in the universe.
CHARLES LAMB

BEGGING

Every country where begging is a profession is ill-governed.
VOLTAIRE

As for begging, it is safer to beg than to take, but is it finer to take than to beg. OSCAR WILDE

BEING

Do not wish to be anything but what you are, and try to be that perfectly.
ST. FRANCIS DE SALES

To be a great philosopher, in the practical and most important sense of the term, little more seems necessary than to be convinced of the truth of the maxim, which the wise man repeated to the daughter of King Cophetua, *That if a thing is, it is,* and there is an end of it!
WILLIAM HAZLITT

Latent genius is just a presumption. Everything that can be, is bound to come into being, and what never comes into being is nothing.
FRÉDÉRIC AMIEL

The nature of things in themselves. A thing 'is' whatever it gives us least trouble to think it is. There is no other 'is' than this.
SAMUEL BUTLER

BELIEF

Man is made by his belief. As he believes, so he is. BHAGAVAD-GITA

Maturity of mind is best shown in slow belief. BALTASAR GRACIÁN

What is your religion? I mean—not what you know about religion but the belief that helps you most?
GEORGE ELIOT

We are born believing. A man bears beliefs, as a tree bears apples.

RALPH WALDO EMERSON

Strong beliefs win strong men, and then make them stronger.

WALTER BAGEHOT

A man is shaped to beliefs long held however uncritically—as the roots of a tree that has grown in the crevices of a rock.

OLIVER WENDELL HOLMES, JR.

I am convinced that if a dozen sceptics were to draw up in parallel columns a list of the events narrated in the gospels which they consider credible and incredible respectively, their lists would be different in several particulars. Belief is literally a matter of taste.

GEORGE BERNARD SHAW

Unfounded beliefs are the homage which impulse pays to reason.

BERTRAND RUSSELL

I do not believe in Belief.

E. M. FORSTER

A well-bred man keeps his beliefs out of his conversation.

ANDRÉ MAUROIS

See also **Believing, Faith, Incredulity, Superstition.**

BELIEVING

Nothing is so firmly believed as that of which we know least.

MONTAIGNE

The clergy would have us believe them against our own reason, as the woman would have had her husband against his own eyes, when he took her with another man, which yet she stoutly denied: 'What? Will you believe your own eyes before your own sweet wife?'

JOHN SELDEN

We are all apt to believe what the world believes about us.

GEORGE ELIOT

The people would not believe in God at all if they were not permitted to believe wrong in Him.

LORD HALIFAX

If you must tell me your opinions, tell me what you believe in. I have plenty of doubts of my own.

GOETHE

It is as absurd to argue men, as to torture them, into believing.

JOHN HENRY NEWMAN

'One *can't* believe impossible things.' 'I daresay you haven't had much practice,' said the Queen. 'When I was your age, I always did it for half-an-hour a day. Why, sometimes I've believed as many as six impossible things before breakfast.'

LEWIS CARROLL

It is undesirable to believe a proposition when there is no ground whatever for supposing it true.

BERTRAND RUSSELL

The most costly of all follies is to believe passionately in the palpably not true. It is the chief occupation of mankind.

H. L. MENCKEN

To believe in God for me is to feel that there is a God, not a dead one, or a stuffed one, but a living one, who with irresistible force urges us towards more loving.

VINCENT VAN GOGH

What a man believes may be ascertained, not from his creed, but from the assumptions on which he habitually acts.

GEORGE BERNARD SHAW

A man can believe a considerable deal of rubbish, and yet go about his daily work in a rational and cheerful manner.

NORMAN DOUGLAS

'You say you *believe*,' said Count de X., an extreme Catholic, to the good Protestant minister. 'You people believe, but we *know*.'
ANDRÉ GIDE

To accomplish great things, we must not only act but also dream, not only plan but also believe.
ANATOLE FRANCE

What is wanted is not the will-to-believe, but the wish to find out, which is its exact opposite.
BERTRAND RUSSELL

Be not afraid of life. Believe that life *is* worth living, and your belief will help create the fact.
WILLIAM JAMES

As a general rule, talking to people about themselves as individuals, I would ask a simple personal question—'What do you believe in most?' In this category too the variety of answers was remarkably profuse. I got a bouncing superabundance of replies—'people' mostly, then 'the' people, then 'the people if you give them an even break,' and also God, Santa Claus, work, children, Thomas Jefferson, the golden rule, the Pythagorean theorem, a high tariff, a low tariff, better agricultural prices, happiness, public power, private power, good roads, bad roads—I could continue almost without end.
JOHN GUNTHER

See also **Belief, Faith, Incredulity, Scepticism, Unbeliever.**

BELLY

Life is a romantic business. It is painting a picture, not doing a sum —but you have to make the romance. And it will come to the question how much fire you have in your belly.
OLIVER WENDELL HOLMES, JR.

To say, 'How could I perceive his inner mental processes?' is not so intelligible as 'How could I know what is going on in his mind?,' and this in turn is decidedly less effective than the Chinese 'Am I a tapeworm in his belly?'   LIN YUTANG

BELOW

He who thinks his place below him will certainly be below his place.
LORD HALIFAX

BENEVOLENCE

He who wishes to be benevolent will not be rich.   MENCIUS

The most melancholy of human reflections, perhaps, is that, on the whole, it is a question whether the benevolence of mankind does more good or harm.
WALTER BAGEHOT

Every genuinely benevolent person loathes almsgiving and mendicity.
GEORGE BERNARD SHAW

See also **Alms, Charity, Philanthropy.**

BEST

I have the simplest tastes. I am always satisfied with the best.
OSCAR WILDE

BETTER

It is a pleasant fact that you will know no man long, however low in the social scale, however poor, miserable, intemperate, and worthless he may appear to be, a mere burden to society, but you will find at last that there is something which he understands and can do better than any other.
HENRY DAVID THOREAU

BETTING

The betting man's is a dedicated life.   ROBERT LYND

BIBLE

The Bible may be the truth, but it is not the whole truth and nothing but the truth. SAMUEL BUTLER

Almost any fool can prove that the Bible ain't so—it takes a wise man to believe it. JOSH BILLINGS

The Bible is the Iliad of religion.
JOSEPH JOUBERT

The total absence of humour from the Bible is one of the most singular things in all literature.
ALFRED NORTH WHITEHEAD

See also **Jeremiah, Old Testament, Ten Commandments.**

BIGOT

Wisdom never has made a bigot but learning has. JOSH BILLINGS

The mind of the bigot is like the pupil of the eye; the more light you pour upon it, the more it will contract.
OLIVER WENDELL HOLMES, JR.

How it infuriates a bigot, when he is forced to drag into the light his dark convictions!
LOGAN PEARSALL SMITH

The people who are most bigoted are the people who have no convictions at all. G. K. CHESTERTON

BIOGRAPHY

Read no history, nothing but biography, for that is life without theory. BENJAMIN DISRAELI

See also **Autobiography, Memoirs.**

BIRD

A bird in the hand is worth what it will bring. AMBROSE BIERCE

I am free to admit that I am the kind of man who would never notice an oriole building a nest unless it came and built it in my hat in the hat room of the club. STEPHEN LEACOCK

BISHOP

How can a bishop marry? How can he flirt? The most he can say is, 'I will see you in the vestry after service.' SYDNEY SMITH

BLESSING

Never undertake anything for which you wouldn't have the courage to ask the blessings of Heaven.
G. C. LICHTENBERG

I am a confirmed believer in blessings in disguise. I prefer them undisguised when I myself happen to be the person blessed; in fact, I can scarcely recognize a blessing in disguise except when it is bestowed upon someone else. ROBERT LYND

BLIND

As soon as you know a man to be blind, you imagine that you can see it from his back.
G. C. LICHTENBERG

BLUNDER

A clever man commits no minor blunders. GOETHE

Most men had rather be charged with malice than with making a blunder. JOSH BILLINGS

See also **Mistake.**

BLUSHING

Man is the only animal that blushes. Or needs to. MARK TWAIN

BODY

My body is that part of the world that my ideas can change. Even imaginary diseases can become real ones. The rest of the world cannot be disturbed by my notions.
G. C. LICHTENBERG

Any good practical philosophy must start out with the recognition of our having a body. LIN YUTANG

See also **Anatomy, Body and Soul, Mind and Body.**

BODY AND SOUL

It is a shameful thing for the soul to faint in the race of life, while the body still perseveres.

MARCUS AURELIUS

Heavy thoughts bring on physical maladies; when the soul is oppressed so is the body.

MARTIN LUTHER

The great art of life is how to turn the surplus life of the soul into life for the body.

HENRY DAVID THOREAU

There is nothing the body suffers that the soul may not profit by.

GEORGE MEREDITH

Happiness is good for the body but sorrow strengthens the spirit.

MARCEL PROUST

Your body is the harp of your soul.

KAHLIL GIBRAN

BOHEMIANISM

Mr. Desmond MacCarthy has said that the hallmark of Bohemianism is a tendency to use things for purposes to which they are not adapted. You are a Bohemian, says Mr. Mac-Carthy, if you would gladly use a razor for buttering your toast at breakfast, and you aren't if you wouldn't.

MAX BEERBOHM

BOLD

The timid man yearns for full value and demands a tenth. The bold man strikes for double value and compromises at par.

MARK TWAIN

BOOK REVIEWING

I never read a book before reviewing it. It prejudices one so!

SYDNEY SMITH

BOOKS

There are more books upon books than upon all other subjects.

MONTAIGNE

The multitude of books is a great evil. There is no measure or limit to this fever for writing; everyone must be an author; some out of vanity to acquire celebrity and raise up a name, others for the sake of lucre and gain.   MARTIN LUTHER

Idle books get born because people don't attend to their proper business, but leap at the chance to divert themselves from it.   MONTAIGNE

There is no book so bad but there is something good in it.   CERVANTES

It is far better to be silent than merely to increase the quantity of bad books.   VOLTAIRE

What harm can a book do that costs a hundred crowns? Twenty volumes folio will never cause a revolution; it is the little portable volumes of thirty sous that are to be feared.

VOLTAIRE

I hate books; they only teach us to talk about things we know nothing about.   ROUSSEAU

What variety, what refreshment, and what interest would be found in books if authors wrote only what they thought!   VAUVENARGUES

In this catalogue of *books which are no books*—*biblia abiblia*—I reckon Court Calendars, Directories, Pocket Books, Draught Boards, bound and lettered on the back, Scientific Treatises, Almanacks, Statutes at Large; the works of Hume, Gibbon, Robertson, Beattie, Soame Jenyns, and, generally, all those volumes which 'no gentleman's library should be without': the Histories of

Flavius Josephus (that learned Jew), and Paley's Moral Philosophy.
CHARLES LAMB

A great wit and statesman said that 'speech was given to man to conceal his thoughts.' So it might be said that books serve as a screen to keep us from a knowledge of things.
WILLIAM HAZLITT

He wrote eight books. He would have done better if he had planted eight trees or fathered eight children.
G. C. LICHTENBERG

What we need most today are *thoughtless* books—books with *things* in them rather than thoughts.
LUDWIG BÖRNE

Each age must write its own books; or rather, each generation for the next succeeding. The books of an older period will not fit this.
RALPH WALDO EMERSON

Books are fatal: they are the curse of the human race. Nine-tenths of existing books are nonsense, and the clever books are the refutation of that nonsense. The greatest misfortune that ever befell man was the invention of printing.
BENJAMIN DISRAELI

Old books, as you well know, are books of the world's youth, and new books are fruits of its age.
OLIVER WENDELL HOLMES, SR.

Homeliness is almost as great a merit in a book as in a house, if the reader would abide there.
HENRY DAVID THOREAU

Books are a finer world within the world.
ALEXANDER SMITH

It is my ambition to say in ten sentences what everyone else says in a whole book—what everyone else does *not* say in a whole book.
FRIEDRICH NIETZSCHE

There are no bad books, any more than there are ugly women.
ANATOLE FRANCE

The world, as I know from my books, is full of abominable evil; even some of these books have never been returned.
LOGAN PEARSALL SMITH

See also **Book Reviewing, Books and Reading, Classics, Literature, Novel.**

BOOKS AND READING

I love such books as are either easy and entertaining, and that tickle my fancy, or such as give me comfort, and offer counsel in reordering my life and death. MONTAIGNE

When I was at Oxford, an old gentleman said to me, 'Young man, ply your book diligently now, and acquire a stock of knowledge, for when years come upon you, you will find that poring upon books will be but an irksome task.'
SAMUEL JOHNSON

People seldom read a book which is given to them. The way to spread a work is to sell it at a low price.
SAMUEL JOHNSON

This man was a very sensible man, who perfectly understood common affairs; a man of a great deal of knowledge of the world, fresh from life, not strained through books.
SAMUEL JOHNSON

No man reads a book of science from pure inclination. The books that we do read with pleasure are light compositions which contain a quick succession of events.
SAMUEL JOHNSON

In a way, the main fault of all books is that they are too long.

SAMUEL JOHNSON
VAUVENARGUES

I am always for getting a boy forward in his learning; for that is a sure good. I would let him at first read *any* English book which happens to engage his attention: because you have done a great deal, when you have brought him to have entertainment from a book. He'll get better books afterwards.

SAMUEL JOHNSON

I feel as if I had read all the books I want to read. Oh! to forget Fielding, Steele, etc., and read 'em new!

CHARLES LAMB

It is one of the misfortunes of life that one must read thousands of books only to discover that one need not have read them.

THOMAS DE QUINCEY

To put away one's original thoughts in order to take up a book is the sin against the Holy Ghost.

SCHOPENHAUER

We live too much in books and not enough in nature, and we are very much like that simpleton of a Pliny the Younger, who went on studying a Greek author while before his eyes Vesuvius was overwhelming five cities beneath the ashes.

ANATOLE FRANCE

Given £400 and five years, and an ordinary man can in the ordinary course, without any undue haste or putting any pressure upon his taste, surround himself with two thousand books, all in his own language, and thenceforward have at least one place in the world in which it is possible to be happy.

AUGUSTINE BIRRELL

I would never read a book if it were possible for me to talk half an hour with the man who wrote it.

WOODROW WILSON

If one cannot enjoy reading a book over and over again, there is no use in reading it at all.

OSCAR WILDE

It is astonishing how many books I find there is no need for me to read at all.   W. SOMERSET MAUGHAM

There is no more merit in having read a thousand books than in having ploughed a thousand fields.

W. SOMERSET MAUGHAM

Sartor Resartus is simply unreadable, and for me that always sort of spoils a book.   WILL CUPPY

I cannot imagine a pleasanter old age than one spent in the not too remote country where I could reread and annotate my favourite books.

ANDRÉ MAUROIS

See also **Books, Reading.**

BOREDOM

We are always bored by those whom we bore.   LA ROCHEFOUCAULD

The only unhappiness is a life of boredom.   STENDHAL

Boredom exists only among those who attach importance to the mind. The more intelligent a man is, the more frequent, painful, and terrible his boredom.

GIACOMO LEOPARDI

One can be bored until boredom becomes a mystical experience.

LOGAN PEARSALL SMITH

When people are bored, it is primarily with their own selves that they are bored.   ERIC HOFFER

See also **Bores, Boring.**

BORES

It is better to be alone than among bores. MONTAIGNE

He has returned from Italy a greater bore than ever; he bores on architecture, painting, statuary and music. SYDNEY SMITH

There is no bore like a clever bore. SAMUEL BUTLER

Bore: A person who talks when you wish him to listen. AMBROSE BIERCE

At some time, I fear, everybody is a bore, because everybody now and again has a fixed idea to impart, and the fixed ideas of the few are the boredom of the many. E. V. LUCAS

Many bores are so obviously happy that it is a pleasure to watch them. ROBERT LYND

BORING

Any subject can be made interesting, and therefore any subject can be made boring. HILAIRE BELLOC

There are books that are at once excellent and boring. Those that at once leap to the mind are Thoreau's *Walden*, Emerson's *Essays*, George Eliot's *Adam Bede* and Landor's *Dialogues*. W. SOMERSET MAUGHAM

The capacity of human beings to bore one another seems to be vastly greater than that of any other animals. Some of their most esteemed inventions have no other apparent purpose: for example, the dinner party of more than two, the epic poem, and the science of metaphysics. H. L. MENCKEN

BORN

It is best never to have been born. But who among us has such luck? One in a million, perhaps. ALFRED POLGAR

BOY

A boy should never be allowed to see an instance of deceit. CONFUCIUS

BRAIN

Agamemnon has not so much brain as ear-wax. SHAKESPEARE
(*Troilus and Cressida*, V, i.)

I not only use all the brains I have, but all I can borrow. WOODROW WILSON

BRANDY

Brandy-and-water spoils two good things. CHARLES LAMB

BRAVE

He whose boldness leads him to venture, will be slain; he who is brave enough not to venture, will live. LAO-TSE

Bravery has no place where it can avail nothing. SAMUEL JOHNSON

We do all stand in the front ranks of the battle every moment of our lives; where there is a brave man there is the thickest of the fight, there the post of honour. HENRY DAVID THOREAU

See also **Courage, Coward.**

BREAKFAST

A simple enough pleasure, surely, to have breakfast alone with one's husband, but how seldom married people in the midst of life achieve it. ANNE MORROW LINDBERGH

BREVITY SEE BRIEF.

BRIDGE

It has always seemed to me that the best symbol of common sense was a bridge. FRANKLIN DELANO ROOSEVELT

It has always seemed to me that the most difficult part of building a bridge would be the start.
ROBERT BENCHLEY

BRIEF

Be brief, for no discourse can please when too long.   CERVANTES

All intelligent people incline to express themselves briefly—to say at once whatever is to be said.
G. C. LICHTENBERG

Brevity is not only the soul of wit, but the soul of making oneself agreeable, and of getting on with people, and indeed of everything that makes life worth having.
SAMUEL BUTLER

As man is now constituted, to be brief is almost a condition of being inspired.   GEORGE SANTAYANA

See also **Short.**

BROODING

The deep-sea diver may fall prey to the ink fish, and the brooder to melancholy.
CHRISTIAN MORGENSTERN

See also **Melancholy.**

BROTHER-IN-LAW

No man was ever so low as to have respect for his brother-in-law.
FINLEY PETER DUNNE

BRUCKNER, ANTON

Somebody once asked Anton Bruckner: 'Master, how, when, where did you think of the divine motif of your Ninth Symphony?' 'Well, it was like this. I walked up the Kahlenberg, and when it got hot and I got hungry, I sat down by a little brook and unpacked my Swiss cheese. And just as I open the greasy paper, that darn tune pops into my head!' PETER ALTENBERG

BUILDING

He that buildeth his house with other men's money is like one that gathereth himself stones against winter.   ECCLESIASTICUS 21

He that buildeth a fair house upon an ill seat, committeth himself to prison.   FRANCIS BACON

Strange it is to think how building do fill my mind and put all other things out of my thoughts.
SAMUEL PEPYS

See also **Dwelling, House.**

BULLDOG

The nose of the bulldog has been slanted backwards so that he can breathe without letting go.
WINSTON S. CHURCHILL

BUSINESS

He that hath little business shall become wise.   ECCLESIASTICUS 38

A man often thinks he has given up business, when he has only exchanged it for another.
MONTAIGNE

The greatest part of the business of the world is the effect of not thinking.   LORD HALIFAX

I find that two days' neglect of business do give more discontent in mind than ten times the pleasure thereof can repair again, be it what it will.   SAMUEL PEPYS

A man is to go about his business as if he had not a friend in the world to help him in it. LORD HALIFAX

Business is so much lower a thing than learning that a man used to the last cannot easily bring his stomach down to the first. LORD HALIFAX

To be at ease is better than to be at business. BALTASAR GRACIÁN

Few people do business well who do nothing else. LORD CHESTERFIELD

It very seldom happens to a man that his business is his pleasure. SAMUEL JOHNSON

A load of cares lies like a weight of guilt upon the mind: so that a man of business often has all the air, the distraction and restlessness and hurry of feeling of a criminal. WILLIAM HAZLITT

Most are engaged in business the greater part of their lives, because the soul abhors a vacuum and they have not discovered any continuous employment for man's nobler faculties. HENRY DAVID THOREAU

Business is really more agreeable than pleasure; it interests the whole mind, the aggregate nature of man more continuously, and more deeply. But it does not *look* as if it did. WALTER BAGEHOT

Business should be like religion and science; it should know neither love nor hate. SAMUEL BUTLER

It is not by any means certain that a man's business is the most important thing he has to do. ROBERT LOUIS STEVENSON

If America is to be civilized, it must be done (at least for the present) by the business class. ALFRED NORTH WHITEHEAD

There is much more hope for humanity from manufacturers who enjoy their work than from those who continue in irksome business with the object of founding hospitals. ALFRED NORTH WHITEHEAD

Half the time when men think they are talking business, they are wasting time. E. W. HOWE

Not a tenth of us who are in business are doing as well as we could if we merely followed the principles that were known to our grandfathers. WILLIAM FEATHER

See also **Affairs, Corporation, Trade.**

BUSY

A busy fool is fitter to be shut up than a downright madman. LORD HALIFAX

As peace is the end of war, so to be idle is the ultimate purpose of the busy. SAMUEL JOHNSON

A bee is never as busy as it seems; it's just that it can't buzz any slower. KIN HUBBARD

The hardest job of all is trying to look busy when you're not. WILLIAM FEATHER

See also **Idle.**

BUTTON

Once you have missed the first buttonhole you'll never manage to button up. GOETHE

BUY

A woman is always buying something. OVID

Not to be covetous is money in your purse; not to be eager to buy is income. CICERO

Never buy a thing you don't want merely because it is dear. OSCAR WILDE

Don't a fellow feel good after he gets out of a store where he nearly bought something? KIN HUBBARD

It don't make no difference what it is, a woman'll buy anything she thinks the store is losing money on.
KIN HUBBARD

See also **Auction, Bargain.**

BYRON
Byron is no poet.
RALPH WALDO EMERSON

C

CALM
Nothing is so aggravating as calmness.
OSCAR WILDE

CAMEL
One shabby camel carries the burdens of many donkeys.
GOETHE

[On the difficulty of convincing a prejudiced man:] You might as well attempt to poultice the lump off a camel's back.
SYDNEY SMITH

Do not free a camel of the burden of his hump: you may be freeing him from being a camel.
G. K. CHESTERTON

CANDIDATE
The election isn't very far off when a candidate can recognize you across the street.
KIN HUBBARD

CANDOUR
The young man turned to him with a disarming candour which instantly put him on his guard.
SAKI

CANNOT
I cannot set about the most indifferent thing without twenty efforts, and had rather write one of these essays than have to seal a letter.
WILLIAM HAZLITT

It is always our inabilities that vex us.
JOSEPH JOUBERT

I cannot decently fold up a letter, and I could never trim a pen, or carve at table worth a pin—or saddle a horse, fly a hawk, or speak to dogs, birds, or horses.
MONTAIGNE

The great pleasure in life is doing what people say you cannot do.
WALTER BAGEHOT

Don't be crazy to do a lot of things you can't do.
E. W. HOWE

It is exactly because a man cannot do a thing that he is the proper judge of it.
OSCAR WILDE

The older I grow the more respect I have for the wise people who cannot read or write.
E. V. LUCAS

Sometimes it is more important to discover what one cannot do, than what one can do.
LIN YUTANG

See also **Clumsy, Ignorance.**

CAPITAL
What is capital? It is what is left over when the primary needs of a society have been satisfied.
ALDOUS HUXLEY

CAPITALISM
Until you understand Capitalism you do not understand human society as it exists at present.
GEORGE BERNARD SHAW

The word Capitalism is misleading. The proper name for our system is Proletarianism.
GEORGE BERNARD SHAW

Capitalism is itself a crisis.
G. K. CHESTERTON

CARD PLAYING

The greatest skill at cards is to know when to discard.
BALTASAR GRACIÁN

I am sorry I have not learned to play at cards. It is very useful in life: it generates kindness and consolidates society.
SAMUEL JOHNSON

In early manhood Coleridge planned a Pantisocracy where all the virtues were to thrive. Lamb did something far more difficult: he played cribbage every night with his imbecile father, whose constant stream of querulous talk and fault-finding might well have goaded a far stronger man into practising and justifying neglect.
AUGUSTINE BIRRELL

To have learnt to play a good game of bridge is the safest insurance against the tedium of old age.
W. SOMERSET MAUGHAM

See also **Games, Play.**

CARD TABLE

No man who has wrestled with a self-adjusting card table can ever be quite the man he once was.
JAMES THURBER

CARICATURE

Caricature is rough truth.
GEORGE MEREDITH

See also **Ridicule.**

CASTLES IN THE AIR

If you have built castles in the air, your work need not be lost; that is where they should be. Now put the foundations under them.
HENRY DAVID THOREAU

There is more pleasure in building castles in the air than on the ground.
EDWARD GIBBON

See also **Daydream.**

CAT

When I play with my cat, who knows but that she regards me more as a plaything than I do her?
MONTAIGNE

See also **Kitten.**

CAUSE AND EFFECT

The thinker makes a great mistake when he asks after cause and effect. They both together make up the indivisible phenomenon. GOETHE

CELEBRITY

A celebrity is one who is known to many persons he is glad he doesn't know. H. L. MENCKEN

See also **Fame.**

CELIBACY

Marriage has many pains, but celibacy has no pleasures.
SAMUEL JOHNSON

CEMETERY

The cast-off clothes of God.
CHRISTIAN MORGENSTERN

See also **Epitaph, Funeral.**

CENSURE

They have a right to censure, that have a heart to help: the rest is cruelty, not justice.
WILLIAM PENN

See also **Criticism.**

CENTRE

Every living creature, even a puppy, is at the centre of the universe.
ANATOLE FRANCE

Every beloved object is the centre of a paradise. NOVALIS

How many years some of us have to spend in this world before we realize that we are not the centre of observation! E. V. LUCAS

CEREMONY

Ceremony keeps up all things. 'Tis like a penny glass to a rich spirit, or some excellent water. Without it the water were split, the spirit lost.
JOHN SELDEN

An age of ignorance is an age of ceremony. SAMUEL JOHNSON

CERTAIN

I have lived in this world just long enough to look carefully the second time into things that I am the most certain of the first time.
JOSH BILLINGS

Absolute uncertainty. We can no more have this than we can have absolute certainty, and so with truth and untruth.
SAMUEL BUTLER

Certitude is not the test of certainty. We have been cocksure of many things that were not so.
OLIVER WENDELL HOLMES, JR.

Certainty generally is illusion, and repose is not the destiny of man.
OLIVER WENDELL HOLMES, JR.

Beware of certitude.
ALFRED NORTH WHITEHEAD

Fear comes from uncertainty. When we are absolutely certain, whether of our worth or worthlessness, we are almost impervious to fear. Thus a feeling of utter unworthiness can be a source of courage.
ERIC HOFFER

Most of the greatest evils that man has inflicted upon man have come through people feeling quite certain about something which, in fact, was false. BERTRAND RUSSELL

See also **Certainty and Doubt, Doubt, Sure, Uncertainty.**

CERTAINTY AND DOUBT

If we begin with certainties we shall end in doubts; but if we begin with doubts, and are patient in them, we shall end in certainties.
FRANCIS BACON

CHAIR

To the discontented man no chair is easy. BENJAMIN FRANKLIN

Chairs and campstools are seats under domestication. Wild seats are seldom comfortable.
SAMUEL BUTLER

A surprising number of the world's rulers have satisfied their sense of fun almost exclusively by the simple expedient of pulling the chair from under the Queen. WILL CUPPY

The lower a chair is, the more comfortable it becomes. LIN YUTANG

The modern artist's supreme aim is to subdue all things to his style, beginning with the simplest, least promising objects. And his emblem is Van Gogh's famous *Chair*.
ANDRÉ MALRAUX

CHANCE

Chance makes us known to others and to ourselves.
LA ROCHEFOUCAULD

He that leaveth nothing to chance will do few things ill, but he will do very few things. LORD HALIFAX

Chance is a nickname for Providence. NICOLAS CHAMFORT

What is called chance is the instrument of Providence and the secret agent that counteracts what men call wisdom, and preserves order and regularity, and continuation in the whole. HORACE WALPOLE

Chance usually favours the prudent man. JOSEPH JOUBERT

In the fields of observation, chance favours only the prepared minds.
LOUIS PASTEUR

Chance works for us when we are good captains. GEORGE MEREDITH

Chance is a name for our ignorance.
LESLIE STEPHEN

It is recorded of SAMUEL BUTLER that on his deathbed he made it plain he wanted to say something and what he wanted to say was that he had written that life was ninety-nine per cent chance and he wished to correct this figure to one hundred per cent.

No fact in human nature is more characteristic than its willingness to live on a chance. WILLIAM JAMES

In life we must all make due allowance for chance. Chance, in the last resort, is God. ANATOLE FRANCE

What is life but a series of inspired follies? The difficulty is to find them to do. Never lose a chance: it doesn't come every day.
GEORGE BERNARD SHAW

The soothing effect of art is mainly due to the fact that a work of art excludes the element of chance.
ARTHUR SCHNITZLER

See also **Accident, Circumstances, Fortune, Luck, Providence.**

CHANGE

Any very great and sudden change is death. SAMUEL BUTLER

There is little relation between our actions, which are perpetually changing, and fixed and unchangeable laws. MONTAIGNE

Such is the state of life that none are happy but by the anticipation of change. The change itself is nothing; when we have made it, the next wish is to change again.
SAMUEL JOHNSON

Nothing is so perfectly amusing as a total change of ideas.
LAURENCE STERNE

We must always change, renew, rejuvenate ourselves; otherwise we harden. GOETHE

One must change one's tactics every ten years if one wishes to maintain one's superiority. NAPOLEON I

People themselves alter so much that there is something new to be observed in them forever.
JANE AUSTEN

In science the important thing is to modify and change one's ideas as science advances.
CLAUDE BERNARD

Wherever we are, it is but a stage on the way to somewhere else, and whatever we do, however well we do it, it is only a preparation to do something else that shall be different. ROBERT LOUIS STEVENSON

Progress is impossible without change; and those who cannot change their minds cannot change anything. GEORGE BERNARD SHAW

We believe we can change things according to our wishes because that's the only happy solution we can see. We don't think of what usually happens and what is *also* a happy solution: things don't change, but by and by our wishes change.
MARCEL PROUST

A man who had not seen Keuner for a long time greeted him with these words: 'You haven't changed at all.' 'Oh,' said Herr Keuner, deeply shocked. BERTOLT BRECHT

See also **Mutability.**

CHARACTER

Character is long-standing habit.
PLUTARCH

It is our duty to compose our character, not to compose books, and to win, not battles and provinces, but order and tranquillity for our conduct of life. MONTAIGNE

Characters must be kept bright as well as clean. LORD CHESTERFIELD

Character, in great and little things, means carrying through what you feel able to do. GOETHE

No one ever changes his character from the time he is two years old; nay, I might say, from the time he is two hours old.
WILLIAM HAZLITT

Persons in a higher or middle rank of life know little or nothing of the characters of those below them, as servants, country people, etc.
WILLIAM HAZLITT

Good and evil lie close together. Seek no artistic unity in character.
LORD ACTON

Few men realize that their life, the very essence of their character, their capabilities and their audacities, are only the expression of their belief in the safety of their surroundings.
JOSEPH CONRAD

You can construct the character of a man and his age not only from what he does and says, but from what he fails to say and do.
NORMAN DOUGLAS

The style of a man's play, plus the normal range of his vices, divided by the square of his work, and multiplied by the coefficient of his nationality, gives, not only his potential resistance under breaking-strain, but indicates, within a few points, how far he may be trusted to pull off a losing game.
RUDYARD KIPLING

Our character in later life is not always, though often, our original character developed or dried up, coarsened or weakened; sometimes it is the very reverse, like a garment turned inside out.
MARCEL PROUST

Many people have character who have nothing else. DON HEROLD

See also **Characteristic, Defect, Fault, Vice, Virtue.**

CHARACTERISTIC

Nothing is more characteristic of a man than the manner in which he behaves towards fools.
FRÉDÉRIC AMIEL

See also **Character.**

CHARITY

Philanthropies and charities have a certain air of quackery.
RALPH WALDO EMERSON

Simple rules for saving money: To save half, when you are fired by an eager impulse to contribute to a charity, wait and count forty. To save three-quarters, count sixty. To save it all, count sixty-five.
MARK TWAIN

Charity, like nature, abhors a vacuum. Next to putting it into the bank, men like to squander their superfluous wealth on those to whom it is sure of doing the least possible good. WILLIAM HAZLITT

You are much surer that you are doing good when you *pay* money to those who work, as the recompense of their labour, than when you *give* money merely in charity.
SAMUEL JOHNSON

This only is charity, to do all, all that we can. JOHN DONNE

I think charitable gifts on a large scale are *prima facie* the worst abuse of private ownership—from the economic point of view.
OLIVER WENDELL HOLMES, JR.

Something happened recently that reminded me of a rich woman's exclamation once in New York. 'Socialism! But wouldn't it do away with charity? And what would we do without charities? I love my work for the poor more than anything else I can do. I think charity is just swell!' LINCOLN STEFFENS

Charity is faith in what is alike. It is not put off by contrary evidence; therefore it pays homage to humanity in the fool, the idiot, the criminal, the unhappy; but also in the rich, the powerful, the frivolous, the unjust, the drunkard, the brute, the jealous, the envious; it reaches across to decide in their favour, to help them, above all, to love them.
ALAIN

Charity deals with symptoms instead of causes. LORD SAMUEL

Charity should be opposed on the grounds of principle, not of stinginess. KARL KRAUS

I rather think there is an immense shortage of Christian charity among so-called Christians.
HARRY S. TRUMAN

See also **Alms, Benevolence, Philanthropy.**

CHARMING

When men give up saying what is charming, they cease thinking what is charming. OSCAR WILDE

Charming people live up to the very edge of their charm, and behave as outrageously as the world will let them. LOGAN PEARSALL SMITH

CHASTITY

An unattempted woman cannot boast of her chastity. MONTAIGNE

People will say that a book which offends virtue is bad. I admit it; and I confess that those whose favourite virtue is chastity, who shudder at the thought of the pleasure they had in love when young, who are revolted by amorous ecstasy and believe that it defiles the soul, had better refrain from reading me.
CASANOVA

CHEAP

All good things are cheap: all bad very dear. HENRY DAVID THOREAU

See also **Expensive.**

CHEATING

Tzu-lu asked how to serve the king. The Master said: 'Never cheat him: withstand him to the face.'
SAYINGS OF CONFUCIUS

Many men *swallow* the being cheated, but no man could ever endure to chew it. LORD HALIFAX

Commerce is the school of cheating. VAUVENARGUES

It is almost always worth while to be cheated; people's little frauds have an interest which amply repays what they cost us.
LOGAN PEARSALL SMITH

CHEQUE

Every one, even the richest and most munificent of men, pays much by cheque more lightheartedly than he pays little in specie.

MAX BEERBOHM

CHEERFUL

In cheerfulness is the success of our studies. PLINY THE ELDER

The most certain sign of wisdom is a continual cheerfulness. Her state is like that of things in the regions above the moon, always clear and serene. MONTAIGNE

Morose men hate the cheerful.

SAMUEL JOHNSON

The highest wisdom and the highest genius have been invariably accompanied with cheerfulness. We have sufficient proofs on record that Shakespeare and Socrates were the most festive companions.

THOMAS LOVE PEACOCK

My religion of life is always to be cheerful. GEORGE MEREDITH

See also **Gay, Good Humour, Merry.**

CHEESE

Send me some preserved cheese, that when I like I may have a feast.

EPICURUS

The obscure man's reflections may be as wise as the rich cheese-maker's, on everything but cheese.

HENRY S. HASKINS

CHESTERFIELD, LORD

His letters teach the morals of a whore, and the manners of a dancing master. SAMUEL JOHNSON

CHEWING

Never chew your pills.

C. H. SPURGEON

It has never ceased to be a source of wonderment to me why a man should prefer to chew pencils when food that is far more wholesome and filling can be procured at a trifling cost.

FRANK SULLIVAN

CHILDHOOD

Every man remembers his childhood as a kind of mythical age, just as every nation's childhood is its mythical age. GIACOMO LEOPARDI

Hors d'oeuvres have always a pathetic interest for me: they remind me of one's childhood that one goes through, wondering what the next course is going to be like—and during the rest of the menu one wishes one had eaten more of the hors d'oeuvres. SAKI

See also **Children, Infancy.**

CHILDREN

We think our children a part of ourselves, though as they grow up they might very well undeceive us.

LORD HALIFAX

You are to have as strict a guard upon yourself amongst your children, as if you were amongst your enemies. LORD HALIFAX

Children think not of what is past, nor what is to come, but enjoy the present time, which few of us do.

JEAN DE LA BRUYÉRE

Nothing seems to have been more universally dreaded by the ancients than orbity, or want of children.

SAMUEL JOHNSON

A child thinks twenty shillings and twenty years can scarce ever be spent. BENJAMIN FRANKLIN

Babies do not want to hear about babies; they like to be told of giants and castles, and of somewhat which can stretch and stimulate their little minds. SAMUEL JOHNSON

You have to ask children and birds how cherries and strawberries taste. GOETHE

Children stand more in need of example than criticism. JOSEPH JOUBERT

Children naturally want to be like their parents, and do what they do. WILLIAM COBBETT

There is more happiness in a multitude of children than safety in a multitude of counsellors; and if I were a rich man, I should like to have twenty children. SYDNEY SMITH

Children are hopes. NOVALIS

Children are all foreigners. We treat them as such. RALPH WALDO EMERSON

I believe the power of observation in numbers of very young children to be quite wonderful for its closeness and accuracy. Indeed, I think that most grown men who are remarkable in this respect, may with greater propriety be said not to have lost the faculty, than to have acquired it; the rather, as I generally observe such men to retain a certain freshness, and gentleness, and capacity of being pleased, which are also an inheritance they have preserved from their childhood. CHARLES DICKENS

Feel the dignity of a child. Do not feel superior to him, for you are not. ROBERT HENRI

Raising children is like making biscuits: it is as easy to raise a big batch as one, while you have your hands in the dough. E. W. HOWE

If you want to see what children can do, you must stop giving them things. NORMAN DOUGLAS

We like little children, because they tear out as soon as they get what they want. KIN HUBBARD

Your children are not your children. KAHLIL GIBRAN

All children are natural, but some are more so than others and are therefore known as natural children. WILL CUPPY

I would rather see one of my children's faces kindle at the sight of the quay at Calais than be offered the chance of exploring by myself the palaces of Peking. J. B. PRIESTLEY

See also **Babies, Boy, Childhood, Infancy, Parents.**

CHINESE

All Chinese are Confucianists when successful, and Taoists when they are failures. The Confucianist in us builds and strives, while the Taoist in us watches and smiles. LIN YUTANG

Given extensive leisure, what do not the Chinese do? They eat crabs, drink tea, taste spring water, sing operatic airs, fly kites, play shuttlecock, match grass blades, make paper boxes, solve complicated wire puzzles, play *mahjong*, gamble and pawn clothing, stew *ginseng*, watch cock-fights, romp with their children, water flowers, plant vegetables, graft fruits, play chess, take baths, hold conversations, keep cage-birds, take afternoon naps, have three meals in one, guess fingers, play at palmistry, gossip about fox spirits, go to operas, beat drums and gongs, play the flute, practise on calligraphy, munch duck-gizzards, salt carrots, fondle walnuts, fly eagles, feed carrier pigeons, quarrel with their tailors, go on pilgrimages, visit temples, climb mountains, watch boat races, hold bull fights, take aphrodisiacs, smoke opium, gather at street corners, shout at aeroplanes, fulminate against the Japanese, wonder at the white people, criticize their politicians, read Buddhist classics, practise deep-breathing, hold Buddhist séances, consult fortune tellers, catch crickets, eat melon seeds, gamble for moon cakes, hold lantern competitions, burn rare incense, eat noodles, solve literary riddles, train pot-flowers, send one another birthday presents, kow-tow to one another, produce children, and sleep. LIN YUTANG

CHRISTIAN

Most people believe that the Christian commandments are intentionally a little too severe—like setting a clock half an hour ahead to make sure of not being late in the morning. SÖREN KIERKEGAARD

People in general are equally horrified at hearing the Christian religion doubted, and at seeing it practised. SAMUEL BUTLER

Christian: One who believes that the New Testament is a divinely inspired book admirably suited to the spiritual needs of his neighbour. AMBROSE BIERCE

I often think the Christian church suffers from a too ardent monotheism. E. B. WHITE

See also **Anglican Church, Christianity, Protestant.**

CHRISTIANITY

He who begins by loving Christianity better than truth will proceed by loving his own sect of church better than Christianity, and end in loving himself better than all. SAMUEL TAYLOR COLERIDGE

We can never see Christianity from the catechism—from the pastures, from a boat in the pond, from amidst the songs of wood-birds we possibly may. RALPH WALDO EMERSON

Imagine a fortress, absolutely impregnable, provisioned for an eternity. Then comes a new commandant. He conceives that it might be a good idea to build bridges over the moats—so as to be able to attack the besiegers. *Charmant!* He transforms the fortress into a country seat—and naturally the enemy takes it.
So it is with Christianity. They changed the method—and naturally the world conquered. SÖREN KIERKEGAARD

Christianity. As an instrument of warfare against vice, or as a tool for making morality, it is a mere flint implement. SAMUEL BUTLER

After all, what is the essence of Christianity? What is the kernel of the nut? Surely common sense and cheerfulness, with unflinching opposition to the charlatanisms and Pharisaisms of a man's own times. SAMUEL BUTLER

Infidel: In New York, one who does not believe in the Christian religion; in Constantinople, one who does. AMBROSE BIERCE

The idea of Christ is much older than Christianity.

GEORGE SANTAYANA

See also **Religion.**

CHURCH

It were better to be of no church than to be bitter for any.

WILLIAM PENN

Campbell is a good man, a pious man. I am afraid he has not been in the inside of a church for many years, but he never passes a church without pulling off his hat. This shows that he has good principles.

SAMUEL JOHNSON

A sparrow fluttering about the church is an antagonist which the most profound theologian in Europe is wholly unable to overcome.

SYDNEY SMITH

There are not many people who would care to sleep in a church. I don't mean at sermon-time in warm weather (when the thing has actually been done, once or twice) but in the night, and alone.

CHARLES DICKENS

It is a law of human nature that the Church should wish to do everything and be everything.

CHARLES BAUDELAIRE

If you go to church, and like the singing better than the preaching, that's not orthodox. E. W. HOWE

So she goes to church. It's cheaper than the psychoanalyst and more convenient, being only once a week.

AUBREY MENEN

See also **Sunday School.**

CICERO

Cicero's style bores me. When I have spent an hour reading him—a good deal for me—and try to recollect what I have extracted, I usually find it nothing but wind.

MONTAIGNE

CIGAR

I have made it a rule never to smoke more than one cigar at a time.

MARK TWAIN

See also **Smoking.**

CIGARETTE

A cigarette is the perfect type of perfect pleasure. It is exquisite and it leaves one unsatisfied.

OSCAR WILDE

See also **Smoking.**

CIRCUMLOCUTION

There lives no man who at some period has not been tormented by an earnest desire to tantalize a listener by circumlocution.

EDGAR ALLAN POE

CIRCUMSTANCES

Control ircumstances, and do not allow them to control you.

THOMAS À KEMPIS

Our acts and thoughts and all must be determined by circumstances.

BALTASAR GRACIÁN

See also **Destiny, Fate.**

CITIZEN

The small state exists so that there may be a spot on earth where the largest possible proportion of the inhabitants are citizens in the fullest sense of the word.

JAKOB BURCKHARDT

CITY

City life: Millions of people being lonesome together.

HENRY DAVID THOREAU

Everything that's worth having goes to the city; the country takes what's left. Everything that's worth having goes to the city and is iced.

FINLEY PETER DUNNE

At length the dead cities, Troy, Mycenae, Argos, Amphipolis, Corinth, Sparta, will do a *danse macabre* with New York, Berlin, London, Paris.   HENRY S. HASKINS

See also **London, New York.**

CIVILIZATION

A decent provision for the poor is the true test of civilization.
     SAMUEL JOHNSON

The next Augustan age will dawn on the other side of the Atlantic. There will, perhaps, be a Thucydides at Boston, a Xenophon at New York, in time a Virgil at Mexico, and a Newton at Peru. At last some curious traveller from Lima will visit England, and give a description of the ruins of St. Paul's, like the editions of Baalbec and Palmyra.   HORACE WALPOLE

Civilization is a limitless multiplication of unnecessary necessaries.
     MARK TWAIN

Civilization is the process of reducing the infinite to the finite.
     OLIVER WENDELL HOLMES, JR.

Civilization is nothing more than politeness, industry and fairness. Savages are always thieves, always loafers, and always impolite and unfair.   E. W. HOWE

The aim of civilization is to make politics superfluous and science and art indispensable.
     ARTHUR SCHNITZLER

The only place I know where European man can still create civilization on the grand scale is in the American Midwest.
     ALFRED NORTH WHITEHEAD

We must not stay as we are, doing always what was done last time, or we shall stick in the mud. Yet neither must we undertake a new world as catastrophic Utopians, and wreck our civilization in our hurry to mend it.
     GEORGE BERNARD SHAW

Does any thoughtful man suppose that the present experiment in civilization is the last the world will see?   GEORGE SANTAYANA

Like its predecessor, our present civilization may be no more than one of those crops farmers sow to improve their land by the fixation of nitrogen from the air; it may have grown only that, accumulating certain traditions, it may be ploughed into the soil again for better things to follow.   H. G. WELLS

Civilization, in the real sense of the term, consists not in the multiplication, but in the deliberate and voluntary reduction of wants. This alone promotes real happiness and contentment, and increases the capacity for service.   GANDHI

The military superiority of Europe to Asia is not an eternal law of nature, as we are tempted to think, and our superiority in civilization is a mere delusion.
     BERTRAND RUSSELL

Many clever men like you have trusted to civilization. Many clever Babylonians, clever Egyptians, many clever men at the end of Rome. Can you tell me, in a world that is flagrant with the failures of civilization, what there is particularly immortal about yours?
     G. K. CHESTERTON

It is only an uncivilized world which would worship civilization.
     HENRY S. HASKINS

You think that a wall as solid as the earth separates civilization from barbarism. I tell you the division is a thread, a sheet of glass. A touch here, a push there, and you bring back the reign of Saturn.

JOHN BUCHAN

The fate of civilization is like needle-work. You can take it up and worry about it at odd moments.

FRANK SULLIVAN

See also, **Civilized, Culture, Progress.**

CIVILIZED

The Widow Douglas she took me for her son, and allowed she would sivilize me; but it was rough living in the house all the time, considering how dismal regular and decent the widow was in all her ways; and so when I couldn't stand it no longer I lit out. MARK TWAIN

The civilized is far simpler than the primeval. JOHN BUCHAN

Neither St. Francis, nor Dante, nor Blake, nor Cézanne, nor Dostoyevsky was completely civilized, nor, given his work and all its implications, could he have been.

CLIVE BELL

By being civilized we mean that there is a certain list of things about which we permit a man to have an opinion different from ours. Usually they are things which we have ceased to care about: for instance, the worship of God.

AUBREY MENEN

See also **Civilization, Culture.**

CLARITY SEE CLEAR.

CLASS

The lower classes of men, though they do not think it worth while to record what they perceive, nevertheless perceive everything that is worth noting; the difference between them and a man of learning often consists in nothing more than the latter's facility for expression.

G. C. LICHTENBERG

I have always been inclined to believe the ruck of hard-working people rather than to believe the special and troublesome literary class to which I belong.

G. K. CHESTERTON

CLASSIC AND ROMANTIC

Classicism is health, romanticism is sickness. GOETHE

CLASSICS

A classic is something that everybody wants to have read and nobody wants to read. MARK TWAIN

I always had scruples lest I was wasting time when I read the classics.

OLIVER WENDELL HOLMES, JR.

Have I uttered the fundamental blasphemy, that once said, sets the spirit free? The literature of the past is a bore—when one has said that frankly to oneself, then one can proceed to qualify and make exceptions.

OLIVER WENDELL HOLMES, JR.

The ideas of the classics, so far as living, are our commonplaces. It is the modern books that give us the latest and most profound conceptions. It seems to me rather a lazy makeshift to mumble over the familiar.

OLIVER WENDELL HOLMES, JR.

My friend the professor of Greek tells me that he truly believes the classics have made him what he is. This is a very grave statement, if well founded. STEPHEN LEACOCK

Books are always the better for not being read. Look at our classics.
GEORGE BERNARD SHAW

Men turn to the classics to escape from their contemporaries.
FRANK MOORE COLBY

To read the great books of the past with intelligent appreciation is one of the last achievements of a studious life.
OLIVER WENDELL HOLMES, JR.

Midnight is the time when one can recall, with ribald delight, the names of all the Great Works which every gentleman ought to have read, but which some of us have not. For there is almost as much clotted nonsense written about literature as there is about theology.
H. M. TOMLINSON

Classical literature is the literature of which we do not expect anything new.
KAREL CAPEK

See also **Ancient, Books, Cicero, Homer, Literature, Plato, Shakespeare.**

CLASSIFICATION

The arrangement of our ideas is as much a matter of convenience as the packing of goods in a druggist's or draper's store and leads to exactly the same kind of difficulties in the matter of classifying them.
SAMUEL BUTLER

Probably a crab would be filled with a sense of personal outrage if it could hear us class it without ado or apology as a crustacean, and thus dispose of it. 'I am no such thing.' it would say; 'I am MYSELF, MYSELF alone.'
WILLIAM JAMES

A classification is a repertory of weapons for attack upon the future and the unknown.
JOHN DEWEY

Crude classifications and false generalizations are the curse of organized human life.
H. G. WELLS

There may be said to be two classes of people in the world: those who constantly divide the people of the world into two classes, and those who do not.
ROBERT BENCHLEY

See also **Logic.**

CLEAR

In language clarity is everything.
CONFUCIUS

When the eye is cleared of obstacles it sees sharply. When the ear is cleared of obstacles it hears well. When the nose is not blocked up, it smells well. When the mouth is cleared, it tastes well. When the mind is clear, it thinks well.
CHUANG-TSE

Whatever is clearly expressed is well wrote.
LADY MARY WORTLEY MONTAGU

Clarity is the good faith of philosophers.
VAUVENARGUES

Microscopes and telescopes confuse clear sight.
GOETHE

It is better to be profound in clear terms than in obscure terms.
JOSEPH JOUBERT

I see but one rule: to be clear. If I am not clear, all my world crumbles to nothing.
STENDHAL

Clarity is the supreme politeness of him who wields a pen.
JEAN HENRI FABRE

I don't care how incorrect language may be if it only has fitness of epithet, energy, and clearness.
WILLIAM JAMES

Everything that can be thought at all can be thought clearly. Everything that can be said can be said clearly. LUDWIG WITTGENSTEIN

See also **Intelligible, Obscure, Plain.**

CLEOPATRA

Caesar might have married Cleopatra, but he had a wife at home. There's always something.
WILL CUPPY

CLERGYMAN

Clergymen understand the least, and take the worst measure of human affairs, of all mankind that can read and write.
EARL OF CLARENDON

A man who is good enough to go to heaven, is good enough to be a clergyman. SAMUEL JOHNSON

Don't you know, as the French say, there are three sexes—men, women, and clergymen. SYDNEY SMITH

A congregation who can't afford to pay a clergyman enough want a missionary more than they do a clergyman. JOSH BILLINGS

See also **Bishop, Minister, Parson, Priest.**

CLEVER

What makes us so bitter against people who outwit us is that they think themselves cleverer than we are. LA ROCHEFOUCAULD

Clever men are the tools with which bad men work. WILLIAM HAZLITT

Only the sick in mind crave cleverness, as a morbid body turns to drink. H. M. TOMLINSON

See also **Intelligent, Wise.**

CLICHÉS

Q. What does an autopsy do? A. An autopsy reveals. Q. What do the police suspect? A. Foul play. Q. What do the neighbours do? A. They report that they heard a shot during the night but thought nothing of it, believing it to be the backfire of an automobile. Q. What is there no sign of after the crime? A. There is no sign of a weapon. Q. What does a murder do to the police? A. It baffles them.
FRANK SULLIVAN

CLOTHES

There are some on whom fine clothes weep. MONTAIGNE

If you have any enterprise before you, try it in your old clothes.
HENRY DAVID THOREAU

Modesty died when clothes were born. MARK TWAIN

Neatness is the asepsis of clothes.
SIR WILLIAM OSLER

To most people a savage nation is one that doesn't wear uncomfortable clothes. FINLEY PETER DUNNE

'When Suetonius wasn't busying himself with scandal he had an interesting nose for detail. Did you know what Augustus Caesar wore under his Imperial toga?' I said that I didn't. 'Flannel drawers.'
AUBREY MENEN

See also **Fashion, Sarong.**

CLUMSY

My hands are so clumsy I cannot write so as to read myself what I have written, and I'd rather scribble it over again than take the trouble to decipher it. MONTAIGNE

See also **Cannot.**

COCKTAIL

Whiskey and vermouth cannot meet as friends and the Manhattan is an offense against piety.
BERNARD DEVOTO

COFFEE

If you want to improve your understanding, drink coffee.
SYDNEY SMITH

COINCIDENCE

It is only in literature that coincidences seem unnatural.
ROBERT LYND

COLLECTING

It is perhaps a more fortunate destiny to have a taste for collecting shells than to be born a millionaire.
ROBERT LOUIS STEVENSON

One cannot collect all the beautiful shells on the beach.
ANNE MORROW LINDBERGH

COLOUR

(Of Cézanne:) The good conscience of those reds, of those blues, their simple truthfulness educates one.
RAINER MARIA RILKE

See also **Grey, Green.**

COMFORT

The scholar who cherishes a love of comfort is not fit to be deemed a scholar.
CONFUCIUS

A chief thing which thou hast to study and endeavour in this world is, to make thy life comfortable.
DR. THOMAS FULLER

(Of America:) Your diffusion of literacy and average comfort and well-being among the masses, in my opinion, is one of the major achievements in human history.
ALFRED NORTH WHITEHEAD

We have all sinned and come short of the glory of making ourselves as comfortable as we easily might have done.
SAMUEL BUTLER

COMIC

Man is a very comic creature, and most of the things he does are comic—eating, for instance. And the most comic things of all are exactly the things that are most worth doing—such as making love.
G. K. CHESTERTON

Human life is basically a comedy. Even its tragedies often seem comic to the spectator, and not infrequently they actually have comic touches to the victim. Happiness probably consists largely in the capacity to detect and relish them.
H. L. MENCKEN

See also **Funny, Joke, Laugh.**

COMMAND

It is always a great mistake to command when you are not sure you will be obeyed.
MIRABEAU

The reward of the general is not a bigger tent, but command.
OLIVER WENDELL HOLMES, JR.

COMMITTEE

Living movements do not come of committees.
JOHN HENRY NEWMAN

COMMON SENSE

Learning is the art of knowing how to use common sense to advantage.
JOSH BILLINGS

Common sense is the measure of the possible.
FRÉDÉRIC AMIEL

The voice of the Lord is the voice of common sense, which is shared by all that is.
SAMUEL BUTLER

After dinner we talked of India. The Duke gave an account of his attack at Assaye and of his acting on the conclusion that there must be a ford at a particular point of the river because he there saw two villages on the opposite sides of it. 'That,' he added, 'is common sense. And when one is strongly intent on an object, common sense will usually direct one to the right means.'
CONVERSATIONS WITH WELLINGTON

Academic and aristocratic people live in such an uncommon atmosphere that common sense can rarely reach them. SAMUEL BUTLER

Common sense is genius in homespun.
ALFRED NORTH WHITEHEAD

I think that common sense, in a rough dogged way, is technically sounder than the special schools of philosophy, each of which squints and overlooks half the facts and half the difficulties in its eagerness to find in some detail the key to the whole. GEORGE SANTAYANA

I don't know why it is that the religious never ascribe common sense to God. W. SOMERSET MAUGHAM

This country is where it is today on account of the real common sense of the big normal majority.
WILL ROGERS
See also **Sense.**

COMMONPLACE
An orator can hardly get beyond *commonplaces:* if he does, he gets beyond his hearers.
WILLIAM HAZLITT

Most remarks that are worth making are commonplace remarks. The thing that makes them worth saying is that we really mean them.
ROBERT LYND

Little minds are interested in the extraordinary; great minds in the commonplace. ELBERT HUBBARD

See also **Platitude, Truism.**

COMMUNISM
The mind of the universe is communistic. MARCUS AURELIUS

Advice to non-Communists: Everything is communal, even God.
CHARLES BAUDELAIRE

What a Communist he is! He would have an equal distribution of sin as well as property. OSCAR WILDE

Communists are frustrated Capitalists. ERIC HOFFER

See also **Socialism.**

COMPANY
A man is known by the company he organizes. AMBROSE BIERCE

See also **Corporation.**

COMPARISON
Comparison is the expedient of those who cannot reach the heart of the things compared.
GEORGE SANTAYANA

COMPASSION
The wretched have no compassion.
SAMUEL JOHNSON

Oh Thou who art! Ecclesiastes names thee the Almighty; Maccabees names thee Creator; the Epistle to the Ephesians names thee Liberty; Baruch names thee Immensity; the Psalms name thee Wisdom and Truth; John names thee Light; the Book of Kings names thee Lord; Exodus calls thee Providence; Leviticus, Holiness; Esdras, Justice; Creation calls thee God; Man names thee Father; but Solomon names thee Compassion, and that is the most beautiful of all thy names.

VICTOR HUGO

See also **Pity.**

COMPENSATION

The whole of what we know is a system of compensations. Every suffering is rewarded; every sacrifice is made up; every debt is paid.

RALPH WALDO EMERSON

COMPETITION

The wise man doesn't compete; therefore nobody can compete with him. LAO-TSE

Never compete.

BALTASAR GRACIÁN

COMPLAIN

He who complains, sins.

ST. FRANCIS DE SALES

When any fit of gloominess, or perversion of mind, lays hold upon you, make it a rule not to publish it by complaints, but exert your whole care to hide it. By endeavouring to hide it you will drive it away.

SAMUEL JOHNSON

To hear complaints is wearisome alike to the wretched and the happy.

SAMUEL JOHNSON

This life is not for complaint, but for satisfaction.

HENRY DAVID THOREAU

COMPLETE

God keep me from ever completing anything. This whole book is but a draft—nay, but the draft of a draft. Oh Time, Strength, Cash, and Patience! HERMAN MELVILLE

See also **Finish, Unfinished.**

COMPLEX

He who asks too much and enjoys complexities is likely to fall into error. GOETHE

Each human being is a more complex structure than any social system to which he belongs.

ALFRED NORTH WHITEHEAD

See also **Simple.**

COMPLIMENT

Some fellows pay a compliment like they expected a receipt.

KIN HUBBARD

COMPREHENSION

Oh! what blockheads are those wise persons who think it necessary that a child should comprehend everything he reads. ROBERT SOUTHEY

See also **Understanding.**

CONCEIT

Those who are wise in their own conceit seldom humbly accept guidance from others.

THOMAS À KEMPIS

Conceit is just as natural a thing to human minds as a centre is to a circle.

OLIVER WENDELL HOLMES, SR.

See also **Vanity.**

CONCESSION

All concession is lying.

ROBERT HENRI

CONCLUSION

Conclusions are not often reached by talk any more than by private thinking.

ROBERT LOUIS STEVENSON

CONDEMN

There is a law in human nature which draws us to be like what we passionately condemn.

G. W. RUSSELL (Æ)

CONDITIONS

The reigning error of mankind is, that we are not content with the conditions on which the goods of life are granted. SAMUEL JOHNSON

Conditions are never just right.
WILLIAM FEATHER

CONFESSION

Confess your sins to the Lord and you will be forgiven; confess them to man and you will be laughed at.
JOSH BILLINGS

All the good writers of confessions, from Augustine onwards, are men who are still a little in love with their sins. ANATOLE FRANCE

It is the confession, not the priest, that gives us absolution.
OSCAR WILDE

Confession is good for the soul only in the sense that a tweed coat is good for dandruff—it is a palliative rather than a remedy.
PETER DE VRIES

CONGRESS

It could probably be shown by facts and figures that there is no distinctively native American criminal class except Congress.
MARK TWAIN

CONQUER

I think Caesar was too old to set about amusing himself with conquering the world. Such sport was good for Augustus or Alexander. They were still young men, and thus difficult to restrain. But Caesar should have been more mature.
PASCAL

A conquered foe should be watched.
E. W. HOWE

The conquered almost always conquer. G. K. CHESTERTON

We wholly conquer only what we assimilate. ANDRÉ GIDE

See also **Conquest, Victory.**

CONQUEROR

A conqueror, like a cannon-ball, must go on. If he rebounds, his career is over.
DUKE OF WELLINGTON

CONQUEST

To delight in conquest is to delight in slaughter. LAO-TSE

The moral for conquerors of empires is that if they substitute savagery for civilization they are doomed.
GEORGE BERNARD SHAW

See also **Victory.**

CONSCIENCE

The laws of conscience, though we ascribe them to nature, actually come from custom. MONTAIGNE

There is another man within me that's angry with me.
SIR THOMAS BROWNE

Conscience and cowardice are really the same things. Conscience is the trade-name of the firm.
OSCAR WILDE

Men would rather be in error with the sanction of their conscience, than be right with the mere judgment of their reason.
JOHN HENRY NEWMAN

And what saved her virtue? The voice of her conscience? Oh no. The voice of her neighbour.
FRIEDRICH NIETZSCHE

The conscience has morbid sensibilities; it must be employed but not indulged, like the imagination or the stomach.
ROBERT LOUIS STEVENSON

Conscience is the most changeable of guides. VAUVENARGUES

All a man can betray is his conscience. JOSEPH CONRAD

Intensive activity blunts the doer to the sense of sin; it is only when his activity is thwarted that his conscience has opportunity to gnaw.
W. SOMERSET MAUGHAM

Nothing is better than frustration for waking up the conscience.
HENRY S. HASKINS

In artistic work one needs nothing so much as conscience: it is the sole standard. RAINER MARIA RILKE

Conscience is the inner voice which warns us that someone may be looking. H. L. MENCKEN

Conscience is a mother-in-law whose visit never ends.
M. L. MENCKEN

CONSCIOUS

I swear, gentlemen, that to be too conscious is an illness—a real thorough-going illness.
FEODOR DOSTOEVSKI

CONSERVATIVE

Some fellows get credit for being conservative when they are only stupid. KIN HUBBARD

See also **Radical.**

CONSISTENCY

Don't be 'consistent,' but be simply true.
OLIVER WENDELL HOLMES, SR.

Predicament: The wage of consistency. AMBROSE BIERCE

Consistency is the last refuge of the unimaginative. OSCAR WILDE

I think what has chiefly struck me in human beings is their lack of consistency. I have never seen people all of a piece. W. SOMERSET MAUGHAM
See also **Constancy, Inconsistency**

CONSTANCY

Steadfastness should be for the will, not for the mind.
BALTASAR GRACIÁN

Constancy, far from being a virtue, seems often to be the besetting sin of the human race, daughter of laziness and self-sufficiency, sister of sleep, the cause of most wars and practically all persecutions.
FREYA STARK

CONSTITUTION

A constitution is a vestment which accommodates itself to the body.
EDMUND BURKE

No society can make a perpetual constitution, or even a perpetual law. THOMAS JEFFERSON

A constitution is the work of time; one cannot provide in it too broad a power of amendment. NAPOLEON I

CONSULTATION

We sometimes deliberate when we want to commit some folly and call our friends together for consultation, just as rulers assume all the formalities of justice when they are most determined to violate it.
VAUVENARGUES

Consult: To seek another's approval of a course already decided on.
AMBROSE BIERCE

See also **Advice.**

CONTEMPT

Contempt is a kind of gangrene, which if it seizes one part of a character corrupts all the rest by degrees. SAMUEL JOHNSON

CONTENTMENT

There is no sin greater than yielding to ambition; no calamity greater than discontent; no vice greater than covetousness. He who has known the contentment of being contented will always be content.
LAO-TSE

All those who are contented with this life pass like a shadow and a dream, or wither like the flower of the field. CERVANTES

My motto is 'Contented with little, yet wishing for more.'
CHARLES LAMB

While a man is contented with himself and his own resources, all is well. When he undertakes to play a part on the stage, and to persuade the world to think more about him than they do about themselves, he is got into a track where he will find nothing but briars and thorns, vexation and disappointment.
WILLIAM HAZLITT

True contentment is the power of getting out of any situation all that there is in it. G. K. CHESTERTON

See also **Accept, Enough, Satisfaction.**

CONTRADICTION

Do not contradict the contradictor.
BALTASAR GRACIÁN

There is nothing contradictory in nature. VAUVENARGUES

To be contradicted, in order to force you to talk, is mighty unpleasing. You *shine*, indeed; but it is by being *ground*. SAMUEL JOHNSON

If anyone accuses me of contradicting myself, I reply: Because I have been wrong once, or several times, I don't intend to be wrong forever.
VAUVENARGUES

We cannot possibly imagine the variety of contradictions in every heart. LA ROCHEFOUCAULD

The well-bred contradict other people. The wise contradict themselves. OSCAR WILDE

If a man never contradicts himself, it is because he never says anything.
MIGUEL DE UNAMUNO

The contradictions the mind comes up against, these are the only realities, the criterion of the real. There is no contradiction in what is imaginary. Contradiction is the test of necessity. SIMONE WEIL

CONTRARY

Some folks are so contrary that if they fell in a river, they'd insist on floating upstream. JOSH BILLINGS

Method of investigation: As soon as we have thought something, try to see in what way the contrary is true.
SIMONE WEIL

CONTROVERSY

When a thing ceases to be a subject of controversy, it ceases to be a subject of interest. WILLIAM HAZLITT

It is not he who gains the exact point in dispute who scores most in controversy—but he who has shown the better temper.
SAMUEL BUTLER

See also **Arguing, Dispute, Quarrel.**

CONVENT

All severity that does not tend to increase good, or prevent evil, is idle. I said to the Lady Abbess of a convent, 'Madam, you are here, not for the love of virtue, but the fear of vice.' SAMUEL JOHNSON

If convents should be allowed at all. they should only be retreats for persons unable to serve the public, or who have served it. It is our first duty to serve society; and, after we have done that, we may attend wholly to the salvation of our own souls. A youthful passion for abstracted devotion should not be encouraged. SAMUEL JOHNSON

CONVERSATION

In my opinion, the most fruitful and natural play of the mind is conversation. The study of books is a drowsy and feeble exercise which does not warm you up.
MONTAIGNE

When I complained of having dined at a splendid table without hearing one sentence of conversation worthy of being remembered, Doctor Johnson said, 'Sir, there seldom is any such conversation.' Boswell: 'Why then meet at table?' Johnson: 'Why, to eat and drink together, and to promote kindness; and, sir, this is better done when there is no solid conversation; for when there is, people differ in opinion, and get into bad humour, or some of the company who are not capable of any such conversation, are left out, and feel themselves uneasy. It was for this reason, Sir Robert Walpole said, he always talked bawdy at his table, because in that all could join.'
BOSWELL (*Life of Johnson*)

'Let me not live,' saith Aretine's Antonia, 'if I had not rather hear thy discourse than see a play.'
ROBERT BURTON

There is not in the world a kind of life more sweet and delightful than that of a continual conversation with God. BROTHER LAWRENCE

One of the reasons that we find so few persons rational and agreeable in conversation is that there is hardly a person who does not think more of what he wants to say than of his answer to what is said.
LA ROCHEFOUCAULD

I never desire to converse with a man who has written more than he has read. SAMUEL JOHNSON

The misfortune of Goldsmith in conversation is this: he goes on without knowing how he is to get off. SAMUEL JOHNSON

It is the good of public life that it supplies agreeable topics and general conversation.
SAMUEL JOHNSON

Contradiction and flattery both make poor conversation. GOETHE

It is a very bad sign (unless where it arises from singular modesty) when you cannot tell a man's profession from his conversation. Such persons either feel no interest in what concerns them most, or do not express what they feel.
WILLIAM HAZLITT

Repose is as necessary in conversation as in a picture.
WILLIAM HAZLITT

The soul of conversation is sympathy. WILLIAM HAZLITT

If you are ever at a loss to support a flagging conversation, introduce the subject of eating. LEIGH HUNT

'What is the use of a book,' thought Alice, 'without pictures or conversations?' LEWIS CARROLL

Conversation should touch everything but should concentrate itself on nothing. OSCAR WILDE

After all, the only proper intoxication is conversation. OSCAR WILDE

Conversation between Adam and Eve must have been difficult at times because they had nobody to talk about. AGNES REPPLIER

The heart and the strength of the democratic way of living are the processes of effective give-and-take communication, of conference, of consultation, of exchange and pooling of experiences,—of free conversation if you will.

JOHN DEWEY

One half of our best society is always telling the other half what it does not wish to know, but the two halves take turns, and this establishes the conversation, usually on a peaceful basis.

FRANK MOORE COLBY

I have a notion that it is pleasanter to read Boswell's record of the conversations than it ever was to listen to Dr. Johnson.

W. SOMERSET MAUGHAM

Woman have simple tastes. They can get pleasure out of the conversation of children in arms and men in love. H. K. MENCKEN

See also **Talk.**

CONVERSION

Men often take their imagination for their heart; and they believe they are converted as soon as they think of being converted. PASCAL

A Protestant preacher's idea of great success in his work is to convert a Catholic. E. W. HOWE

To go through life without ever being converted to anything seems a mark of insensitiveness. The ideal world would be a world in which everybody was capable of conversion and in which at the same time the converts would admit the possibility that they might be mistaken.

ROBERT LYND

Tolerance cannot afford to have anything to do with the fallacy that evil may convert itself to good.

FREYA STARK

CONVICTION

Every fool is fully convinced, and everyone fully persuaded is a fool.

BALTASAR GRACIÁN

I have better uses for my leisure than to try to bring others round to any convictions of mine, such as they are. NORMAN DOUGLAS

See also **Opinion.**

COOKING

Cooking is one of those arts which most require to be done by persons of a religious nature.

ALFRED NORTH WHITEHEAD

See also **Food, Kitchen.**

CORPORATION

Corporate bodies are more corrupt and profligate than individuals, because they have more power to do mischief, and are less amenable to disgrace and punishment.

WILLIAM HAZLITT

Corporation: An ingenious device for obtaining individual profit without individual responsibility.

AMBROSE BIERCE

It is idle to suppose that corporations will not be brought more and more under public control.

ALFRED NORTH WHITEHEAD

See also **Company.**

CORRUPTION

Some places have such a corrupting influence upon the man that it is a supernatural thing to resist it.

LORD HALIFAX

See also **Incorruptibility.**

COST OF LIVING

I haven't heard of anybody who wants to stop living on account of the cost. KIN HUBBARD

COUNTRY

No wise man will go to live in the country, unless he has something to do which can be better done in the country. SAMUEL JOHNSON

I have no relish for the country; it is a kind of healthy grave.

SYDNEY SMITH

O let no native Londoner imagine that health, and rest, and innocent occupation, interchange of converse, sweet and recreative study, can make the country anything better than altogether odious and detestable. CHARLES LAMB

See also **City, Nature, Scenery, Town and Country, Tree.**

COURAGE

Valour lies just half-way between rashness and cowardice.

CERVANTES

We have more respect for a man who robs boldly on a highway than for a fellow who jumps out of a ditch and knocks you down behind your back. Courage is a quality so necessary for maintaining virtue, that it is always respected even when it is associated with vice.

SAMUEL JOHNSON

Nothing but courage can guide life.

VAUVENARGUES

Perfect courage means doing unwitnessed what one would be capable of doing before the whole world. LA ROCHEFOUCAULD

A man who has never been in danger cannot answer for his courage.

LA ROCHEFOUCAULD

As to moral courage, I have very rarely met with the *two o'clock in the morning kind*. I mean unprepared courage, that which is necessary on an unexpected occasion, and which, in spite of the most unforeseen events, leaves full freedom of judgment and decision. NAPOLEON I

A great part of courage is the courage of having done the thing before.

RALPH WALDO EMERSON

What is more mortifying than to feel that you've missed the plum for want of courage to shake the tree?

LOGAN PEARSALL SMITH

Courage is rightly esteemed the first of human qualities because it is the quality which guarantees all others.

WINSTON S. CHURCHILL

Courage can be a very difficult neurosis. GRAHAM GREENE

See also **Brave, Coward, Pluck.**

COURTESY

Hail, ye small sweet courtesies of life, for smooth do ye make the road of it; like grace and beauty, which beget inclinations to love at first sight: 'tis ye who open this door and let the stranger in.

LAURENCE STERNE

The pleasure of courtesy is like the pleasure of good dancing. ALAIN

See also **Manners, Politeness.**

COW

Some people want to see God with their eyes as they see a cow, and love Him as they love a cow—for the milk and cheese and profit it brings them.   MEISTER ECKHART

My cow milks me.
RALPH WALDO EMERSON

Oh, labour is the curse of the world, and nobody can meddle with it without becoming proportionately brutified. Is it a praiseworthy matter that I have spent five golden months in providing food for cows and horses? It is not so.
NATHANIEL HAWTHORNE

COWARD

There are not many cowards who know the whole of their fear.
LA ROCHEFOUCAULD

There are cowards who will make one effort to exert their courage, that they may have a pretence to avoid danger the rest of their lives.
ROUSSEAU

See also **Brave, Courage, Fear.**

CRACK

There is a crack in everything God has made.
RALPH WALDO EMERSON

It is through the cracks in our brains that ecstasy creeps in.
LOGAN PEARSALL SMITH

CREATIVE

In the creative state a man is taken out of himself. He lets down as it were a bucket into his subconscoius, and draws up something which is normally beyond his reach. He mixes this thing with his normal experiences, and out of the mixture he makes a work of art.
E. M. FORSTER

Man is preeminently a creative animal, predestined to strive consciously for an object and to engage in engineering—that is, incessantly and eternally to make new roads, *wherever they may lead.*
FEODOR DOSTOEVSKI

When you follow nature, you get everything. . . . The point is not to create. Creation and improvisation are useless words. Genius only comes to the man who understands with his eye and his brain.
RODIN

The so-called progressive gogues, in the days of their glory, had a large and bristling vocabulary of their own, much of it lifted from the lingo of the psychoanalysts, the various warring wings of psychologists, the Rotarians and the Boy Scouts. One of its favourite terms was *creative.*   H. L. MENCKEN

See also **Art.**

CREDIT

No man's credit is as good as his money.   E. W. HOWE

See also **Creditors, Debt.**

CREDITORS

No man is impatient with his creditors.   TALMUD

See also **Credit, Debt.**

CREED

The best creed we can have is charity towards the creeds of others.
JOSH BILLINGS

Those who enter heaven may find the outer walls plastered with creeds, but they won't find any on the inside.   JOSH BILLINGS

See also **Belief, Faith, Religion.**

CRIME

We are only to relieve the afflicted, to look on their distress, and not on their crimes.   CERVANTES

Those who are incapable of committing great crimes do not easily suspect others.
                    LA ROCHEFOUCAULD

There are crimes which become innocent and even glorious by their brilliancy, their number, or their excess: thus it happens that public robbery is called financial skill, and the unjust capture of provinces is called a conquest.
                    LA ROCHEFOUCAULD

Nobody ever commits a crime without doing something stupid.
                        OSCAR WILDE

People have got so accustomed to having life seasoned with crime and poverty that they cannot contemplate a life without it.
                    GEORGE BERNARD SHAW

A transgression, a crime, entering a man's existence, eats it up like a malignant growth, consumes it like a fever.   JOSEPH CONRAD

The real significance of crime is in its being a breach of faith with the community of mankind.
                    JOSEPH CONRAD

See also **Murder, Thief.**

CRIMINAL

Every criminal is an atheist, though he doesn't always know it.
                    HONORÉ DE BALZAC

Our criminal system is an organized attempt to produce white by two blacks.   GEORGE BERNARD SHAW

CRITIC

To be a good critic demands more brains and judgment than most men possess.   JOSH BILLINGS

To feel himself freer than his neighbour is the reward of the critic.
                    FRÉDÉRIC AMIEL

See also **Criticism.**

CRITICISM

'Tis a very excellent piece of work, madam lady. Would 'twere done.
                    SHAKESPEARE
        (*The Taming of the Shrew*, I, i)

There is always an appeal open from criticism to nature.
                    SAMUEL JOHNSON

Of all the cants which are canted in this canting world, though the cant of hypocrites may be the worst, the cant of criticism is the most tormenting.   LAURENCE STERNE

Criticism is the adventure of the soul among masterpieces.
                    ANATOLE FRANCE

The imagination imitates; it is the critical spirit that creates.
                        OSCAR WILDE

The entertainer suffers from no criticism whatever. No one has told P. G. Wodehouse which is his best book or his worst, what are his faults or how he should improve them. The fate of the entertainer is simply to go on till he wakes up one morning to find himself obscure.
                    CYRIL CONNOLLY

See also **Critic, Censure.**

CROSS

If you bear the cross unwillingly, you make it a burden, and load yourself more heavily; but you must needs bear it. If you cast away one cross, you will certainly find another, and perhaps a heavier.
                    THOMAS À KEMPIS

To repel one's cross is to make it heavier.   FRÉDÉRIC AMIEL

CROWD

There is an accumulative cruelty in a number of men, though none in particular are ill-natured.
LORD HALIFAX

Wherever there is a crowd there is untruth. SÖREN KIERKEGAARD

When a hundred men stand together, each of them loses his mind and gets another one.
FRIEDRICH NIETZSCHE

See also **Multitude.**

CRUELTY

I cruelly hate cruelty, both by nature and reason, as the worst of all the vices. MONTAIGNE

Scarce anything awakens attention like a tale of cruelty.
SAMUEL JOHNSON

CULTURE

Launch your boat, blest youth, and flee at full speed from every form of culture. EPICURUS

Culture is like the sum of special knowledge that accumulates in any large united family and is the common property of all its members. When we of the great Culture Family meet, we exchange reminiscences about Grandfather Homer, and that awful old Dr. Johnson, and Aunt Sappho, and poor Johnny Keats. ALDOUS HUXLEY

The poor have no business with culture and should beware of it. They cannot eat it; they cannot sell it; they can only pass it on to others and that is why the world is full of hungry people ready to teach us anything under the sun.
AUBREY MENEN

See also **Civilized.**

CURIOSITY

The secret of happiness is curiosity.
NORMAN DOUGLAS

A free curiosity has more efficacy in learning than a frightful enforcement. ST. AUGUSTINE

Beware of being over-curious about matters beyond your knowledge.
THOMAS À KEMPIS

Curiosity is, in great and generous minds, the first passion and the last.
SAMUEL JOHNSON

Curiosity is one of the permanent and certain characteristics of a vigorous intellect. SAMUEL JOHNSON

The public have an insatiable curiosity to know everything, except what is worth knowing.
OSCAR WILDE

History may be read as the story of the magnificent rearguard action fought during several thousand years by dogma against curiosity.
ROBERT LYND

CUT

Never cut what you can untie.
JOSEPH JOUBERT

Every writer hits now and then upon a thought that seems to him so happy, a repartee that amuses him so much, that to cut it is worse than having a tooth out; it is then that it is well to have engraved on his heart the maxim, If you can, cut.
W. SOMERSET MAUGHAM

CYNIC

To the true cynic nothing is ever revealed. OSCAR WILDE

Cynicism is intellectual dandyism.
GEORGE MEREDITH

Cynics are only happy in making the world as barren for others as they have made it for themselves.
GEORGE MEREDITH

A cold and cynical wisdom particularly disapproves of most men's best actions.   WALTER BAGEHOT

The opposite of the religious fanatic is not the fanatical atheist but the gentle cynic who cares not whether there is a God or not.
ERIC HOFFER

A cynic is just a man who found out when he was about ten that there wasn't any Santa Claus, and he's still upset. JAMES GOULD COZZENS

D

DAMN

Damn braces. Bless relaxes.
WILLIAM BLAKE

CHARLES LAMB was once bored by a lady praising to him 'such a charming man!' etc., etc., ending with 'I know him, bless him!' on which Lamb said, 'Well, I don't, but damn him, at a hazard,'
When we say *damn*, it relieves us because it is a strong word and yet means nothing; we do not intend the person or thing or event that we damn to be burnt in hell fire; far from it; but the faint aroma of brimstone that hangs forever about the word is savoury in wrathful nostrils.
H. W. FOWLER

See also **Profanity.**

DANCING

The Earl of Leicester, knowing that Queen Elizabeth was much delighted to see gentlemen dance well, brought the master of the dancing school to dance before her. 'Pish,' said the Queen, 'it is his profession, I will not see him.'
THOMAS FULLER

DANGER

A heart full of courage and cheerfulness needs a little danger from time to time, or the world gets unbearable.   FRIEDRICH NIETZSCHE

DARK AGES

Perhaps in time the so-called Dark Ages will be thought of as including our own. G. C. LICHTENBERG

See also **Middle Ages.**

DARKNESS

Give light, and the darkness will disappear of itself.   ERASMUS

Hans Sachs, in describing Chaos, said it was so pitchy dark, that even the very cats ran against each other.
SAMUEL TAYLOR COLERIDGE

DAY

Nothing is worth more than this day.   GOETHE

We are told, 'Let not the sun go down on your wrath.' This, of course, is best; but, as it generally does, I would add, Never act or write till is has done so. This rule has saved me from many an act of folly. It is wonderful what a different view we take of the same event four-and-twenty hours after it has happened.   SYDNEY SMITH

The days run through me as water through a sieve.   SAMUEL BUTLER

When one has much to put into them, a day has a hundred pockets.
FRIEDRICH NIETZSCHE

DAYDREAM

Reverie is the Sunday of thought.
FRÉDÉRIC AMIEL

How many of our daydreams would darken into nightmares, were there a danger of their coming true!   LOGAN PEARSALL SMITH

See also **Castles in the Air.**

DEAD

After supper she got out her book and learned me about Moses and the Bulrushers, and I was in a sweat to find out all about him; but by and by she let out that Moses had been dead a considerable long time; so then I didn't care no more about him, because I don't take no stock in dead people.   MARK TWAIN

See also **Death, Dying.**

DEATH

We don't know life: how can we know death?   CONFUCIUS

There is no man so blessed that some who stand by his deathbed won't hail the occasion with delight.   MARCUS AURELIUS

As a well-spent day brings happy sleep, so a life well used brings happy death.   LEONARDO DA VINCI

It is certain that to most men the preparation for death has been a greater torment than the suffering of it.   MONTAIGNE

Death is only a larger kind of going abroad.   SAMUEL BUTLER

I knew a man who had been virtually drowned and then revived. He said that his death had not been painful.   ANDRÉ MAUROIS

See also **Dead, Dying, Funeral.**

DEBT

Debts shorten life.
JOSEPH JOUBERT

He who has a claim for money upon his neighbour and knows that the latter is unable to pay, must not pass by him constantly.   TALMUD

Small debts are like smallshot; they are rattling on every side, and can scarcely be escaped without a wound: great debts are like cannon; of loud noise, but little danger.
SAMUEL JOHNSON

It is a sure sign of an improved character if you like paying debts as much as getting money.
G. C. LICHTENBERG

A man in debt is so far a slave.
RALPH WALDO EMERSON

If I had the privilege of making the Eleventh Commandment it would be this—*Owe no man.*
JOSH BILLINGS

See also **Credit, Creditors.**

DECEIVING

The art of pleasing is the art of deceiving.   VAUVENARGUES

We are never deceived: we deceive ourselves.   GOETHE

Our senses don't deceive us: our judgment does.   GOETHE

The secret of life is to appreciate the pleasure of being terribly deceived.   OSCAR WILDE

DECISION

It is better to stir up a question without deciding it, than to decide it without stirring it up.
JOSEPH JOUBERT

In financial matters, no decision is often better than a hasty decision.
WILLIAM FEATHER

The man who insists upon seeing with perfect clearness before he decides, never decides. Accept life, and you must accept regret.
FRÉDÉRIC AMIEL

The soul of dispatch is decision.
WILLIAM HAZLITT

All human acts involve more chance than decision. ANDRÉ GIDE

The fine art of executive decision consists in not deciding questions that are not now pertinent, in not deciding prematurely, in not making decisions that cannot be made effective, and in not making decisions that others should make.
CHESTER I. BARNARD

See also **Indecision.**

DEFECT
We only work out our way to excellence by being imprisoned in defects. JAMES NORTHCOTE

He tries, not without success, to compensate for his lack of talent by defects of character.
ALFRED POLGAR

See also **Fault.**

DEFENSE
It is a fixed rule with the wise never to defend themselves with the pen.
BALTASAR GRACIÁN

DEFINITION
'If the Prince of Wei were to ask you to take over the government, what would you put first on your agenda?' 'The one thing needed.' replied the Master, 'is the definition of terms. If terms are ill-defined, statements disagree with facts; when statements disagree with facts, business is mismanaged: when business is mismanaged, order and harmony do not flourish; when order and harmony do not flourish, then justice becomes arbitrary; and when justice becomes arbitrary, the people do not know how to move hand or foot.' CONFUCIUS

'Then, Sir, what is poetry?' 'Why. Sir, it is much easier to say what it is not. We all *know* what light is, but it is not easy to *tell* what it is.'
BOSWELL
(*Life of Johnson*)

Definitions might be good things, if only we did not employ words in making them. ROUSSEAU

Definitions are a kind of scratching, and generally leave a sore place more sore than it was before.
SAMUEL BUTLER

Although it may be very difficult to define in law what is or what is not a trade union, most people of common sense know a trade union when they see one. It is like trying to define a rhinoceros: it is difficult enough, but if one is seen, everybody can recognize it.
WINSTON S. CHURCHILL

DELICACY
If a person has no delicacy, he has you in his power.
WILLIAM HAZLITT

DEMOCRACY
Were there a people of gods, their government would be democratic.
ROUSSEAU

All real democracy is an attempt (like that of a jolly hostess) to bring the shy people out.
G. K. CHESTERTON

A fanatical belief in democracy makes democratic institutions impossible. BERTRAND RUSSELL

The democratic faith is this: that the most terribly important things must be left to ordinary men themselves—the mating of the sexes, the rearing of the young, the laws of the state. G. K. CHESTERTON

If the government was as afraid of disturbing the consumer as it is of disturbing business, this would be some democracy.   KIN HUBBARD

The first of all democratic doctrines is that all men are interesting.
G. K. CHESTERTON

Two cheers for democracy: one because it admits variety and two because it permits criticism.
E. M. FORSTER

Democracy is the recurrent suspicion that more than half of the people are right more than half of the time.   E. B. WHITE

See also **Congress, Electorate, Parliament.**

DENIAL

It is always easy to be on the negative side. If a man were not to deny that there is salt upon the table, you could not reduce him to an absurdity.   SAMUEL JOHNSON

See also **No.**

DENTIST

Dentists and solicitors. These are the people to whom we always show our best side.   SAMUEL BUTLER

DESCRIPTION

It is a rule to never be forgotten, that whatever strikes strongly, should be described while the first impression remains fresh upon the mind.   SAMUEL JOHNSON

Description is always a bore, both to the describer and the describee.
BENJAMIN DISRAELI

When a man acts he is a puppet. When he describes he is a poet.
OSCAR WILDE

Stephen Thorle recounted a slum experience in which two entire families did all their feeding out of one damaged soup-plate. 'The gratitude of those poor creatures when I presented them with a set of table crockery apiece, the tears in their eyes and in their voices when they thanked me, would be impossible to describe.' 'Thank you all the same for describing it,' said Comus.
SAKI

DESIRE

It would not be better for mankind if they were given their desires.
HERACLITUS

I have made it my habit to alter my desires rather than the order of the world, and to consider that what has not come about is, so far as I was concerned, an absolute impossibility.   DESCARTES

If there is nothing left to desire, there is everything to fear, an unhappy state of happiness.
BALTASAR GRACIÁN

There are two tragedies in life. One is to lose your heart's desire. The other is to gain it.
GEORGE BERNARD SHAW

Some desire is necessary to keep life in motion.   SAMUEL JOHNSON

That man is truly free who desires what he is able to perform, and does what he desires.   ROUSSEAU

He who desires but acts not, breeds pestilence.   WILLIAM BLAKE

Sooner murder an infant in its cradle than nurse unacted desires.
WILLIAM BLAKE

Our duty is to be useful, not according to our desires but according to our powers.
FRÉDÉRIC AMIEL

The stoical scheme of supplying our wants by lopping off our desires is like cutting off our feet when we want shoes. JONATHAN SWIFT

A man who has had his way is seldom happy, for generally he finds that the way does not lead very far on this earth of desires which can never be fully satisfied. JOSEPH CONRAD

I like to walk down Bond Street, thinking of all the things I don't desire. LOGAN PEARSALL SMITH

See also **Wish**.

DESPAIR

One must never despair if something is lost to one, a person or a joy or a happiness; everything comes back again more gloriously. RAINER MARIA RILKE

Life begins on the other side of despair. JEAN-PAUL SARTRE

See also **Desperate, Discouragement, Hope**.

DESPERATE

It is a characteristic of wisdom not to do desperate things. HENRY DAVID THOREAU

See also **Despair**.

DESTINY

People born to be hanged are safe in water. MARK TWAIN'S MOTHER

Lots of folks confuse bad management with destiny. KIN HUBBARD

It is a mistake to look too far ahead. Only one link in the chain of destiny can be handled at a time. WINSTON S. CHURCHILL

Destiny is an invention of the cowardly and the resigned. IGNAZIO SILONE

See also **Fate, Happen, Providence**.

DETACHMENT

A man that steps aside from the world and has leisure to observe it without interest and design, thinks all mankind as mad as they think him. LORD HALIFAX

Every scene, even the commonest, is wonderful, if only one can detach oneself, casting off all memory of use and custom, and behold it (as it were) for the first time; in its right, authentic colours; without making comparisons. ARNOLD BENNETT

See also **Spectator**.

DETAILS

One should absorb the colour of life, but one should never remember its details. Details are always vulgar. OSCAR WILDE

DETERMINISM

This then is determinism: to learn to understand the causes of evil, so that we may induce the causes of reform. Not to be a fatalist, or a slave, a slave of oneself, or a slave of one's surroundings. Wherever we are, not to act and work blindly, but freely and consciously, to anticipate and plan like a worker and collaborator of God. THOMAS G. MASARYK

See also **Fatalism, Fate, Free Will**.

DEVIL

The devil does not tempt unbelievers and sinners who are already his own. THOMAS À KEMPIS

All religions issue Bibles against Satan, and say the most injurious things against him, but we never hear his side. MARK TWAIN

It is the devil's masterstroke to get us to accuse him.

GEORGE MEREDITH

An apology for the devil. It must be remembered that we have only heard one side of the case. God has written all the books.

SAMUEL BUTLER

See also **God and the Devil.**

DEWEY, JOHN

(On his *Experience and Nature:*) So methought God would have spoken had He been inarticulate but keenly desirous to tell you how it was.

OLIVER WENDELL HOLMES, JR.

DIAGNOSIS

Diagnosis is one of the commonest diseases. KARL KRAUS

See also **Doctor, Medicine, Physician.**

DICKENS, CHARLES

I have no sense of humour. In illustration of this fact I will say this— by way of confession—that if there is a humorous passage in the *Pickwick Papers* I have never been able to find it. MARK TWAIN

One must have a heart of stone to read the death of Little Nell without laughing. OSCAR WILDE

DICTIONARY

Dictionaries are like watches: the worst is better than none, and the best cannot be expected to go quite true. SAMUEL JOHNSON

The trouble with the dictionary is that you have to know how a word is spelled before you can look it up to see how it is spelled.

WILL CUPPY

DIET

They keep ordering us not merely a new diet, but the very opposite to that we are accustomed to: a change that not even a healthy man can suffer. . . . If they do no other good they do this at least, that they prepare their patients betimes for death, by gradually undermining and cutting off their enjoyment of life. MONTAIGNE

Sermons on diet ought to be preached in the churches at least once a week. G. C. LICHTENBERG

When a man diets, he eats oatmeal in addition to everything else he usually eats. E. W. HOWE

If specific exercises in self-denial are undertaken, they should be inconspicuous, non-competitive and uninjurious to health. Thus, in the matter of diet, most people will find it sufficiently mortifying to refrain from eating all the things which the experts in nutrition condemn as unwholesome. ALDOUS HUXLEY

See also **Eating, Food, Regime, Vegetarianism, Vitamins.**

DIFFERENCE

We boil at different degrees.

RALPH WALDO EMERSON

An unlearned carpenter of my acquaintance once said in my hearing: 'There is very little difference between one man and another; but what little there is, *is very important.*'

WILLIAM JAMES

See also **Distinction.**

DIFFICULT

To sow is less difficult than to reap.

GOETHE

Seek not things that are too hard for thee, and search not out things that are above thy strength.
ECCLESIASTICUS 3

Do what is easy as if it were difficult, and what is difficult as if it were easy.   BALTASAR GRACIÁN

Exercise, exercise your powers: what is now difficult will finally become routine.
G. C. LICHTENBERG

Never do a thing that you find difficult, because another person who finds it easy will beat you at the game.   WILLIAM MORRIS

Blame it, this whole thing is just as easy and awkward as it can be. And so it makes it so rotten difficult to get up a difficult plan.
MARK TWAIN

No man who is occupied in doing a very difficult thing, and doing it very well, ever loses his self-respect.
GEORGE BERNARD SHAW

What is required of us is that we *love the difficult* and learn to deal with it. In the difficult are the friendly forces, the hands that work on us.   RAINER MARIA RILKE

A great many people, maybe most people, confronted by a difficult situation, one in which they don't know what to do, get nowhere because they are so busy pointing out that the situation should be remade so they *will* know what to do.
JAMES GOULD COZZENS

See also **Difficulty, Easy, Problem.**

DIFFICULTY

Wanting to change, to improve, a person's situation means offering him, for difficulties in which he is

practiced and experienced, other difficulties that will find him perhaps even more bewildered.
RAINER MARIA RILKE

I sometimes suspect that half our difficulties are imaginary and that if we kept quiet about them they would disappear.   ROBERT LYND

See also **Difficult, Problem, Trouble.**

DIGESTION

Digestion is the great secret of life.
SYDNEY SMITH

Happiness for me is largely a matter of digestion.   LIN YUTANG

See also **Dyspepsia, Indigestion, Stomach.**

DIGRESSION

Digressions, incontestably, are the sunshine;—they are the life, the soul of reading!—take them out of this book, for instance,—you might as well take the book along with them;—one cold eternal winter would reign in every page of it; restore them to the writer;—he steps forth like a bridegroom,—bids All-hail; brings in variety, and forbids the appetite to fail.
LAURENCE STERNE

DIMINISHING RETURNS

The law of diminishing returns holds good in almost every part of our human universe.
ALDOUS HUXLEY

DINNER

A man seldom thinks with more earnestness of anything than he does of his dinner.
SAMUEL JOHNSON

When a man is invited to dinner, he is disappointed if he does not get something good. Everybody loves to have things which please the palate put in their way, without trouble or preparation.

SAMUEL JOHNSON

A man's own dinner is to himself so important that he cannot bring himself to believe that it is a matter utterly indifferent to anyone else.

ANTHONY TROLLOPE

See also **Eating, Meals.**

DISAGREEABLE

If the truth were known, the most disagreeable people are the most amiable. WILLIAM HAZLITT

See also **Agreeable.**

DISAGREEMENT

To disagree with three-fourths of the British public on all points is one of the first elements of sanity, one of the deepest consolations in all moments of spiritual doubt.

OSCAR WILDE

A disagreement may be the shortest cut between two minds.

KAHLIL GIBRAN

DISCIPLINE

It is one thing to praise discipline, and another to submit to it.

CERVANTES

DISCONTENT

Let thy discontents be secrets.

BENJAMIN FRANKLIN

All the discontented people I know are trying sedulously to be something they are not, to do something they cannot do. DAVID GRAYSON

See also **Contentment.**

DISCOURAGEMENT

Nothing resembles pride so much as discouragement.

FRÉDÉRIC AMIEL

Discouragement serves no possible purpose; it is simply the despair of wounded self-love.

FRANÇOIS DE FÉNELON

See also **Despair.**

DISCRETION

Thy friend has a friend, and thy friends' friend has a friend; be discreet. TALMUD

See also **Indiscretion.**

DISCUSSION

It is nearly always difficulties born of his own ideas, not those born of the nature of things, with which man is struggling in the discussions that torment the mind of himself and his fellows.

JOSEPH JOUBERT

Discussion: A method of confirming others in their errors.

AMBROSE BIERCE

DISEASE

We ought to give diseases free access to us; and I have found that they stay a shorter time with me, who give them a free hand. And some have left me, even of those reputed among the most tenacious and stubborn, dying of their own decay, without the help of the art of medicine, and in spite of its rules.

MONTAIGNE

Diseases are the price of ill pleasures.

THOMAS FULLER

To talk of diseases is a sort of Arabian Nights' entertainment.

SIR WILLIAM OSLER

There is a nobility of disease as there is a nobility of health.

THOMAS MANN

See also **Distemper, Dyspepsia, Epidemic, Health, Sick, Rheumatism.**

DISHONEST

A man who only does what everyone of the society to which he belongs would do, is not a dishonest man.   SAMUEL JOHNSON

See also **Honesty.**

DISLIKE

If people are made to do what they dislike, you must allow for a little ill-humour.   LORD MELBOURNE

There are two ways of disliking art. One is to dislike it. The other is to like it rationally.   OSCAR WILDE

Too many moralists begin with a dislike of reality: a dislike of men as they are.   CLARENCE DAY

DISORDERLY

There are some enterprises in which a careful disorderliness is the true method.   HERMAN MELVILLE

One of the advantages of being disorderly is that one is constantly making exciting discoveries.   A. A. MILNE

See also **Orderliness.**

DISPLACED

Most men are displaced.   LE SAGE

DISPLAY

If there were no such thing as display in the world, my private opinion is, and I hope you agree with me, that we might get on a great deal better than we do, and might be infinitely more agreeable company than we are.   CHARLES DICKENS

DISPUTE

A long dispute means that both parties are wrong.   VOLTAIRE

Nothing was ever learnt by either side in a dispute.   WILLIAM HAZLITT

Truths turn into dogmas the instant that they are disputed.   G. K. CHESTERTON

See also **Controversy, Disagreement, Quarrel.**

DISTANT

There are charms made only for distant admiration. No spectacle is nobler than a blaze.   SAMUEL JOHNSON

I look on distant objectives as decoys for fools.   ROUSSEAU

DISTEMPER

Every age, like every human body, has its own distemper.   RALPH WALDO EMERSON

DISTINCTION

When a doubt is propounded, you must learn to distinguish, and show wherein a thing holds, and wherein it doth not hold. Ay, or no, never answered any question. The not distinguishing where things should be distinguished, and the not confounding where things should be confounded, is the cause of all the mistakes in the world.   JOHN SELDEN

A distinction that does not further understanding is no distinction.   GOETHE

See also **Difference.**

DISTRUST

He who distrusts God is not worthy to be His instrument.   FRANÇOIS DE FÉNELON

DIVINE

Not he that adorns but he that adores makes a divinity.

BALTASAR GRACIÁN

What is there of the divine in a load of bricks? What is there of the divine in a barber's shop? . . . Much. All.

RALPH WALDO EMERSON

It is a maxim of our fathers that there is in every god an element of the divine.　ANATOLE FRANCE

See also **God, Holy.**

DIVORCE

The worst reconciliation is preferable to the best divorce.

CERVANTES

DOCTOR

All the happy effects that the patient feels, who is under their care, is due to them. . . . When an unfortunate accident occurs, they will disclaim all responsibility, and lay the blame on the patient; and they take care never to be at a loss for any number of frivolous reasons, such as, 'he must have left his arm uncovered; he has heard the rattling of a coach; somebody has opened the window; he has been lying on his left side; he has been thinking of something painful.'　MONTAIGNE

The medical art is not so cut and dried that we cannot find some authority for doing whatever we please. If your doctor does not think it good for you to sleep, to drink wine, or to eat of a particular dish, do not worry; I will find you another who will not agree with him.　MONTAIGNE

There's another advantage of being poor—a doctor will cure you faster.

KIN HUBBARD

The best doctor is the one you run for and can't find.　DIDEROT

One of the most advanced types of human being on earth today is the *good* American doctor.

ALFRED NORTH WHITEHEAD

Live so that you stick out your tongue at the insurance doctor.

DON MARQUIS

Doctors know what you tell them.

DON HEROLD

See also **Medicine, Patient, Physician.**

DOCTRINE

A clash of doctrines is not a disaster —it is an opportunity.

ALFRED NORTH WHITEHEAD

See also **Theory.**

DOG

I had rather see the portrait of a dog that I know than all the allegorical paintings they can show me in the world.　SAMUEL JOHNSON

When a dog runs at you, whistle for him.　HENRY DAVID THOREAU

Money will buy a pretty good dog but it won't buy the wag of his tail.

JOSH BILLINGS

The great pleasure of a dog is that you may make a fool of yourself with him and not only will he not scold you, but he will make a fool of himself too.　SAMUEL BUTLER

A dog teaches a boy fidelity, perseverance, and to turn around three times before lying down.

ROBERT BENCHLEY

See also **Animals, Bulldog.**

DOGMA

The greater the ignorance the greater the dogmatism.

SIR WILLIAM OSLER

The man who has a dogmatic creed has more time left for his business.
HENRY S. HASKINS

DOING

Whoever loves much, does much.
THOMAS À KEMPIS

No man is obliged to do as much as he can do. A man is to have part of his life to himself.
SAMUEL JOHNSON

All our business in life is with doing: enjoyment and suffering come by themselves.   GOETHE

Even in science we can never really know. We must always do.
GOETHE

How many years you have to keep on doing, until you know what to do and how to do it!   GOETHE

Our main business is not to see what lies dimly at a distance, but to do what lies clearly at hand.
THOMAS CARLYLE

We do what we must, and call it by the best names.
RALPH WALDO EMERSON

Our chief want in life, is, somebody who shall make us do what we can.
RALPH WALDO EMERSON

The art of life, of a poet's life, is, not having anything to do, to do something.   HENRY DAVID THOREAU

I came into this world, not chiefly to make this a good place to live in, but to live in it, be it good or bad. A man has not everything to do, but something; and because he cannot do *everything*, it is not necessary that he should do *something* wrong.
HENRY DAVID THOREAU

To find out what one is fitted to do and to secure an opportunity to do it is the key to happiness.
JOHN DEWEY

'What shall I think of it?' a common person says to himself about a vexed question; but in a 'cranky' mind 'What must I do about it?' is the form the question tends to take.
WILLIAM JAMES

The doer alone learneth.
FRIEDRICH NIETZSCHE

To know just what has to be done, then to do it, comprises the whole philosophy of practical life.
SIR WILLIAM OSLER

Never learn to do anything. If you don't learn you'll always find someone else to do it for you.
MARK TWAIN'S MOTHER

Do whatever you do intensely.
ROBERT HENRI

If a thing is worth doing, it is worth doing badly.   G. K. CHESTERTON

We sin grievously against ourselves when we get somebody to do something for us which we could do.
HENRY S. HASKINS

Many of the things we are struggling to do would be much obliged to us if we took our minds off them.
HENRY S. HASKINS

He who wants to do everything will never do anything.
ANDRÉ MAUROIS

The great thing in life is not to be able to do things, because then they are always done for you.
ANGELA THIRKELL

Men weary as much of not doing the things they want to do as of doing the things they do not want to do.
ERIC HOFFER

See also **Action, Activity, Doing Good, Doing Nothing.**

DOING GOOD

Few can do us good, almost any can do us harm. BALTASAR GRACIÁN

It is not so dangerous to do wrong to most men, as to do them too much good. LA ROCHEFOUCAULD

As it is said of the greatest liar, that he tells more truth than falsehood; so it may be said of the worst man, that he does more good than evil.
SAMUEL JOHNSON

You cannot spend money in luxury without doing good to the poor. Nay, you do more good to them by spending it in luxury, than by giving it; for by spending it in luxury, you make them exert industry, whereas by giving it, you keep them idle.
SAMUEL JOHNSON

The usual pretext of those who make others unhappy is that they do it for their own good.
VAUVENARGUES

We see the wisdom of Solon's remark, that no more good must be attempted than the nation can bear.
THOMAS JEFFERSON

Try to do no good and then you won't get into any scrapes.
LORD MELBOURNE

No people do so much harm as those who go about doing good.
BISHOP MANDELL CREIGHTON

We should do only those righteous actions which we cannot stop ourselves from doing. SIMONE WEIL

See also **Charity, Good, Philanthropy.**

DOING NOTHING

Positively, the best thing a man can have to do is nothing, and, *next to that*, perhaps, good works.
CHARLES LAMB

Hard is the case of him who will stuff himself with food the whole day without applying his mind to anything. Are there not gamesters and chess-players? To be one of those would be still better than doing nothing at all. CONFUCIUS

The perfect man does nothing, the sage takes no action. CHUANG-TSE

Abstention from doing is often as noble as doing, but is less exposed to the light of day. MONTAIGNE

To be occupied in what does not concern you is worse than doing nothing. BALTASAR GRACIÁN

A man can never have too much time to himself, nor too little to do. Had I a little son, I would christen him 'Nothing-to-do'; he should do nothing. Man, I verily believe, is out of his element as long as he is operative. CHARLES LAMB

To do nothing is the wisdom of those who have seen fools perish.
GEORGE MEREDITH

It is to do nothing that the elect exist. OSCAR WILDE

Let me say to you that to do nothing at all is the most difficult thing in the world, the most difficult, and the most intellectual.
OSCAR WILDE

The most precious, the most consoling, the most pure and holy, the noble habit of doing nothing at all.
G. K. CHESTERTON

See also **Idle, Indolence, Leisure, Loafing, Passivity.**

DOLLAR

If you wish to give a man a sense of poverty, give him a thousand dollars. The next hundred dollars he gets will not be worth more than ten that he used to get.
HENRY DAVID THOREAU

I cannot easily buy a blank book to write thoughts in; they are commonly ruled for dollars and cents.
HENRY DAVID THOREAU

The happiest time in any man's life is when he is in red-hot pursuit of a dollar with a reasonable prospect of overtaking it. JOSH BILLINGS

It is a commonplace among thinking economists that a dollar bill will go just so far and no farther at a given time and place, the same law of nature holding true for bills of other denominations, such as $2 bills, $5 bills, and so on, and even truer for the more familiar nickel, dime, and quarter. WILL CUPPY

See also **Money.**

DONE

For a thing to remain undone nothing more is needed than to think it done. BALTASAR GRACIÁN

Wonderful maxim: Not to talk of things any more after they are done.
MONTESQUIEU

To feel that you have done what should be done raises you in your own eyes. EUGÈNE DELACROIX

Nothing is done. Everything in the world remains to be done or done over. LINCOLN STEFFENS

See also **Complete, Doing, Finish, Over, Unfinished.**

DOUBT

A philosopher is one who doubts.
MONTAIGNE

Let go the things in which you are in doubt for the things in which there is no doubt. MOHAMMED

Doubt everything at least once, even the statement that two times two makes four.
G. C. LICHTENBERG

With most people, doubt about one thing is simply blind belief in another. G. C. LICHTENBERG

Believe the doubter, and doubt when you are told to believe.
LUDWIG BÖRNE

Ten thousand difficulties do not make one doubt.
JOHN HENRY NEWMAN

The method which begins by doubting in order to philosophize is just as suited to its purpose as making a soldier lie down in a heap in order to teach him to stand up straight. SÖREN KIERKEGAARD

Faith keeps many doubts in her pay. If I could not doubt, I should not believe. HENRY DAVID THOREAU

To begin to act, you must first have your mind completely at ease and no trace of doubt left in it.
FEODOR DOSTOEVSKI

When in doubt, tell the truth.
MARK TWAIN

We go on our way, doubtful that that is what it is.
HENRY S. HASKINS

See also **Certain, Certainty and Doubt, Hesitate, Incredulity.**

DOZING

If we can develop some way in which a man can doze and still keep from making a monkey of himself, we have removed one of the big obstacles to human happiness in modern civilization.

ROBERT BENCHLEY

See also **Nap, Sleep.**

DREAM

If we dreamt the same thing every night, it would affect us as much as the objects we see every day. And if a workman were sure to dream every night for twelve hours' duration that he was a king, I believe he would be almost as happy as a king, who should dream every night for twelve hours on end that he was a workman. PASCAL

The inquiry into a dream is another dream. LORD HALIFAX

The poverty of my dreams mortifies me. There is Coleridge, at his will can conjure up icy domes, and pleasure houses for Kubla Khan, and Abyssinian maids, and songs of Abara . . . to solace his night solitudes—when I cannot muster a fiddle. CHARLES LAMB

Existence would be intolerable if we were never to dream.

ANATOLE FRANCE

You see things; and you say 'Why?' But I dream things that never were; and I say 'Why not?'

GEORGE BERNARD SHAW

Sanity is a madness put to good uses; waking life is a dream controlled. GEORGE SANTAYANA

An artist is a dreamer consenting to dream of the actual world.

GEORGE SANTAYANA

A child, awakened out of a deep sleep, expressed all the crying babies and all the weeping idealists in the world. 'Oh, dear,' he said, 'I have lost my place in my dream.'

LINCOLN STEFFENS

See also **Sleep.**

DRINKING

Water, taken in moderation, cannot hurt anybody. MARK TWAIN

Drinking may be practised with great prudence; a man who exposes himself when he is intoxicated, has not the art of getting drunk.

SAMUEL JOHNSON

Drink because you are happy, but never because you are miserable.

G. K. CHESTERTON

See also **Alcohol, Cocktail, Coffee, Prohibition, Teetotalism, Wine.**

DROP

Mrs. Montagu has dropt me. Now, sir, there are people whom one should like very well to drop, but would not wish to be dropt by.

SAMUEL JOHNSON

DRUDGERY

The test of a vocation is the love of the drudgery it involves.

LOGAN PEARSALL SMITH

See also **Routine, Work.**

DUTY

Common duties become religious acts when performed with fervour.

ST. FRANCIS DE SALES

There are persons who have so far outgrown their catechism as to believe that their only duty is to themselves. SAMUEL JOHNSON

If you assign people duties without granting them any rights, you must pay them well.   GOETHE

When once a rigid idea of duty has made its way into a narrow mind, it can never get out again.
    JOSEPH JOUBERT

We must find our duties in what comes to us, not in what we imagine might have been.
    GEORGE ELIOT

The habit of doing one's duty drives away fear.
    CHARLES BAUDELAIRE

It is seldom very hard to do one's duty when one knows what it is, but it is often exceedingly difficult to find this out.   SAMUEL BUTLER

Duties are not performed for duty's sake, but because their neglect would make the man uncomfortable. A man performs but one duty —the duty of contenting his spirit, the duty of making himself agreeable to himself.   MARK TWAIN

Make it a point to do something every day that you don't want to do. This is the golden rule for acquiring the habit of doing your duty without pain.   MARK TWAIN

Duty is what one expects from others, it is not what one does oneself.   OSCAR WILDE

One's immediate duty is happily, as a rule, clear enough. 'Do the next thing,' says the old shrewd motto.
    A. C. BENSON

The true source of rights is duty. If we all discharge our duties, rights will not be far to seek.   GANDHI

A sense of duty is useful in work, but offensive in personal relations.
    BERTRAND RUSSELL

In a free country it is the duty of writers to pay no attention to duty.
    E. B. WHITE

See also **Job.**

DWELLING

Small rooms or dwellings set the mind in the right path, large ones cause it to go astray.
    LEONARDO DA VINCI

We shape our dwellings, and afterwards our dwellings shape us.
    WINSTON S. CHURCHILL

See also **Home, House, Palace.**

DYING

If you do not know how to die, don't worry, Nature herself will teach you in the proper time; she will discharge that work for you; don't trouble yourself.
    MONTAIGNE

We say, 'He will die soon,' when a man, in doing something, departs from his customary ways.
    GOETHE

When a man takes to his bed, almost all his friends secretly hope to see him die: some to prove that his health was inferior to theirs; others in a disinterested wish to study an agony.   CHARLES BAUDELAIRE

We die daily. Happy those who daily come to life as well.
    GEORGE MACDONALD

When you are going to be drowned you can think of nothing but how they will be puzzled at home when

you don't turn up for tea, or what
will happen because you haven't
made your will.

GEORGE BERNARD SHAW

Few men ever drop dead from overwork, but many quietly curl up and
die because of undersatisfaction.

SYDNEY HARRIS

The hour of dying is only one of
our hours and not exceptional: our
being is continually undergoing and
entering upon changes that are
perhaps of no less intensity than the
new, the next, and next again, that
death brings with it.

RAINER MARIA RILKE

When a man dies, he dies not just of
the disease he has. He dies of his
whole life.   CHARLES PÉGUY

'If ye just about half-live, ye just the
same as half-die; and if ye spend yer
time half-dyin', some day ye turn in
and die all over, without rightly
meanin' to at all—just a kind o' bad
habit ye've got yerself inter.'

DOROTHY CANFIELD FISHER

See also **Death.**

DYSPEPSIA

No dyspeptic can have a sane outlook on life.   SIR WILLIAM OSLER

See also **Indigestion.**

E

EAGER

The eagerness of a knave makes
him often as catchable as ignorance
makes a fool.   LORD HALIFAX

EARLY RISING

Well enough for old folks to rise
early, because they have done so
many mean things all their lives they
can't sleep anyhow.   MARK TWAIN

There is not a single proverb in favour of early rising that appeals to
the higher nature of man.

ROBERT LYND

Rise early and at the same hour
every morning, how late soever you
may have sat up the night before.

LORD CHESTERFIELD

We can heat the body, we can cool
it; we can give it tension or relaxation; and surely it is possible to
bring it into a state in which rising
from bed will not be a pain.

JAMES BOSWELL

No man practices so well as he
writes. I have, all my life long, been
lying till noon; yet I tell all young
men, and tell them with great sincerity, that nobody who does not
rise early will ever do any good.

SAMUEL JOHNSON

See also **Alarm Clock, Bed.**

EARS

What a mercy it would be if we
were able to open and close our
ears as easily as we open and close
our eyes!   G. C. LICHTENBERG

See also **Listening.**

EARTH

And God hath spread the earth as a
carpet for you, that ye may walk
therein through spacious paths.

KORAN

Do not despise your situation: in it
you must act, suffer, and conquer.
From every point on earth we are
equally near to heaven and to the
infinite.   FRÉDÉRIC AMIEL

It is just as well to be a little giddy-
pated, if you are to feel at home on
this turning earth.

LOGAN PEARSALL SMITH

What you cannot find on earth is not worth seeking. NORMAN DOUGLAS

See also **World.**

EASY

It is easier to ruin a kingdom than to set up a greengrocer's stall.
WILLIAM HAZLITT

My friend, the human race is always trying this dodge of making everything entirely easy; but the difficulty which it shifts off one thing it shifts on to another.
G. K. CHESTERTON

What is easy is seldom excellent.
SAMUEL JOHNSON

Psychology has its Gresham's Law; its bad money drives out the good. Most people tend to perform the actions that require least effort, to think the thoughts that are easiest, to feel the emotions that are most vulgarly commonplace, to give the rein to desires that are most nearly animal. ALDOUS HUXLEY

See also **Difficult.**

EATING

In eating, a third of the stomach should be filled with food, a third with drink and the rest left empty.
TALMUD

The spirit cannot endure the body when overfed but, if underfed, the body cannot endure the spirit.
ST. FRANCIS DE SALES

I saw few die of hunger, of eating—100,000. BENJAMIN FRANKLIN

In general, mankind, since the improvement of cookery, eat twice as much as nature requires.
BENJAMIN FRANKLIN

Some people have a foolish way of not minding, or of pretending not to mind, what they eat. For my part, I mind my belly very studiously and very carefully; for I look upon it that he who does not mind his belly will hardly mind anything else.
SAMUEL JOHNSON

I have heard it remarked by a statesman of high reputation, that most great men have died of over-eating themselves. SIR HENRY TAYLOR

Part of the secret of success in life is to eat what you like and let the food fight it out inside. MARK TWAIN

More people are killed by over-eating and drinking than by the sword. SIR WILLIAM OSLER

Most people eat as though they were fattening themselves for market. E. W. HOWE

See also **Breakfast, Diet, Dinner, Food, Lunch, Meals, Vegetarianism, Vitamins.**

ECONOMICS

Only one fellow in ten thousand understands the currency question, and we meet him every day.
KIN HUBBARD

Nine out of ten economic laws are economic laws only till they are found out. ROBERT LYND

ECONOMY

Economy is the art of making the most of life. The love of economy is the root of all virtue.
GEORGE BERNARD SHAW

See also **Frugality.**

EDUCATED

If any man will sum us up according to our actions and behaviour, he will find many more excellent men among the ignorant than among the educated; I mean as regards any kind of virtue. MONTAIGNE

There is no common language or medium of understanding between people of education and without it—between those who judge of things from books or from their senses. WILLIAM HAZLITT

A child educated only at school is an uneducated child.
GEORGE SANTAYANA

An educated man is one who has the right loves and hatreds.
LIN YUTANG

See also **Education, Uneducated.**

EDUCATION (DEFINITIONS)

Education is a kind of begetting.
G. C. LICHTENBERG

Education: That which discloses to the wise and disguises from the foolish their lack of understanding.
AMBROSE BIERCE

Education is the acquisition of the art of the utilization of knowledge.
ALFRED NORTH WHITEHEAD

The main fact about education is that there is no such thing. Education is a word like 'transmission' or 'inheritance'; it is not an object, but a method. G. K. CHESTERTON

The wit was not wrong who defined education in this way: 'Education is that which remains, if one has forgotten everything he learned in school.' ALFRED EINSTEIN

Education is our sixth sense.
CLIVE BELL

An education isn't how much you have committed to memory, or even how much you know. It's being able to differentiate between what you do know and what you don't. It's knowing where to go to find out what you need to know; and it's knowing how to use the information once you get it.
WILLIAM FEATHER

EDUCATION

In true education, anything that comes to our hand is as good as a book: the prank of a page-boy, the blunder of a servant, a bit of table-talk—they are all part of the curriculum. MONTAIGNE

The usual education of young people is to inspire them with a second self-love.
LA ROCHEFOUCAULD

I hate by-roads in education. Education is as well known, and has long been as well known, as ever it can be. SAMUEL JOHNSON

Any one who has passed through the regular gradations of a classical education, and is not made a fool by it, may consider himself as having had a very narrow escape.
WILLIAM HAZLITT

The things taught in colleges and schools are not an education, but the means of education.
RALPH WALDO EMERSON

The greatest innovation in the world is the demand for education as a right of man; it is a disguised demand for comfort.
JAKOB BURCKHARDT

Education consists mainly in what we have unlearned. MARK TWAIN

With half an hour's reading in bed every night as a steady practice, the busiest man can get a fair education before the plasma sets in the periganglionic spaces of his grey cortex. SIR WILLIAM OSLER

Half of the little education people have is usually wrong.
E. W. HOWE

Education is an admirable thing, but it is well to remember from time to time that nothing that is worth knowing can be taught.
OSCAR WILDE

Just as the philanthropist is the nuisance of the ethical sphere, so the nuisance of the intellectual sphere is the man who is so occupied in trying to educate others, that he has never had any time to educate himself. OSCAR WILDE

The result of the educative process is capacity for further education.
JOHN DEWEY

Education with inert ideas is not only useless; it is, above all things, harmful.
ALFRED NORTH WHITEHEAD

The great difficulty in education is to get experience out of ideas.
GEORGE SANTAYANA

You can't impose education on anyone. ROBERT HENRI

The only real education comes from what goes counter to you.
ANDRÉ GIDE

To my mind, education is an absurdly overrated affair. At least, one never took it very seriously at school, where everything was done to bring it prominently under one's notice. Anything that is worth knowing one practically teaches oneself, and the rest obtrudes itself sooner or later. SAKI

The chief object of education is not to learn things but to unlearn things. G. K. CHESTERTON

Without a gentle contempt for education, no gentleman's education is complete. G. K. CHESTERTON

Plasticine and self-expression will not solve the problems of education. Nor will technology and vocational guidance; nor the classics and the Hundred Best Books.
ALDOUS HUXLEY

Like every meddler with children who ever lived, Rousseau wanted to educate poor Emile for a better world than this one.
AUBREY MENEN

There are no new ideas in education. The last and final one was thought of by James I, who shut up a boy from the age of one in a cellar to see if he would talk Hebrew when he let him out ten years later. Modern educational theories are no more than timorous adaptions of the same bold idea. The most advanced teacher of the most advanced school believes nothing more profound than that the best way of teaching a boy is to leave him to his own devices.
AUBREY MENEN

See also **Educated, Education (Definitions), Learning (Studying), School, Teaching, University.**

EFFICIENT
It's pretty hard to be efficient without being obnoxious.
KIN HUBBARD

EGG

The hen is an egg's way of producing another egg.

SAMUEL BUTLER

Put all thine eggs in one basket and—watch that basket.

MARK TWAIN

An egg is always an adventure: it may be different. OSCAR WILDE

If I were given my choice between an egg and ambrosia for breakfast, I should choose an egg.

ROBERT LYND

Vasari, in his *Lives of the Painters*, describes how Piero di Cosimo, finding that eating interfered with his work, took to living entirely on hard-boiled eggs. He cooked these a hundred at a time, and kept a basketful beside his easel. That is one way of simplifying the pursuit of beauty. AUBREY MENEN

EGO

Wherever I climb I am followed by a dog called 'Ego.'

FRIEDRICH NIETZSCHE

See also **I, Self.**

EGOTISM

If a man lacks a streak of kindly egotism, beware of him.

CHARLES HORTON COOLEY

Mastery is often taken for egotism.

GOETHE

Take egotism out, and you would castrate the benefactors. Luther, Mirabeau, Napoleon, John Adams, Andrew Jackson.

RALPH WALDO EMERSON

Egotism itself, which is so necessary to a proper sense of human dignity, is entirely the result of an indoor life. OSCAR WILDE

Egotism speaks all sorts of languages and plays all sorts of roles, even that of disinterestedness.

LA ROCHEFOUCAULD

See also **Mine, Self, Selfish.**

EIGHTY

Grandmother, about eighty, is visiting in the East and sends home things she has bought for her house. 'I don't suppose I shall live forever,' she says, 'but while I do live I don't see why I shouldn't live as if I expected to.'

CHARLES HORTON COOLEY

ELABORATE

To elaborate is of no avail. Learned and unlearned feel that this is so.

WALT WHITMAN

ELECTORATE

The electorate is the jury writ large.

LORD SAMUEL

See also **Democracy.**

ELOQUENCE

Continued eloquence wearies.

PASCAL

See also **Rhetoric, Speech.**

EMBARRASSING

It's always embarrassing to run unexpectedly into a girl you used to be engaged to. P. G. WODEHOUSE

EMERSON, RALPH WALDO

I doubt if Emerson could trundle a wheelbarrow through the streets, because it would be out of character. One needs to have a comprehensive character.

HENRY DAVID THOREAU

Few authors read so well on first meeting as Emerson, and then seem to be so specious and empty on re-acquaintance. One page of the dour Thoreau is worth an entire volume of the expansive Emerson.

SYDNEY HARRIS

EMOTION

Emotion has taught mankind to reason. VAUVENARGUES

When a person has an inborn genius for certain emotions, his life differs strangely from that of ordinary people, for none of their usual deterrents check him.

WILLIAM JAMES

The secret of remaining young is never to have an emotion that is unbecoming. OSCAR WILDE

Intellect is to emotion as our clothes are to our bodies: we could not very well have civilized life without clothes, but we would be in a poor way if we had only clothes without bodies.

ALFRED NORTH WHITEHEAD

See also **Feeling, Heart.**

EMPIRE

A great empire, like a great cake, is most easily diminished at the edges.

BENJAMIN FRANKLIN

EMPLOYMENT

Employment, sir, and hardships, prevent melancholy.

SAMUEL JOHNSON

See also **Job, Work.**

ENDURE

Nothing befalls a man except what is in his nature to endure.

MARCUS AURELIUS

He who can endure all can dare all.

VAUVENARGUES

See also **Put Up.**

ENEMY

Predestined enemies will always meet in a narrow alleyway.

CHINESE PROVERB

A wise man gets more use from his enemies than a fool from his friends.

BALTASAR GRACIÁN

Nothing would more contribute to make a man wise than to have always an enemy in his view.

LORD HALIFAX

There is no better weapon against an enemy than another enemy.

FRIEDRICH NIETZSCHE

There is some advice that is too good. That advice to love your enemies, for example.

E. W. HOWE

A man cannot be too careful in the choice of his enemies.

OSCAR WILDE

See also **Enmity.**

ENERGY

We might make ourselves spiritual by detaching ourselves from action, and become perfect by the rejection of energy. OSCAR WILDE

ENGLAND AND AMERICA

In England, if something goes wrong—say, if one finds a skunk in the garden—he writes to the family solicitor, who proceeds to take the proper measures; whereas in America, you telephone the fire department. Each satisfies a characteristic need; in the English, love of order and legalistic procedure; and here in America what you like, is something vivid, and red, and swift.

ALFRED NORTH WHITEHEAD

See also **America, American.**

ENGLISH LANGUAGE

It is certain that more people speak English correctly in the United States than in Britain.

RALPH WALDO EMERSON

'Vich I call addin' insult to injury, as the parrot said ven they not only took him from his native land, but made him talk the English langwidge arterwards.'

CHARLES DICKENS

The world was made before the English language and seemingly upon a different design.

ROBERT LOUIS STEVENSON

Our study of English begins with years and years of the silly stuff called grammar and rhetoric. All the grammar that any human being ever needs, or that is of any use as an intellectual training, can be learned in a few weeks from a little book as thin as a Ritz-Carlton sandwich. . . . Rhetoric is worse. It lays down laws for the writing of sentences and paragraphs about as reasonable and as useful as a set of directions telling how to be a gentleman, or how to have a taste for tomatoes.   STEPHEN LEACOCK

I would make boys all learn English; and then I would let the clever ones learn Latin as an honour and Greek as a treat. But the only thing I would whip them for is not knowing English. I would whip them hard for that.

WINSTON S. CHURCHILL

A great many people use faulty English without knowing it. Ain't you?   ROBERT BENCHLEY

See also **Ain't, Grammar, Language, Sentence, Spelling, Split Infinitive, Words.**

ENGLISHMEN

Not only England, but every Englishman is an island.   NOVALIS

It is not at all easy (humanly speaking) to wind up an Englishman to a dogmatic level.

JOHN HENRY NEWMAN

Napoleon described the English as a nation of shopkeepers. He would have come nearer the truth if he had described them as a nation of goalkeepers.   ROBERT LYND

The atmosphere of English casualness is most attractive. It is pleasant to see things done without fuss. It is engaging to meet a man (as I once did in Naples) who will casually discuss Plato's *Republic* for an hour and then indolently arise and announce: 'I must push on; my boat leaves for India in half an hour.'

IRWIN EDMAN

Mad dogs and Englishmen go out in the midday sun. NOEL COWARD

ENJOYMENT

The greatest blessing is created and enjoyed at the same moment.

EPICURUS

I am content to enjoy the world, without busying myself with it; to live no more than an excusable life, a life that will be no burden to myself or others.   MONTAIGNE

A man who can rightly and truly enjoy his existence is absolutely and almost divinely perfect.
          MONTAIGNE

Whilst ye are upon earth, enjoy the good things that are here (to that end were they given) and be not melancholy, and wish yourself in heaven.   JOHN SELDEN

If there are no books in this world, then nothing need be said, but since there are books, they must be read; if there is no wine, then nothing need be said, but since there is wine, it must be drunk; if there are no famous hills, then nothing need be said, but since there are, they must be visited; if there are no flowers and no moon, then nothing need be said, but since there are, they must be enjoyed; if there are no talented men and beautiful women, then nothing need be said, but since there are, they must be loved and protected.   CHANG CH'AO

The fullest possible enjoyment is to be found by reducing our ego to zero.   G. K. CHESTERTON

He has spent his life best who has enjoyed it most. God will take care that we do not enjoy it any more than is good for us.
          SAMUEL BUTLER

People are always good company when they are doing what they really enjoy.   SAMUEL BUTLER

All of the animals, excepting man, know that the principal business of life is to enjoy it.
          SAMUEL BUTLER

There is no cure for birth and death save to enjoy the interval.
          GEORGE SANTAYANA

There are two things to aim at in life: first, to get what you want; and, after that, to enjoy it. Only the wisest of mankind achieve the second.   LOGAN PEARSALL SMITH

He who enjoys doing and enjoys what he has done is happy.
          GOETHE

Certainly we ought to be discontented, we ought not simply to find out ways of making the best of a bad job, and yet if we kill all pleasure in the actual process of life, what sort of future are we preparing for ourselves? If a man cannot enjoy the return of spring, why should he be happy in a labour-saving Utopia?   GEORGE ORWELL

See also **Joy, Pleasure.**

ENMITY

A man who values a good night's rest will not lie down with enmity in his heart, if he can help it.
          LAURENCE STERNE

See also **Enemy, Hate.**

ENOUGH

That which is competency for one man, is not enough for another, no more than that which will keep one man warm, will keep another man warm; one man can go in doublet and hose, when another man cannot be without a cloak, and yet have no more clothes than is necessary for him.   JOHN SELDEN

You never know what is enough until you know what is more than enough.   WILLIAM BLAKE

See also **Contentment.**

ENTERPRISE

Mr. Skimpole then betook himself to lying down on his back under a tree, and looking at the sky. . . . 'Enterprise and effort,' he would say to us (on his back), 'are delightful to me. I believe I am truly cosmopolitan, I have the deepest sympathy with them. I lie in a shady place like this and think of adventurous spirits going to the North Pole, or penetrating to the heart of the Torrid Zone, with admiration.'

CHARLES DICKENS

ENTERTAIN

Men that cannot entertain themselves want somebody, though they care for nobody. LORD HALIFAX

The trouble in civilized life of entertaining company, as it is called too generally without much regard to strict veracity, is so great that it cannot but be a matter of wonder that people are so fond of attempting it. ANTHONY TROLLOPE

ENTHUSIASM

Enthusiasm is not always the companion of total ignorance, it is often that of erroneous information.

VOLTAIRE

A cold man without enthusiasm is like someone who has eaten too much and then is disgusted by the sight of the most delicious food; is that the fault of the food or of his stomach? VAUVENARGUES

There are incompetent enthusiasts, and they are a mighty dangerous lot. G. C. LICHTENBERG

It requires so infinitely much tact to handle enthusiasm.

JENS PETER JACOBSEN

Nothing will dispel enthusiasm like a small admission fee.

KIN HUBBARD

Enthusiasm is the most beautiful word on earth.

CHRISTIAN MORGENSTERN

ENVY

Envy is more irreconcilable than hatred. LA ROCHEFOUCAULD

Envy, among other ingredients, has a mixture of the love of justice in it. We are more angry at undeserved than at deserved good fortune.

WILLIAM HAZLITT

Envy and fear are the only passions to which no pleasure is attached.

JOHN CHURTON COLLINS

Envy makes strange bed-fellows.

NORMAN DOUGLAS

EPICURE

You should be an epicure as to your work. EUGÈNE DELACROIX

Epicure: An opponent of Epicurus, an abstemious philosopher who, holding that pleasure should be the chief aim of man, wasted no time in gratification of the senses.

AMBROSE BIERCE

EPIDEMIC

Some people are so sensitive that they feel snubbed if an epidemic overlooks them. KIN HUBBARD

EPIGRAM

He asked me how to make an epigram. Since he was in the flying corps it seemed natural enough to answer: 'You merely loop the loop on a commonplace and come down between the lines.'

W. SOMERSET MAUGHAM

See also **Aphorism, Maxim, Paradox.**

EPITAPH

CHARLES LAMB, when a little boy, walking in a church-yard with his sister, and reading the epitaphs, said to her, 'Mary, where are all the naughty people buried?'

EQUALITY

One man alone was brought forth at the time of Creation in order that thereafter none should have the right to say to another, 'My father was greater than your father.'

TALMUD

One man is no more than another if he does no more than another.

CERVANTES

So far is it from being true that men are naturally equal, that no two people can be half an hour together but one shall acquire an evident superiority over the other.

SAMUEL JOHNSON

Men are born unequal. The great benefit of society is to diminish this inequality as much as possible by procuring for everybody security, the necessary property, education, and succour. JOSEPH JOUBERT

Of Equality—as if it harm'd me, giving others the same chances and rights as myself—as if it were not indispensable to my own rights that others possess the same.

WALT WHITMAN

But this august dignity I treat of, is not the dignity of kings and robes, but that abounding dignity which has no robed investiture. Thou shalt see it shining in the arm that wields a pick or drives a spike; that democratic dignity which, on all hands, radiates without end from God; Himself! The great God ab-solute! The centre and circumference of all democracy! His omni-presence, our divine equality!

HERMAN MELVILLE

In sport, in courage, and the sight of Heaven, all men meet on equal terms. WINSTON S. CHURCHILL

Equality is essential to good breeding, but unfortunately equality is incompatible with differences in income, as the people on the lower income level always tend to consider themselves superior to those above them.

GEORGE BERNARD SHAW

See also **Level.**

EQUATION

Nothing requires a rarer intellectual heroism than willingness to see one's equation written out.

GEORGE SANTAYANA

EQUATOR

There isn't a parallel of latitude but thinks it would have been the equator if it had had its rights.

MARK TWAIN

ERROR

The cautious seldom err.

CONFUCIUS

There are as many errors of temper as of mind. LA ROCHEFOUCAULD

The progress of rivers to the sea is not as rapid as that of man to error.

VOLTAIRE

If all errors were clearly stated, they would perish by themselves.

VAUVENARGUES

To err is human—the animals never err, except for the smartest among them. G. C. LICHTENBERG

We have to pay dearly to get rid of our errors and even then we are lucky. GOETHE

To discover an error means to invent retroactively. GOETHE

An error is the more dangerous in proportion to the degree of truth which it contains. FRÉDÉRIC AMIEL

If wise men never erred, fools would have to despair. GOETHE

Next to the promulgation of a truth, the best thing I can conceive that a man can do is the recantation of a public error. LORD LISTER

Error itself may be the happy chance. ALFRED NORTH WHITEHEAD

It is not in our power to 'take off' an error, as we take off clothes because we prefer to wear others; the power to get rid of our errors comes to us only when we cannot use them any more, when they are really 'worn out'. EGON FRIEDELL

See also **Fallacy, Truth and Error.**

ESCAPE

There are various routes of escape from responsibility: escape into death, escape into disease, and escape into stupidity. The last is the safest and easiest, for even intelligent people are usually closer to the goal than they would like to think. ARTHUR SCHNITZLER

ETHICS

He who defines his conduct by ethics imprisons his song-bird in a cage. KAHLIL GIBRAN

See also **Morality.**

ETIQUETTE

Etiquette means behaving yourself a little better than is absolutely essential. WILL CUPPY

See also **Manners, Politeness.**

EVENT

I claim not to have controlled events, but confess plainly that events have controlled me. ABRAHAM LINCOLN

See also **Circumstances, Happen.**

EVERYDAY

The most instructive experiences are those of everyday life. FRIEDRICH NIETZSCHE

See also **Ordinary.**

EVIDENCE

Some circumstantial evidence is very strong, as when you find a trout in the milk. HENRY DAVID THOREAU

See also **Proof.**

EVIL

The greatest penalty of evil-doing is to grow into the likeness of bad men. PLATO

The oldest and best known evil is ever more tolerable than a fresh and unexperienced mischief. MONTAIGNE

Never open the door to a lesser evil, for other and greater ones invariably slink in after it. BALTASAR GRACIÁN

No man is clever enough to know all the evil he does. LA ROCHEFOUCAULD

There is nothing that makes us feel so good as the idea that someone else is an evildoer.   ROBERT LYND

If our imaginations were filled from waking to sleeping with a sense of the evil in the world, we should scarcely be able to work or to eat our meals.   ROBERT LYND

As soon as we do evil, the evil appears as a sort of duty.
SIMONE WEIL

See also **Good and Evil.**

EXAGGERATE

There are people so addicted to exaggeration that they can't tell the truth without lying.
JOSH BILLINGS

Sir, it is amazing how things are exaggerated. A gentleman was lately telling in a company where I was present, that in France as soon as a man of fashion marries he takes an opera girl into keeping; and this he mentioned as a general custom. 'Pray, sir,' said I, 'how many opera girls may there be?' He answered, 'About four-score.' 'Well, then, sir,' said I, 'you see there can be no more than four-score men of fashion who can do this.'
SAMUEL JOHNSON

Exaggeration is a branch of lying.
BALTASAR GRACIÁN

Nothing lays itself open to the charge of exaggeration more than the language of naked truth.
JOSEPH CONRAD

Exaggeration is the definition of art.
G. K. CHESTERTON

See also **Lying.**

EXAMPLE

Nothing is so infectious as example, and we never do great good or evil without producing the like.
LA ROCHEFOUCAULD

Example is not only the best way of propagating an opinion, but it is the only way worth taking into account.   SAMUEL BUTLER

Few things are harder to put up with than the annoyance of a good example.   MARK TWAIN

The only rational way of educating is to be an example—if one can't help it, a warning example.
ALBERT EINSTEIN

EXCESS

Excess, like defect of intellect, is accused of madness.   PASCAL

Wisdom has its excesses and, no less than folly, needs to be moderated.
MONTAIGNE

The road of excess leads to the palace of wisdom.   WILLIAM BLAKE

Intellectual overindulgence is the most gratuitous and disgraceful form which excess can take, nor is there any the consequences of which are more disastrous.
SAMUEL BUTLER

Moderation is a fatal thing. Nothing succeeds like excess.
OSCAR WILDE

There seems to be an excess of everything except parking space and religion.   KIN HUBBARD

EXERCISE

The only possible form of exercise is to talk, not to walk.
OSCAR WILDE

The need of exercise is a modern superstition, invented by people who ate too much, and had nothing to think about. Athletics don't make anybody either long-lived or useful. GEORGE SANTAYANA

As for exercise, if you have to take it, take it and put up with it. But as long as you have the price of a hack and can hire other people to play baseball for you and run races and do gymnastics when you sit in the shade and smoke and watch them— great heavens what more do you want? STEPHEN LEACOCK

EXILE

Exile: One who serves his country by residing abroad, yet is not an ambassador. AMBROSE BIERCE

EXPECT

Gifts much expected are paid, not given. BENJAMIN FRANKLIN

When I take up the end of a web, and find it packthread, I do not expect, by looking further, to find embroidery. SAMUEL JOHNSON

A fool or idiot is one who expects things to happen that never can happen. GEORGE ELIOT

A thing long expected takes the form of the unexpected when at last it comes. MARK TWAIN

It is always nice to be expected and not to arrive. OSCAR WILDE

Our conduct is influenced not by our experience but by our expectation of life.
GEORGE BERNARD SHAW

Blessed is he that expecteth nothing, for he shall be gloriously surprised.
G. K. CHESTERTON

'Go love without the help of anything on earth; and that's real horse meat. A man is more independent that way, when he doesn't expect anything for himself. And it's just possible he may avoid getting in a state.' JOYCE CARY

See also **Surprise, Unexpected.**

EXPENSE

I live from hand to mouth, content to have enough for my ordinary expenses. As to extraordinary contingencies, not all the scrimping in the world would suffice.
MONTAIGNE

See also **Cost of Living, Pay.**

EXPENSIVE

A man often pays dear for a small frugality. RALPH WALDO EMERSON

Keeping up appearances is the most expensive thing in the world.
A. C. BENSON

See also **Cheap.**

EXPERIENCE

Experience never misleads; what you are misled by is only your judgment, and this misleads you by anticipating results from experience of a kind that is not produced by your experiments.
LEONARDO DA VINCI

We reach quite inexperienced the different stages of life, and often, in spite of the number of our years, we lack experience.
LA ROCHEFOUCAULD

Few men are worthy of experience. The majority let it corrupt them.
JOSEPH JOUBERT

To most men, experience is like the stern lights of a ship, which illumine only the track it has passed.
SAMUEL TAYLOR COLERIDGE

Nobody learns anything from experience; everybody does the same thing over and over again.
LORD MELBOURNE

June 8, 1838. (Age 35) A man must have aunts and cousins, must buy carrots and turnips, must have barn and woodshed, must go to market and to the blacksmith's shop, must saunter and sleep and be inferior and silly.
RALPH WALDO EMERSON

February 4, 1841. (Age 37) If I judge from my own experience I should unsay all my fine things, I fear, concerning the manual labour of literary men. They ought to be released from every species of public or private responsibility. To them the grasshopper is a burden.
RALPH WALDO EMERSON

The cat, having sat upon a hot stove lid, will not sit upon a hot stove lid again. Nor upon a cold stove lid.
MARK TWAIN

The burnt child shuns the fire until the next day. MARK TWAIN

Experience is in the fingers and head. The heart is inexperienced.
HENRY DAVID THOREAU

We always exempt ourselves from the common laws. When I was a boy and the dentist pulled out a second tooth I thought to myself that I would grow a third if I needed it. Experience discouraged this prophecy.
OLIVER WENDELL HOLMES, JR.

We are constantly misled by the ease with which our minds fall into the ruts of one or two experiences.
SIR WILLIAM OSLER

Experience is a question of instinct about life. OSCAR WILDE

Personal experience is the most vicious and limited circle.
OSCAR WILDE

Experience is the name everyone gives to their mistakes.
OSCAR WILDE

We learn from experience that men never learn anything from experience. GEORGE BERNARD SHAW

The sense of antecedent probability is the sixth sense.... An Italian picture is put under my nose and I am told it is a Leonardo, a Raphael, a Titian, a Botticelli, as happens often enough. My sixth sense, that is to say my previous experience of the painter in question, runs to the window, as it were, to see, and almost immediately decides for or against the attribution.
BERNARD BERENSON

Has any man ever attained to inner harmony by pondering the experience of others? Not since the world began! He must pass through the fire. NORMAN DOUGLAS

Experience is a poor guide to man, and is seldom followed. What really teaches a man is not experience, but observation. H. L. MENCKEN

Some people have had nothing else but experience. DON HEROLD

Experience is not what happens to a man. It is what a man does with what happens to him.
ALDOUS HUXLEY

EXPERIMENT

The true worth of an experimenter consists in his pursuing not only what he seeks in his experiment, but also what he did not seek.

CLAUDE BERNARD

When we think that we are experimenting on others, we are really experimenting on ourselves.

OSCAR WILDE

EXPLAIN

It is beyond our power to explain either the prosperity of the wicked or the afflictions of the righteous.

TALMUD

Do not explain overmuch.

BALTASAR GRACIÁN

'Explain all that.' said the Mock Turtle. 'No, no! The adventures first,' said the Gryphon in an impatient tone: 'explanations take such a dreadful time.'

LEWIS CARROLL

Many things are not believed because their current explanation is not believed.

FRIEDRICH NIETZCHE

I may have said the same thing before. . . . But my explanation, I am sure, will always be different.

OSCAR WILDE

A good rule for writers: do not explain overmuch.

W. SOMERSET MAUGHAM

As if explanations can help anybody. The facts may be right, but the explanations are nearly always wrong, because they have to be in terms of our limited intelligence.

GEORGE BERNARD SHAW

EXTREME

Push right to the extreme and it becomes wrong: press all the juice from an orange and it becomes bitter.   BALTASAR GRACIÁN

EXUBERANCE

Exuberance is beauty.

WILLIAM BLAKE

EYES

Mr. Squeers had but one eye, whereas popular prejudice runs in favour of two.

CHARLES DICKENS

Only those who get into scrapes with their eyes open can find the safe way out.

LOGAN PEARSALL SMITH

See also **Seeing.**

F

FABLE

Whether it is a parable or a fable depends on oneself.

HENRY S. HASKINS

FACE

Dr. Burney having remarked that Mr. Garrick was beginning to look old, he said, 'Why, sir, you are not to wonder at that; no man's face has had more wear and tear.'

BOSWELL (*Life of Johnson*)

One of those characteristic British faces that, once seen, are never remembered.   OSCAR WILDE

FACING IT

Facing it—always facing it—that's the way to get through. Face it! That's enough for any man!

JOSEPH CONRAD

FACT

Reporting facts is the refuge of those who have no imagination.
VAUVENARGUES

Oh, don't tell me of facts—I never believe facts: you know Canning said nothing was so fallacious as facts, except figures.
SYDNEY SMITH

The fact will one day flower into a truth. HENRY DAVID THOREAU

Sit down before fact as a little child, be prepared to give up every preconceived notion, follow humbly wherever and to whatever abyss nature leads, or you shall learn nothing. T. H. HUXLEY

Life is one long struggle between conclusions based on abstract ways of conceiving cases, and opposite conclusions prompted by our instinctive perception of them as individual facts. WILLIAM JAMES

I have no general philosophy. All my life I have thought only in connection with facts that came before me. LOUIS D. BRANDEIS

A fact, in science, is not a mere fact, but an instance.
BERTRAND RUSSELL

Ugly facts are a challenge to beautify them. HENRY S. HASKINS

Knowledge is power only if a man knows what facts not to bother about. ROBERT LYND

FAILURE

Everything fails with the unfortunate—himself, his words, and his luck. BALTASAR GRACIÁN

I never knew a man of merit neglected; it was generally his own fault that he failed of success.
SAMUEL JOHNSON

A man's life is interesting primarily when he has failed—I well know. For it's a sign that he tried to surpass himself.
GEORGES CLÉMENCEAU

Those who fail, no matter how ingloriously, have their revenge on the successful few, by having kept themselves free from vulgarity, or by having died unknown.
R. B. CUNNINGHAME GRAHAM

Failure is instructive. The person who really thinks learns quite as much from his failures as from his successes. JOHN DEWEY

Failure sometimes enlarges the spirit. You have to fall back upon humanity and God.
CHARLES HORTON COOLEY

There is nothing more disappointing than failing to accomplish a thing, unless it is to see somebody else accomplish it.
HENRY S. HASKINS

We need to teach the highly educated person that it is not a disgrace to fail and that he must analyze every failure to find its cause. He must learn how to fail intelligently, for failing is one of the greatest arts in the world.
CHARLES F. KETTERING

See also **Success, Success and Failure.**

FAITH

Faith. You can do very little with it, but you can do nothing without it.
SAMUEL BUTLER

It is the heart which experiences God, and not the reason. This, then, is faith: God felt by the heart, not by the reason. PASCAL

Men must be saved in this world by their want of faith.
LORD HALIFAX

Faith is hidden household capital.
GOETHE

Faith is the soul riding at anchor.
JOSH BILLINGS

To win true peace, a man needs to feel himself directed, pardoned, and sustained by a supreme power, to feel himself in the right road, at the point where God would have him be—in order with God and the universe. This faith gives strength and calm. I have not got it.
FRÉDÉRIC AMIEL

What is faith but a kind of betting or speculation after all? It should be, 'I bet that my Redeemer liveth.'
SAMUEL BUTLER

I admire the serene assurance of those who have religious faith. It is wonderful to observe the calm confidence of a Christian with four aces.
MARK TWAIN

There are those who scoff at the schoolboy, calling him frivolous and shallow. Yet it was the schoolboy who said, 'Faith is believing what you know ain't so.'
MARK TWAIN

The great act of faith is when a man decides that he is not God.
OLIVER WENDELL HOLMES, JR.

'Faith' means not *wanting* to know what is true.
FRIEDRICH NIETSCHE

Faith in our associates is part of our faith in God.
CHARLES HORTON COOLEY

We think we believe, but is our faith really awake, or is it lying bedridden in some dormitory of our souls?
W. R. INGE

A man who has faith must be prepared not only to be a martyr, but to be a fool.   G. K. CHESTERTON

Treat the other man's faith gently; it is all he has to believe with. His mind was created for his own thoughts, not yours or mine.
HENRY S. HASKINS

Faith may be relied upon to produce sustained action and, more rarely, sustained contemplation. There is, however, no guarantee that it will produce good art. ALDOUS HUXLEY

Faith in a holy cause is to a considerable extent a substitute for the lost faith in ourselves.
ERIC HOFFER

Where there is the necessary technical skill to move mountains, there is no need for the faith that moves mountains.
ERIC HOFFER

See also **Belief, Believing, Creed, Religion, Trust.**

FAITHFUL
Faithfulness is to the emotional life what consistency is to the life of the intellect—simply a confession of failure.   OSCAR WILDE

FALLACY
Far from feeling glad when I see some time-honoured fallacy exploded, I think of the new one that will come to take its place, and ask myself the anxious question, Will it not perhaps be more inconvenient and dangerous than the other?
ANATOLE FRANCE

See also **Error.**

FAME

All the fame I look for in life is to have lived it quietly.   MONTAIGNE

The fame of great men ought always to be estimated by the means used to acquire it.
LA ROCHEFOUCAULD

There are names written in her immortal scroll, at which Fame blushes!   WILLIAM HAZLITT

Fame is climbing a greasy pole for $10 and ruining trousers worth $15.
JOSH BILLINGS

Being famous is like having a string of pearls given you. It's nice, but after a while, if you think of it at all, it's only to wonder if they're real or cultured.
W. SOMERSET MAUGHAM

Fame isn't a thing. It's a feeling. Like what you get after a pill.
JOYCE CARY

See also **Celebrity, Notoriety, Obscure, Reputation.**

FAMILY

It is not possible for one to teach others who cannot teach his own family.   CONFUCIUS

He that loves not his wife and children, feeds a lioness at home, and broods a nest of sorrow.
JEREMY TAYLOR

I was ever of opinion, that the honest man who married and brought up a large family, did more service than he who continued single and only talked of population.   OLIVER GOLDSMITH

All happy families are alike, but every unhappy one is unhappy in its own way.   LEO TOLSTOY

The families of one's friends are always a disappointment.
NORMAN DOUGLAS

Perhaps the greatest social service that can be rendered by anybody to the country and to mankind is to bring up a family. But here again, because there is nothing to sell, there is a very general disposition to regard a married woman's work as no work at all, and to take it as a matter of course that she should not be paid for it.
GEORGE BERNARD SHAW

Don't try to marry an entire family or it may work out that way.
GEORGE ADE

Every family has prize kin.
E. W. HOWE

Many a family tree needs trimming.
KIN HUBBARD

The same motives which lead men to marry late also lead them to limit their families.   BERTRAND RUSSELL

The family is a good institution because it is uncongenial.
G. K. CHESTERTON

A family is a unit composed not only of children, but of men, women, an occasional animal, and the common cold.   OGDEN NASH

See also **Brother-in-law, Children, Father, Mother, Parents, Relatives.**

FANATIC

There is no strong performance without a little fanaticism in the performer.   RALPH WALDO EMERSON

Fanaticism consists in redoubling your effort when you have forgotten your aim.   GEORGE SANTAYANA

A fanatic is a man that does what he thinks the Lord would do if he knew the facts of the case.

FINLEY PETER DUNNE

A fanatic is one who can't change his mind and won't change the subject.   WINSTON S. CHURCHILL

FARM

Even if a farmer intends to loaf, he gets up in time to get an early start.

E. W. HOWE

Life on the farm is a school of patience: you can't hurry the crops or make an ox in two days.   ALAIN

A farm is an irregular patch of nettles bounded by short-term notes, containing a fool and his wife who didn't know enough to stay in the city.   S. J. PERELMAN

FASHION

Even knowledge has to be in fashion, and where it is not it is wise to affect ignorance.

BALTASAR GRACIÁN

When a man is once in fashion all he does is right.   LORD CHESTERFIELD

It is not proper for an older man to dress or think according to fashion.

GOETHE

Fashion is like God, man cannot see into its holy of holies and live.

SAMUEL BUTLER

OSCAR WILDE claimed that he once saw in a French journal, under a drawing of a bonnet, the words: 'With this style the mouth is worn slightly open'.

For an idea ever to be fashionable is ominous, since it must afterwards be always old-fashioned.

GEORGE SANTAYANA

He who goes against the fashion is himself its slave.

LOGAN PEARSALL SMITH

FASTING

Fasting is a medicine.

ST. JOHN CHRYSOSTOM

See also **Abstain, Diet, Hunger.**

FATALISM

Fatalism is always apt to be a double-edged philosophy; for while, on the one hand, it reveals the minutest occurrences as the immutable results of a rigid chain of infinitely predestined causes, on the other, it invests the wildest incoherencies of conduct or of circumstance with the sanctity of eternal law.   LYTTON STRACHEY

See also **Destiny, Determinism, Fate.**

FATE

Whatever the universal nature assigns to any man at any time is for the good of that man at that time.

MARCUS AURELIUS

It often amuses me to hear men impute all their misfortunes to fate, luck, or destiny, whilst their successes or good fortune they ascribe to their own sagacity, cleverness, or penetration.

SAMUEL TAYLOR COLERIDGE

See also **Circumstances, Destiny, Determinism, Fatalism, Free Will, Happen.**

FATHER

Few fathers care much for their sons, or at least, most of them care more for their money. . . . Of those who really love their sons, few know how to do it.

LORD CHESTERFIELD

As fathers commonly go, it is seldom a misfortune to be fatherless, and considering the general run of sons as seldom a misfortune to be childless.   LORD CHESTERFIELD

The severity of the master is more useful than the indulgence of the father.   SADI

When I was a boy of fourteen, my father was so ignorant I could hardly stand to have the old man around. But when I got to be twenty-one, I was astonished at how much he had learned in seven years.   MARK TWAIN

Fathers and sons are much more considerate of one another than mothers and daughters.   FRIEDRICH NIETZSCHE

Many a man spanks his children for things his own father should have spanked out of him.   DON MARQUIS

See also **Children, Parents.**

FATHERLAND
I would give something to know for whose sake precisely those deeds were really done that supposedly were done for the fatherland.   G. C. LICHTENBERG

FAULT
A man's faults all conform to his type of mind. Observe his faults and you may know his virtues.   CONFUCIUS

We confess to small faults only to convey the impression that we have no big ones.   LA ROCHEFOUCAULD

If we had no faults, we should take less pleasure in noticing those of others.   LA ROCHEFOUCAULD

There are people whose faults become them, and others whose very virtues disgrace them.   LA ROCHEFOUCAULD

Men so like to be talked about that a discussion of their faults delights them.   ANDRÉ MAUROIS

Fortune cures us of many faults that reason could not.   LA ROCHEFOUCAULD

As soon as men have understanding enough to find a fault, they have enough to see the danger of mending it.   LORD HALIFAX

Men do not suspect faults which they do not commit.   SAMUEL JOHNSON

A man has virtues enough if he deserves pardon for his faults on account of them.   G. C. LICHTENBERG

I like a friend better for having faults that one can talk about.   WILLIAM HAZLITT

It is idle to talk to people of their faults, for, if they knew them, they wouldn't commit them.   LORD MELBOURNE

If you want a person's faults, go to those who love him. They will not tell you, but they know.   ROBERT LOUIS STEVENSON

Always remember that the person that you find fault with a great deal, will finally rebel.   E. W. HOWE

Misfortunes one can endure—they come from outside, they are accidents. But to suffer for one's own faults—ah!—there is the sting of life!   OSCAR WILDE

Don't tell your friends their social faults; they will cure the fault and never forgive you.   LOGAN PEARSALL SMITH

We give ourselves credit for the opposite faults of those we have: when we are weak, we boast of being obstinate. LA ROCHEFOUCAULD

We have to try to cure our faults by attention and not by will.
SIMONE WEIL

See also **Defect, Foible, Vice.**

FAVOUR

With many persons it is not necessary to do more than overburden them with favours to lose them altogether: they cannot repay you, and so they retire, preferring rather to be enemies than perpetual debtors. BALTASAR GRACIÁN

Learn how to refuse favours. This is a great and very useful art.
DR. THOMAS FULLER

Never claim as a right what you can ask as a favour.
JOHN CHURTON COLLINS

Never let your inferiors do you a favour. It will be extremely costly.
H. L. MENCKEN

FEAR

A man who causes fear cannot be free from fear. EPICURUS

As courage endangers life even so fear preserves it.
LEONARDO DA VINCI

He who fears he will suffer, already suffers because of his fear.
MONTAIGNE

Fear is one of the passions of human nature of which it is impossible to divest it. You remember the Emperor Charles V, when he read upon the tombstone of a Spanish nobleman, 'Here lies one who never knew fear.' wittily said, 'Then he never snuffed a candle with his fingers.' SAMUEL JOHNSON

Fear is faithlessness.
GEORGE MACDONALD

Fear of life in one form or another is the great thing to exorcise.
WILLIAM JAMES

There is often less danger in the things we fear than in the things we desire. JOHN CHURTON COLLINS

Worry is a form of fear, and all forms of fear produce fatigue. A man who has learned not to feel fear will find the fatigue of daily life enormously diminished.
BERTRAND RUSSELL

See also **Afraid, Fret, Scare, Terrified, Worry.**

FEELING

Sentiments are for the most part traditional; we feel them because they were felt by those who preceded us. WILLIAM HAZLITT

'It is certainly very cold,' said Peggotty. 'Everybody must feel it so.' 'I feel it more than other people,' said Mrs. Gummidge.
CHARLES DICKENS

See also **Emotion, Heart, Passion, Sensibility, Sentiment.**

FELICITY

Many in this world run after felicity like an absent man hunting for his hat, while all the time it is on his head or in his hand.
SYDNEY SMITH

Great felicities are often great misfortunes. LOGAN PEARSALL SMITH

See also **Happiness.**

FICTION SEE TRUTH AND FICTION

FIDDLE

Had I learnt to fiddle, I should have done nothing else.
SAMUEL JOHNSON

FIFTY

He that has seen both sides of fifty has lived to little purpose if he has not other views of the world than he had when he was much younger.
WILLIAM COWPER

As many a too industrious millionaire has discovered, one cannot learn to idle at the age of fifty.
ROBERT LYND

A man of fifty looks as old as Santa Claus to a girl of twenty.
WILLIAM FEATHER

To me personally, the only function of philosophy is to teach us to take life more lightly and gaily than the average business man does, for no business man who does not retire at fifty, if he can, is in my eyes a philosopher.
LIN YUTANG

FIGHT

The wise man thinks it better not to enter the fight than to win.
LA ROCHEFOUCAULD

He that wrestles with us strengthens our nerves and sharpens our skill. Our antagonist is our helper.
EDMUND BURKE

On not knowing when one is beaten. This is all very well, but one of the first businesses of a sensible man is to know when he is beaten, and to leave off fighting at once.
SAMUEL BUTLER

If this life be not a real fight, in which something is eternally gained for the universe by success, it is no better than a game of private theatricals from which one may withdraw at will. But it *feels* like a real fight—as if there were something really wild in the universe. . . .
WILLIAM JAMES

A man should stand up to his bad luck, to his mistakes, to his conscience and all that sort of thing. Why—what else would you have to fight against.
JOSEPH CONRAD

You cannot love a thing without wanting to fight for it.
G. .K. CHESTERTON

It is a perplexing and unpleasant truth that when men already have 'something worth fighting for,' they do not feel like fighting.
ERIC HOFFER

FIND

The essential thing is not to find, but to absorb what we find.
PAUL VALÉRY

See also **Seek.**

FINISH

One always has to spoil a picture a little bit, in order to finish it.
EUGÈNE DELACROIX

See also **Complete, Unfinished.**

FIRE

What makes a fire so pleasant is, I think, that it is a live thing in a dead room.
SYDNEY SMITH

FIRST

The great man is the man who does a thing for the first time.
ALEXANDER SMITH

FISH

Suppose a man were eating rotten stockfish, the very smell of which would choke another, and yet believed it a dish for the gods, what difference is there as to his happiness? ERASMUS

FISHING

As I thus sat, joying in my own happy condition, and pitying this poor rich man that owned this and many other pleasant groves and meadows about me, I did thankfully remember what my Saviour said, that the meek possess the earth; or rather, they enjoy what the others possess and enjoy not; for anglers and meek, quiet-spirited men are free from those high, those restless thoughts, which corrode the sweets of life. IZAAK WALTON

Every man, deep down, is a fisherman. STEPHEN LEACOCK

FLATTERY

If we did not flatter ourselves, the flattery of others would do us no harm. LA ROCHEFOUCAULD

If we never flattered ourselves we should have but scant pleasure. LA ROCHEFOUCAULD

FLEAS

Fleas are, like the remainder of the universe, a divine mystery. ANATOLE FRANCE

FLIRT

One kind of flirtation is to boast we never flirt. LA ROCHEFOUCAULD

FLY

King James said to the fly, Have I three kingdoms, and thou must needs fly into my eye? JOHN SELDEN

A fly is as untamable as a hyena. RALPH WALDO EMERSON

FLYING

What can you conceive more silly and extravagant than to suppose a man racking his brains, and studying night and day how to fly? WILLIAM LAW

Flying. Whatever any other organism has been able to do man should surely be able to do also, though he may go a different way about it. SAMUEL BUTLER

FOIBLE

A man's foibles are what makes him lovable. GOETHE

FOLLOW

He who follows another sees nothing, learns nothing, nay, seeks nothing. SIR WILLIAM OSLER

See also **Lead.**

FOLLY

There are follies as catching as infections. LA ROCHEFOUCAULD

Folly is often more cruel in the consequence than malice can be in the intent. LORD HALIFAX

The most exquisite folly is made of wisdom spun too fine. BENJAMIN FRANKLIN

Every man has his follies—and often they are the most interesting things he has got. JOSH BILLINGS

An act of folly isn't foolish, when you know it for the folly it is. LOGAN PEARSALL SMITH

See also **Fool, Wisdom and Folly.**

FOOD

Soup and fish explain half of the emotions of life.   SYDNEY SMITH

Nothing helps scenery like ham and eggs.   MARK TWAIN

To be without a sense of taste is to be deficient in an exquisite faculty, that of appreciating the qualities of food, just as a person may lack the faculty of appreciating the quality of a book or a work of art. It is to want a vital sense, one of the elements of human superiority.
    GUY DE MAUPASSANT

If a man will be sensible and one fine morning, while he is lying in bed, count at the tips of his fingers how many things in this life truly give him enjoyment, invariably he will find food is the first one.
    LIN YUTANG

We (the Chinese) eat food for its texture, the elastic or crisp effect it has on our teeth, as well as for fragrance, flavour and colour.
    LIN YUTANG

See also **Apple Dumplings, Cheese, Egg, Fish, Milk, Vegetarianism, Vitamins.**

FOOL

A man who knows he is a fool is not a great fool.   CHUANG-TSE

The fool who knows his foolishness is wise at least so far. But a fool who thinks himself wise, he is called a fool indeed.   DHAMMAPADA

You must play the fool a little, if you would not be thought wholly a fool.   MONTAIGNE

To learn that we have said or done a foolish thing, that is nothing; we must learn that we are but fools: a much fuller and more important lesson.   MONTAIGNE

It is the fool's misfortune to fail in obtaining the position, the employment, and the circle of friends that suit him.   BALTASAR GRACIÁN

Nothing is more like a wise man than a fool who holds his tongue.
    ST. FRANCIS DE SALES

He that does not know a fool when he sees him is one himself.
    BALTASAR GRACIÁN

The greatest fool is he who thinks he is not one and all others are.
    BALTASAR GRACIÁN

There are more fools than knaves in the world, else the knaves would not have enough to live upon.
    SAMUEL BUTLER   (1612-1680)

A fool has not stuff in him to be good.   LA ROCHEFOUCAULD

A fool has no dialogue within himself; the first thought carries him without the reply of a second.
    LORD HALIFAX

A fool does not enter a room, nor leave it, nor sit down, nor rise up, nor is he silent, nor does he stand on his legs, like a man of sense.
    JEAN DE LA BRUYÈRE

Most fools think they are only ignorant.   BENJAMIN FRANKLIN

It is ill manners to silence a fool, and cruelty to let him go on.
    BENJAMIN FRANKLIN

Fools cannot understand intelligent people.   VAUVENARGUES

If the fool would persist in his folly he would become wise.
    WILLIAM BLAKE

I am always afraid of a fool. One cannot be sure that he is not a knave as well.   WILLIAM HAZLITT

Every man is a damn fool for at least five minutes every day; wisdom consists in not exceeding the limit. ELBERT HUBBARD

Neither man nor woman can be worth anything until they have discovered that they are fools. This is the first step towards becoming either estimable or agreeable; and until it be taken there is no hope. The sooner the discovery is made the better. LORD MELBOURNE

Taciturnity in a fool would already be the sign of a mind.
EUGÈNE DELACROIX

Let us be thankful for the fools. But for them the rest of us could not succeed. MARK TWAIN

See also **Folly, Foolish, Imbecile, Stupid.**

FOOLISH

To be intimate with a foolish friend is like going to bed with a razor.
BENJAMIN FRANKLIN

If others had not been foolish, we should be so. WILLIAM BLAKE

If forty million people say a foolish thing it does not become a wise one, but the wise man is foolish to give them the lie.
W. SOMERSET MAUGHAM

See also **Folly, Fool, Muddle-Headed, Silly, Stupid.**

FOOTBALL

There is a function of a quasi religious nature performed by a few experts but followed in spirit by the whole university world, serving indeed as a symbol to arouse in the students and in the alumni certain congregate and hieratic emotions. I refer, of course, to football.
CHARLES HORTON COOLEY

FOOTNOTES

When you get to the footnote at the bottom of the page, like as not all you find is *ibid*. FRANK SULLIVAN

FORCE

The more I study the world, the more I am convinced of the inability of brute force to create anything durable. NAPOLEON I

The only justification in the use of force is to reduce the amount of force necessary to be used.
ALFRED NORTH WHITEHEAD

FOREIGN

To know a foreign country at all you must not only have lived in it and in your own, but also lived in at least one other.
W. SOMERSET MAUGHAM

See also **Abroad, Travel.**

FORGET

Forget injuries, never forget kindnesses. CONFUCIUS

I am forced to call my servants by their occupation or birthplace, for names are hard for me to retain. I can tell, indeed, if a name has three syllables, or a harsh sound, or if it begins or ends with a certain letter —but that is all. If I live long enough, I shall no doubt forget my own. MONTAIGNE

'The horror of that moment,' the King went on, 'I shall never, never forget!' 'You will, though,' the Queen said, 'if you don't make a memorandum of it.'
LEWIS CARROLL

The existence of forgetting has never been proved: we only know that some things don't come to mind when we want them to.
FRIEDRICH NIETZSCHE

Blessed are those who forget, for they thus surmount even their mistakes.   FRIEDRICH NIETZSCHE

We never forget things so well as when we are tired of talking about them.   LA ROCHEFOUCAULD

The world, like an accomplished hostess, pays most attention to those whom it will soonest forget.
    JOHN CHURTON COLLINS

Nobody ever forgets where he buried a hatchet.   KIN HUBBARD

It's sweet to be remembered, but it's often cheaper to be forgotten.
    KIN HUBBARD

We soon forget what we have not deeply thought about.
    MARCEL PROUST

Forgetfulness is a form of freedom.
    KAHLIL GIBRAN

See also **Memory, Remember.**

FORGIVE

The memory and conscience never did, nor never will agree about forgiving injuries.   LORD HALIFAX

We never ask God to forgive anybody except where we haven't.
    ELBERT HUBBARD

FORMULA

It is awkward to carry uncoined gold: that's what a thinker does who has no formulas.
    FRIEDRICH NIETZSCHE

A formula is something that worked once, and keeps trying to do it again.   HENRY S. HASKINS

To suppose that people can be saved by studying and giving assent to formulae is like supposing that one can get to Timbuctoo by poring over a map of Africa.
    ALDOUS HUXLEY

FORTUNE

Fortune brings in some boats that are not steer'd.
    SHAKESPEARE (*Cymbeline*, IV, iii)

Court not felicity too far, and weary not the favourable hand of fortune.   SIR THOMAS BROWNE

Dame Fortune plays with a man who surrenders himself to her caprices as a child plays with an ivory ball on a billiard table, pushing it hither and thither, and laughing with joy, when by chance he sends it into the pocket; and an expert player, who calculates speed, reaction, distance, angles, and a crowd of other things, does what he pleases with the ball; but Fortune is not a learned geometrician, and he who abandons himself to her must stand the hazard of the die. She seems, indeed, to take a malicious pleasure in proving that she is not blind; she has never raised me up except with the intention of casting me down afterwards.
    CASANOVA

In general, the greatest reverses of fortune are the most easily borne from a sort of dignity belonging to them.   WILLIAM HAZLITT

See also **Chance, Destiny, Fate.**

FORTY

Any man of forty who is endowed with moderate intelligence has seen—in the light of the uniformity of nature—the entire past and future.   MARCUS AURELIUS

Every man over forty who acquiesces is a scoundrel.
    GEORGE BERNARD SHAW

When a man is past forty and does not become a crook, he is either feeble-minded or a genius.
    LIN YUTANG

FORTY-FIVE

Forty-five is the age of recklessness for many men, as if in defiance of the decay and death waiting with open arms in the sinister valley at the bottom of the inevitable hill. For every age is fed on illusions, lest men should renounce life early and the human race come to an end.

JOSEPH CONRAD

FORTY-SIX

Old age begins at forty-six years, according to the common opinion.

CICERO

FORWARDS

The business of life is to go forwards. SAMUEL JOHNSON

It is perfectly true, as philosophers say, that life must be understood backwards. But they forget the other proposition, that it must be lived forwards.

SÖREN KIERKEGAARD

I have a perhaps unreasonable amount of belief, not in a millennium, but in the world on the whole blundering rather forwards than backwards. LESLIE STEPHEN

FRATERNITY

A 'fraternity' is the antithesis of *fraternity*. E. B. WHITE

FREE

To free oneself is nothing; it's being free that is hard. ANDRÉ GIDE

He is free who knows how to keep in his own hands the power to decide, at each step, the course of his life, and who lives in a society which does not block the exercise of that power.

SALVADOR DE MADARIAGA

FREE WILL

Submit to fate of your own free will. MARCUS AURELIUS

All theory is against freedom of the will; all experience for it.

SAMUEL JOHNSON

Sir, as to the doctrine of necessity, no man believes it. If a man should give me arguments that I do not see, though I could not answer them, should I believe that I do not see? SAMUEL JOHNSON

Dr. Johnson shunned tonight any discussion of the perplexed question of fate and free will, which I attempted to agitate: 'Sir,' said he, 'we *know* our will is free, and *there's* an end on't.'

BOSWELL (*Life of Johnson*)

A horse that is hitched with others to a wagon is not free not to walk in front of the wagon; and if it will not draw, the wagon will strike its legs, and it will go whither the wagon goes, and will pull it involuntarily. But, in spite of this limited freedom, it is free itself to pull the wagon, or be dragged along by it. The same is true of man. LEO TOLSTOY

He who *feels* that his will is not free is insane: he who *denies* it is foolish.

FRIEDRICH NIETZSCHE

See also **Determinism, Fatalism, Fate, Will.**

FREEDOM

Freedom is more precious than any gifts for which you may be tempted to give it up. BALTASAR GRACIÁN

It is my certain conviction that no man loses his freedom except through his own weakness.

GANDHI

In our country we have those three unspeakably precious things: freedom of speech, freedom of conscience, and the prudence never to practice either.   MARK TWAIN

The essence of freedom is the practicability of purpose.
ALFRED NORTH WHITEHEAD

(To Franklin D. Roosevelt, on freedom from want:) You are referring, I presume, Mr. President, to deprivation, not to desire.
WINSTON S. CHURCHILL

The basic test of freedom is perhaps less in what we are free to do than in what we are free not to do.
ERIC HOFFER

See also **Free, Liberty.**

FRENCH LANGUAGE

'Is a Frenchman a man?' 'Yes.' '*Well*,' den! Dad blame it, why doan' he *talk* like a man? You answer me *dat*!'   MARK TWAIN

It is good to be on your guard against an Englishman who speaks French perfectly; he is very likely to be a card-sharper or an attaché in the diplomatic service.
W. SOMERSET MAUGHAM

FRENCHMEN

Frenchmen are very pleasant at the age when they begin to believe in God for the second time.
G. C. LICHTENBERG

FRET

Fret not thyself, else shalt thou be moved to do evil.
BOOK OF COMMON PRAYER.
PSALM 37

See also **Fear, Worry.**

FRIEND

Do not remove a fly from your friend's forehead with a hatchet.
CHINESE PROVERB

The best preservative to keep the mind in health is the faithful admonition of a friend.
FRANCIS BACON

Friends are a second existence.
BALTASAR GRACIÁN

It is more shameful to distrust our friends than to be deceived by them.
LA ROCHEFOUCAULD

When our best friends are in trouble, there is always something that is not wholly displeasing to us.
LA ROCHEFOUCAULD

I set it down as a fact that if all men knew what each said of the other, there would not be four friends in the world.   PASCAL

It is a misfortune for a man not to have a friend in the world, but for that reason he shall have no enemy.
LORD HALIFAX

Most people enjoy the inferiority of their best friends.
LORD CHESTERFIELD

Prosperity makes few friends.
VAUVENARGUES

It is better to be deceived by one's friends than to deceive them.
GOETHE

When my friends lack an eye, I look at them in profile.
JOSEPH JOUBERT

The discussing the character and foibles of common friends is a great sweetener and cement of friendship.   WILLIAM HAZLITT

To accept a favour from a friend is to confer one.
JOHN CHURTON COLLINS

A man's growth is seen in the successive choirs of his friends.
RALPH WALDO EMERSON

A man cannot be said to succeed in this life who does not satisfy one friend. HENRY DAVID THOREAU

A friend who cannot at a pinch remember a thing or two that never happened is as bad as one who does not know how to forget.
SAMUEL BUTLER

It takes your enemy and your friend, working together, to hurt you to the heart, the one to slander you and the other to get the news to you.
MARK TWAIN

Instead of loving your enemies, treat your friends a little better.
E. W. HOWE

Anybody can sympathize with the sufferings of a friend, but it requires a very fine nature to sympathize with a friend's success.
OSCAR WILDE

One's friends are that part of the human race with which one can be human. GEORGE SANTAYANA

I might give my life for my friend, but he'd better not ask me to do up a parcel. LOGAN PEARSALL SMITH

There are no friends at cards or world politics.
FINLEY PETER DUNNE

A friend that ain't in need is a friend indeed. KIN HUBBARD

FRIENDSHIP

Of all the things which wisdom provides to make life entirely happy, much the greatest is the possession of friendship. EPICURUS

However rare true love is, true friendship is rarer.
LA ROCHEFOUCAULD

Friendship cannot live with ceremony, nor without civility.
LORD HALIFAX

If a man does not make new acquaintances as he advances through life, he will soon find himself left alone. A man, sir, should keep his friendship in constant repair.
SAMUEL JOHNSON

Old friendships are like meats served up repeatedly, cold, comfortless, and distasteful. The stomach turns against them.
WILLIAM HAZLITT

Contracting a real friendship is one of the most completely involuntary things a man can do.
HENRY S. HASKINS

Nothing so fortifies a friendship as a belief on the part of one friend that he is superior to the other.
HONORÉ DE BALZAC

Friendship is like money, easier made than kept. SAMUEL BUTLER

See also **Acquaintance, Friend, Love and Friendship.**

FRIVOLITY

Much that is achieved by faith can also be achieved by utmost frivolity.
ERIC HOFFER

FROGS

My Aunt Maria asked me to read the life of Dr. Chalmers, which, however, I did not promise to do. Yesterday, Sunday, she was heard through the partition shouting to my Aunt Jane, who is deaf, 'Think of it! He stood half an hour today

to hear the frogs croak, and he wouldn't read the life of Chalmers.'
HENRY DAVID THOREAU

FROLIC

A man cannot spend all his life in frolick.　SAMUEL JOHNSON

FRUGALITY

Frugality too has a limit, and to disregard it is just as wrong as to err through excess.　EPICURUS

See also **Economy.**

FUN

Fun is like life insurance: the older you get, the more it costs.
KIN HUBBARD

See also **Amusement, Funny, Pleasure.**

FUNERAL

I assisted, with several others of his friends, in escorting the body of Monsieur de Grammont to Soissons, from the siege of La Fère, where he was killed. I observed that, in all the places we passed through, the people we met with were moved to tears and lamentations by the mere solemn pomp of our convoy; for they did not know even the name of the departed.　MONTAIGNE

A solemn funeral is inconceivable to the Chinese mind. LIN YUTANG

See also **Death, Grief.**

FUNNY

When a thing is funny, search it for a hidden truth.
GEORGE BERNARD SHAW

Everything is funny as long as it is happening to somebody else.
WILL ROGERS

See also **Comic, Laugh, Joke.**

FUTURE

If you wish to live a life free from sorrow, think of what is going to happen as if it had already happened.　EPICTETUS

Sorrow upon sorrow can be the only result if you worry about the future.　THOMAS À KEMPIS

The future is hidden even from those who make it.
ANATOLE FRANCE

The silly vanity of being abreast with the ideas of the day after tomorrow.　JOSEPH CONRAD

To the being fully alive, the future is not ominous but a promise; it surrounds the present like a halo.
JOHN DEWEY

Nothing has any sense for a man except in so far as it is directed toward the future.
JOSÉ ORTEGA Y GASSET

In the management of our own personal affairs, we are proceeding on the theory that what happens will be something we didn't expect, and that any worry about the future is a waste of time.　WILLIAM FEATHER

See also **Past, Past and Future, Present, Prophecy, Prophet.**

G

GAIETY SEE GAY.

GALLANT

If anyone complains of not succeeding in affairs of gallantry, we will venture to say, it is because he is not gallant. He has mistaken his talent.　WILLIAM HAZLITT

GALLERY

I never visit a gallery without wanting to cry to the sad spectators: 'Stop tip-toeing! Have some fun! Find some delight in this place—or march straight out!'

J. B. PRIESTLEY

How often my soul visits the National Gallery, and how seldom I go there myself!

LOGAN PEARSALL SMITH

See also **Painting, Picture.**

GAMBLE

Life has only one real charm—the charm of *gambling*. But what if we do not care whether we win or lose?

CHARLES BAUDELAIRE

See also **Speculate.**

GAMES

Games lubricate the body and the mind. BENJAMIN FRANKLIN

Some men are so mean that when they attend a ball game, they want to see the home team beaten.

E. W. HOWE

I am afraid I play no outdoor games at all, except dominoes. I have sometimes played dominoes outside French cafés. OSCAR WILDE

It is in games that many men discover their paradise.

ROBERT LYND

See also **Play.**

GARDEN

Should a garden look as if the gardener worked on his knees? I ask you. LINCOLN STEFFENS

GAY

Live merrily as thou canst, for by honest mirth we cure many passions of the mind. A gay companion is as a wagon to him that is wearied by the way. ROBERT BURTON

Gaiety, especially literary gaiety, clears the mind. Boredom confuses it; extreme tension strains it; sublimity revives it. JOSEPH JOUBERT

Gaiety alone, as it were, is the hard cash of happiness; everything else is just a promissory note.

SCHOPENHAUER

In godless times one must be gay. It is a duty. FRANZ KAFKA

See also **Laugh, Humour, Merry, Mirth.**

GENERALITY

Generalities and great conceit are always likely to cause calamity.

GOETHE

General propositions do not decide concrete cases.

OLIVER WENDELL HOLMES, JR.

The chief end of man is to frame general propositions and no general proposition is worth a damn.

OLIVER WENDELL HOLMES, JR.

For parlour use the vague generality is a life-saver. GEORGE ADE

GENERALIZATION

All universal judgments are weak, loose, and dangerous.

MONTAIGNE

General notions are generally wrong.

LADY MARY WORTLEY MONTAGU

All general reflections upon nations and societies are the trite, threadbare jokes of those who set up for wit without having any.

LORD CHESTERFIELD

One of the perils of a great war is that it revives the passionate faith of the common man in generalizations. ROBERT LYND

See also **Generality.**

GENERATION

The man who sees two or three generations is like one who sits in the conjurer's booth at a fair, and sees the tricks two or three times. They are meant to be seen only once. SCHOPENHAUER

See also **History.**

GENEROSITY

The reputation for generosity is to be purchased pretty cheap. It does not depend so much upon a man's general expense as upon his giving handsomely where it is proper to give at all. LORD CHESTERFIELD

Generosity gives help rather than advice. VAUVENARGUES

True generosity gives recognition. GOETHE

Note how perverse is the attitude of the weak toward their benefactors. They feel generosity as oppression; they want to retaliate. They say to their benefactors: 'May the day come when you shall be weak and we will send bundles to America.' ERIC HOFFER

See also **Alms, Benevolence, Charity, Give, Philanthropy.**

GENIUS

Passion holds up the bottom of the universe and genius paints up its roof. CHANG CH'AO

Genius is patience. BUFFON

At least once a year everybody is a genius. G. C. LICHTENBERG

If it were not for respect for human opinions, I would not open my window to see the bay of Naples for the first time, whilst I would go five hundred leagues to talk with a man of genius whom I had not seen. MADAME DE STAËL

God did not rest after the six days of creation: He is still continuously at work, as on the first day. Surely it wouldn't have been much fun for Him to build this lumbering world out of simple elements and let it roll about in the sunshine year in, year out, if He hadn't had the plan to build upon this material basis a training ground for higher spirits. And so He is continually at work in great geniuses, so as to pull the common people *up*. GOETHE

When thou seest an eagle, thou seest a portion of genius; lift up thy head! WILLIAM BLAKE

Execution is the chariot of genius. WILLIAM BLAKE

There is in genius itself an unconscious activity; nay, that is the genius in the man of genius. SAMUEL TAYLOR COLERIDGE

The definition of genius is that it acts unconsciously; and those who have produced immortal works, have done so without knowing how or why. The greatest power operates unseen. WILLIAM HAZLITT

The world has a standing pique against genius. WILLIAM HAZLITT

What makes men of genius, or rather, what they make, is not new ideas, it is that idea—possessing them—that what has been said has still not been said enough. EUGÈNE DELACROIX

Genius is the capacity for seeing relationships where lesser men see none.   WILLIAM JAMES

What is called genius is the abundance of life or health.
HENRY DAVID THOREAU

'Genius is patience,' as Buffon said. And patience after all is a man's nearest approach to nature's process of creation. What is art but nature concentrated?
HONORÉ DE BALZAC

Great geniuses have the shortest biographies. Their cousins can tell you nothing about them.
RALPH WALDO EMERSON

Genius ain't anything more than elegant common sense.
JOSH BILLINGS

It's stupid to say that genius is merely long-drawn-out patience. Because in the first place patience itself doesn't mean anything—it requires more than patience to get what you want—you must go straight for it. And secondly, there is one kind of genius, perhaps the best and most precious, into which not a grain of patience enters. But there is another kind which is due to effort, a fierce application, and to that, for my part, I pay respect.
GEORGES CLÉMENCEAU

Genius is a promontory jutting out into the future.   VICTOR HUGO

Genius is born, not paid.
OSCAR WILDE

Every man of genius is considerably helped by being dead.
ROBERT LYND

See also **Artist, Genius and Talent.**

GENIUS AND TALENT

Talent differs from genius, as voluntary differs from involuntary power.   WILLIAM HAZLITT

Genius learns from nature; talent from books.   JOSH BILLINGS

To do easily what is difficult for others is the mark of talent. To do what is impossible for talent is the mark of genius.   FRÉDÉRIC AMIEL

GENTLEMAN

A gentleman never contends in anything he does—except perhaps in archery.   CONFUCIUS

A gentleman is mindful no less of the freedom of others than of his own dignity.   LIVY

Poverty may partly eclipse a gentleman, but cannot totally obscure him.   CERVANTES

My master hath been an honourable gentleman; tricks he hath had in him which gentlemen have.
SHAKESPEARE (*All's Well That Ends Well*, V, iii)

A gentleman may love like a lunatic, but not like a beast.
LA ROCHEFOUCAULD

The Swiss are offended at being called gentlemen.   PASCAL

It is almost a definition of a gentleman to say that he is one who never inflicts pain.
JOHN HENRY NEWMAN

Repose and cheerfulness are the badges of the gentleman—repose in energy.   RALPH WALDO EMERSON

If we are asked what is the most essential characteristic that underlies this word, the word itself will guide us to gentleness, absence of browbeating or overbearing manners, absence of fuss, and generally consideration for other people.

SAMUEL BUTLER

No real gentleman will tell the naked truth in the presence of ladies.

MARK TWAIN

A gentleman is a man, more often a woman, who owes nothing and leaves the world in debt to him. It is better to die a gentleman than a martyr.

GEORGE BERNARD SHAW

To ignore, to disdain to consider, to overlook, are the essence of the gentleman. WILLIAM JAMES

This is the private man, in other words the gentleman, who will neither love nor remember in common. ALICE MEYNELL

If a man is a gentleman, he knows quite enough, and if he is not a gentleman, whatever he knows is bad for him. OSCAR WILDE

A gentleman never looks out of the window. OSCAR WILDE

When an English man is totally incapable of doing any work whatsoever, he describes himself in the income-tax form as a 'gentleman'.

ROBERT LYND

One never thinks of Habakkuk, John the Baptist, Epictetus, Martin Luther or Calvin as gentlemen; they were prophets, saints, heroes, if you like, but not gentlemen.

HENRY DWIGHT SEDGWICK

Give a man a secure position and you will note an access of self-confidence and ease of intercourse; he feels the social order bearing him

up. It will go far to make a very common man a gentleman.

CHARLES HORTON COOLEY

A real gentleman is at a big disadvantage these days.

KIN HUBBARD

When I was young the conception of a gentleman had value; now not only what it stood for, but the word itself have become vaguely objectionable. Outside lavatories you will often see *Ladies* on the door of one, but *Men* on the door of another. W. SOMERSET MAUGHAM

No gentleman can be a philosopher and no philosopher a gentleman: to the philosopher everything is fluid —even himself. The gentleman is a little God over against the Cosmos.

OLIVER WENDELL HOLMES, JR.

A woman in a London police court once said: 'My husband is no gentleman: he puts on his trousers before his socks.' ROBERT LYND

See also **Lady, Well-Bred.**

GERMAN LANGUAGE

My philological studies have satisfied me that a gifted person ought to learn English (barring spelling and pronouncing) in thirty hours, French in thirty days, and German in thirty years. MARK TWAIN

Some German words are so long that they have a perspective. Observe these examples: *Freundschaftsbezeigungen, Dilettantenaufdringlichkeiten, Stadtverordnetenversammlungen.*

MARK TWAIN

GETTING

In this world there are only two tragedies. One is not getting what one wants and the other is getting it.

OSCAR WILDE

GETTING OUT

There is a certain perverseness, of which I believe all men have a share—I mean that temper, or humour, or whatever it is to be called, that indisposes us to a situation, though not unpleasant in itself, merely because we cannot get out of it.   WILLIAM COWPER

It is easier to stay out than get out.
MARK TWAIN

See also **Leaving.**

GHOST

(To a lady who asked whether he believed in ghosts:) No, ma'am, I've seen too many.
SAMUEL TAYLOR COLERIDGE

We do not believe in ghosts, but to talk about them scares us.
E. W. HOWE

I do not see ghosts, I only see their inherent possibility.
G. K. CHESTERTON

See also **Spiritualism, Supernatural.**

GHOSTLY

There is something ghostly in all great art.   LAFCADIO HEARN

See also **Ghost, Supernatural.**

GIBBON, EDWARD

Gibbon's style is detestable, but his style is not the worst thing about him. His history has proved an effective bar to all real familiarity with the temper and habits of imperial Rome.
SAMUEL TAYLOR COLERIDGE

GIVING

The wise man does not lay up treasure. The more he gives to others, the more he has for his own.
LAO-TSE

A wise lover values not so much the gift of the lover as the love of the giver.   THOMAS À KEMPIS

Who gives much does not give but sells.   BALTASAR GRACIÁN

Never give beyond the possibility of return.   BALTASAR GRACIÁN

Giving is the business of the rich.
GOETHE

You cannot afford to have things given to you.   E. W. HOWE

We do not quite forgive a giver. The hand that feeds us is in some danger of being bitten.
RALPH WALDO EMERSON

To a right-minded man nothing costs more dear than what is given him.   BALTASAR GRACIÁN

He who gives money he has not earned is generous with other people's labour.
GEORGE BERNARD SHAW

If ever you have a lump of money large enough to be of any use, and can spare it, don't give it away: find some needed job that nobody is doing and get it done.
GEORGE BERNARD SHAW

It is certainly more agreeable to have power to give than to receive.
WINSTON S. CHURCHILL.

It is well to give when asked, but it is better to give unasked, through understanding.   KAHLIL GIBRAN

In the jungles of South India live the Bhils, who are said to have been there before the last ice age. . . . I am told that they will give away anything they have for the mere asking, and know neither avarice nor envy. For they look upon objects as we look upon air and sunlight and the other free gifts of God. FREYA STARK

See also **Generosity, Presents.**

GLITTER

Dirt glitters when the sun happens to shine. GOETHE

GLOOMY

Austerity is a disease. I would a thousand times rather be stricken with fever than think gloomily. VOLTAIRE

See also **Brooding, Melancholy.**

GOD (DEFINITIONS)

A comprehended God is no God. ST. JOHN CHRYSOSTOM

Why dost thou prate of God? Whatever thou sayest of Him is untrue. MEISTER ECKHART

God is the denial of denials. MEISTER ECKHART

The most beautiful of all emblems is that of God, whom Timaeus of Locris describes under the image of 'A circle whose centre is everywhere and circumference nowhere.' VOLTAIRE

After all, is our idea of God anything more than personified incomprehensibility? G. C. LICHTENBERG

Dare I put it so? It is easy to know God, so long as you do not vex yourself to define Him. JOSEPH JOUBERT

God is within us: He is that inner presence which makes us admire the beautiful, which rejoices us when we have done right and consoles us for not sharing the happiness of the wicked. EUGÈNE DELACROIX

To know God better is only to realize more fully how impossible it is that we should ever know Him at all. I know not which is the more childish—to deny Him, or the define Him. SAMUEL BUTLER

God is our expression for all forces and powers which we do not understand, or with which we are unfamiliar. SAMUEL BUTLER

God is that indefinable something which we all feel but which we do not know. To me God is truth and love, God is ethics and morality, God is fearlessness, God is the source of light and life and yet He is above and beyond all these. God is conscience. He is even the atheism of the atheist. GANDHI

See also **Divine, God, God and the Devil, God and Man, Love of God, Will of God.**

GOD

The foundation of all foundations, the pillar supporting all wisdoms, is the recognition of the reality of God. MOSES MAIMONIDES

Those who attempt to search into the majesty of God will be overwhelmed with its glory. THOMAS À KEMPIS

Belief in God is an instinct as natural to man as walking on two legs. G. C. LICHTENBERG

To stand on one leg and prove God's existence is a very different thing from going on one's knees and thanking Him. SÖREN KIERKEGAARD

If Henry Ward Beecher knows so much more about God than another, if he has made some discovery of truth in this direction, I would thank him to publish it in *Silliman's Journal*, with as few flourishes as possible.

HENRY DAVID THOREAU

The true laws of God are the laws of our own well-being.

SAMUEL BUTLER

God is *in* the world, or nowhere, creating continually in us and a-round us.

ALFRED NORTH WHITEHEAD

Speculation about God is for the most part slightly morbid or merely curious; a clear flow of life and purpose is Himself, and all we need.

CHARLES HORTON COOLEY

The true God is the God of things as they are.   G. K. CHESTERTON

See also **Divine, God (Definitions), God and the Devil, God and Man, Gods, Love of God, Will of God.**

GOD AND THE DEVIL

God and the devil are an effort after specialization and division of labour.   SAMUEL BUTLER

See also **Devil.**

GOD AND MAN

The sage looks up to God, but does not offer to aid.   CHUANG-TSE

God never deceives; but man is deceived whenever he puts too much trust in himself.

THOMAS À KEMPIS

He to whom God is not adequate is very greedy.

ST. FRANCIS DE SALES

There is practically nothing that men do not prefer to God. A tiresome detail of business, an occupation utterly pernicious to health, the employment of time in ways one does not dare to mention. Anything rather than God.

FRANÇOIS DE FÉNELON

There needs neither art nor science for going to God, but only a heart resolutely determined to apply itself to nothing but Him.

BROTHER LAWRENCE

Lift up your heart to Him, sometimes even at your meals, and when you are in company; the least little remembrance will always be acceptable to Him. You need not cry very loud; He is nearer to us than we are aware of.

BROTHER LAWRENCE

Live to seek God, and life will not be without God.   LEO TOLSTOY

It is only by forgetting yourself that you draw near to God.

HENRY DAVID THOREAU

It is terrible to watch a man who has the incomprehensible in his grasp, does not know what to do with it, and sits playing with a toy called God.   LEO TOLSTOY

Resist God and He will fly from you.   SAMUEL BUTLER

Verily, verily, I say unto thee, he who longs for God finds Him. Go and verify this in thine own life; try for three consecutive days with genuine earnestness and thou art sure to succeed.   RAMAKRISHNA

God must love those who defy Him.   JOHN BURROUGHS

I once heard a lady describe the pleasure it gave her to think that she 'could always cuddle up to God.'   WILLIAM JAMES

Beware of the man whose god is in the skies. GEORGE BERNARD SHAW

I believe in God as I believe in my friends, because I feel the breath of His affection, feel His invisible and intangible hand drawing me, leading me, grasping me; because I possess an inner consciousness of a particular providence and of a universal mind that marks out for me the course of my own destiny.
MIGUEL DE UNAMUNO

He who waits for God fails to understand that he possesses Him. Believe that God and happiness are one, and put all your happiness in the present moment.
ANDRÉ GIDE

People ought to talk about God only naturally. ANDRÉ GIDE

'Indeed, the times are troubled,' he said, 'but we must remember that we are all in God's hands.' 'I know we are,' said Mrs. Brandon earnestly, laying her hand on the Vicar's sleeve, 'and that is just what is so perfectly *dreadful*.'
ANGELA THIRKELL

My father was a God-fearing man, but he never missed a copy of the New York *Times* either.
E. B. WHITE

Of two men who have no experience of God, he who denies Him is perhaps nearer to Him than the other. SIMONE WEIL

See also **God (Definitions), God, Man.**

GODS

Even those who worship other deities, and sacrifice to them with faith in their hearts, are really worshipping me, though with a mistaken approach. For I am the only enjoyer and the only God of all sacrifices. BHAGAVAD-GITA

Man cannot make a worm, yet he will make gods by the dozen.
MONTAIGNE

It is Socrates' opinion, and mine too, that the wisest theory about the gods is to have no theory at all.
MONTAIGNE

As nations improve, so do their gods. G. C. LICHTENBERG

See also **Religions.**

GOING

A man never goes so far as when he does not know whither he is going.
OLIVER CROMWELL

Never come unasked and only go when sent for. BALTASAR GRACIÁN

See also **Not Going.**

GOLDEN RULE

Absolutely speaking, *Do unto others as you would that they should do unto you* is by no means a golden rule, but the best of current silver. An honest man would have but little occasion for it.
HENRY DAVID THOREAU

The golden rule is that there are no golden rules.
GEORGE BERNARD SHAW

See also **Rules of Life.**

GOLF

It is almost impossible to remember how tragic a place the world is when one is playing golf.
ROBERT LYND

GOOD

Do good, and evil shall not find you. Good is prayer with fasting and alms and righteousness.
BOOK OF TOBIT, 12

No evil can happen to a good man, either in life or after death.
SOCRATES (Plato, *Apology*)

Put an end once and for all to this discussion of what a good man should be, and be one.
MARCUS AURELIUS

What is good only because it pleases cannot be pronounced good until it has been found to please.
SAMUEL JOHNSON

We have no right to make those miserable whom we cannot make good.
VAUVENARGUES

The greatest pleasure I know is to do a good action by stealth and to have it found out by accident.
CHARLES LAMB

God does not intend people, and does not like people, to be too good. He likes them neither too good nor too bad, but a little too bad is more venial with him than a little too good.
SAMUEL BUTLER

Men have a singular desire to be good without being good for anything.
HENRY DAVID THOREAU

Men should not try to overstrain their goodness more than any other faculty, bodily or mental.
SAMUEL BUTLER

Be good and you will be lonely.
MARK TWAIN

There is no good fishing, and there are no good times.
E. W. HOWE

The longer I live the more keenly I feel that whatever was good enough for our fathers is not good enough for us.
OSCAR WILDE

When we are happy we are always good but when we are good we are not always happy.
OSCAR WILDE

There's too many folks of limited means who think that nothing's too good for them.
KIN HUBBARD

A never failing way to get rid of a fellow is to tell him something for his own good.
KIN HUBBARD

Good behaviour is the last refuge of mediocrity.
HENRY S. HASKINS

See also **Best, Better, Doing Good, Good and Bad, Good and Evil, Good Humour, Good Temper, Good Will, Good Works.**

GOOD AND BAD

Do not become bad from sheer goodness—that is, by never getting into a temper.
BALTASAR GRACIÁN

If you have called a bad thing bad, you have done no great matter; but if you call a good thing good, you have accomplished much.
GOETHE

There are bad people who would be less dangerous if they had no good in them.
LA ROCHEFOUCAULD

Good and bad men are each less so than they seem.
SAMUEL TAYLOR COLERIDGE

See also **Good, Wicked.**

GOOD AND EVIL

Often we are good so that we can do evil with impunity.
LA ROCHEFOUCAULD

To do evil, that good may come of it, is for bunglers in politics, as well as morals.   WILLIAM PENN

Good is the passive that obeys reason. Evil is the active springing from energy.   WILLIAM BLAKE

Evil, no doubt, is a form of good of which the results are not immediately manifest.   HONORÉ DE BALZAC

Public good is made of many private evils.   ANATOLE FRANCE

Good is that which makes for unity; evil is that which makes for separateness.   ALDOUS HUXLEY

See also **Evil, Good.**

GOOD HUMOUR

Think not that any good act is contemptible, though it be but your brother's coming to you with an open countenance and good humour.   MOHAMMED

A man's being in a good or bad humour depends upon his will.   SAMUEL JOHNSON

What I value more than all things is good humour.   THOMAS JEFFERSON

See also **Cheerful, Good Temper.**

GOOD TEMPER

Good temper is an estate for life.   WILLIAM HAZLITT

GOOD WILL

The chief stress of Jesus' teaching was not laid upon poverty and humility, though they have a high place in the Beatitudes. The thing He taught mainly, first and last, was simple goodwill between man and man—simple friendliness, simple decency.   H. L. MENCKEN

GOOD WORKS

He who has more learning than good deeds is like a tree with many branches but weak roots; the first great storm will throw it to the ground. He whose good works are greater than his knowledge is like a tree with fewer branches but with strong and spreading roots, a tree which all the winds of heaven cannot uproot.   TALMUD

In contemplation, you serve only yourselves. In good works, you serve many people.   MEISTER ECKHART

So long as you wear this mortal body, you will be subject to weariness and sadness of heart. . . . When this happens, you will be wise to resort to humble, exterior tasks, and to restore yourself by good works.   THOMAS À KEMPIS

See also **Service, Work.**

GOSSIP

Gossip is none the less gossip because it comes from venerable antiquity.   BISHOP MANDELL CREIGHTON

Gossip is charming! History is merely gossip. But scandal is gossip made tedious by morality.   OSCAR WILDE

See also **Scandal.**

GOVERNMENT

Govern a great nation as you would fry small fish.   LAO-TSE

When Tzu Lu asked about the art of government, the Master replied: 'Be in advance of the people; show them how to work.' On his asking for something more, the Master added: 'Untiringly.'   SAYINGS OF CONFUCIUS

They that govern most make least noise. JOHN SELDEN

The government of the world is a great thing, but a very coarse one, too, compared with the fineness of speculative knowledge. LORD HALIFAX

In general, the art of government consists in taking as much money as possible from one party of the citizens to give it to the other. VOLTAIRE

I would not give half a guinea to live under one form of government rather than another. It is of no moment to the happiness of an individual. SAMUEL JOHNSON

It is a maxim of wise government to deal with men not as they ought to be but as they are. GOETHE

Ruling is easy, governing difficult. GOETHE

What government is best? That which teaches us to govern ourselves. GOETHE

The art of government is not to let men grow stale. NAPOLEON I

The whole duty of government is to prevent crime and to preserve contracts. LORD MELBOURNE

We must remember that the machinery of government would not work if it were not allowed a little play in its joints. OLIVER WENDELL HOLMES, JR.

England has been in a dreadful state for some weeks. Lord Coodle would go out, Sir Thomas Doodle wouldn't come in, and there being nobody in Great Britain (to speak of) except Coodle and Doodle, there has been no Government. CHARLES DICKENS

I heartily accept the motto, 'That government is best which governs least;' . . . Carried out, it finally amounts to this, which I also believe,—'That government is best which governs not at all;' and when men are prepared for it, that will be the kind of government which they will have. HENRY DAVID THOREAU

I know not how better to describe our form of government in a single phrase than by calling it a government by the chairmen of the Standing Committees of Congress. WOODROW WILSON

There is no government without mumbo-jumbo. HILAIRE BELLOC

While the Pobble was in the water some unidentified creatures came and ate his toes off, and when he got home his aunt remarked:
It's a fact the whole world knows,
That Pobbles are happier without their toes,
which is funny because it has a meaning, and one might even say a political significance. For the whole theory of authoritarian government is summed up in the statement that Pobbles are happier without their toes. GEORGE ORWELL

See also **Politics, Ruler, State.**

GRACE

I have never found anyone, however religious and devout, who did not sometimes experience withdrawal of grace, or feel a lessening of devotion. THOMAS À KEMPIS

The breeze of divine grace is blowing upon us all. But one needs to set the sail to feel this breeze of grace. RAMAKRISHNA

GRACEFUL

How inimitably graceful children are in general—before they learn to dance.

SAMUEL TAYLOR COLERIDGE

There is no true gracefulness which is not epitomized goodness.

SAMUEL BUTLER

GRACES

Every man of any education would rather be called a rascal than accused of deficiency in the graces.

SAMUEL JOHNSON

GRADUAL

Firstly, gradualness. About this most important condition of fruitful scientific work I never can speak without emotion. Gradualness, gradualness, and gradualness. From the very beginning of your work, school yourselves to severe gradualness in the accumulation of knowledge.

IVAN PAVLOV

GRAMMAR

No man forgets his original trade: the rights of nations, and of kings, sink into questions of grammar, if grammarians discuss them.

SAMUEL JOHNSON

It is well to remember that grammar is common speech formulated. Usage is the only test. I would prefer a phrase that was easy and unaffected to a phrase that was grammatical.

W. SOMERSET MAUGHAM

See also **Ain't, Split Infinitive, We.**

GRATITUDE

The gratitude of most men is only a secret wish to get greater benefits.

LA ROCHEFOUCAULD

Gratitude is expensive.

EDWARD GIBBON

'I feel a very unusual sensation,' said Mr. St. Barbe, after dining with the Neufchatels. 'If it is not indigestion, I think it must be gratitude.'

BENJAMIN DISRAELI

'It's only you, the generous creatures, whom I envy,' said Mr. Skimpole. 'I envy you your power of doing what you do. It is what I should revel in, myself. I don't feel any vulgar gratitude to you. I almost feel as if *you* ought to be grateful to me, for giving you the opportunity of enjoying the luxury of generosity. I know you like it. For anything I can tell, I may have come into the world expressly for the purpose of increasing your stock of happiness. I may have been born to be a benefactor to you, by sometimes giving you an opportunity of assisting me in my little perplexities. Why should I regret my incapacity for details and worldly affairs, when it leads to such pleasant consequences? I don't regret it therefore.'

CHARLES DICKENS

I believe the best definition of man is the ungrateful biped.

FEODOR DOSTOEVSKI

Nothing tires a man more than to be grateful all the time.

E. W. HOWE

GREY

The enemy of all painting is the grey: a painting will almost always appear greyer than it is, on account of its oblique position under the light. EUGÈNE DELACROIX

GRAY, THOMAS

Sir, he was dull in company, dull in his closet, dull everywhere, He was dull in a new way, and that made many people think him great.

SAMUEL JOHNSON

GREAT MEN

A great man is he who has not lost the heart of a child. MENCIUS

Eminent posts make great men greater, and little men less.

JEAN DE LA BRUYÈRE

Great men, like nature, use simple language. VAUVENARGUES

If I had succeeded I should have been the greatest man the world has known. NAPOLEON I

No really great man ever thought himself so. WILLIAM HAZLITT

No great man ever complains of want of opportunity.

RALPH WALDO EMERSON

Great men are the true men, the men in whom nature has succeeded. They are not extraordinary—they are in the true order. It is the other species of men who are not what they ought to be.

FRÉDÉRIC AMIEL

All great men are bad.

LORD ACTON

Eleven out of twelve great men of history were only agents of a great cause. FRIEDRICH NIETZSCHE

The narrower the age, the greater the great men. AUBREY MENEN

I studied the lives of great men and famous women; and I found that the men and women who got to the top were those who did the jobs they had in hand, with everything they had of energy and enthusiasm and hard work. HARRY S. TRUMAN

There is a great man who makes every man feel small. But the real great man is the man who makes every man feel great.

G. K. CHESTERTON

See also **Genius, Hero.**

GREED

It is partly to avoid consciousness of greed that we prefer to associate with those who are at least as greedy as ourselves. Those who consume much less are a reproach.

CHARLES HORTON COOLEY

GREEN

Constable said that the superiority of the green he uses for his meadows derives from the fact that it is composed of a multitude of different greens. What causes the lack of intensity and of life in verdure as it is painted by the common run of landscapists is that they ordinarily do it with a uniform tint.—What he said about the green of the meadows can be applied to all the other tones.

EUGÈNE DELACROIX

GREENHORN

Gullibility is the key to all adventures. The greenhorn is the ultimate victor in everything; it is he that gets the most out of life.

G. K. CHESTERTON

GRIEF

Work makes a callus to grief.

CICERO

Grief is a species of idleness.

SAMUEL JOHNSON

It is dangerous to abandon oneself to the luxury of grief; it deprives one of courage, and even of the wish for recovery.

FRÉDÉRIC AMIEL

And being come to the grave as above, Dr. Pierson, the minister of the parish, did read the service for burial, and so I saw my poor brother laid into the grave; and so all broke up, and I and my wife and Madam Turner and her family to my brother's, and by and by fell to a barrel of oysters, cake, and cheese, being too merry for so late a sad work. But, Lord! to see how the world makes nothing of the memory of a man an hour after he is dead! And, indeed, I must blame myself; for though at the sight of him dead and dying, I had real grief for a while, while he was in my sight, yet presently after, and ever since, I have had very little grief indeed for him. SAMUEL PEPYS

See also **Funeral, Sorrow.**

GROUCH

A grouch escapes so many little annoyances that it almost pays to be one. KIN HUBBARD

GROWING OLD

To know how to grow old is the master work of wisdom, and one of the most difficult chapters in the great art of living.
FRÉDÉRIC AMIEL

The mere process of growing old together will make the slightest acquaintance seem a bosom-friend.
LOGAN PEARSALL SMITH

It is only in our eyes that animals grow old. G. C. LICHTENBERG

When we grow older, we must deliberately remain at a certain stage.
GOETHE

Some folks as they grow older grow wise, but most folks simply grow stubborner. JOSH BILLINGS

In ageing, the mind grows constipated and thick. MONTAIGNE

In growing old, we become more foolish—and more wise.
LA ROCHEFOUCAULD

The older one gets, the larger one's horizon. But the possibilities of life get smaller and smaller.
FRANZ KAFKA

See also **Old Age, Young and Old.**

GROWTH

Study, in all its manifestations, in the works of nature and the works of man, the universal and eternal law of growth by degrees, of 'little by little' or 'one thing at a time'—a growth accompanied by a steady quickening acccumulation of strength, like the accumulation of money at compound interest.
CHARLES BAUDELAIRE

See also **Gradual.**

GUEST

A man who stays a week with another makes him a slave for a week.
SAMUEL JOHNSON

Fish and visitors smell in three days.
BENJAMIN FRANKLIN

Mankind is divisible into two great classes; hosts and guests.
MAX BEERBOHM

See also **Host.**

GULLIVER'S TRAVELS

When you have once thought of big men and little men, it is easy to do the rest. SAMUEL JOHNSON

GYPSIES

Are you not scared by seeing that the gypsies are more attractive to us than the apostles?
RALPH WALDO EMERSON

H

HABIT

He who wishes to benefit by a habit, let him avoid continuing it.
MONTAIGNE

It is too bad if you have to do everything upon reflection and can't do anything from early habit.
G. C. LICHTENBERG

Habit makes everything, even love.
VAUVENARGUES

It seems, in fact, as though the second half of a man's life is made up of nothing but the habits he has accumulated during the first half.
FEODOR DOSTOEVSKI

Habit is habit and not to be flung out of the window by any man, but coaxed downstairs a step at a time.
MARK TWAIN

A man may have no bad habits and have worse. MARK TWAIN

The most unendurable thing, to be sure, the really terrible thing, would be a life without habits, a life which continually required improvisation. FRIEDRICH NIETZSCHE

The worse our habits the more we have what is called good legislation. When there are good habits in a country, the business of the state dwindles. G. W. RUSSELL (Æ)

Wise living consists perhaps less in acquiring good habits than in acquiring as few habits as possible.
ERIC HOFFER

The man who interferes with another's habits has the worst one.
HENRY S. HASKINS

What is most contrary to salvation is not sin but habit.
CHARLES PÉGUY

Habit converts luxurious enjoyments into dull and daily necessities. ALDOUS HUXLEY

See also **Routine, Rut, Used to.**

HANDLE

Everything has two handles, one by which it may be borne, the other by which it may not. EPICTETUS

Take things always by their smooth handle. THOMAS JEFFERSON

HANGING

There is no man so good who, were he to submit all his thoughts and actions to the laws, would not deserve hanging ten times in his life.
MONTAIGNE

Men are not hanged for stealing horses, but that horses may not be stolen. LORD HALIFAX

Talking of our feeling for the distresses of others. . . . Why, there's Baretti, who is to be tried for his life tomorrow, friends have risen up for him on every side; yet if he should be hanged, none of them will eat a slice of plum-pudding the less.
SAMUEL JOHNSON

HAPPEN

The important events in the world are not deliberately brought about; they simply happen.
G. C. LICHTENBERG

We are all like Scheherazade's husband, in that we want to know what happens next. E. M. FORSTER

Nothing happens to you that hasn't happened to someone else.
WILLIAM FEATHER

HAPPINESS

Perfect happiness is the absence of the striving for happiness; perfect renown is the absence of concern for renown. CHUANG-TSE

It is the chiefest point of happiness that a man is willing to be what he is. ERASMUS

Man is meant for happiness and this happiness is in him, in the satisfaction of the daily needs of his existence. LEO TOLSTOY

Happiness is in the taste, and not in the things themselves; we are happy from possessing what we like, not from possessing what others like. LA ROCHEFOUCAULD

Sir, that all who are happy, are equally happy, is not true. A peasant and a philosopher may be equally *satisfied*, but not equally *happy*. Happiness consists in the multiplicity of agreeable consciousness. A peasant has not the capacity for having equal happiness with a philosopher. SAMUEL JOHNSON

Blest is that nation whose silent course of happiness furnishes nothing for history to say. This is what I ambition for my own country. THOMAS JEFFERSON

No temper could be more cheerful than hers, or possess, in a greater degree, that sanguine expectation of happiness which is happiness itself. JANE AUSTEN

All happiness depends on courage and work. I have had many periods of wretchedness, but with energy, and above all, with illusions, I pulled through them all. HONORÉ DE BALZAC

To fill the hour, and leave no crevice for a repentance or an approval—that is happiness. RALPH WALDO EMERSON

If an Arab in the desert were suddenly to discover a spring in his tent, and so would always be able to have water in abundance, how fortunate he would consider himself—so too, when a man, who as a physical being is always turned toward the outside, thinking that his happiness lies outside him, finally turns inward and discovers that the source is within him; not to mention his discovery that the source is his relation to God. SÖREN KIERKEGAARD

Surfeits of happiness are fatal. BALTASAR GRACIÁN

Happiness is a Swedish sunset—it is there for all, but most of us look the other way and lose it. MARK TWAIN

There are people who can do all fine and heroic things but one: keep from telling their happinesses to the unhappy. MARK TWAIN

Happiness and misery consist in a progression towards better or worse; it does not matter how high up or low down you are, it depends not on this, but on the direction in which you are tending. SAMUEL BUTLER

What we call happiness is what we do not know. ANATOLE FRANCE

Every little while we see this heading in the newspapers: 'The Secret of Happiness.' There is no such secret. E. W. HOWE

Happiness and beauty are by-products. Folly is the direct pursuit of happiness and beauty. GEORGE BERNARD SHAW

Happiness is the only sanction of life; where happiness fails, existence remains a mad and lamentable experiment.   GEORGE SANTAYANA

Happiness is a wine of the rarest vintage, and seems insipid to a vulgar taste.
LOGAN PEARSALL SMITH

It's pretty hard to tell what does bring happiness; poverty and wealth have both failed.   KIN HUBBARD

Contempt for happiness is usually contempt for other people's happiness, and is an elegant disguise for hatred of the human race.
BERTRAND RUSSELL

The true test of happiness is whether you know what day of the week it is. A miserable man is aware of this even in his sleep. To be as cheerful and rosycheeked on Monday as on Saturday, and at breakfast or dinner is to—well, make an ideal husband.   W. N. P. BARBELLION

Some of us might find happiness if we would quit struggling so desperately for it.
WILLIAM FEATHER

Happiness is like coke—something you get as a by-product in the process of making something else.
ALDOUS HUXLEY

I have always been impressed by the fact that the most studiously avoided subject in western philosophy is that of happiness.   LIN YUTANG

The search for happiness is one of the chief sources of unhappiness.
ERIC HOFFER

They taught me that happiness could be simply attained. I could either do my duty in that station of life to which it has pleased God to call me: or I could take evening classes in book-keeping and go one better than He intended.
AUBREY MENEN

See also **Felicity, Happy, Unhappy**.

HAPPY

We are never so happy or so unhappy as we suppose.
LA ROCHEFOUCAULD

We are apt to call things by wrong names. We will have prosperity to be happiness, and adversity to be misery. If thou wouldst be happy, bring thy mind to thy condition and have an indifference for more than what is sufficient.   WILLIAM PENN

Happy are the people whose annals are tiresome.   MONTESQUIEU

There are men who are happy without knowing it.   VAUVENARGUES

He is the happiest man who can connect the end of his life with its beginning.   GOETHE

Mankind are always happier for having been happy; so that if you make them happy now, you make them happy twenty years hence, by the memory of it.   SYDNEY SMITH

To live we must conquer incessantly, we must have the courage to be happy.   FRÉDÉRIC AMIEL

We are never happy: we can only remember that we were so once.
ALEXANDER SMITH

There is no duty we so much underrate as the duty of being happy.
ROBERT LOUIS STEVENSON

The happiest people seem to be those who have no particular cause for being happy except that they are so.   W. R. INGE

The happiest life, seen in perspective, can hardly be better than a stringing together of odd little moments. NORMAN DOUGLAS

Happy creatures do not know a great deal about life.
ANATOLE FRANCE

See also **Happiness, Unhappy.**

HAT

Never run after your own hat—others will be delighted to do it: why spoil their fun?
MARK TWAIN

When a man buys a new hat, he wants one just like the one he has had before. But a woman isn't that way. E. W. HOWE

HATE

We are nearer loving those who hate us than those who love us more than we wish.
LA ROCHEFOUCAULD

We not only love ourselves in others, but hate ourselves in others too. G. C. LICHTENBERG

CHARLES LAMB was once hotly assailing the character and reputation of a certain person, when his hearer, rather surprised at his outburst, interrupted it to say that he had no idea that Lamb knew the man in question. 'Know him!' Lamb exclaimed. 'Of course I don't know him. I never could hate anyone I knew.'

Those whom we can love, we can hate; to others we are indifferent.
HENRY DAVID THOREAU

It does not matter much what a man hates provided he hates something.
SAMUEL BUTLER

I hate them which hate God but I don't find God sufficiently hating them which hate me.
SAMUEL BUTLER

There is a jealousy in hating too: we want to have our enemy for ourselves. FRIEDRICH NIETZSCHE

Hatred is the coward's revenge for being intimidated.
GEORGE BERNARD SHAW

Men must learn to be kind and just to those whom they very properly hate. GEORGE BERNARD SHAW

Hate is a dead thing. Who of us would be a tomb? KAHLIL GIBRAN

Passionate hatred can give meaning and purpose to an empty life.
ERIC HOFFER

To wrong those we hate is to add fuel to our hatred. Conversely, to treat an enemy with magnanimity is to blunt our hatred for him.
ERIC HOFFER

Those of little faith are of little hatred. ERIC HOFFER

See also **Antipathy, Enmity, Love and Hate.**

HEAD

Some men's heads are as easily blown away as their hats.
LORD HALIFAX

See also **Head and Heart.**

HEAD AND HEART

The head does not know what the heart is after. VAUVENARGUES

See also **Head, Heart, Mind and Heart.**

HEAL

There is as much healing power in a Beethoven sonata or a painting by

Constable as in excerpts from the Bible.   GEORGE BERNARD SHAW

See also **Medicine.**

HEALTH

The feeling of health can only be gained by sickness.

G. C. LICHTENBERG

With me health means keeping up my accustomed way of living without discomfort. I find that sickness upsets my balance in one direction; if I take the advice of the doctors they will upset it in the other.

MONTAIGNE

A man's own observation, what he finds good of, and what he finds hurt of, is the best physic to preserve health.   FRANCIS BACON

There is no curing a sick man who believes himself in health.

FRÉDÉRIC AMIEL

See also **Disease, Medicine, Sick, Turkish Bath.**

HEART

Men may tire themselves in a labyrinth of search, and talk of God; but if we would know Him indeed, it must be from the impressions we receive of Him; and the softer our hearts are, the deeper and livelier those will be upon us.

WILLIAM PENN

Great ideas come from the heart.

VAUVENARGUES

The worst of all misalliances is that of the heart.   NICOLAS CHAMFORT

Everybody's heart is open, you know, when they have recently escaped from severe pain, or are recovering the blessing of health.

JANE AUSTEN

It is a misfortune to have to manoeuvre one's heart as a general has to manoeuvre his army.

ALEXANDER SMITH

Many a man does not find his heart until he has lost his head.

FRIEDRICH NIETZSCHE

It is wisdom to believe the heart.

GEORGE SANTAYANA

See also **Emotion, Feel, Head and Heart, Mind and Heart.**

HEAVEN

There are souls who aspire to build their nest in heaven.

THOMAS À KEMPIS

It is not so difficult to live the life which leads to heaven as is believed.

EMANUEL SWEDENBORG

Heaven is for those who think of it.

JOSEPH JOUBERT

There are people who, if they ever reach heaven, will commence at once looking for their own set.

JOSH BILLINGS

A German's idea of heaven is painted blue and has cast-iron dogs on the lawn.

FINLEY PETER DUNNE

As soon as Herr and Frau Mueller get to heaven, they'll ask for picture postcards.

CHRISTIAN MORGENSTERN

See also **Heaven and Hell.**

HEAVEN AND HELL

Many might go to heaven with half the labour they go to hell.

BEN JONSON

Heaven for climate, hell for society.

MARK TWAIN

Asked what he thought about the existence of heaven or hell, MARK TWAIN replied: 'I don't want to express an opinion. You see, I have friends in both places.'

Men have feverishly conceived a heaven only to find it insipid, and a hell to find it ridiculous.
GEORGE SANTAYANA

See also **Heaven, Hell.**

HELL
The Lord casts no one down to hell, but the spirit casts himself thither.   EMANUEL SWEDENBORG

Fathers and teachers, I ponder 'What is hell?' I maintain that it is the suffering of being unable to love.   FEODOR DOSTOEVSKI

We are each our own devil, and we make this world our hell.
OSCAR WILDE

If you get gloomy, just take an hour off and sit and think how much better this world is than hell. Of course, it won't cheer you up much if you expect to go there.
DON MARQUIS

Every man is his own hell.
H. L. MENCKEN

See also **Heaven and Hell.**

HELP
It is not so much our friends' help that helps us as the confidence of their help.   EPICURUS

He who sees a need and waits to be asked for help is as unkind as if he had refused it.
DANTE (*Purgatorio*, XVII, 59)

HELPLESS
No one can feel as helpless as the owner of a sick goldfish.
KIN HUBBARD

HENRY VIII
Henry VIII had so many wives because his dynastic sense was very strong whenever he saw a maid of honour.   WILL CUPPY

HEREDITY
Heredity is nothing but stored environment.   LUTHER BURBANK

HERETIC
That is the whole trouble with being a heretic. One usually must think out everything for oneself.
AUBREY MENEN

See also **Orthodox.**

HERO
Calculation never made a hero.
JOHN HENRY NEWMAN

Every hero becomes a bore at last.
RALPH WALDO EMERSON

A hero is no braver than an ordinary man, but he is brave five minutes longer.
RALPH WALDO EMERSON

We cannot have heroes to dine with us. There are none. And were these heroes to be had, we should not like them.   ANTHONY TROLLOPE

As Chas. Lamb says, there is nothing so nice as doing good by stealth and being found out by accident, so I now say it is even nicer to make heroic decisions and to be prevented by 'circumstances beyond your control' from even trying to execute them.
WILLIAM JAMES

See also **Brave, Courage, Great Men.**

HESITATE
Leave undone whatever you hesitate to do.   YOSHIDA KENKO

He who hesitates is sometimes saved. JAMES THURBER

See also **Doubt.**

HIGH

Many have lost their devotion by attempting to pry into matters too high for them. THOMAS À KEMPIS

The mind reaches great heights only by spurts. VAUVENARGUES

The length of things is vanity, only their height is joy. GEORGE SANTAYANA

A cathedral, a wave in a storm, a dancer's leap never turn out to be as high as we had hoped. MARCEL PROUST

HIGHBROW

A highbrow is a person educated beyond his intelligence. BRANDER MATTHEWS

The giraffe may surely be regarded as an example of uplift, and is even, in a manner of speaking, a highbrow. G. K. CHESTERTON

The lowbrow is a person who often believes that a bad book is good; the highbrow is a person who as often believes that a good book is bad. ROBERT LYND

A highbrow is the kind of person who looks at a sausage and thinks of Picasso. A. P. HERBERT

HISTORIAN

The historian looks backward. In the end he also believes backward. FRIEDRICH NIETZSCHE

Historian: An unsuccessful novelist. H. L. MENCKEN

See also **History Writing.**

HISTORY (DEFINITIONS)

History is only a confused heap of facts. LORD CHESTERFIELD

All history is little else than a long succession of useless cruelties. VOLTAIRE

History supplies little beyond a list of those who have accommodated themselves with the property of others. VOLTAIRE

History is little more than the register of the crimes, follies, and misfortunes of mankind. EDWARD GIBBON

History is on every occasion the record of that which one age finds worthy of note in another. JAKOB BURCKHARDT

History is nothing but a collection of fables and useless trifles, cluttered up with a mass of unnecessary figures and proper names. LEO TOLSTOY

History is from day to day; and it is not events, it is sociology; it is the progress of thought. ALFRED NORTH WHITEHEAD

History is made out of the failures and heroism of each insignificant moment. FRANZ KAFKA

Generalized history is a branch of speculation, connected (often rather arbitrarily and uneasily) with certain facts about the past. ALDOUS HUXLEY

See also **Historian, History, History Writing.**

HISTORY

Not to know what has been transacted in former times is to continue always a child. CICERO

We must consider how very little history there is; I mean real authentic history. That certain kings reigned, and certain battles were fought, we can depend upon as true; but all the colouring, all the philosophy of history, is conjecture.   SAMUEL JOHNSON

When we look back upon our forefathers, we seem to look back upon the people of another nation, almost upon creatures of another species.   WILLIAM COWPER

You cannot understand history without having lived through history yourself.   GOETHE

The best thing we get from history is the enthusiasm it rouses.
          GOETHE

In analyzing history do not be too profound, for often the causes are quite superficial.
          RALPH WALDO EMERSON

There is properly no history, only biography.
          RALPH WALDO EMERSON

The first lesson of history is the good of evil.
          RALPH WALDO EMERSON

Our ignorance of history makes us libel our own times. People have always been like this.
          GUSTAVE FLAUBERT

History would be an excellent thing if only it were true. LEO TOLSTOY

I'd like to have been around in the times the historical novelists write about—but I wouldn't like to be in the life insurance business.
          FINLEY PETER DUNNE

Studying history warns against making it. HENRY S. HASKINS

In history, what we consider causes are really consequences—consequences of causes that lie beyond history. The true course of history does not consist of events.
          EGON FRIEDELL

See also **Ancient, Athens, Attila, Civilization, Cleopatra, Dark Ages, Event, Generation, Gibbon, Happen, Henry VIII, Historian, History (Definitions), History Writing, Louis XIV, Marie Antoinette, Middle Ages, Napoleon, Nero, Period, Prehistoric, Pyramids, Revolution, Trojan War, War, Waterloo.**

HISTORY WRITING

Writing history is a way of getting rid of the past.   GOETHE

The secret of historical composition is to know what to neglect.
          LORD BRYCE

When a history book contains no lies it is always tedious.
          ANATOLE FRANCE

History is always written wrong, and so always needs to be rewritten.   GEORGE SANTAYANA

The one duty we owe to history is to rewrite it.   OSCAR WILDE

Anybody can make history; only a great man can write it.
          OSCAR WILDE

We teach history only when it can be made into an entertaining anecdote, a procedure which is about as sound as leaving the teaching of sexual hygiene to a commercial traveller.   AUBREY MENEN

See also **Historian, History (Definitions), History.**

HOLIDAY

I have a great confidence in the revelations which holidays bring forth.　BENJAMIN DISRAELI

See also **Leisure.**

HOLY

Even the merest gesture is holy if it is filled with faith.　FRANZ KAFKA

See also **Divine.**

HOLY SPIRIT

Many are deceived in the end, who at first seemed to be led by the Holy Spirit.　THOMAS À KEMPIS

HOME

Home is not where you live but where they understand you.
CHRISTIAN MORGENSTERN

To the moderately poor the home is the only place of liberty.
G. K. CHESTERTON

Home was quite a place when people stayed there.　E. B. WHITE

See also **House.**

HOMER

A man who has not read Homer is like a man who has not seen the ocean. There is a great object of which he has no idea.
WALTER BAGEHOT

HONEST

In this age, when it is said of a man, he knows *how to live*, it may be implied he is not very honest.
LORD HALIFAX

I suppose there is not a man in the world who, when he becomes a knave for the sake of $1,000, would not rather have remained an honest man for half the money.
G. C. LICHTENBERG

I have not observed men's honesty to increase with their riches.
THOMAS JEFFERSON

Honesty is the best policy, but he who is governed by that maxim is not an honest man.
ARCHBISHOP WHATELY

Honesty can be useful when it is skillfully employed or when people don't believe in it because it is so rare.　GIACOMO LEOPARDI

Honesty pays, but it don't seem to pay enough to suit a lot of people.
KIN HUBBARD

See also **Dishonest.**

HONOUR

A man of honour knows no false pride.　JEAN DE LA BRUYÈRE

HOPE

Everything that is done in the world is done by hope.　MARTIN LUTHER

Notwithstanding the sight of all our miseries, which press upon us and take us by the throat, we have an instinct which we cannot repress, and which lifts us up.　PASCAL

Men should do with their hopes as they do with tame fowl, cut their wings that they may not fly over the wall.　LORD HALIFAX

Hope is generally a wrong guide, though it is very good company by the way.　LORD HALIFAX

The natural flights of the human mind are not from pleasure to pleasure, but from hope to hope.
SAMUEL JOHNSON

Hope is itself a species of happiness, and, perhaps, the chief happiness which this world affords.
SAMUEL JOHNSON

I never knew a man who lived on hope but what spent his old age at somebody else's expense.
JOSH BILLINGS

Every man knows better than he hopes. E. W. HOWE

See also **Despair, Optimism.**

HOST

To mankind in general Macbeth and Lady Macbeth stand out as the supreme type of all that a host and hostess should not be.
MAX BEERBOHM
See also **Guest.**

HOT WATER

I believe in getting into hot water. I think it keeps you clean.
G. K. CHESTERTON

See also **Trouble.**

HOUSE

A fool knows more in his own house than a wise body in another man's. CERVANTES

As every normal man desires a woman, and children born of a woman, every normal man desires a house of his own to put them into.
G. K. CHESTERTON

See also **Dwelling, Home.**

HUMAN

I can stand any kind of society. All I care to know is that a man is a human being—that is enough for me; he can't be any worse.
MARK TWAIN

A person who is going to commit an inhuman act invariably excuses himself by saying. 'I'm only human, after all.' SYDNEY HARRIS

HUMAN NATURE

There is in human nature generally more of the fool than of the wise.
FRANCIS BACON

There is in human nature a general inclination to make people stare; and every wise man has himself to cure of it, and does cure himself.
SAMUEL JOHNSON

Man's chief merit consists in resisting the impulses of his nature.
SAMUEL JOHNSON

The more one analyzes people, the more all reasons for analysis disappear. Sooner or later one comes to that dreadful universal thing called human nature.
OSCAR WILDE
See also **Man, Nature, People.**

HUMAN RACE

It is not by sitting still at a grand distance and calling the human race *larvae*, that men are to be helped.
RALPH WALDO EMERSON

Etiquette requires us to admire the human race. MARK TWAIN

Leonardo da Vinci ruled his notebooks in columns headed fox, wolf, bear, and monkey and made notes of human faces by ticking them off in these columns.
GEORGE BERNARD SHAW

Such is the human race. Often it does seem such a pity that Noah and his party didn't miss the boat.
MARK TWAIN
See also **Man, People.**

HUMANITY

Those thinkers who cannot believe in any gods often assert that the love of humanity would be in itself

sufficient for them; and so, perhaps, it would, if they had it.
G. K. CHESTERTON

HUMILITY

Do not consider yourself to have made any spiritual progress, unless you account yourself the least of all men. THOMAS À KEMPIS

Humility is a virtue all men preach, none practise, and yet everybody is content to hear. The master thinks it good doctrine for his servants, the laity for the clergy, and the clergy for the laity. JOHN SELDEN

Many people want to be devout, but no one wants to be humble.
LA ROCHEFOUCAULD

There is small chance of truth at the goal where there is not a child-like humility at the starting post.
SAMUEL TAYLOR COLERIDGE

The landscape painter must walk in the fields with a humble mind.
JOHN CONSTABLE

Acquire the art of detachment, the virtue of method, and the quality of thoroughness, but above all the grace of humility.
SIR WILLIAM OSLER

Humility is not renunciation of pride but the substitution of one pride for another. ERIC HOFFER

It is always the secure who are humble. G. K. CHESTERTON

See also **Meek.**

HUMOUR

A sense of humour keen enough to show a man his own absurdities as well as those of other people will keep a man from the commission of all sins, or nearly all, save those that are worth committing.
SAMUEL BUTLER

The secret source of humour is not joy but sorrow; there is no humour in heaven. MARK TWAIN

Men will confess to treason, murder, arson, false teeth, or a wig. How many of them will own up to a lack of humour?
FRANK MOORE COLBY

The total absence of humour from the Bible is one of the most singular things in all literature.
ALFRED NORTH WHITEHEAD

The only thing worth having in an earthly existence is a sense of humour. LINCOLN STEFFENS

Humour is the contemplation of the finite from the point of view of the infinite. CHRISTIAN MORGENSTERN

A sense of humour is a sense of proportion. KAHLIL GIBRAN

This I conceive to be the chemical function of humour: to change the character of our thought.
LIN YUTANG

See also **Comic, Gay, Irony, Laugh, Merry, Wit, Wit and Humour.**

HUNGER

Hunger is not only the best cook, but also the best physician.
PETER ALTENBERG

Hunger is the handmaid of genius.
MARK TWAIN

See also **Fasting.**

HURRY

A constant smirk upon the face, and a whiffling activity of the body, are strong indications of futility. Whoever is in a hurry, shows that the thing he is about is too big for him.
LORD CHESTERFIELD

A man of sense may be in haste, but can never be in a hurry.
LORD CHESTERFIELD

God travels at a snail's pace. Those who want to do good are not selfish, they are not in a hurry, they know that to impregnate people with good requires a long time.
GANDHI

HUSBAND

A wife is to thank God her husband has faults; a husband without faults is a dangerous observer.
LORD HALIFAX

Mrs. Norris consoled herself for the loss of her husband by considering that she could do very well without him.
JANE AUSTEN

The majority of husbands remind me of an orang-outang trying to play the violin.
HONORÉ DE BALZAC

A woman might as well propose: her husband will claim she did.
E. W. HOWE

A married man forms married habits and becomes dependent on marriage just as a sailor becomes dependent on the sea.
GEORGE BERNARD SHAW

Among a husband's other uses, most wives find him a handy thing with which to impress other women.
CHARLES W. MORTON

See also **Marriage, Wife.**

HYBRID

Hybrids are what makes the world go forward. LUTHER BURBANK

HYPOCRITE

No man is a hypocrite in his pleasures. SAMUEL JOHNSON

The greatest hypocrites are the greatest dupes.
WILLIAM HAZLITT

See also **Insincere, Pretense.**

I

I am my world.
LUDWIG WITTGENSTEIN

He who is afraid to use an 'I' in his writing will never make a good writer. LIN YUTANG

See also **Ego, Self.**

IDEA

Ideas often flash across our minds more complete than we could make them after much labour.
LA ROCHEFOUCAULD

An emotion ceases to be a passion as soon as we form a clear and distinct idea of it. SPINOZA

Man can have only a certain number of teeth, hair, and ideas. There comes a time when he necessarily loses his teeth, his hair, and his ideas. VOLTAIRE

That fellow seems to me to possess but one idea, and that is a wrong one. SAMUEL JOHNSON

Our ideas are for the most part like bad sixpences, and we spend our lives in trying to pass them on one another. SAMUEL BUTLER

The wise only possess ideas; the greater part of mankind are possessed by them.
SAMUEL TAYLOR COLERIDGE

He is stupid, like all heartless people. For ideas do not come from the head but from the heart.
HEINRICH HEINE

Every idea is of itself endowed with an immortal life, just as a person is.
CHARLES BAUDELAIRE

Everybody lives and acts partly according to his own, partly according to other people's ideas.
LEO TOLSTOY

Daring ideas are like chessmen moved forward; they may be beaten, but they may start a winning game.
GOETHE

The thing that gives people courage is ideas.   GEORGES CLÉMENCEAU

When we are tired, we are attacked by ideas we conquered long ago.
FRIEDRICH NIETZSCHE

It is by acts and not by ideas that people live.   ANATOLE FRANCE

An idea that is not dangerous is unworthy of being called an idea at all.   OSCAR WILDE

The kind of man who wants the government to adopt and enforce his ideas is always the kind of man whose ideas are idiotic.
H. L. MENCKEN

The average length of time it takes, I think, for any great discovery in the realm of ideas to pass into general currency or to receive any practical effectuation is a thousand years.
ALFRED NORTH WHITEHEAD

No idea is so outlandish that it should not be considered with a searching but at the same time with a steady eye.
WINSTON S. CHURCHILL

Ideas won't keep. Something must be done about them.
ALFRED NORTH WHITEHEAD

Ideas interest me more than men. They live; they fight; they perish like men. Of course it may be said that our only knowledge of them is through men, just as our only knowledge of the wind is through the reeds that it bends; but all the same the wind is of more importance than the reeds.   ANDRÉ GIDE

It (Rousseau's *Émile*) is the greatest book on the education of children ever written. I do not say that all his ideas can be put into practice; but that is because he has too many of them, not because they are bad.
AUBREY MENEN

See also **Ingenuity, New Idea, Notion, Opinion, Thought.**

IDEAL

An ideal is often but a flaming vision of reality.   JOSEPH CONRAD

Those who would sacrifice a generation to realize an ideal are the enemies of mankind.
ERIC HOFFER

IDEALIST

When they come downstairs from their ivory towers, idealists are apt to walk straight into the gutter.
LOGAN PEARSALL SMITH

See also **Ideal.**

IDIOT

Idiots and lunatics see only their own wit.   LA ROCHEFOUCAULD

See also **Fool, Imbecile.**

IDLE

I have been an idle fellow all my life.   SAMUEL JOHNSON

As peace is the end of war, so to be idle it the ultimate purpose of the busy.   SAMUEL JOHNSON

If it be difficult to persuade the idle to be busy, it is likewise not easy to convince the busy that it is better to be idle.   SAMUEL JOHNSON

Boswell: 'We grow weary when idle.' Johnson: 'That is, sir, because, others being busy, we want company; but if we were all idle, there would be no growing weary; we should all entertain one another.'   BOSWELL (*Life of Johnson*)

I love idleness. I love to busy myself about trifles, to begin a hundred things and not finish one of them, to come and go as my fancy bids me, to change my plan every moment, to follow a fly in all its circlings, to try and uproot a rock to see what is underneath, eagerly to begin on a ten-years' task and to give it up after ten minutes: in short, to fritter away the whole day inconsequentially and incoherently, and to follow nothing but the whim of the moment.   ROUSSEAU

Too much idleness, I have observed, fills up a man's time much more completely, and leaves him less his own master, than any sort of employment whatsoever.   EDMUND BURKE

There is one piece of advice, in a life of study, which I think no one will object to; and that is, every now and then to be completely idle—to do nothing at all.   SYDNEY SMITH

It is not that I am idle in my nature neither; but propose to me to do one thing, and it is inconceivable the desire I have to do something else.   SIR WALTER SCOTT

What I like best is to lie whole mornings on a sunny bank on Salisbury Plain, without any object before me, neither knowing nor caring how time passes, and thus 'with light-winged toys of feathered idleness' to melt down hours to moments.   WILLIAM HAZLITT

Work is not always required of a man. There is such a thing as a sacred idleness, the cultivation of which is now fearfully neglected.   GEORGE MACDONALD

Few women and fewer men have enough character to be idle.   E. V. LUCAS

There is nothing worse than an idle hour, with no occupation offering.   H. L. MENCKEN

See also **Doing Nothing, Idler, Indolence, Lazy, Loafing.**

IDLER

Every man is, or hopes to be, an idler.   SAMUEL JOHNSON

IGNORANCE

There is simple ignorance, which is the source of lighter offenses, and double ignorance, which is accompanied by a conceit of wisdom.   PLATO

O what a soft and easy and wholesome pillow is ignorance and freedom from care to rest a well-screwed-on headpiece!   MONTAIGNE

Many of the delusions of the world, or to speak more boldly, all the delusions in the world, are begotten of our being taught to be afraid of professing our ignorance, and thinking ourselves bound to accept everything we cannot refute.   MONTAIGNE

Whoever will be cured of ignorance, let him confess it.   MONTAIGNE

I was born and bred in the country and among field-labourers; I have had the business of husbandry in my own hands ever since my predecessors in the possession of the property I enjoy left me to succeed in it. And yet I can add up neither with counters nor with a pen. Most of our coins are unknown to me. I cannot differentiate between one grain and another, either in the ground or in the barn, unless the difference be too glaring; and can scarcely distinguish between the cabbages and lettuces in my garden. I do not even know the names of the chief implements of husbandry, nor the rude principles of agriculture, which the boys know. I know still less of the mechanical arts, of trade and merchandise, of the nature and diversity of fruits, wines and foodstuffs, of training a hawk or physicking a horse or a hound. And, to complete my disgrace, only a month ago I was caught in ignorance of the fact that leaven is used in making bread, and of the meaning of allowing wine to ferment.   MONTAIGNE

There is a happy pitch of ignorance that a man of sense might pray for.
    LORD HALIFAX

(To a lady who asked him how he came to define *pastern* as the *knee* of a horse in his dictionary:) Ignorance, madam, pure ignorance.
    SAMUEL JOHNSON

Keep this truth ever before you—ignorance never did anyone any harm, error alone is fatal, and we do not lose our way through ignorance but through self-confidence.
    ROUSSEAU

Ignorance is the mother of devotion.   JEREMY TAYLOR

Nothing is more terrible than ignorance in action.   GOETHE

I am always made uneasy when the conversation turns in my presence upon popular ignorance and the duty of adapting our writings to the mind of the people. 'Tis all pedantry and ignorance. The people know as much and reason as well as we do.   RALPH WALDO EMERSON

Ignorance is the best of law reformers.
    OLIVER WENDELL HOLMES, JR.

The fine role is sometimes to be the dupe. Life teaches that one is never happy save at the price of some ignorance.   ANATOLE FRANCE

Ignorance is the condition necessary, I do not say for happiness, but for existence itself. If we knew all, we could not endure life for an hour.   ANATOLE FRANCE

When a man considers all that he doesn't know, the immeasurable abundance of things of which he has no or only the vaguest idea, he gets downcast. And yet, he also feels free and great. In the vastness of his ignorance, he stands trembling with the feeling of infinity, as under the starry sky.   ALFRED POLGAR

All our loves, all our hero-worships, all our dreams of coming peace, all our visions of fortune, are the fruits of ignorance.
    HILAIRE BELLOC

According to a charming law of nature which is evident even in the most sophisticated societies, we live in complete ignorance of whatever we love.   MARCEL PROUST

Ignorance and error are necessary to life, like bread and water.
ANATOLE FRANCE

Ignorance is like a delicate exotic fruit; touch it and the bloom is gone. OSCAR WILDE

Ignorance is the first requisite of the historian—ignorance which simplifies and clarifies, which selects and omits, with a placid perfection unattainable by the highest art.
LYTTON STRACHEY

Most ignorance is vincible ignorance. We don't know because we don't want to know.
ALDOUS HUXLEY

See also **Cannot, Greenhorn, Ignorant, Knowledge and Ignorance, Not Knowing, Wisdom and Ignorance.**

IGNORANT

Mankind have a great aversion to intellectual labour; but even supposing knowledge to be easily attainable, more people would be content to be ignorant than would take even a little trouble to acquire it. SAMUEL JOHNSON

Nowadays a parlourmaid as ignorant as Queen Victoria was when she came to the throne would be classed as mentally defective.
GEORGE BERNARD SHAW

The true art of self-training is the art of making yourself ignorant: the finest and most useful of the arts but one that is rarely and poorly practised. LUDWIG BÖRNE

Ignoramus: A person unacquainted with certain kinds of knowledge familiar to yourself, and having certain other kinds that you know nothing about. AMBROSE BIERCE

Everybody is ignorant, only on different subjects. WILL ROGERS

Be honest and humble; learn how to be ignorant, then you will never deceive yourself or others. ROUSSEAU

When a situation is so unprecedented that no amount of knowledge or experience is adequate to master it, then the ignorant and inexperienced are more fit to deal with it than the learned and experienced.
ERIC HOFFER

One of the best and fastest ways of acquiring knowledge is to insist on remaining ignorant about things that aren't worth knowing.
SYDNEY HARRIS

See also **Ignorance.**

ILLUSION

There is no more dangerous illusion than the fancies by which people try to avoid illusion.
FRANÇOIS DE FÉNELON

Don't part with your illusions. When they are gone you may still exist but you have ceased to live.
MARK TWAIN

Life is full of its disappointments, and I suppose the art of being happy is to disguise them as illusions. SAKI

Nothing is more sad than the death of an illusion. ARTHUR KOESTLER

ILLUSTRATION

To illustrate a principle you must exaggerate much and you must omit much. WALTER BAGEHOT

IMAGINATION

If the greatest philosopher in the world found himself upon a plank wider than actually necessary, but hanging over a precipice, his imagination would prevail, though his reason convinced him of his safety.   PASCAL

Were it not for imagination, sir, a man would be as happy in the arms of a chambermaid as of a duchess.
SAMUEL JOHNSON

There is nothing more horrible than imagination without taste.
GOETHE

To make a thing tangible is the next thing to making it clear; and to make it imaginable the next thing to making it tangible. So you render a great service to the truth when you present it to the imagination.
JOSEPH JOUBERT

He who has imagination without learning, has wings and no feet.
JOSEPH JOUBERT

Imagination is the eye of the soul.
JOSEPH JOUBERT

What is now proved was once only imagined.   WILLIAM BLAKE

Keep the imagination sane—that is one of the truest conditions of communion with heaven.
NATHANIEL HAWTHORNE

Imagination is too often accompanied by somewhat irregular logic.
BENJAMIN DISRAELI

The ingenious are always fanciful, and the *truly* imaginative never otherwise than analytic.
EDGAR ALLAN POE

He (Don Quixote) rides forth, his head encircled by a halo—the patron saint of all lives spoiled or saved by the irresistible grace of imagination. But he was not a good citizen.   JOSEPH CONRAD

Often it is just lack of imagination that keeps a man from suffering very much.   MARCEL PROUST

Let us leave pretty women to men without imagination.
MARCEL PROUST

IMBECILE

Nothing betrays imbecility so much as the being insensible of it.
THOMAS JEFFERSON

See also **Fool, Idiot.**

IMITATION

The most complete revenge is not to imitate the aggressor.
MARCUS AURELIUS

Almost all absurdity of conduct arises from the imitation of those whom we cannot resemble.
SAMUEL JOHNSON

Life imitates art far more than art imitates life.   OSCAR WILDE

IMMEDIATE

Immediacy is happiness, because in immediacy there is no contradiction; the immediate is essentially happy, and the philosophy of immediacy is happiness.
SÖREN KIERKEGAARD

IMMORAL

Starvation, overwork, and dirt are as immoral as prostitution and as unromantic.
GEORGE BERNARD SHAW

We are told by moralists with the plainest faces that immorality will spoil our looks.
LOGAN PEARSALL SMITH

See also **Morality.**

IMMORTALITY

Preoccupation with immortality is for the upper classes, particularly ladies with nothing to do. An able man, who has a regular job and must toil and produce day by day, leaves the future world to itself, and is active and useful in this one.

GOETHE

When THOREAU was questioned as to his beliefs in a life beyond the grave, he answered impatiently: 'Oh, one world at a time.'

The average man, who does not know what to do with this life, wants another one which shall last forever. ANATOLE FRANCE

The late F. W. H. Myers used to tell how he asked a man at a dinner table what he thought would happen to him when he died. The man tried to ignore the question, but, on being pressed, replied: 'Oh well, I suppose I shall inherit eternal bliss, but I wish you wouldn't talk about such unpleasant subjects.'

BERTRAND RUSSELL

See also **Other World.**

IMPARTIAL

I can promise to be frank, but I can't promise to be impartial.

GOETHE

I cannot undertake to be impartial as between the fire brigade and the fire. WINSTON S. CHURCHILL

IMPERISHABLE

Everything that seems to us imperishable tends toward its destruction. MARCEL PROUST

IMPERSONAL

The world's deepest misfortune is the unhappy objectivity (in the sense of the absence of personality)

characteristic of all speech and teaching, and that one great mechanical discovery after the other has made it possible to expound doctrines impersonally in constantly increasing measure.

SÖREN KIERKEGAARD

IMPIETY

Impiety: Your irreverence toward my deity. AMBROSE BIERCE

IMPORTANT

Every individual has a place to fill in the world, and is important, in some respect, whether he chooses to be so or not.

NATHANIEL HAWTHORNE

The momentous topics of human life are always of secondary importance to the business in hand, just as carpenters discuss politics between the strokes of the hammer while they are shingling a roof.

HENRY DAVID THOREAU

'Unimportant, of course, I meant,' the King hastily said, and went on to himself in an undertone, 'important—unimportant—important—' as if he were trying which words sounded best. LEWIS CARROLL

Nothing that actually occurs is of the smallest importance.

OSCAR WILDE

One of the most serious thoughts that life provokes is the reflection that we can never tell, at the time, whether a word, a look, a touch, an occurrence of any kind, is trivial or important. E. V. LUCAS

It is not merely the trivial which clutters our lives but the important as well.

ANNE MORROW LINDBERGH

See also **Irrelevant, Self-Important, Trifle.**

IMPROBABLE

Beware of telling an improbable truth.   DR. THOMAS FULLER

One should always be a little improbable.   OSCAR WILDE

Man can believe the impossible, but can never believe the improbable.
OSCAR WILDE

Literature must in some sense be believable, whereas experiences of human beings in fact develop beyond all powers of conjecture. Thus social literature is conventional, while history exceeds all limitations of common sense.
ALFRED NORTH WHITEHEAD

It is not the impossible that I object to in detective novels; it is the improbable that destroys all suspension of disbelief.
HAROLD NICOLSON

IMPROVEMENT

By a man without passions I mean one who does not permit likes and dislikes to disturb his inner economy, but rather falls in with what happens and does not try to improve upon life.   CHUANG-TSE

'So, sir, you laugh at schemes of political improvement?' 'Why, sir, most schemes of political improvement are very laughable things.'
BOSWELL (*Life of Johnson*)

Ask yourself always: How can this be done better?
G. C. LICHTENBERG

Improvement makes straight roads; but the crooked roads without improvement are roads of genius.
WILLIAM BLAKE

Possibly we might even improve the world a little, if we got up early in the morning, and took off our coats to the work.
CHARLES DICKENS

The improvements of ages have had but little influence on the essential laws of man's existence.
HENRY DAVID THOREAU

If you think that I am going to bother myself again before I die about social improvement or read any of those stinking upward and onwarders—you err. I mean to have some good out of being old.
OLIVER WENDELL HOLMES, JR.

Half a man's life is devoted to what he calls improvements, yet the original had some quality which is lost in the process.   E. B. WHITE

See also **Self-Improvement.**

INACCESSIBLE

There is in nature what is within reach and what is beyond reach. He who is unaware of the distinction may waste himself in lifelong toil trying to get at the inaccessible without ever getting close to truth. But he who knows it and is wise will stick to what is accessible; and in exploring this region in all directions and confirming his gains he will even push back the confines of the inaccessible.   GOETHE

INACCURACY

I do not mind lying, but I hate inaccuracy.   SAMUEL BUTLER

INATTENTION

When a neighbour is in your fruit garden, inattention is the truest politeness.   CHINESE PROVERB

See also **Attention, Overlook, Unnoticed.**

INCOME

Live within your income. Always have something saved at the end of the year. Let your imports be more than your exports, and you'll never go far wrong,   SAMUEL JOHNSON

It is better to have a permanent income than to be fascinating.

OSCAR WILDE

There are few sorrows, however poignant, in which a good income is of no avail. LOGAN PEARSALL SMITH

I'm living so far beyond my income that we may almost be said to be living apart. SAKI

There are several ways in which to apportion the family income, all of them unsatisfactory.

ROBERT BENCHLEY

See also **Money, Poor, Rich, Rich and Poor.**

INCOME TAX

To produce an income tax return that has any depth to it, any feeling, one must have Lived—and Suffered. FRANK SULLIVAN

See also **Income, Tax.**

INCOMPREHENSIBLE

The nearer we get to any natural object the more incomprehensible it becomes. A grain of sand is undoubtedly not what I take it to be.

G. C. LICHTENBERG

Man must cling to the belief that the imcomprehensible is comprehensible; otherwise he would give up research. GOETHE

To say that a work of art is good, but incomprehensible to the majority of men, is the same as saying of some kind of food that is it very good but that most people can't eat it. LEO TOLSTOY

See also **Intelligible, Understanding.**

INCONSISTENCY

I find nothing harder to believe than man's consistency and nothing easier than his inconsistency.

MONTAIGNE

The great point is to know one's own inconsistencies, and to keep those which are the most conducive to happiness. ROUSSEAU

It matters little what profession, whether of religion or irreligion, a man may make, provided only he follows it out with charitable inconsistency, and without insisting on it to the bitter end.

SAMUEL BUTLER

Inconsistency. Characters in a novel or a play who act all the way through exactly as one expects them to. . . . This consistency of theirs which is held up to our admiration, is on the contrary the very thing which makes us recognize that they are artificially composed.

ANDRÉ GIDE

See also **Consistency.**

INCONVENIENCE

We sometimes inconvenience people when it seems impossible.

LA ROCHEFOUCAULD

An adventure is only an inconvenience rightly considered. An inconvenience is only an adventure wrongly considered.

G. K. CHESTERTON

It is a good maxim to ask of no one more than he can give without inconvenience to himself.

W. SOMERSET MAUGHAM

INCORRUPTIBILITY

Most people who have been done a favour consider it an opportunity to show their incorruptibility rather than their gratitude. This is not only considerably cheaper morally, but it sometimes increases their pride so much that pretty soon they look down on their benefactor.

ARTHUR SCHNITZLER

Incorruptibility is the fetish of the half-civilized.   NORMAN DOUGLAS

INCREDULITY

Tepid incredulity acts as an emetic on secrets.   BALTASAR GRACIÁN

Incredulity is the wisdom of a fool.
JOSH BILLINGS

See also **Believing, Doubt.**

INDECISION

Indecision: The chief element of success; 'for whereas,' saith Sir Thomas Brewbold, 'there is but one way to do nothing and divers ways to do something, whereof, to a surety, only one is the right way, it followeth that he who from indecision standeth still hath not so many chances of going astray as he who pusheth forwards'—a most clear and satisfactory exposition of the matter.   AMBROSE BIERCE

See also **Hesitate.**

INDEPENDENT

Aim to be independent of any one vote, of any one fashion, of any one century.   BALTASAR GRACIÁN

See also **Free.**

INDIFFERENT

Almost all women, and many men too, particularly proud men, can be won over by indifference and contempt—even, if necessary, feigned indifference and contempt.
GIACOMO LEOPARDI

The worst sin towards our fellow creatures is not to hate them, but to be indifferent to them; that's the essence of inhumanity.
GEORGE BERNARD SHAW

Where moderation is a fault, indifference is a crime.
G. C. LICHTENBERG

A man's intelligence can be gauged mainly by his ability to make himself indifferent toward many things that could interest or even excite him if he gave in to them.   ALAIN

INDIGESTION

An indigestion is an excellent commonplace for two people that never met before.   WILLIAM HAZLITT

See also **Digestion, Dyspepsia.**

INDISCRETION

Nothing looks so like innocence as an indiscretion.   OSCAR WILDE

For lack of a topic of conversation we commit the meanest acts of tactlessness and indiscretion.
PETER ALTENBERG

It's almost got so you can't speak the truth without committing an indiscretion.   KIN HUBBARD

See also **Discretion.**

INDIVIDUAL

The individual is always mistaken.
RALPH WALDO EMERSON

Had I to carve an inscription on my tombstone I would ask for none other than 'The Individual'.
SÖREN KIERKEGAARD

INDIVIDUALITY

Learn to limit yourself, to content yourself with some definite thing, and some definite work; dare to be what you are, and learn to resign with a good grace all that you are not, and to believe in your own individuality.   FRÉDÉRIC AMIEL

No member of a crew is praised for the rugged individuality of his rowing.   RALPH WALDO EMERSON

Individualism is the death of individuality. It is so, if only because it is an 'ism.'

G. K. CHESTERTON

INDOLENCE

I wish that all the year were holiday. I am sure that indolence, indefeasible indolence is the true state of man, and business the invention of the Old Teaser, who persuaded Adam's Master to give him an apron and set him ahoeing.

CHARLES LAMB

See also **Idle, Lazy, Loafing.**

INDUSTRY

Industry without art is brutality.

JOHN RUSKIN

Industry is the root of all ugliness.

OSCAR WILDE

We might just as well have had the Industrial Age in the time of Archimedes; everything necessary was known; the only things lacking were tea and coffee. That fact so affected the habits of people that the Industrial Age had to wait centuries until people in Scotland watched their kettles boil and so invented the steam engine.

ALFRED NORTH WHITEHEAD

INEVITABLE

The higher a man's place in the social scale, the more connections he has with others, and the more power he has over them, the more conspicuous is the inevitability and predestination of every act he commits.

LEO TOLSTOY

I not only bow to the inevitable; I am fortified by it.

THORNTON WILDER

It is the mark of a good action that it appears inevitable in the retrospect. ROBERT LOUIS STEVENSON

See also **Necessity.**

INFANCY

One cannot love lumps of flesh, and little infants are nothing more.

SAMUEL JOHNSON

Infancy: The period of our lives when, according to Wordsworth, 'Heaven lies about us.' The world begins lying about us pretty soon afterward. AMBROSE BIERCE

See also **Babies, Childhood, Children.**

INFERIOR

By an inferior man I mean one who knows nothing that is not known to every adult, who can do nothing that could not be learned by anyone in a few weeks, and who meanly admires mean things.

H. L. MENCKEN

See also **Superiority.**

INFINITE

The eternal silence of these infinite spaces frightens me. PASCAL

If the doors of perception were cleansed, everything would appear to man as it is, infinite.

WILLIAM BLAKE

INFORMATION

We have more useless information than ignorance of what is useful.

VAUVENARGUES

The mind of a thoroughly well-informed man is a dreadful thing. It is like a bric-a-brac shop, all monsters and dust, with everything priced above its proper value.

OSCAR WILDE

A wise man will not go out of his way for information.
HENRY DAVID THOREAU

I once knew an old manufacturer who said: 'All information is false.' And he was right, for almost everything is exaggerated, distorted, or suppressed. ANDRÉ MAUROIS

One has information only to the extent to which one has tended to communicate one's experience.
HARRY STACK SULLIVAN

See also **Knowledge, Learning.**

INGENUITY

The idea that only a limited number of people can live in a country is a profound illusion. It all depends on their cooperative and inventive power. There is no limit to the ingenuity of man if it is properly and vigorously applied under conditions of peace and justice.
WINSTON S. CHURCHILL

See also **Invention.**

INHERIT

To inherit property is not to be born—it is to be still-born, rather.
HENRY DAVID THOREAU

INITIATE

The wise man never initiates any action. BHAGAVAD-GITA

INJUSTICE

Injustice is impiety.
MARCUS AURELIUS

See also **Justice.**

INK

For several days after my first book was published I carried it about in my pocket, and took surreptitious peeps at it to make sure the ink had not faded. JAMES M. BARRIE

INN

There is nothing which has yet been contrived by man, by which so much happiness is produced as by a good tavern or inn; a tavern chair is the throne of human felicity.
SAMUEL JOHNSON

Inns are the mirror and at the same time the flower of a people.
HILAIRE BELLOC

INNOCENCE

'Therefore,' I said rather carelessly, 'we would have to eat again the fruit of the tree of knowledge, so as to return to the state of innocence?' 'Quite so,' he replied; 'this is the last chapter of the history of the world.' HEINRICH VON KLEIST

The truly innocent are those who not only are guiltless themselves but who think others are.
JOSH BILLINGS

Innocence, most often, is a good fortune and not a virtue.
ANATOLE FRANCE

It would be so awkward in heaven, after all one had discovered, to have to put on a perfect innocence.
GEORGE SANTAYANA

INNOVATION

Nothing presses so hard upon a state as innovation; mere change gives scope to injustice and tyranny.
MONTAIGNE

When an innovation is very difficult to establish, it is unnecessary.
VAUVENARGUES

We must beware of needless innovations, especially when guided by logic. WINSTON S. CHURCHILL

See also **New, New Idea.**

INSECT

It makes all the difference whether you hear an insect in the bedroom or in the garden.   ROBERT LYND

INSIGHT

In a moment of insight you can *perceive* everything; but it takes years for exactitude to give it expression.
JOSEPH JOUBERT

INSINCERE

The most exhausting thing in life is being insincere.
ANNE MORROW LINDBERGH

See also **Affectation, Hypocrite, Pretense.**

INSOMNIA

(Of constitutional melancholy:) A man so afflicted must divert distressing thoughts, and not combat with them. To attempt to *think them down* is madness. He should have a lamp constantly burning in his bed chamber during the night, and if wakeful or disturbed, take a book and read, and compose himself to rest. To have the management of the mind is a great art, and it may be attained in a considerable degree by experience and habitual exercise.
SAMUEL JOHNSON

Bob Davis wrote that one night thirty years ago he was unable to sleep. Rising, he looked in the mirror and noticed that he needed a shave. He shaved leisurely, turned back to bed, and slept soundly. Since then he has not fought wakefulness but has accepted it. He reads, makes notes, bathes, or goes to the kitchen for a bite to eat.
WILLIAM FEATHER

See also **Sleep.**

INSPIRATION

Perpetual inspiration is as necessary to the life of goodness, holiness and happiness as perpetual respiration is necessary to animal life.
WILLIAM LAW

After investigating a problem in all directions, happy ideas come unexpectedly, without effort, like an inspiration. So far as I am concerned, they have never come to me when my mind was fatigued, or when I was at my working table. . . . They came particularly readily during the slow ascent of wooded hills on a sunny day.
H. L. VON HELMHOLTZ

Inspiration is never genuine if it is known as inspiration at the time. True inspiration always steals on a person, its importance not being fully recognized for some time.
SAMUEL BUTLER

The man who turns inspiration to his own account is embezzling his cargo.   HENRY S. HASKINS

Here is the secret of inspiration. Tell yourself that thousands and tens of thousands of people, not very intelligent and certainly no more intelligent than the rest of us, have mastered problems as difficult as those that now baffle you.
WILLIAM FEATHER

See also **Creative, Idea, Ingenuity.**

INSTITUTION

As a snow-drift is formed where there is a lull in the wind, so, one would say, where there is a lull of truth an institution springs up. But the truth blows right on over it, nevertheless, and at length blows it down.   HENRY DAVID THOREAU

The whole history of civilization is strewn with creeds and institutions which were invaluable at first, and deadly afterwards.

WALTER BAGEHOT

INTELLIGENCE

To perceive things in the germ is intelligence. LAO-TSE

Honest, unaffected distrust of the powers of man is the surest sign of intelligence. G. C. LICHTENBERG

There is a kinship, a kind of free-masonry, between all persons of intelligence, however antagonistic their moral outlook.

NORMAN DOUGLAS

If we could learn how to utilize all the intelligence and patent good-will children are born with, instead of ignoring much of it—why—*there might be enough to go around*!

DOROTHY CANFIELD FISHER

If an animal does something they call it instinct. If we do exactly the same thing for the same reason they call it intelligence. I guess what they mean is that we all make mistakes, but intelligence enables us to do it on purpose. WILL CUPPY

See also **Intelligent, Knowledge, Wisdom.**

INTELLIGENCE TESTS

This intelligence-testing business reminds me of the way they used to weigh hogs in Texas. They would get a long plank, put it over a cross-bar, and somehow tie the hog on one end of the plank. They'd search all around till they found a stone that would balance the weight of the hog and they'd put that on the other end of the plank. Then they'd guess the weight of the stone.

JOHN DEWEY

INTELLIGENT

An intelligent man never snubs anybody. VAUVENARGUES

Intelligent people are the best encyclopaedia. GOETHE

What is an intelligent man? A man who enters with ease and completeness into the spirit of things and the intention of persons, and who arrives at an end by the shortest route. FRÉDÉRIC AMIEL

Intelligent people are always on the unpopular side of anything.

KIN HUBBARD

See also **Clever, Wise.**

INTELLIGIBLE

Nowadays to be intelligible is to be found out. OSCAR WILDE

See also **Clear.**

INTENTION

Everything works for the best, even the worst intentions.

LORD MELBOURNE

It is always with the best intentions that the worst work is done.

OSCAR WILDE

Hell is paved with good intentions, not bad ones. All men mean well.

GEORGE BERNARD SHAW

INTEREST

What you make it to the interest of men to do, that they will do.

EDMUND BURKE

When a person takes you aside and asks you what rent you pay and whether your boots pinch, you know that he is interested in you.

GEORGE BERNARD SHAW

Human passions are quite as strongly agitated by small interests as by great ones. HONORÉ DE BALZAC

A man's interest consists of whatever he takes interest in. He is a good man or a bad, according as he prefers one class of his interests to another. JOHN STUART MILL

The thousand mysteries around us would not trouble but interest us, if only we had cheerful, healthy hearts. FRIEDRICH NIETZSCHE

The very first step towards success in any occupation is to become interested in it. SIR WILLIAM OSLER

Interest is immeasurably better and more important than beauty.
G. K. CHESTERTON

There are no uninteresting things, there are only uninterested people.
G. K. CHESTERTON

See also **Absorbed, Self-Interest.**

INTERFERE

Leave all things to take their natural course, and do not interfere.
LAO-TSE

Do not interfere when your opinion is not sought. THOMAS À KEMPIS

INTERRUPTION

Nobody kicks on being interrupted if it's by applause. KIN HUBBARD

Interruptions are the spice of life.
DON HEROLD

INTOLERABLE

When human relations last long enough, the intolerable becomes the indispensable. ALFRED POLGAR

INTOLERANCE

No human trait deserves less tolerance in everyday life, and gets less, than intolerance.
GIACOMO LEOPARDI

See also **Tolerance.**

INVENTION

Civil reformation seldom is carried on without violence and confusion, whilst inventions are a blessing and a benefit without injuring or afflicting any. FRANCIS BACON

'Necessity is the mother of invention' is a silly proverb. 'Necessity is the mother of futile dodges' is much nearer to the truth. The basis of the growth of modern invention is science, and science is almost wholly the outgrowth of pleasurable intellectual curiosity.
ALFRED NORTH WHITEHEAD

It has been said that necessity is the mother of invention. If true, it seems strange that the world contains so many people in desperate circumstances. I rather suspect that relaxation is the mother of invention. WILLIAM FEATHER

In anything at all, perfection is finally attained not when there is no longer anything to add, but when there is no longer anything to take away, when a body has been stripped down to its nakedness. It results from this that perfection of invention touches hands with absence of invention, as if that line which the human eye will follow with effortless delight were a line that had not been invented but simply discovered, had in the beginning been hidden by nature and in the end been found by the engineer.
ANTOINE DE SAINT-EXUPÉRY

I invent nothing; I rediscover.
RODIN

Inventor: A person who makes an ingenious arrangement of wheels, levers and springs, and believes it civilization. AMBROSE BIERCE

Nature has never invented a wheel.
SIR CHARLES SHERRINGTON

The greatest invention of the nineteenth century was the invention of the method of invention.

ALFRED NORTH WHITEHEAD

INVISIBLE

Invisible threads are the strongest ties. FRIEDRICH NIETZSCHE

See also **Seeing.**

IRONY

Irony is the last phase of disillusion.
ANATOLE FRANCE

Irony is the gaiety of reflection and the joy of wisdom.
ANATOLE FRANCE

The ironic philosopher reflects with a smile that Sir Walter Raleigh is more safely enshrined in the memory of mankind because he set his cloak for the Virgin Queen to walk upon than because he carried the English name to undiscovered countries.
W. SOMERSET MAUGHAM

A taste for irony has kept more hearts from breaking than a sense of humour—for it takes irony to appreciate the joke which is on oneself. JESSAMYN WEST

See also **Humour, Irony and Pity.**

IRONY AND PITY

The more I reflect upon human life, the more I believe that we should give it as witnesses and judges Irony and Pity. ANATOLE FRANCE

IRRATIONAL

Anything which is rational is always difficult for the lay mind. But the thing which is irrational anyone can understand.
G. K. CHESTERTON

See also **Reason.**

IRRELEVANT

Experience has shown, and a true philosophy will always show, that a vast, perhaps the larger, portion of the truth arises from the seemingly irrelevant. EDGAR ALLAN POE

See also **Important.**

IS SEE BEING.

ITALY

A man who has not been in Italy is always conscious of an inferiority, from his not having seen what it is expected a man should see.
SAMUEL JOHNSON

J

JAMES, HENRY

Mr. Henry James writes fiction as if it were a painful duty.
OSCAR WILDE

JEREMIAH

In private life he was very likely a person of the most playful humour, brimful of fun and merriment.
SAMUEL BUTLER

JEWS

Sublimity is Hebrew by birth.
SAMUEL TAYLOR COLERIDGE

When Jews are good, they are better than Christians, but when they are bad, they are worse.
HEINRICH HEINE

They are an ancient people, a famous people, an enduring people, and a people who in the end have generally attained their objects. I hope Parliament may endure forever, and sometimes I think it will; but I cannot help remembering that the Jews have outlived Assyrian kings, Egyptian Pharaohs, Roman Caesars, and Arabian Caliphs.
BENJAMIN DISRAELI

Jews differ from all the peoples of the earth in that their fatherland is history itself.

SALVADOR DE MADARIAGA

JOB

It is good to follow a workaday occupation as well as to study the Torah, for between the two one forgets to sin.   TALMUD

As soon as a man is detailed for a particular job—that is to say, a duty that he has to perform for somebody else's sake—he gets, whether he likes it or not, the beginnings of an ideal of conduct. He may loathe the job; but his reasoning mind makes him uncomfortable within himself if he neglects the job.

RUDYARD KIPLING

See also **Duty, Work.**

JOKE

A drunk sometimes cracks funnier jokes than the best comedians.

VAUVENARGUES

There are certain queer times and occasions in this strange mixed affair we call life when a man takes this whole universe for a vast practical joke, though the wit thereof he but dimly discerns, and more than suspects that the joke is at nobody's expense but his own.

HERMAN MELVILLE

Nothing reveals a man's character better than the kind of joke at which he takes offense.

G. C. LICHTENBERG

You could read Kant by yourself, if you wanted; but you must share a joke with someone else.

ROBERT LOUIS STEVENSON

It is only the dull who like practical jokes.   OSCAR WILDE

See also **Anecdote, Funny, Laugh, Pun, Story.**

JOURNEY

For a small reward a man will hurry away on a long journey, while for eternal life many will hardly take a single step.   THOMAS À KEMPIS

I was especially fascinated by the notion of hurried journeys. . . . A long journey, even with the most lofty purpose, may be a dull thing to read of if it is made at leisure; but a hundred yards may be a breathless business if only a few seconds are granted to complete it.

JOHN BUCHAN

See also **Travel.**

JOY

Weak is the joy which is never wearied.   WILLIAM BLAKE

Excess of joy is harder to bear than any amount of sorrow.

HONORÉ DE BALZAC

Our sadness is not sad, but our cheap joys.

HENRY DAVID THOREAU

All real works of art look as if they were done in joy.

ROBERT HENRI

Grief can take care of itself, but to get the full value of a joy you must have somebody to divide it with.

MARK TWAIN

To miss the joy is to miss all. In the actors lies the sense of any action. That is the explanation, that the excuse.   ROBERT LOUIS STEVENSON

The joy of life is to put out one's power in some natural and useful or harmless way. There is no other. And the real misery is not to do this.

OLIVER WENDELL HOLMES, JR.

See also **Enjoyment.**

JUST

I have found men more kind than I expected, and less just.

SAMUEL JOHNSON

Men are just only toward those they love.   JOSEPH JOUBERT

You have no tenderness, nothing but truth, and so you judge unjustly.   FEODOR DOSTOEVSKI

JUSTICE

The love of justice is simply in the majority of men the fear of suffering injustice.   LA ROCHEFOUCAULD

Justice and truth are of too fine a quality to be measured by our clumsy human instruments.

PASCAL

Justice is always violent to the party offending, for every man is innocent in his own eyes.

DANIEL DEFOE

Of Justice—as if Justice could be anything but the same ample law, expounded by natural judges and saviours,
    As if it might be this thing or that thing, according to decisions.

WALT WHITMAN

Liberty, equality—bad principles! The only true principle for humanity is justice, and justice toward the weak becomes necessarily protection or kindness.

FRÉDÉRIC AMIEL

Injustice is relatively easy to bear; what stings is justice.

H. L. MENCKEN

See also **Injustice, Mercy.**

JUSTIFIED

A man knows when he is justified, and not all the wits in the world can enlighten him on that point.

HENRY DAVID THOREAU

K

KINDNESS

Requite injury with kindness.

LAO-TSE

Someone said. "What do you say concerning the principle that injury should be returned with kindness?" The Master said, "With what, then, will you recompense kindness? Recompense injury with justice, and recompense kindness with kindness."

SAYINGS OF CONFUCIUS

Whoever gives a small coin to a poor man has six blessings bestowed upon him, but he who speaks a kind word to him obtains eleven blessings.   TALMUD

Kindness is in our power, but fondness is not.   SAMUEL JOHNSON

A part of kindness consists in loving people more than they deserve.   JOSEPH JOUBERT

Sympathy is a thing to be encouraged, because it supplies us with materials for wisdom. It is probably more instructive to entertain a sneaking kindness for any unpopular person than to give way to perfect raptures of moral indignation against his abstract vices.

ROBERT LOUIS STEVENSON

We cannot be just if we are not kind-hearted.   VAUVENARGUES

Truth generally is kindness, but where the two diverge and collide, kindness should override truth.

SAMUEL BUTLER

One can always be kind to people about whom one cares nothing.

OSCAR WILDE

The kindness of the American people is, so far as I know, something unique in the history of the world, and it is the justification of your existence.
ALFRED NORTH WHITEHEAD

Loving-kindness is the better part of goodness.
W. SOMERSET MAUGHAM

Be kind and considerate to others, depending somewhat upon who they are.
DON HEROLD

KING

To call a king 'prince' is pleasing, because it diminishes rank.
PASCAL

Everyone is born a king, and most people die in exile, like most kings.
OSCAR WILDE

Vulgarity in a king flatters the majority of the nation.
GEORGE BERNARD SHAW

See also **Ruler.**

KISS

When women kiss it always reminds one of prize-fighters shaking hands.
H. L. MENCKEN

KITCHEN

Such is life. It is no cleaner than a kitchen; it reeks of a kitchen; and if you mean to cook your dinner, you must expect to soil your hands; the real art is in getting them clean again, and therein lies the whole morality of our epoch.
HONORÉ DE BALZAC

Give me the provisions and whole apparatus of a kitchen, and I would starve.
MONTAIGNE

See also **Cooking.**

KITTEN

A kitten is so flexible that she is almost double; the hind parts are equivalent to another kitten with which the forepart plays. She does not discover that her tail belongs to her until you tread upon it.
HENRY DAVID THOREAU

See also **Cat.**

KNOW THYSELF

A humble knowledge of oneself is a surer road to God than a deep searching of the sciences.
THOMAS À KEMPIS

'Know thyself' is indeed a weighty admonition. But in this, as in any science, the difficulties are discovered only by those who set their hands to it. We must push against a door to find out whether it is bolted or not.
MONTAIGNE

We usually know quite well what we ought to do, but we don't know what we *would* do. It is a sign of presumption to imagine ourselves able to handle hot coal without burning ourselves.
ST. FRANCIS DE SALES

People tell me to be frank, but how can I be when I don't dare to know myself?
FINLEY PETER DUNNE

No man ever understands quite his own artful dodges to escape from the grim shadow of self-knowledge.
JOSEPH CONRAD

He that knows himself knows how to strengthen his weakness, and the wise man conquers everything, even the stars in their courses.
BALTASAR GRACIÁN

All ages have said and repeated that one should strive to know one's self. This is a strange demand which no one up to now has measured up to and, strictly considered, no one should. With all his study and effort, man is directed to what is outside, to the world about him, and he is kept busy coming to know this and to master it to the extent that his purposes require. GOETHE

How can you come to know yourself? Never by thinking; always by doing. Try to do your duty, and you'll know right away what you amount to. And what is your duty? Whatever the day calls for.
GOETHE

Even when I am reading my lectures I often think to myself, 'What a humbug you are,' and I wonder the people don't find it out.
WILLIAM MAKEPEACE THACKERAY

Only the shallow know themselves.
OSCAR WILDE

Know thyself. A Yale undergraduate left on his door a placard for the janitor on which was written, 'Call me at 7 o'clock; it is absolutely necessary that I get up at seven. Make no mistake. Keep knocking until I answer.' Under this he had written: 'Try again at ten.'
WILLIAM LYON PHELPS

It is thus with most of us: we are what other people say we are. We know ourselves chiefly by hearsay.
ERIC HOFFER

Know thyself: to what depths of vain, egocentric brooding has that dictum led! NORMAN DOUGLAS

See also **Knowing, Self.**

KNOWING

The fox knows many things, but the hedgehog knows one big thing.
ARCHILOCHUS

A man may know everything for others and nothing for himself.
BALTASAR GRACIÁN

A man that excels in any one thing has a kind of arbitrary power over all that hear him upon that subject, and no man's life is too short to know any one thing perfectly.
LORD HALIFAX

All knowledge is of itself of some value. There is nothing so minute or inconsiderable, that I would not rather know it than not. In the same manner, all power, of whatever sort, is of itself desirable. A man would not submit to learn to hem a ruffle, of his wife's, or his wife's maid; but if a mere wish could attain it, he would rather wish to be able to hem a ruffle.
SAMUEL JOHNSON

He who knows nothing is nearer the truth than he whose mind is filled with falsehoods and errors.
THOMAS JEFFERSON

Knowing is not enough; we must apply. Willing is not enough; we must do. GOETHE

Can a sparrow know how a stork feels? GOETHE

To know where a thing is we must have found it. GOETHE

We don't get to know anything but what we love. GOETHE

We do not really know anything at all until a long time after we have learned it. JOSEPH JOUBERT

He who has suffered you to impose on him, knows you.
WILLIAM BLAKE

Macaulay. No person ever knew so much that was so little to the purpose. RALPH WALDO EMERSON

It is better to know nothing than to know what ain't so. JOSH BILLINGS

We are often unable to tell people what they *need* to know, because they *want* to know something else.
GEORGE MACDONALD

It is madness not to try to know, but it is almost as much madness to try to do so. God will not have any human being know what will sell, nor when anyone is going to die, nor even whether or not it is going to rain. SAMUEL BUTLER

To know is to know the things belonging to one's peace.
SAMUEL BUTLER

There are only two kinds of people who are really fascinating—people who know absolutely everything and people who know absolutely nothing. OSCAR WILDE

No student knows his subject. The most he knows is where and how to find out the things he does not know. WOODROW WILSON

It's what a fellow thinks he knows that hurts him. KIN HUBBARD

Ask your neighbour only about things you know better. His advice might be valuable. KARL KRAUS

We know lots of things we used to didn't know, but we don't know any way to prevent them happening. WILL ROGERS

See also **Knowledge, Not Knowing, Unknowable.**

KNOWLEDGE

One who knows how to stop at where he cannot know has reached the limit of knowledge.
CHUANG-TSE

Book knowledge is a mere nuisance. It may do for an ornament, but never for a foundation.
MONTAIGNE

Even in the search for knowledge there should be moderation, lest we learn things better left unknown.
BALTASAR GRACIÁN

Pat knowledge helps some more than the seven arts.
BALTASAR GRACIÁN

Knowledge without courage is sterile. BALTASAR GRACIÁN

Knowledge without sense is double folly. BALTASAR GRACIÁN

The struggling for knowledge has a pleasure in it like that of wrestling with a fine woman.
LORD HALIFAX

Knowledge is divided among the Scots like bread in a besieged town —to every man a mouthful, to no man a bellyful. SAMUEL JOHNSON

Knowledge is of two kinds. We know a subject ourselves, or we know where we can get information upon it. SAMUEL JOHNSON

Knowledge, in most of its branches, and in most affairs, is like music in an Italian street, whereof those may partake who pay nothing.
LAURENCE STERNE

No man can reveal to you aught but that which already lies half asleep in the dawning of your knowledge.
KAHLIL GIBRAN

Mediocre men often have the most acquired knowledge.
CLAUDE BERNARD

Pupils must not be encouraged to think that there are short cuts to knowledge. BERTRAND RUSSELL

An empty head has room for much knowledge. KARL KRAUS

See also **Knowing, Knowledge and Ignorance, Knowledge and Learning, Knowledge and Wisdom, Omniscience.**

KNOWLEDGE AND IGNORANCE

Ignorance is bold, and knowledge reserved. THUCYDIDES

There is an ABC ignorance that precedes knowledge and a doctoral ignorance that comes after it. MONTAIGNE

Ignorance lies at the bottom of all human knowledge, and the deeper we penetrate the nearer we arrive unto it. C. C. COLTON

There are as many strange truths of ignorance as of knowledge. LEIGH HUNT

What is most of our boasted so-called knowledge but a conceit that we know something, which robs us of the advantage of our actual ignorance? HENRY DAVID THOREAU

A man's ignorance sometimes is not only useful but beautiful, while his knowledge is oftentimes worse than useless, besides being ugly. HENRY DAVID THOREAU

I would rather have my ignorance than another man's knowledge, because I have got so much more of it. MARK TWAIN

The pleasures of ignorance are as great, in their way, as the pleasures of knowledge. ALDOUS HUXLEY

See also **Ignorance, Knowledge.**

KNOWLEDGE AND LEARNING

It is only when we forget all our learning that we begin to know. HENRY DAVID THOREAU

See also **Knowledge, Learning (Scholarship).**

KNOWLEDGE AND WISDOM

The farther one pursues knowledge, the less one knows. LAO-TSE

Abundance of knowledge does not teach men to be wise. HERACLITUS

See also **Knowledge, Wisdom.**

L

LABOUR SEE WORK

LADY

Ladies grow handsome by looking at themselves in the glass. WILLIAM HAZLITT

A true lady or gentleman remains at home with a grouch same as if they had pneumonia. KIN HUBBARD

A lady is a woman who makes a man behave like a gentleman. RUSSELL LYNES

See also **Gentleman, Well-Bred.**

LANGUAGE

Language is part of a man's character. FRANCIS BACON

He who knows no foreign language knows nothing of his own. GOETHE

Because everybody can talk, everybody thinks he can talk about language. GOETHE

Anything living is easily and naturally expressed in popular language.
HENRY DAVID THOREAU

The language ranks highest which goes farthest in the art of accomplishing much with little means, or, in other words, which is able to express the greatest amount of meaning with the simplest mechanism.   OTTO JESPERSEN

The individual's whole experience is built upon the plan of his language.   HENRI DELACROIX

Their eldest son was such a disappointment to them; they wanted him to be a linguist, and spent no end of money on having him taught to speak—oh, dozens of languages! —and then he became a Trappist monk.   SAKI

See also **English Language, French Language, German Language, Latin, Spelling, Translation, Words.**

LAO-TSE

Lao-tse, perhaps the first of the great mystics, wrote his book (so tradition avers) at a custom-house while he was waiting to have his baggage examined; and, as might be expected, it is full of the doctrine that action is futile.
BERTRAND RUSSELL

See also **Taoism.**

LARGE AND SMALL

The telescope makes the world smaller; it is only the microscope that makes it larger.
G. K. CHESTERTON

LAST WILL

Waked this morning with news, brought me by a messenger on purpose, that my uncle Robert is dead, and died yesterday; so I rose sorry in some respect, glad in my expectations in another respect. . . . My father and I lay together tonight, I greedy to see the will, but did not ask to see it till tomorrow.
SAMUEL PEPYS

LATIN

The Romans would never have found time to conquer the world if they had been obliged first to learn Latin.   HEINRICH HEINE

LAUGH

When the highest type of men hear the truth, they try hard to live in accordance with it; when the mediocre type hear the truth, they seem to be aware and yet unaware of it. When the lowest type hear the truth they break into loud laughter. If it were not laughed at, it would not be the truth.   LAO-TSE

Were it not for bunglers in the manner of doing it, hardly any man would ever find out he was laughed at.   LORD HALIFAX

I am sure that, since I have had the full use of my reason, nobody has ever heard me laugh.
LORD CHESTERFIELD

Men have been wise in very different modes; but they have always laughed the same way.
SAMUEL JOHNSON

She laughs at everything you say. Why? Because she has fine teeth.
BENJAMIN FRANKLIN

Nothing shows a man's character more than what he laughs at.
GOETHE

A stupid story or idea will sometimes make one laugh more than wit.   HORACE WALPOLE

If you want to make people weep, you must weep yourself. If you want to make people laugh, your face must remain serious.

CASANOVA

Danger is a good teacher, and makes apt scholars. So are disgrace, defeat, exposure to immediate scorn and laughter. WILLIAM HAZLITT

Man is the only animal that laughs and weeps; for he is the only animal that is struck with the difference between what things are and what they might have been.

WILLIAM HAZLITT

He who has the courage to laugh is almost as much the master of the world as he who is ready to die.

GIACOMO LEOPARDI

I enjoy a good laugh—one that rushes out of a man's soul like the breaking up of a Sunday School.

JOSH BILLINGS

Laughing is the sensation of feeling good all over, and showing it principally in one spot.

JOSH BILLINGS

. . . that older and greater church to which I belong: the church where the oftener you laugh the better, because by laughter only can you destroy evil without malice, and affirm good fellowship without mawkishness.

GEORGE BERNARD SHAW

The young man who has not wept is a savage, and the old man who will not laugh is a fool.

GEORGE SANTAYANA

Laughter, as I have come to see in my old age, is the innocent youthful side of repentance, of disillusion, of understanding.

GEORGE SANTAYANA

Nothing, no experience good or bad, no belief, no cause, is in itself momentous enough to monopolize the whole of life to the exclusion of laughter.

ALFRED NORTH WHITEHEAD

If the animals suddenly got the gift of laughter, they would begin by laughing themselves sick about man, that most ridiculous, most absurd, most foolish of all animals.

EGON FRIEDELL

See also **Comic, Funny, Gay, Humour, Irony, Joke, Merry, Mirth, Ridicule.**

LAW

The greater the number of statutes, the greater the number of thieves and brigands. LAO-TSE

There is nothing so much, nor so grossly, nor so ordinarily faulty as the laws. MONTAIGNE

It is the rule of rules, and the general law of laws, that everyone observe those of the place wherein he lives. MONTAIGNE

Men seldom understand any laws but those they *feel*.

LORD HALIFAX

I love the University of Salamanca; for when the Spaniards were in doubt as to the lawfulness of their conquering America, the University of Salamanca gave it as their opinion that it was not lawful.

SAMUEL JOHNSON

It was the old notion that justice should not arise from laws, but laws from justice. JOSEPH JOUBERT

When men are pure, laws are useless; when men are corrupt, laws are broken. BENJAMIN DISRAELI

Every actual state is corrupt. Good men must not obey laws too well.
RALPH WALDO EMERSON

The best laws grow out of usages.
JOSEPH JOUBERT

In law, nothing is certain but the expense.
SAMUEL BUTLER

Law is a statement of the circumstances in which the public force will be brought to bear upon men through the courts.
OLIVER WENDELL HOLMES, JR.

There are few grave legal questions in a poor estate.
E. W. HOWE

See also **Constitution, Justice, Lawyer, Natural Law.**

LAWYER

The first thing we do, let's kill all the lawyers.
SHAKESPEARE
(*King Henry VI*, Pt. 2, IV ii)

If the laws could speak for themselves, they would complain of the lawyers in the first place.
LORD HALIFAX

A countryman between two lawyers is like a fish between two cats.
BENJAMIN FRANKLIN

LAZY

Laziness: Unwarranted repose of manner in a person of low degree.
AMBROSE BIERCE

See also **Idle, Indolence, Loafing, Sluggard.**

LEADING

I remember what a very able man who made a fortune on the Stock Exchange once said to me. 'They talk about our leading the procession—we only *follow it ahead* like little boys. If we turn down a side street it doesn't.'
OLIVER WENDELL HOLMES, JR.

Those who try to lead the people can only do so by following the mob.
OSCAR WILDE

No leader, however great a personality he may be, is as important to a people as their own intellectual development.
G. W. RUSSELL (Æ)

Charlatanism of some degree is indispensable to effective leadership.
ERIC HOFFER

See also **Follow.**

LEANING

All are apt to shrink from those that lean upon them.
LORD HALIFAX

LEARNED

The learned tradition is not concerned with truth, but with the learned adjustment of learned statements of antecedent learned people.
ALFRED NORTH WHITEHEAD

See also **Learning (Scholarship).**

LEARNING (SCHOLARSHIP)

Abandon learning, and you will be free from trouble and distress.
LAO-TSE

Learning: The kind of ignorance distinguishing the studious.
AMBROSE BIERCE

To the neglect of learning, genius sometimes owes its greater glory.
EDWARD YOUNG

Wear your learning like your watch, in a private pocket; and do not pull it out, and strike it, merely to show that you have one.
LORD CHESTERFIELD

Learned men are the cisterns of knowledge, not the fountainheads.
JAMES NORTHCOTE

(Of Macaulay's conversation:) He not only overflowed with learning, but stood in the slop.
SYDNEY SMITH

We need but little learning to live happily. MONTAIGNE

Like Leporello learned literary men keep a list, but the point is what they lack; while Don Juan seduces girls and enjoys himself—Leporello notes down the time, the place and a description of the girl.
SÖREN KIERKEGAARD

The most learned among us differ only from the ignorant by their faculty of finding amusement in multifarious and complicated errors. ANATOLE FRANCE

In order to acquire learning, we must first shake ourselves free of it.
ALFRED NORTH WHITEHEAD

Learning preserves the errors of the past as well as its wisdom.
ALFRED NORTH WHITEHEAD

Once learning solidifies, all is over with it.
ALFRED NORTH WHITEHEAD

See also **Knowledge and Learning, Learning (Studying), Scholarship, Study, Wisdom and Learning.**

LEARNING (STUDYING)

A man who has learned little, grows old like an ox; his flesh grows, but his knowledge does not grow. DHAMMAPADA

I am still learning.
MOTTO OF MICHELANGELO

The eagle never lost so much time as when he submitted to learn of the crow. WILLIAM BLAKE

Never try and find out anything, or try to learn anything till you have found the not knowing it to be a nuisance to you for some time. Then you will remember it, but not otherwise. SAMUEL BUTLER

In all things we learn only from those we love. GOETHE

I didn't begin to learn anything until after I had finished my studies.
ANATOLE FRANCE

Do not learn more than you absolutely need to get through life.
KARL KRAUS

To learn, a man must subtract himself from the study of any solid and objective thing.
G. K. CHESTERTON

The man who is too old to learn was probably always too old to learn. HENRY S. HASKINS

The brighter you are, the more you have to learn. DON HEROLD

See also **Learning (Scholarship), School, Study, Teaching.**

LEAVING

'Tis a maxim of the wise to leave things before things leave them.
BALTASAR GRACIÁN

If there is one pleasure on earth which surpasses all others, it is leaving a play before the end. I might perhaps except the joy of taking tickets for a play, dining well, sitting on after dinner, and finally not going at all. That, of course, is very heaven.
ANGELA THIRKELL

See also **Not Going.**

LEISURE

Only those who take leisurely what the people of the world are busy about can be busy about what the people of the world take leisurely.
CHANG CH'AO

Leisure in time is like unoccupied floor space in a room.
SHU PAIHSIANG

He enjoys true leisure who has time to improve his soul's estate.
HENRY DAVID THOREAU

What is liberty? Leisure. What is leisure? Liberty.
GEORGE BERNARD SHAW

If you are losing your leisure, look out! You may be losing your soul.
LOGAN PEARSALL SMITH

Michael Foster, the English physiologist, once remarked that 'leisure is the mother of discovery.'
WALTER B. CANNON

Do not mistake a crowd of big wage-earners for a leisure class.
CLIVE BELL

See also **Doing Nothing, Idle, Relax.**

LEND

He who lends without interest is more worthy than he who gives charity, and he who invests money in the business of a poor man is the most worthy of all.   TALMUD

'Boswell, *lend* me sixpence—*not to be repaid.*'   SAMUEL JOHNSON

If you'd lose a troublesome visitor, lend him money.
BENJAMIN FRANKLIN

The human species, according to the best theory I can form of it, is composed of two distinct races, *the men who borrow, and the men who lend.*   CHARLES LAMB

No one will set heartily to work, who has the face to enter a strange house, ask the master of it for a considerable loan, and walk off with it in his pocket. You might as well suspect a highwayman of addicting himself to hard study in the intervals of his profession.
WILLIAM HAZLITT

Acquaintance: A person whom we know well enough to borrow from, but not well enough to lend to.
AMBROSE BIERCE

Brutus, that exemplar of republican virtue, lent money to a city at forty per cent, and hired a private army to besiege it when it failed to pay the interest.   BERTRAND RUSSELL

See also **Banker, Credit.**

LETTER

There is a pleasure annexed to the communication of one's ideas, whether by word of mouth or by letter, which nothing earthly can supply the place of.
WILLIAM COWPER

When I began this letter I thought I had something to say: but I believe the truth was I had nothing to do.
EDWARD FITZGERALD

A pleasant letter I hold to be the pleasantest thing that this world has to give.   ANTHONY TROLLOPE

The best letters of our time are those that can never be published.
VIRGINIA WOOLF

Sydney Smith, or Napoleon or Marcus Aurelius (somebody about that time) said that after ten days any letter would answer itself. You see what he meant.   A. A. MILNE

LETTING ALONE

'Tis by no means the least of life's rules: to let things alone.

BALTASAR GRACIÁN

If you attend to your work, and let your enemy alone, some one else will come along some day, and do him up for you.　E. W. HOWE

A man is rich in proportion to the things he can afford to let alone.

HENRY DAVID THOREAU

My boy, about seventy-five years ago I learned I was not God. And so, when the people of the various states want to do something and I can't find anything in the Constitution expressly forbidding them to do it, I say, whether I like it or not: 'Damn it, let 'em do it!'

OLIVER WENDELL HOLMES, JR.

One thing I am coming to learn in this world, and that is to let people haggle along with their lives as I haggle along with mine.

DAVID GRAYSON

LEVEL

Your levellers wish to level down as far as themselves, but they cannot bear levelling up to themselves.

SAMUEL JOHNSON

See also **Equality.**

LEVITY

A little levity will save many a good heavy thing from sinking.

SAMUEL BUTLER

My method is to take the utmost trouble to find the right thing to say. And then say it with the utmost levity.　GEORGE BERNARD SHAW

See also **Frivolity, Light and Heavy, Serious.**

LIBERTY

It is not good to have too much liberty. It is not good to have all one wants.　PASCAL

Liberty can neither be got nor kept but by so much care that mankind are generally unwilling to give the price for it.　LORD HALIFAX

When the people contend for their liberty, they seldom get anything by their victory but new masters.

LORD HALIFAX

Liberty means responsibility. That is why most men dread it.

GEORGE BERNARD SHAW

The excessive worship of liberty is usually a materialistic passion. It is founded on a belief that man is the prisoner of external forces, and that, if he were released from them, it would be into a heaven upon earth.

ROBERT LYND

See also **Free, Freedom, Independent.**

LIFE

Most men employ the first part of life to make the rest miserable.

JEAN DE LA BRUYÈRE

Were it offered to my choice, I should have no objection to a repetition of the same life from its beginning, only asking the advantages authors have in a second edition to correct some faults of the first.　BENJAMIN FRANKLIN

Life finds its end in itself, and laughs at what is thought of it.

GOETHE

A man's life of any worth is a continual allegory, and very few eyes can see the mystery of his life.

JOHN KEATS

There are many people who reach their conclusions about life like schoolboys: they cheat their teacher by copying the answer out of a book without having worked out the sum for themselves.
SÖREN KIERKEGAARD

However mean your life is, meet it and live it; do not shun it and call it hard names.
HENRY DAVID THOREAU

Life consists not in holding good cards but in playing those you do hold well. JOSH BILLINGS

Life is a hospital, in which every patient is possessed by the desire of changing his bed. One would prefer to suffer near the fire, and another is certain he would get well if he were by the window.
CHARLES BAUDELAIRE

Nothing is in general more gloomy and monotonous than declamations on the hollowness and transitoriness of human life and grandeur.
MATTHEW ARNOLD

I looked more widely around me, I studied the lives of the masses of humanity, and I saw that, not two or three, or ten, but hundreds, thousands, millions, had so understood the meaning of life that they were able both to live and to die. All these men were well acquainted with the meaning of life and death. quietly laboured, endured privation and suffering, lived and died, and saw in all this, not a vain, but a good thing. LEO TOLSTOY

Life is a matter about which we are lost if we reason either too much or too little. SAMUEL BUTLER

Life is like playing a violin in public and learning the instrument as one goes on. SAMUEL BUTLER

Life is the art of drawing sufficient conclusions from insufficient premises. SAMUEL BUTLER

Is life worth living? This is a question for an embryo, not for a man.
SAMUEL BUTLER

We are here to add what we can to, not to get what we can from life.
SIR WILLIAM OSLER

On the whole I am on the side of the unregenerate who affirm the worth of life as an end in itself as against the saints who deny it.
OLIVER WENDELL HOLMES, JR.

I bid myself accept the common lot; an adequate vitality would say daily: 'God—what a good sleep I've had.' 'My eye, that was a dinner.' 'Now for a rattling walk,'—in short, realize life as an end in itself. Functioning is all there is—only our keenest pleasure is in what we call the higher sort.
OLIVER WENDELL HOLMES, JR.

The truth is that life is delicious, horrible, charming, frightful, sweet, bitter, and that it is everything.
ANATOLE FRANCE

Life is composed of the most dissimilar things, the most unforeseen, the most contradictory, the most incongruous; it is merciless, without sequence or connection, full of inexplicable, illogical and contradictory catastrophes, such as can only be classed as miscellaneous facts. GUY DE MAUPASSANT

One's real life is often the life that one does not lead. OSCAR WILDE

Life, happy or unhappy, successful or unsuccessful, is extraordinarily interesting.
GEORGE BERNARD SHAW

Life is not a spectacle or a feast; it is a predicament.

GEORGE SANTAYANA

Life is a series of relapses and recoveries. GEORGE ADE

Life also is a school of philosophy, but it is like one of those modern kindergartens in which children are left to their own devices and work only at the subjects that arouse their interest. W. SOMERSET MAUGHAM

When man at the end of the road casts up his accounts, he finds that, at best, he has used only half his life, for good or bad purposes. The other half was lost inadvertently, like money dropped through a hole in the pocket. ALFRED POLGAR

Our portion of life is the whole thing for us. HENRY S. HASKINS

Your daily life is your temple and your religion. KAHLIL GIBRAN

At any given moment life is completely senseless. But viewed over a long period, it seems to reveal itself as an organism existing in time, having a purpose, tending in a certain direction. ALDOUS HUXLEY

What is this strange and bitter miracle of life? Is it to feel, when furious day is done, the evening hush, the sorrow, of lost, fading light, far sounds and broken cries, and footsteps, voices, music, and all lost—and something murmurous, immense and mighty in the air? THOMAS WOLFE

When I hear somebody sigh that 'Life is hard,' I am always tempted to ask, 'Compared to what?'

SYDNEY HARRIS

See also **Art of Living, Living, Rules of Life.**

LIGHT AND HEAVY

It is easy to be heavy: hard to be light. G. K. CHESTERTON

See also **Levity, Serious.**

LIKING

As for social pleasures, one of the highest enjoyments is agreeable company and good conversation; and I especially like men, women and children.

WILLIAM LYON PHELPS

We would all rather be in the company of somebody we like than in the company of the most superior being of our acquaintance.

FRANK SWINNERTON

See also **Dislike.**

LIMIT

There is nothing that helps a man in his conduct through life more than a knowledge of his own characteristic weaknesses (which guarded against become his strength), as there is nothing that tends more to the success of a man's talents than his knowing the limits of his faculties, which are thus concentrated on some practicable object. WILLIAM HAZLITT

The safest way to hide the limits of your knowledge is not to transgress them. GIACOMO LEOPARDI

If you want to succeed, limit yourself.

CHARLES AUGUSTIN SAINTE-BEUVE

Art consists of limitation. The most beautiful part of every picture is the frame. G. K. CHESTERTON

Genius is, as a rule, a response to apparently hostile limitations.

ROBERT LYND

LINE

The line that is straightest offers most resistance.

LEONARDO DA VINCI

The firmest line that can be drawn upon the smoothest paper has still jagged edges if seen through a microscope. This does not matter until important deductions are made on the supposition that there are no jagged edges. SAMUEL BUTLER

The English never draw a line without blurring it.

WINSTON S. CHURCHILL

The great and golden rule of art, as well as of life, is this; that the more distinct, sharp and wiry the bounding line, the more perfect the work of art, and the less keen and sharp, the greater is the evidence of weak imagination, plagiarising, and bungling. . . . What is it that distinguishes honesty from knavery but the hard and wiry line of rectitude and certainty in the actions and intentions? Leave out this line and you leave out life itself.

WILLIAM BLAKE

See also **Outline.**

LISTENING

A woman would rather marry a poor provider any time than a poor listener. KIN HUBBARD

The only way to entertain some folks is to listen to them.

KIN HUBBARD

He began to realize the deep truth that no one, broadly speaking, ever wishes to hear what you have been doing. ANGELA THIRKELL

See also **Ears.**

LITERATURE

Never pursue literature as a trade.

SAMUEL TAYLOR COLERIDGE

The only sensible ends of literature are, first, the pleasurable toil of writing; second, the gratification of one's family and friends; and, lastly, the solid cash.

NATHANIEL HAWTHORNE

Literature always anticipates life. It does not copy it, but moulds it to its purpose. The nineteenth century, as we know it, is largely an invention of Balzac. OSCAR WILDE

To turn events into ideas is the function of literature.

GEORGE SANTAYANA

For the ordinary half-educated man, all poetry (except political verse) and, in the literature of the past, even the greatest creations of humour (Aristophanes, Rabelais, Don Quixote, etc.) are incomprehensible and tedious because none of all this literature was written specifically for him, as presentday novels are.

JAKOB BURCKHARDT

It is one of the functions of literature to turn truisms into truths.

G. K. CHESTERTON

Literature is but language; it is only a rare and amazing miracle by which a man really says what he means.

G. K. CHESTERTON

Literature is the art of writing something that will be read twice.

CYRIL CONNOLLY

See also **Books, Classics, Novel, Writing.**

LITTLE

Three things are good in little measure and evil in large: yeast, salt, and hesitation. TALMUD

While I am busy with little things, I am not required to do greater things. ST. FRANCIS DE SALES

Little and good is twice good.
BALTASAR GRACIÁN

Those who apply themselves too closely to little things often become incapable of great things.
LA ROCHEFOUCAULD

Little minds are wounded by the smallest things.
LA ROCHEFOUCAULD

Cardinal de Retz very sagaciously marked out Cardinal Chigi for a little mind, from the moment that he told him he had wrote three years with the same pen, and that it was an excellent good one still.
LORD CHESTERFIELD

The variations of life consist of little things.
SAMUEL JOHNSON

I mentioned that I was afraid I put into my journal too many little incidents. Johnson: 'There is nothing, sir, too little for so little a creature as man. It is by studying little things that we attain the great art of having as little misery and as much happiness as possible.'
BOSWELL (*Life of Johnson*)

To great evils we submit; we resent little provocations.
WILLIAM HAZLITT

Life is a great bundle of little things.
OLIVER WENDELL HOLMES, SR.

Nothing can be done except little by little.
CHARLES BAUDELAIRE

The importance of little things. This is all very true but so also is the un-importance even of great things—sooner or later.
SAMUEL BUTLER

See also **Large and Small, Small, Trifle.**

LIVING

Swim with the tide, so as not to offend others. Do this day by day without break, and live in peace with mankind. Thus you will be ready for all contingencies, and may be said to have your talents perfect.
CHUANG-TSE

My trade and art is to live.
MONTAIGNE

If you are wise, live as you can, if you cannot live as you would.
BALTASAR GRACIÁN

To achieve great things, we must live as though we were never going to die.
VAUVENARGUES

Everything living forms an atmosphere around itself.
GOETHE

When they asked Plato how he had lived in this world he answered: 'I entered with pain. I never ceased to marvel. I depart with reluctance. And I have learned nothing except that I know nothing.'
GOETHE

The great majority of men exist but do not live.
BENJAMIN DISRAELI

The great end of living is to harmonize man with the order of things.
OLIVER WENDELL HOLMES, SR.

We live but a fraction of our life.
HENRY DAVID THOREAU

To live is like to love—all reason is against it, and all healthy instinct for it.
SAMUEL BUTLER

To live is to function. That is all there is in living.
OLIVER WENDELL HOLMES, JR.

One must really think of nothing in order not to feel cruelly the tragic absurdity of living.
ANATOLE FRANCE

There is one phrase by which the dishonest man invariably reveals himself: 'You have to live.' Why?
SYDNEY HARRIS

See also **Art of Living, Life, Rules of Life.**

LOAFING

It is better to have loafed and lost than never to have loafed at all.
JAMES THURBER

See also **Doing Nothing, Idle, Lazy.**

LOGIC

Logic is nothing more than a knowledge of words.   CHARLES LAMB

Even logical consequences just happen.   HENRY S. HASKINS

Logic is like the sword—those who appeal to it, shall perish by it.
SAMUEL BUTLER

There is a logic of colours, and it is with this alone, and not with the logic of the brain, that the painter should conform.   PAUL CÉZANNE

There is nothing in reality that conforms strictly to logic.
FRIEDRICH NIETZSCHE

See also **Classification.**

LONDON

No man fond of letters leaves London without regret.
SAMUEL JOHNSON

When a man is tired of London, he is tired of life; for there is in London all that life can afford.
SAMUEL JOHNSON

LONELINESS

I value more the privilege of seeing great things in loneliness than the fame of a prophet.   JOHN KEATS

See also **Alone, Solitude.**

LONG

I find all books too long.
VOLTAIRE

A long happiness loses by its mere length.   G. C. LICHTENBERG

LOOKING

Pythagoras used to say life resembles the Olympic Games: a few men strain their muscles to carry off a prize; others bring trinkets to sell to the crowd for a profit; and some there are (and not the worst) who seek no further advantage than to look at the show and see how and why everything is done.
MONTAIGNE

A leaf swept along by the wind often looks like a bird.   GOETHE

The person that has acted, fears; the person that looks on is formidable.
RALPH WALDO EMERSON

There is an unexplored side to everything, because instead of looking at things with our eyes we look at them with the memory of what others have thought.
GUSTAVE FLAUBERT

There are men and women born into the world to do its work and win its prizes; others, simply to look on and see what happens. These two kinds of people feel ashamed when they meet each other.
LOGAN PEARSALL SMITH

Suppose you watch a man split wood from a hundred yards away. You'll see the two pieces fall to the right and left—and then you'll hear the sound. Just so we may look at the world for half our lives until we hear it speak to us with the language of its soul.
CHRISTIAN MORGENSTERN

(Of Cézanne:) 'He sat in front of it like a dog and simply looked, without any nervousness or ulterior motive.'   RAINER MARIA RILKE

See also **Spectator.**

LORD'S PRAYER

The Lord's Prayer says all that is necessary and is very proper for all occasions.   MONTAIGNE

See also **Prayer.**

LORDS

Most lords are feeble and forlorn.
WALTER BAGEHOT

LOSING

It's the good loser that finally loses out.   KIN HUBBARD

If you want to know what a man is really like, take notice how he acts when he loses money.
NEW ENGLAND PROVERB

Always imitate the behaviour of the winners when you lose.
GEORGE MEREDITH

LOUIS XIV

Those of my readers who may feel that the social life of today is rather demanding should consider that at least they don't have to get up at seven-thirty to go and see Louis XIV put on his pants.
WILL CUPPY

LOVE

Love, and do what you like.
ST. AUGUSTINE

Love is a power too strong to be overcome by anything but flight.
CERVANTES

In their first passions women are in love with their lover; in the rest, with love.   LA ROCHEFOUCAULD

Love is to the soul of him who loves, what the soul is to the body which it animates.   LA ROCHEFOUCAULD

When one loves one doubts even what one most believes.
LA ROCHEFOUCAULD

No disguise can long conceal love where it exists, or long feign it where it is lacking.
LA ROCHEFOUCAULD

There are people who would never have fallen in love had they never heard love discussed.
LA ROCHEFOUCAULD

Love concedes in a moment what we can hardly attain by effort after years of toil.   GOETHE

It is as safe to play with fire as it is to dally with gallantry. Love is a passion that has friends in the garrison.
LORD HALIFAX

Love is the wisdom of the fool and the folly of the wise.
SAMUEL JOHNSON

If you would shut up any man with any woman, so as to make them derive their whole pleasure from each other, they would inevitably fall in love, as it is called, with each other.
SAMUEL JOHNSON

It is commonly a weak man who marries for love. SAMUEL JOHNSON

The gentle delights of peace are preferable by far to the charms of love: but one does not think so when one is in love.   CASANOVA

If we spend our lives in loving, we have no leisure to complain, or to feel unhappiness. JOSEPH JOUBERT

No person who is in love can ever be entirely persuaded that the passion is not reciprocal; as no one

who does not feel it ever believes that it is sincere in others.
WILLIAM HAZLITT

Love is to the moral nature exactly what the sun is to the earth.
HONORÉ DE BALZAC

First love is a kind of vaccination which saves a man from catching the complaint a second time.
HONORÉ DE BALZAC

Young men make great mistakes in life; for one thing, they idealize love too much. BENJAMIN JOWETT

Love is like measles: you can get it only once, and the later in life it occurs the tougher it gets.
JOSH BILLINGS

Doubt of the reality of love ends by making us doubt everything.
FRÉDÉRIC AMIEL

It is not customary to love what one has. ANATOLE FRANCE

The best way to know God is to love many things.
VINCENT VAN GOGH

Love does not consist in gazing at each other but in looking outward together in the same direction.
ANTOINE DE SAINT-EXUPÉRY

Love can canonize people. The saints are those who have been most loved. OSCAR WILDE

He who comes to do good knocks at the gate; he who loves finds the door open.
RABINDRANATH TAGORE

People who are not in love fail to understand how an intelligent man can suffer because of a very ordinary woman. This is like being surprised that anyone should be stricken with cholera because of a creature so insignificant as the comma bacillus.
MARCEL PROUST

The real value of love is the increased general vitality it produces.
PAUL VALÉRY

Love consists in this that two solitudes protect and touch and greet each other. RAINER MARIA RILKE

This is the miracle that happens every time to those who really love: the more they give, the more they possess of that precious nourishing love from which flowers and children have their strength and which could help all human beings if they would take it without doubting. . . .
RAINER MARIA RILKE

Love doesn't grow on the trees like apples in Eden—it's something you have to make. And you must use your imagination to make it too, just like anything else. It's all work, work. JOYCE CARY

It is difficult not to be unjust to what one loves. OSCAR WILDE

See also **Affection, Love and Friendship, Love of God, Love and Hate, Lover.**

LOVE AND FRIENDSHIP

If we judge of love by the majority of its results it rather resembles hatred than friendship.
LA ROCHEFOUCAULD

However rare true love is, true friendship is rarer.
LA ROCHEFOUCAULD

The feeling of friendship is like that of being comfortably filled with roast beef; love, like being enlivened with champagne.
SAMUEL JOHNSON

Friendship is like earthenware, once broken it can be mended; love is like a mirror, once broken that ends it. JOSH BILLINGS

LOVE OF GOD

Any old woman can love God better than a doctor of theology can. ST. BONAVENTURA

We ought to love our Maker for His own sake, without either hope of good or fear of pain. CERVANTES

To love God is to have good health, good looks, good sense, experience, a kindly nature and a fair balance of cash in hand. We know that all things work together for good to them that love God. SAMUEL BUTLER

The knowledge of God is very far from the love of Him. PASCAL

He who loves God cannot endeavour to bring it about that God should love him in return. SPINOZA

See also **God, Love.**

LOVE AND HATE

Love makes everything lovely; hate concentrates itself on the one thing hated. GEORGE MACDONALD

LOVER

Most part of a lover's life is full of agony, anxiety, fear and grief, complaints, sighs, suspicions, and cares (heigh-ho my heart is woe), full of silence and irksome solitariness. ROBERT BURTON

We keep our first lover for a long time—if we do not get a second. LA ROCHEFOUCAULD

LUCK

The superior man lives quietly and calmly, waiting for the will of Heaven, while the mean man does what is full of risk, looking out for turns of luck. CONFUCIUS

When I contemplate the common lot of mortality, I must acknowledge that I have drawn a high prize in the lottery of life. The far greater part of the globe is overspread with barbarism and slavery. In the civilized world, the most numerous class is condemned to ignorance and poverty; and the double fortune of my birth in a free and enlightened country in an honourable and wealthy family, is the lucky chance of a unit against millions. EDWARD GIBBON

To a brave man, good and bad luck are like his right and left hand. He uses both. ST. CATHERINE OF SIENA

People are lucky and unlucky, not according to what they get absolutely, but according to the ratio between what they get and what they have been led to expect. SAMUEL BUTLER

It would be a very fine thing for the world if everyone were entitled, in some slight degree, to be lucky. E. B. WHITE

See also **Chance, Circumstances, Fortune.**

LUNCH

Let us consider for a moment lunch in the country. I do not mean lunch in the open air, for it is obvious that there is no meal so heavenly as lunch thus eaten, and I have no time to dwell upon the obvious. A. A. MILNE

When ordering lunch, the big executives are just as indecisive as the rest of us. WILLIAM FEATHER

LUXURY

Every degree of luxury hath some connection with evil. JOHN WOOLMAN

Never economise on luxuries.
ANGELA THIRKELL

See also **Necessary**.

LYING

As universal a practice as lying is,
and as easy a one as it seems, I do
not remember to have heard three
good lies in all my conversation,
even from those who were most
celebrated in that faculty.
JONATHAN SWIFT

He who is not very strong in memory should not meddle with lying.
MONTAIGNE

'There are inexcusable lies, and consecrated lies. For instance, we are
told that on the arrival of the news
of the unfortunate battle of Fonte-
noy, every heart beat, and every eye
was in tears. Now we know that no
man ate his dinner the worse, but
there *should* have been all this concern; and to say there *was* (smiling)
may be reckoned a consecrated lie.'
BOSWELL (*Life of Johnson*)

If I make a mistake, anyone can see
it, but not if I lie.   GOETHE

A person who does not tell lies, will
not believe that others tell them.
From old habit, he cannot break the
connection between words and
things.   WILLIAM HAZLITT

The man who can't tell a lie thinks
he is the best judge of one.
MARK TWAIN

George Washington was ignorant
of the commonest accomplishments
of youth. He could not even lie.
MARK TWAIN

Any fool can tell the truth, but it
requires a man of some sense to lie
well.   SAMUEL BUTLER

Lying has a kind of respect and
reverence with it. We pay a person
the compliment of acknowledging
his superiority whenever we lie to
him.   SAMUEL BUTLER

Lies are essential to humanity. They
are perhaps as important as the pursuit of pleasure and moreover are
necessary to that pursuit.
MARCEL PROUST

He who does not need to lie is
proud of not being a liar.
FRIEDRICH NIETZSCHE

Many a young man starts in life
with a natural gift for exaggeration,
which, if nurtured in congenial and
sympathetic surroundings, or by
the imitation of the best models,
might grow into something really
great and wonderful. But, as a rule,
he comes to nothing. He either falls
into careless habits of accuracy, or
takes to frequenting the society of
the aged and the well-informed.
Both things are equally fatal to his
imagination, and in a short time he
develops a morbid and unhealthy
faculty of truth-telling, begins to
verify all statements made in his
presence, has no hesitation in contradicting people who are much
younger than himself, and often
ends by writing novels that are so
like life that no one can possibly
believe in their probability.
OSCAR WILDE

To pretend that you believe a liar is
a lie too—often the most contemptible of them all.
ARTHUR SCHNITZLER

It takes a wise man to handle a lie.
A fool had better remain honest.
NORMAN DOUGLAS

Someone says it's a lie. Well, I am
reminded by that of the remark of
the witty Irishman who said: 'There

are a terrible lot of lies going about the world, and the worst of it is that half of them are true.'
WINSTON S. CHURCHILL

We lie loudest when we lie to ourselves. ERIC HOFFER

See also **Exaggeration, Sincerity, Telling the Truth, Truth and Lying, Veracity.**

M

MACHIAVELLI

Machiavelli wrote the rules for short term success, of from five to fifteen years.
ALFRED NORTH WHITEHEAD

MACHINE

The arithmetical machine produces effects that approach nearer to thought than all the actions of animals. But it does nothing that would enable us to attribute will to it, as to the animals. PASCAL

The mystery of mysteries is to view machines making machines.
BENJAMIN DISRAELI

See also **Mechanic.**

MAD

Men are so necessarily mad, that not to be mad would amount to another form of madness. PASCAL

Many a man is mad in certain instances, and goes through life without having it perceived.
SAMUEL JOHNSON

There is a pleasure in madness, which none but madmen know.
WILLIAM HAZLITT

Even the madness of gifted people is not that of fools or nobodies.
HONORÉ DE BALZAC

When we remember we are all mad, the mysteries disappear and life stands explained. MARK TWAIN

It is his reasonable conversation which mostly frightens us in a madman. ANATOLE FRANCE

The madman is the man who has lost everything except his reason.
G. K. CHESTERTON

See also **Sanity.**

MAJORITY

Whenever you find that you are on the side of the majority, it is time to reform. MARK TWAIN

MAKE-BELIEVE

Man is a make-believe animal—he is never so truly himself as when he is acting a part.
WILLIAM HAZLITT

In the child's world of dim sensation, play is all in all. 'Making believe' is the gist of his whole life, and he cannot so much as take a walk except in character.
ROBERT LOUIS STEVENSON

MALTHUS

Philosopher Malthus came here last week. I got an agreeable party for him of unmarried people. There was only one lady who had had a child; but he is a good-natured man, and, if there are no appearances of approaching fertility, is civil to every lady. SYDNEY SMITH

MAMMON

Mammon: The god of the world's leading religion. His chief temple is in the holy city of New York.
AMBROSE BIERCE

Those who set out to serve God and Mammon soon discover that there is no God. LOGAN PEARSALL SMITH

The spread of atheism among the young is something awful; I give no credit, however, to the report that some of them do not believe in Mammon.   LOGAN PEARSALL SMITH

See also **Money.**

MAN

There is all Africa and her prodigies in us.   SIR THOMAS BROWNE

It is easier to know a man in general than to know a particular man.
      LA ROCHEFOUCAULD

There are hardly two creatures of a more different species than the same man, when he is pretending to a place, and when he is in possession of it.   LORD HALIFAX

'I wonder what pleasure men can take in making beasts of themselves!' 'I wonder, madam, that you have not penetration enough to see the strong inducement to this excess; for he who makes a *beast* of himself gets rid of the pain of being a man.'   SAMUEL JOHNSON

We should expect the best and the worst from mankind, as from the weather.   VAUVENARGUES

Man is made not only of what he has inherited, but also of what he has acquired.   GOETHE

All men are bizarre and inexplicable composites of contraries; that is what those fellows who turn out novels and plays refuse to understand. Their men are all of one piece. There are no such creatures. There are ten men in one man, and often they all show themselves within one hour, under certain circumstances.   EUGÈNE DELACROIX

God defend me from ever looking at a man as an animal.
      RALPH WALDO EMERSON

Man is God's highest present development. He is the latest thing in God.   SAMUEL BUTLER

Mankind is a tribe of animals, living by habits and thinking in symbols; and it can never be anything else.   GEORGE SANTAYANA

When one thinks coldly, I see no reason for attributing to man a significance different in kind from that which belongs to a baboon or to a grain of sand.
      OLIVER WENDELL HOLMES, JR.

I sometimes think that God in creating man somewhat overestimated his ability.   OSCAR WILDE

Man will become better when you show him what he is like.
      ANTON CHEKHOV

Every man is the descendant of every king and every slave that ever lived.   KAHLIL GIBRAN

Advice to young writers who want to get ahead without any annoying delays: don't write about Man, write about *a* man.   E. B. WHITE

See also **God and Man, Human Nature, Man and Himself, Men.**

MAN AND GOD SEE GOD AND MAN

MAN AND HIMSELF
He who exalts himself does not rise high.   LAO-TSE

One is not obliged to belong so much to all as not to belong at all to oneself.   BALTASAR GRACIÁN

There is as much difference between us and ourselves as between us and others.   MONTAIGNE

It is a malady confined to man, and not seen in any other creatures, to hate and despise ourselves.

MONTAIGNE

When all is summed up, a man never speaks of himself without losing thereby. His self-accusations are always believed; his self-praise disbelieved. MONTAIGNE

God defend me from myself.

SPANISH PROVERB

All censure of a man's self is oblique praise. SAMUEL JOHNSON

We can really respect a man only if he doesn't always *look out for himself*. GOETHE

It is a great mistake to think you are more than you are and yet to underrate your real value. GOETHE

He who doesn't think too much of himself is much more than he thinks.

GOETHE

The fox condemns the trap, not himself. WILLIAM BLAKE

As long as a man stands in his own way, everything seems to be in his way, governments, society, and even the sun and moon and stars, as astrology may testify.

HENRY DAVID THOREAU

Most men are like eggs, too full of themselves to hold anything else.

JOSH BILLINGS

When a man gets talking about himself, he seldom fails to be eloquent and often reaches the sublime.

JOSH BILLINGS

By despising himself too much a man comes to be worthy of his own contempt. FRÉDÉRIC AMIEL

Anybody at all has a right to talk about himself—provided he knows how to be entertaining.

CHARLES BAUDELAIRE

He is a poor creature who does not believe himself to be better than the whole world else. No matter how ill we may be, nor how low we may have fallen, we should not change identity with any other person.

SAMUEL BUTLER

You've no idea what a poor opinion I have of myself—and how little I deserve it. W. S. GILBERT

It is not selfish to think for oneself. A man who does not think for himself does not think at all.

OSCAR WILDE

To love oneself is the beginning of a life-long romance. OSCAR WILDE

When people talk to us about others they are usually dull. When they talk to us about themselves they are nearly always interesting.

OSCAR WILDE

Perhaps the only true dignity of man is his capacity to despise himself. GEORGE SANTAYANA

It is the best thing in life that each should have everything in himself: his fate, his future, his whole expanse and world.

RAINER MARIA RILKE

A man by himself is in bad company. ERIC HOFFER

See also **Know Thyself, Man, Self.**

MANAGEMENT

The man who escapes with clean hands from the management of the world's affairs, escapes by a miracle.

PLATO

The commonest precaution I take with my servants is to remain ignorant of what they do. I had rather be told at the end of two months that I had spent four hundred crowns than have three or five or seven crowns dinned in my ears every night.   MONTAIGNE

The great requisite for the prosperous management of ordinary business is the want of imagination.
WILLIAM HAZLITT

Every person who manages another is a hypocrite.
WILLIAM MAKEPEACE THACKERAY

Those who cannot miss an opportunity of saying a good thing are not to be trusted with the management of any great question.
WILLIAM HAZLITT

MANNER

A bad manner spoils everything, even reason and justice.
BALTASAR GRACIÁN

MANNERS

Good manners is the art of making those people easy with whom we converse. Whoever makes the fewest persons uneasy, is the best bred in the company. JONATHAN SWIFT

As manners make laws, manners likewise repeal them.
SAMUEL JOHNSON

Manners are of more importance than laws.   EDMUND BURKE

Manners are the shadows of virtue.
SYDNEY SMITH

Good manners are made up of petty sacrifices.
RALPH WALDO EMERSON

See also **Courtesy, Etiquette, Graces, Politeness, Rude.**

MARCUS AURELIUS

Marcus Aurelius departed from the rule (of adoptive successors) by appointing his own son Commodus,
which happened to be a bad appointment. Marcus would have fared very ill with posterity if he hadn't written those amiable memoirs, which, however edifying and delightful, had nothing to do with the point. His job was to find a good successor.
ALFRED NORTH WHITEHEAD

It is generally thought that no Christians were thrown to the lions until the reign of Marcus Aurelius Antoninus, whose meditations you ought to read. Great stuff.
WILL CUPPY

MARIE ANTOINETTE

Marie Antoinette is devoted to pleasure and expense and not remarkable for any other vices or virtues.   THOMAS JEFFERSON

MARRIAGE

We call a wife good and a marriage happy, not because they are, but because no one says to the contrary.
MONTAIGNE

A good marriage, if there is such a thing, rejects the company and conditions of love. It tries to imitate those of friendship.   MONTAIGNE

Marriage is a desperate thing. The frogs in Aesop were extreme wise; they had a great mind to some water, but they would not leap into the well, because they could not get out again.   JOHN SELDEN

Being married to a sleepy-souled woman is just like playing at cards for nothing; no passion is excited, and the time is filled up.
SAMUEL JOHNSON

There are but two objects in marriage, love or money. If you marry for love, you will certainly have some very happy days, and probably many very uneasy ones; if for money, you will have no happy days and probably no uneasy ones. LORD CHESTERFIELD

I believe marriages would in general be as happy, and often more so, if they were all made by the Lord Chancellor, upon a due consideration of the characters and circumstances, without the parties having any choice in the matter.
SAMUEL JOHNSON

There may be good but there are no exquisite marriages.
LA ROCHEFOUCAULD

No man will be fond of what forces him daily to feel himself inferior.
SAMUEL JOHNSON

Marriage is not commonly unhappy, otherwise than as life is unhappy.
SAMUEL JOHNSON

Sir, it is so far from being natural for a man and woman to live in a state of marriage, that we find all the motives which they have for remaining in that connection, and the restraints which civilized society imposes to prevent separation, are hardly sufficient to keep them together. SAMUEL JOHNSON

Keep your eyes wide open before marriage, and half-shut afterwards.
BENJAMIN FRANKLIN

Only choose in marriage a woman whom you would choose as a friend if she were a man. JOSEPH JOUBERT

Marriage resembles a pair of shears, so joined that they cannot be separated, often moving in opposite directions, yet always punishing anyone who comes between them.
SYDNEY SMITH

It is better to know as little as possible of the defects of the person with whom you are to pass your life. JANE AUSTEN

Matrimony and bachelorhood are both of them at once equally wise and equally foolish.
SAMUEL BUTLER

Marriage: The state or condition of a community consisting of a master, a mistress and two slaves, making in all, two. AMBROSE BIERCE

At the beginning of a marriage ask yourself whether this woman will be interesting to talk to from now until old age. Everything else in marriage is transitory: most of the time is spent in conversation.
FRIEDRICH NIETZSCHE

It is not lack of love but lack of friendship that makes unhappy marriages. FRIEDRICH NIETZSCHE

Marriage is one long conversation, chequered by disputes.
ROBERT LOUIS STEVENSON

The one charm of marriage is that it makes a life of deception absolutely necessary for both parties.
OSCAR WILDE

Marriage is hardly a thing one can do now and then—except in America. OSCAR WILDE

Marriage is popular because it combines the maximum of temptation with the maximum of opportunity.
GEORGE BERNARD SHAW

If one wants marriage to be a refuge, friendship must gradually replace love. ALAIN

I should be interested to discover what proportion of unsatisfactory marriages is due to the bare fact that the male partner does not know his business. NORMAN DOUGLAS

Often and often, a marriage hardly differs from prostitution, except being harder to escape from.
BERTRAND RUSSELL

It does not occur to anyone to expect a single person to be 'happy'—but if he marries, people are much surprised if he *isn't*!
RAINER MARIA RILKE

A good marriage is that in which each appoints the other guardian of his solitude. RAINER MARIA RILKE

Let there be spaces in your togetherness. KAHLIL GIBRAN

'Our union has been blest with issues,' I said. PETER DE VRIES

See also **Husband, Married, Marry, Wedding, Wife.**

MARRIED

All the world feels that a man when married acquires some of the attributes of an old woman—he becomes, to a certain extent, a motherly sort of being; he acquires a conversance with women's ways and women's wants, and loses the wilder and offensive sparks of his virility.
ANTHONY TROLLOPE

A married man forms married habits and becomes dependent on marriage just as a sailor becomes dependent on the sea.
GEORGE BERNARD SHAW

No matter how happily a woman may be married, it always pleases her to discover that there is a nice man who wishes that she were not.
H. L. MENCKEN

See also **Husband, Wife.**

MARRY

I believe it will be found that those who marry late are best pleased with their children, and those who marry early, with their partners.
SAMUEL JOHNSON

It is not from reason and prudence that people marry, but from inclination. A man is poor; he thinks, 'I cannot be worse, and so I'll take Peggy.' SAMUEL JOHNSON

I have always thought that every woman should marry, and no man.
BENJAMIN DISRAELI

Those who marry to escape something usually find something else.
GEORGE ADE

Nobody works as hard for his money as the man who marries it.
KIN HUBBARD

See also **Marriage, Married, Wedding.**

MASK

A mask tells us more than a face.
OSCAR WILDE

MASS

Men, who are knaves individually, are in the mass very honourable.
MONTESQUIEU

MASTERPIECE

There is something frightful in being required to enjoy and appreciate all masterpieces; to read with equal relish Milton and Dante, and Calderon and Goethe, and Homer, and Scott, and Voltaire, and Wordsworth, and Cervantes, and Molière, and Swift. AGNES REPPLIER

The greatest masterpieces were once only pigments on a palette.
HENRY S. HASKINS

Nothing is a masterpiece—a real masterpiece—till it's about two hundred years old. A picture is like a tree or a church, you've got to let it grow into a masterpiece. Same with a poem or a new religion. They begin as a lot of funny words. Nobody knows whether they're all nonsense or a gift from heaven.
JOYCE CARY

See also **Classics, Work of Art.**

MATHEMATICS

There is no certainty in science where one of the mathematical sciences cannot be applied.
LEONARDO DA VINCI

The mathematicians are a sort of Frenchmen: when you talk to them, they immediately translate it into their own language, and right away it is something utterly different.
GOETHE

The most promising sign in a boy is, I should say, mathematics.
SYDNEY SMITH

I had a feeling once about Mathematics—that I saw it all. Depth beyond Depth was revealed to me—the Byss and the Abyss. I saw—as one might see the transit of Venus or even the Lord Mayor's Show—a quantity passing through infinity and changing its sign from plus to minus. I saw exactly how it happened and why the tergiversation was inevitable—but it was after dinner and I let it go.
WINSTON S. CHURCHILL

See also **Science.**

MATTER SEE MIND AND MATTER.

MAXIM

All good maxims are in the world. We only need to apply them.
PASCAL

Few maxims are true in all respects.
VAUVENARGUES

The conduct of men depends on temperament, not upon a bunch of musty maxims.
BENJAMIN DISRAELI

A maxim has the advantage of being true and untrue at one and the same time, which is equally so of the truth or untruth behind it.
HENRY S. HASKINS

In the conduct of life, habits count for more than maxims.
FRÉDÉRIC AMIEL

It is more trouble to make a maxim than it is to do right.   MARK TWAIN

Maxims of 85-year-old M. Gabriel Hanotaux: 'Anything can happen . . . Everything is forgotten. . . . Every difficulty can be overcome. No one understands anything. . . . If everyone knew what everyone said about everyone, no one would speak to anyone. . . . Above all things, never be afraid. The enemy who forces you to retreat is himself afraid of you at that very moment.'   ANDRÉ MAUROIS

See also **Aphorism, Epigram, Precept, Rules, Rules of Life.**

MEALS

I believe it is best to eat just as one is hungry; but a man who is in business, or a man who has a family, must have stated meals.
SAMUEL JOHNSON

Three good meals a day is bad living.   BENJAMIN FRANKLIN

One pancake for lunch and half a boiled egg for dinner makes a man at sixty able to do anything a college athlete can do.
SIR WILLIAM OSLER

See also **Breakfast, Dinner, Eating, Lunch.**

MEAN

We have but to change the point of view and the greatest action looks mean.
WILLIAM MAKEPEACE THACKERAY

MEANING

Words differently arranged have a different meaning, and meanings differently arranged have different effects. PASCAL

'In that case,' said the Dodo solemnly, rising to its feet, 'I move that the meeting adjourn, for the immediate adoption of more energetic remedies—' 'Speak English!' said the Eaglet. 'I don't know the meaning of half those long words, and, what's more, I don't believe you do either!' LEWIS CARROLL

'If there's no meaning in it,' said the King, 'that saves a world of trouble, you know, as we needn't try to find any.' LEWIS CARROLL

See also **Words.**

MEANINGLESS

The man who regards his own life and that of his fellow creatures as meaningless is not merely unhappy but hardly fit for life.
ALBERT EINSTEIN

Most propositions and questions that have been written about philosophical matters are not false, but senseless. LUDWIG WITTGENSTEIN

MEANS

Use human means as if there were no divine ones, and divine as if there were no human ones. (A masterly rule: it needs no comment.)
BALTASAR GRACIÁN

If one takes care of the means, the end will take care of itself.
GANDHI

Means and end are controvertible terms in my philosophy of life. . . . There is no wall of separation between means and end. Indeed the Creator has given us control over means, none over the end. Realization of the goal is in exact proportion to that of the means. . . . The means may be likened to a seed, the end to a tree; and there is just the same inviolable connection between the means and the end as there is between the seed and the tree. GANDHI

MECHANICS

Mechanics is the paradise of mathematical science, because here we come to the fruits of mathematics.
LEONARDO DA VINCI

The people have a saying that God Almighty is Himself a mechanic.
BENJAMIN FRANKLIN

MEDICINE

I always despise taking medicine, but when I am sick, instead of getting reconciled to it, I begin to hate and fear it as well; and to those who urge me to take it I reply that they may wait at least until I am restored to health and strength, in order to be better able to support the effect and danger of their potions.
MONTAIGNE

My antipathy to the doctor's art is hereditary. My father lived to be seventy-four, my grandfather sixty-nine, my great-grandfather to nearly eighty, without ever tasting any kind of physic. MONTAIGNE

NAPOLEON had no faith in medicine, or its remedies, of which he made no use. 'Doctor,' he said, 'our body is a machine for the purpose of life: it is organized to that end—that is its nature. Leave the life there at its ease, let it take care of itself, it will do better than if your paralyze it by loading it with medicine.'

One of the first duties of the physician is to educate the masses not to take medicine. SIR WILLIAM OSLER

I don't see why any man who believes in medicine would shy at the faith cure. PETER FINLEY DUNNE

For every disease that doctors cure with medicine, they produce ten in healthy people by inoculating them with that virus which is a thousand times more powerful than any microbe: the idea that one is ill. MARCEL PROUST

One of the chief objects of medicine is to save us from the natural consequences of our vices and follies. H. L. MENCKEN

There is no medicine; there are only medicine-men. There are no diseases; there are only patients. SALVADOR DE MADARIAGA

I don't know much about medicine, but I know what I like. S. J. PERELMAN

See also **Diagnosis, Doctor, Healing, Operation, Physician.**

MEDIOCRE

The well-being and happiness of private citizens is based largely on the mediocrity of their talents and incomes. A republic whose laws have produced many mediocre people and which is composed of many happy people—such a republic will be very happy. MONTESQUIEU

Mediocrity is excellence to the mediocre. JOSEPH JOUBERT

Mediocre people have an answer to everything and are astonished at nothing. EUGÈNE DELACROIX

See also **Average, Ordinary.**

MEDITATION

A man doubtful of his dinner, or trembling at a creditor, is not much disposed to abstract meditation, or remote inquiries. SAMUEL JOHNSON

No great work has ever been produced except after a long interval of still and musing meditation. WALTER BAGEHOT

See also **Thinking.**

MEEK

Meekness takes injuries like pills, not chewing, but swallowing them down. SIR THOMAS BROWNE

It's going to be fun to watch and see how long the meek can keep the earth after they inherit it. KIN HUBBARD

See also **Humility.**

MELANCHOLY

If you are melancholy for the first time, you will find upon a little inquiry, that others have been melancholy many times, and yet are cheerful now. If you have been melancholy many times, recollect that you have got over all those times; and try if you cannot find means of getting over them better. LEIGH HUNT

See also **Brooding, Gloomy.**

MEMBERSHIP

Avoid membership in a body of persons pledged to only one side of anything. HENRY S. HASKINS

See also **Party.**

MEMOIRS

There ain't nothing that breaks up homes, country, and nations like somebody publishing their memoirs. WILL ROGERS

See also **Autobiography.**

MEMORY

A strong memory is commonly coupled with infirm judgment.

MONTAIGNE

I have scarcely any memory, and do not think there is another in the world so imperfect as mine. My other faculties are average and ordinary, but in this I think myself rare and singular and entitled to some fame. MONTAIGNE

If I am a man of some reading, I am a man of no retention.

MONTAIGNE

My weakness of memory is so extreme that I have chanced more than once to pick up a book, thinking it was new and unknown to me, and discovered, from notes I had scribbled in it, that I had carefully read it a few years before.

MONTAIGNE

Method is the mother of memory.

THOMAS FULLER

Everyone complains of his memory, but no one complains of his judgment. LA ROCHEFOUCAULD

How is it that our memory is good enough to retain the least triviality that happens to us, and yet not good enough to recollect how often we have told it to the same person?

LA ROCHEFOUCAULD

Some men's memory is like a box where a man should mingle his jewels with his old shoes.

LORD HALIFAX

Where interest lags, memory lags too. GOETHE

Nothing is more common than a fool with a strong memory.

C. C. COLTON

A great memory does not make a mind, any more than a dictionary is a piece of literature.

JOHN HENRY NEWMAN

'The horror of that moment,' the King went on, 'I shall never, *never* forget!' 'You will, though,' the Queen said, 'if you don't make a memorandum of it.'

LEWIS CARROLL

No woman should have a memory. Memory in a woman is the beginning of dowdiness.

OSCAR WILDE

Memory is the diary that chronicles things that never have happened and couldn't possibly have happened. OSCAR WILDE

We find a little of everything in our memory; it is a kind of pharmacy or chemical laboratory in which chance guides our hand now to a calming drug and now to a dangerous poison. MARCEL PROUST

See also **Forget, Remember.**

MEN

Men are what they were.

GEORGE BERNARD SHAW

See also **Human Nature, Man, Men and Women, People.**

MEN AND WOMEN

There never was a man who was not gratified by being told that he was liked by the women.

SAMUEL JOHNSON

Marriage is much more necessary to a man than to a woman; for he is much less able to supply himself with domestic comforts.

SAMUEL JOHNSON

It is always incomprehensible to a man that a woman should ever refuse an offer of marriage.

JANE AUSTEN

Women's most dangerous weapon is their tongue, whether they use it for speech or silence. When they speak you can, if your common sense and your patience are both considerable, reduce them sometimes to silence; but if they are silent (which, in domestic warfare, is called sulking) then all your efforts to make them speak will be useless; you will be compelled to retire and to conclude an armistice on any terms. LUDWIG BÖRNE

Women have less accurate measure of time than men. There is a clock in Adam: none in Eve.

RALPH WALDO EMERSON

We love women in proportion to their degree of strangeness to us.

CHARLES BAUDELAIRE

Men who do not make advances to women are apt to become victims to women who make advances to them. WALTER BAGEHOT

Woman will be the last thing civilized by man.

GEORGE MEREDITH

A man is shorn of his strength if he belongs to one set or one woman.

SAMUEL BUTLER

What attracts us in a woman rarely binds us to her.

JOHN CHURTON COLLINS

A woman wants men to have good times in a woman's way.

E. W. HOWE

How can a woman be expected to be happy with a man who insists on treating her as if she were a perfectly natural being?

OSCAR WILDE

Think what cowards men would be if they had to bear children. Women are an altogether superior species. GEORGE BERNARD SHAW

Women love hotels: men hate them.

GEORGE BERNARD SHAW

Women find their inspiration in the stress of moments that for us are merely awful, absurd, or futile.

JOSEPH CONRAD

When men and women agree, it is only in their conclusions; their reasons are always different.

GEORGE SANTAYANA

None but the brave can live with the fair. KIN HUBBARD

No self-made man ever did such a good job that some woman didn't want to make a few alterations.

KIN HUBBARD

Women prefer to talk in two's, while men prefer to talk in three's.

G. K. CHESTERTON

It is true that all sensible women think all studious men mad. It is true, for the matter of that, all women of any kind think all men of any kind mad. G. K. CHESTERTON

Women lie about their age; men lie about their income.

WILLIAM FEATHER

Man wants a great deal here below, and woman even more.

JAMES THURBER

See also **Women.**

MERCY

Mercy is better than justice.

VAUVENARGUES

A miscarriage of mercy is as much to be guarded against as a miscarriage of justice. ROBERT LYND

See also **Justice.**

MERIT

Man's merit, like the crops, has its season.   LA ROCHEFOUCAULD

What I like about the Order of the Garter is that there is no damned merit about it.   LORD MELBOURNE

MERRY

Our loving Lord God wills that we eat, drink, and be merry, making use of his creatures, for therefore He created them.   MARTIN LUTHER

I never have a merry thought without being vexed at having to keep it to myself, with nobody to share it.   MONTAIGNE

He was a wise Pope, that when one that was used to be merry with him, before he was advanced to the Popedom, refrained afterwards to come at him, presuming he was busy in governing the Christian world, the Pope sends for him, bids him come again; and, says he, we will be merry as we were before, for thou little thinkest what a little foolery governs the whole world.   JOHN SELDEN

There cannot be too much merriment, but it is always good; but, on the other hand, melancholy is always bad.   SPINOZA

At noon a good venison pasty and a turkey to ourselves without anybody as much as invited by us, a thing unusual for so small a family of my condition: but we did it, and were very merry.   SAMUEL PEPYS

I thank God, who has made me poor, that He has made me merry.   SYDNEY SMITH

See also **Fun, Gay, Laugh, Mirth.**

METAPHYSICS

Let us place at the end of every chapter of metaphysics the two letters used by the Roman judges when they did not understand a pleading: N. L.—*non liquet*—it is not clear.   VOLTAIRE

He had learned to play a few pieces on the metaphysics.   G. C. LICHTENBERG

It is remarkable what a fascination metaphysics seems to possess for the human mind. It is like falling in love. But you get over it after a time.   BENJAMIN JOWETT

Metaphysics is the science of proving what we don't understand.   JOSH BILLINGS

Not to be concerned any longer with great questions is like smoking a pipe, a habit which you take to when age is gaining on you, whereby you believe you are becoming a man although the truth is merely that you have grown old. Happy the man who keeps his youthful appetite for metaphysics.   CHARLES PÉGUY

It is never possible for a metaphysician to state his ideas in plain English.   H. L. MENCKEN

See also **Philosophy.**

MIDDLE AGE

The youth gets together materials for a bridge to the moon, and at length the middle-aged man decides to make a woodshed with them.   HENRY DAVID THOREAU

On the whole, I take it that middle age is a happier period than youth.   ALEXANDER SMITH

For real true love, love at first sight, love to devotion, love that robs a man of his sleep, love that 'will gaze an eagle blind,' love that 'will hear the lowest sound when the suspicious tread of theft is stopped,' love that is 'like a Hercules, still climbing trees in the Hesperides,'—we believe the best age is from forty-five to seventy; up to that, men are generally given to mere flirting.

ANTHONY TROLLOPE

Boys will be boys, and so will a lot of middle-aged men.

KIN HUBBARD

Being middle-aged is a nice change from being young.

DOROTHY CANFIELD FISHER

Perhaps middle age is, or should be, a period of shedding shells; the shell of ambition, the shell of material accumulations and possessions, the shell of the ego.

ANNE MORROW LINDBERGH

See also **Growing Old.**

MIDDLE AGES

In the Middle Ages people were more amused than in our own time.

HENRY ADAMS

The Middle Ages were as unaware of what we mean by the word 'art' as were Greece and Egypt, who had no word for it.

ANDRÉ MALRAUX

See also **Dark Ages.**

MILK

Man should go out of this world as he came in—chiefly on milk.

SIR WILLIAM OSLER

MILLIONAIRE

I'm opposed to millionaires, but it would be dangerous to offer me the position.   MARK TWAIN

I love money; just to be in the room with a millionaire makes me less forlorn.

LOGAN PEARSALL SMITH

See also **Rich.**

MILTON

There are, no doubt, many who have found difficulty in reconciling the critical dictum that the 'Paradise Lost' is to be devoutly admired throughout, with the absolute impossibility of maintaining for it, during perusal, the amount of enthusiasm which that critical dictum would demand.

EDGAR ALLAN POE

Milton cannot have been at all the sort of person one would want to know.   ANGELA THIRKELL

MIND

The perfect man uses his mind like a mirror. It grasps nothing: it refuses nothing. It receives, but does not keep.   CHUANG-TSE

A tamed mind brings happiness.

DHAMMAPADA

As for the passions and studies of the mind: avoid envy; anxious fears; anger fretting inwards; subtile and knotty inquisitions; joys and exhilarations in excess; sadness not communicated. Entertain hopes; mirth rather than joy; variety of delights, rather than surfeit of them; wonder and admiration, and therefore novelties; studies that fill the mind with splendid and illustrious objects, as histories, fables, and contemplations of nature.   FRANCIS BACON

The blemishes of the mind, like those of the face, increase by age.

LA ROCHEFOUCAULD

The health of the mind is no less uncertain than that of the body, and when passions seem furthest removed we are no less in danger of infection than of falling ill when we are well. LA ROCHEFOUCAULD

The defects of the mind are like the wounds of the body. Whatever care we take to heal them, the scars ever remain, and there is always danger of their reopening
LA ROCHEFOUCAULD

Our mind holds the same position in the world of thought as our body occupies in the expanse of nature.
PASCAL

The mind must have some worldly objects to excite its attention, otherwise it will stagnate in indolence, sink into melancholy, or rise into visions and enthusiasm.
LORD CHESTERFIELD

There are minds that resemble those convex or concave mirrors, which represent objects just as they receive them, but which never receive them as they really are.
JOSEPH JOUBERT

Every mind has its dregs.
JOSEPH JOUBERT

The mind of man is like a clock that is always running down, and requires to be as constantly wound up. WILLIAM HAZLITT

There is an unseemly exposure of the mind, as well as of the body.
WILLIAM HAZLITT

The wealth of each mind is proportioned to the number and to the precision of its categories and its points of view. FRÉDÉRIC AMIEL

Our minds want clothes as much as our bodies. SAMUEL BUTLER

When everything has its proper place in our minds, we are able to stand in equilibrium with the rest of the world. FRÉDÉRIC AMIEL

A mental waste-paper basket. Everyone should keep one and the older he grows the more things will he the more promptly consign to it—torn up to irrecoverable tatters. SAMUEL BUTLER

We have, or at any rate think we have, a fairly definite idea before us when we talk of matter, but I don't think we ever think we have any definite idea about our own meaning when we talk of mind.
SAMUEL BUTLER

See also **Brain, Head, Head and Heart, Mind and Body, Mind and Heart, Mind and Matter, Neurosis, Open Mind, Psychoanalysis, Psychology, Soul, Spirit, Thinking.**

MIND AND BODY

A weak mind in a sound body is better, or at least more profitable, than a sound mind in a weak or crazy conformation.
WILLIAM HAZLITT

Body and Mind. We shall never get straight till we leave off trying to separate these two things. Mind is not a thing at all or, if it is, we know nothing about it. It is a function of body. Body is not a thing at all or, if it is, we know nothing about it. It is a function of mind. SAMUEL BUTLER

To me as a physiologist, mind and consciousness seem to be equivalent, and the evidence appears to be strong that mind or consciousness is associated with a limited but shifting area of integrated activity in the cortex of the brain.
WALTER B. CANNON

Mens sana in corpore sano is a foolish saying. The sound body is a product of the sound mind.

GEORGE BERNARD SHAW

See also **Body, Mind.**

MIND AND HEART

Those who know their minds do not necessarily know their hearts.

LA ROCHEFOUCAULD

It is well for the heart to be naïve and for the mind not to be.

ANATOLE FRANCE

See also **Head and Heart.**

MIND AND MATTER

O Nature and O soul of man! how far beyond all utterance are your linked analogies! not the smallest atom stirs or lives in matter, but has its cunning duplicate in mind. HERMAN MELVILLE

MINE

Mine is better than ours.

BENJAMIN FRANKLIN

See also **Egotism, Selfish.**

MINISTER

People wouldn't become ministers unless they had rather second-rate minds. GEORGE SANTAYANA

See also **Clergyman, Parson, Priest.**

MINUTE

Sometimes a man can do in a minute what in other circumstances would take a year.

WILLIAM FEATHER

See also **Moment.**

MIRACLE

Miracles arise from our ignorance of nature, not from nature itself.

MONTAIGNE

Many a man who is now willing to be shot down for the sake of his belief in a miracle, would have doubted, if he had been present, the miracle itself.

G. C. LICHTENBERG

Mysteries are not yet miracles.

GOETHE

Men talk about Bible miracles because there is no miracle in their lives. HENRY DAVID THOREAU

A man after fourteen years' penance in a solitary forest obtained at last the power of walking on water. Overjoyed at this, he went to his guru and said, 'Master, Master, I have acquired the power of walking on water.' The master rebukingly replied, 'Fie, O child! is this the result of thy fourteen years' labour? Verily thou hast obtained only that which is worth a penny; for what thou hast accomplished after fourteen years' arduous labour ordinary men do by paying a penny to the boatman.' RAMAKRISHNA

Jesus' teaching has nothing to do with miracles. If his mission had been simply to demonstrate a new method for restoring lost eyesight, the miracle of curing the blind would have been entirely relevant. But to say 'You should love your enemies; and to convince you of this I will now proceed to cure this gentleman of cataract' would have been, to a man of Jesus' intelligence, the proposition of an idiot.

GEORGE BERNARD SHAW

Science which thinks to make belief in miracles impossible is itself belief in miracles—in the miracles best authenticated by history and by daily life.

GEORGE SANTAYANA

The true miracles are those of man.
ALAIN

t would be a miracle, for example,
f I dropped a stone and it rose
upwards. But is it no miracle that
t falls to the ground?
ALFRED POLGAR

MIRROR

All mirrors are magical mirrors;
never can we see our faces in them.
LOGAN PEARSALL SMITH

MIRTH

t is a good sign that corpulence
and intoxication are no longer considered subjects of mirth but are
now considered either a disease or
a breach of good manners.
GEORGE BERNARD SHAW

The thinkers of the world should
by rights be the guardians of the
world's mirth. AGNES REPPLIER

See also **Gay, Laugh, Merry.**

MISANTHROPE

The real misanthropes are to be
found not in solitude but in society.
GIACOMO LEOPARDI

MISERABLE

One kind of happiness is to know
exactly at what point to be miserable. LA ROCHEFOUCAULD

I sometimes try to be miserable
that I may do more work.
WILLIAM BLAKE

It is seldom that the miserable can
help regarding their misery as a
wrong inflicted by those who are
less miserable. GEORGE ELIOT

The secret of being miserable is to
have leisure to bother about
whether you are happy or not.
GEORGE BERNARD SHAW

MISERY

Misery is almost always the result
of thinking. JOSEPH JOUBERT

MISFORTUNE

Experience has taught me this, that
we undo ourselves by impatience.
Misfortunes have their life and
their limits, their sickness and their
health. MONTAIGNE

Do not wake misfortune when she
sleeps. BALTASAR GRACIÁN

Misfortunes occur only when a man
is false to his genius. . . . Events,
circumstances, etc., have their origin in ourselves. They spring from
seeds which we have sown.
HENRY DAVID THOREAU

Man is born with a tendency to
detect a maximum of contributory
negligence in other people's misfortunes, and nothing but blind
chance in his own.
ARTHUR SCHNITZLER

It is well to treasure the memories
of past misfortunes; they constitute
our bank of fortitude.
ERIC HOFFER

See also **Adversity.**

MISQUOTE

We misquote authors so often
because we have not understood
them. GOETHE

MISSIONARY

Missionaries, my dear! Don't you
realise that missionaries are the
divinely provided food for desti-
tute and underfed cannibals?
Whenever they are on the brink of
starvation, Heaven in its infinite
mercy sends them a nice plump
missionary. OSCAR WILDE

MISTAKE

My brethren, by the bowels of Christ I beseech you, bethink you that you may be mistaken.

OLIVER CROMWELL

Nowadays most people die of a sort of creeping common sense, and discover when it is too late that the only things one never regrets are one's mistakes. OSCAR WILDE

Learn from life and correct your mistakes in living.

CHRISTIAN MORGENSTERN

If I am accused of this mistake, I can only say with M. Clémenceau on a celebrated occasion: 'Perhaps I have made a number of other mistakes of which you have never heard.' WINSTON S. CHURCHILL

It is very easy to forgive others their mistakes; it takes more grit and gumption to forgive them for having witnessed your own.

JESSAMYN WEST

See also **Blunder, Slip.**

MISUNDERSTANDING

Nine-tenths of the serious controversies which arise in life result from misunderstanding, result from one man not knowing the facts which to the other man seem important, or otherwise failing to appreciate his point of view.

LOUIS D. BRANDEIS

MODERATION

I find it as easy to avoid passions as I find it difficult to moderate them.

MONTAIGNE

The moderation of the weak is nothing but mediocrity.

VAUVENARGUES

A reasonable man needs only to practice moderation to find happiness. GOETHE

Nine-tenths of mankind are more afraid of violence than of anything else; and inconsistent moderation is always popular, because of all qualities it is most opposite to violence. WALTER BAGEHOT

See also **Self-Restraint, Temperance.**

MODESTY

The man who is ostentatious of his modesty is twin to the statue that wears a fig-leaf. MARK TWAIN

MOMENT

God enables the humble-minded to understand more of the ways of the everlasting truth in a single moment than ten years of study in the schools. THOMAS À KEMPIS

'Tis one of the great gifts of mind to be able to offer what is needed at the moment. BALTASAR GRACIÁN

Happiness is the moment we don't want to trade in for not-being.

MONTESQUIEU

See also **Minute, Now, Present.**

MONEY

To have enough is good luck, to have more than enough is harmful. This is true of all things, but especially of money. CHUANG-TSE

Taking it all in all, I find it is more trouble to watch after money than to get it. MONTAIGNE

Money in a fool's hand exposes him worse than a pied coat.

LORD HALIFAX

They who are of opinion that money will do everything may very well be suspected to do everything for money. LORD HALIFAX

Emptied a £50 bag, and it was a joy to me to see that I am able to part with such a sum, without much inconvenience; at least, without any trouble of mind.
SAMUEL PEPYS

It is a strange thing to observe and fit for me to remember that I am at no time so unwilling to part with money as when I am concerned in the getting of it most.
SAMUEL PEPYS

There are few ways in which a man can be more innocently employed than in getting money.
SAMUEL JOHNSON

A woman of fortune, being used to the handling of money, spends it judiciously; but a woman who gets the command of money for the first time upon her marriage, has such a gust in spending it that she throws it away with great profusion.
SAMUEL JOHNSON

Even the wisest among men welcome people who bring money more than those who take it away.
G. C. LICHTENBERG

Every *bon mot* that I utter costs me a purseful of money; half a million of my private fortune has passed through my hands that I might learn what I know now;—not only the whole of my father's fortune, but my salary, and my large literary income for more than fifty years.
GOETHE

It is a common observation that any fool can get money; but they are not wise that think so.
C. C. COLTON

As a general rule, nobody has money who ought to have it.
BENJAMIN DISRAELI

The sinews of art and literature, like those of war, are money.
SAMUEL BUTLER

It is not the rich man only who is under the dominion of things; they too are slaves who, having no money, are unhappy from the lack of it.
GEORGE MACDONALD

I cannot afford to waste my time making money.
LOUIS AGASSIZ

A drunkard would not give money to sober people. He said they would only eat it, and buy clothes and send their children to school with it.
SAMUEL BUTLER

Money is the last enemy that shall never be subdued. While there is flesh there is money—or the want of money, but money is always on the brain so long as there is a brain in reasonable order.
SAMUEL BUTLER

As soon as any art is pursued with a view to money, then farewell, in ninety-nine cases out of a hundred, all hope of genuine good work.
SAMUEL BUTLER

The lack of money is the root of all evil.
MARK TWAIN

The price we have to pay for money is paid in liberty.
ROBERT LOUIS STEVENSON

Young people, nowadays, imagine that money is everything, and when they grow older they know it.
OSCAR WILDE

When I think of all the sorrow and the barrenness that has been wrought in my life by want of a few more pounds per annum than I was able to earn, I stand aghast at money's significance.
GEORGE GISSING

Two thirds of the people who can make money are mediocre; and at least one half of them are morally at a low level.
ALFRED NORTH WHITEHEAD

Money and sex are forces too unruly for our reason; they can only be controlled by taboos which we tamper with at our peril.
LOGAN PEARSALL SMITH

When we see what people we like will do for money, it is best to be sad and say nothing.
LOGAN PEARSALL SMITH

As a *man*, I should be disgusted if I could not earn plenty of money and the praise of the discriminating.
ARNOLD BENNETT

The safest way to double your money is to fold it over once and put it in your pocket. KIN HUBBARD

The chief value of money lies in the fact that one lives in a world in which it is overestimated.
H. L. MENCKEN

Many beautiful things have been said about money. One of the best was pulled by a man named L'Estrange, who remarked: 'A narrow fortune is a cramp to a great mind.' You said something, Mr. L'Estrange! WILL CUPPY

When a man needs money, he needs money, and not a headache tablet or a prayer. WILLIAM FEATHER

See also **Capital, Cheque, Cost, Credit, Dollar, Economics, Expensive, Income, Lending, Mammon, Pay, Spending.**

MONK

All men cannot be monks; we have different paths allotted to us to mount to the high seat of eternal felicity. CERVANTES

I have often thought that in the old monkish poverty-worship, in spite of the pedantry which infested it there might be something like that moral equivalent of war which we are seeking. WILLIAM JAMES

See also **Convent.**

MONOPOLY

The holder of a monopoly is a sinner and offender. MOHAMMED

MONOTONY

Monotony is the law of nature Look at the monotonous manner in which the sun rises. . . . The monotony of necessary occupations is exhilarating and life-giving.
GANDHI

Nature abhors monotony as much as she abhors a vacuum.
JOSEPH WOOD KRUTCH

MONTAIGNE

He knows that life is full of bitters and he holds it wisdom that a man should console himself, as far as possible, with its sweets, the principal of which are peace, travel leisure, and the writing of essays.
ALEXANDER SMITH

MOON

If you go expressly to look at the moon, it becomes tinsel.
RALPH WALDO EMERSON

Moonlight is sculpture.
NATHANIEL HAWTHORNE

Every one is a moon and has a dark side which he never shows to anybody. MARK TWAIN

Among the more elderly inhabitants of the South I found a melancholy tendency to date every event of importance on the late War. 'How

beautiful the moon is tonight,' I
once remarked to a gentleman
standing near me. 'Yes,' was his
reply, 'but you should have seen it
before the War.'   OSCAR WILDE

Moonshine is all moonshine to me.
LOGAN PEARSALL SMITH

MORAL

'Tut, tut, child!' said the Duchess.
'Everything's got a moral, if only
you can find it.'   LEWIS CARROLL

MORALITY

There is but one morality, as there
is but one geometry.   VOLTAIRE

Go into the street, and give one
man a lecture on morality, and
another a shilling, and see which
will respect you most.
SAMUEL JOHNSON

The only moral lesson which is
suited for a child—the most important lesson for every time of
life—is this: 'Never hurt anybody.'
ROUSSEAU

The world is, and must be, moral;
for when people grow up and get
married, they teach their children
to be *moral*. No man wishes to
have them turn out profligate.
JAMES NORTHCOTE

Many a man has been hindered
from pushing his fortune in the
world by an early cultivation of his
moral sense, and repented of it at
leisure during the rest of his life.
WILLIAM HAZLITT

Morality is the custom of one's
country and the current feeling of
one's peers. Cannibalism is moral
in a cannibal country.
SAMUEL BUTLER

Foundations of morality are like all
other foundations; if you dig too
much about them the superstruc-
ture will come tumbling down.
SAMUEL BUTLER

It is more moral to be behind the
age than in advance of it.
SAMUEL BUTLER

If your morals make you dreary,
depend upon it they are wrong.
ROBERT LOUIS STEVENSON

Morality is simply the attitude we
adopt toward people whom we
personally dislike.   OSCAR WILDE

There is a moral sense and there is
an immoral sense. History shows
us that the moral sense enables us
to perceive morality and how to
avoid it, and that the immoral
sense enables us to perceive immorality and how to enjoy it.
MARK TWAIN

My ideal man never would think
about morality. He naturally would
do the kind, generous, splendid
thing. While in all other depart-
ments we prefer native gifts to
industry (which is also a gift of a
less specialized sort), we have a
queer notion that in morality
industry is better than genius.
OLIVER WENDELL HOLMES, JR.

Moral education is impossible without the habitual vision of greatness.
ALFRED NORTH WHITEHEAD

Morality is moral only when it is
voluntary.   LINCOLN STEFFENS

Morality is the theory that every
human act must be either right or
wrong and that ninety-nine per
cent of them are wrong.
H. L. MENCKEN

'Out with it, Tarrou! What on earth prompted you to take a hand in this?' 'I don't know. My code of morals, perhaps.' 'Your code of morals? What code?' 'Comprehension.' ALBERT CAMUS
See also **Ethics, Golden Rule, Immoral.**

MORNING

Pastime, like wine, is poison in the morning. THOMAS FULLER

MOTHER

A mother who is really a mother is never free. HONORÉ DE BALZAC

Nobody can misunderstand a boy like his own mother
NORMAN DOUGLAS
See also **Parents.**

MOTIVE

Man sees your actions, but God your motives. THOMAS À KEMPIS

Motives are generally unknown.
SAMUEL JOHNSON
When anyone takes great pleasure in doing a thing it is almost always from some motive other than the ostensible one.
G. C. LICHTENBERG
Often we think we believe a thing, and yet do not believe it. Nothing is more impenetrable than the motivation of our actions.
G. C. LICHTENBERG
No man does anything from a single motive.
SAMUEL TAYLOR COLERIDGE
It is a fallacy, I think, to look to any theory for motives—we get our motives from our spontaneity—and the business of philosophy is to show that we are not fools for doing what we do.
OLIVER WENDELL HOLMES, JR.

Whenever a man does a thoroughly stupid thing, it is always from the noblest of motives. OSCAR WILDE

If we always knew from what motives our profoundest convictions have sprung! NORMAN DOUGLAS

He was a man who acted from the best motives. There is one born every minute. P. G. WODEHOUSE

MOUNTAIN

There are many paths to the top of the mountain, but the view is always the same.
CHINESE PROVERB
We are all insane, anyway. Note the mountain climbers. MARK TWAIN

If there be any value in scaling the mountains, it is only that from them one can behold the plains.
G. K. CHESTERTON

MOVE

I don't like disorder, but I am exasperated by those who shout 'Don't move' when no one is yet in place. ANDRÉ GIDE

MOZART

Play Mozart in memory of me.
LAST WORDS OF CHOPIN

MUCH

Too much noise deafens us; too much light dazzles us; too much distance or too much proximity impedes vision; too much length or too much brevity of discourse obscures it; too much truth astonishes us. PASCAL

The greatest secret of good work whether in music, literature or art lies in not attempting too much; if it is asked, 'What is too much?' the answer is, 'Anything that we find difficult or unpleasant.'
SAMUEL BUTLER
See also **Excess.**

MUD

As rivers which run very slowly have always the most mud at the bottom, so a solid stiffness in the constant course of a man's life is a sign of a thick bed of mud at the bottom of his brain.

LORD HALIFAX

MUDDLE-HEADED

It is difficult to be muddle-headed. It is difficult to be clever, but still more difficult to graduate from cleverness into muddle-headedness.

CHENG PANCH'IAO

Muddle-headedness is a condition precedent to independent thought.

ALFRED NORTH WHITEHEAD

MUDDLING THROUGH

The English know how to make the best of things. Their so-called muddling through is simply skill at dealing with the inevitable.

H. L. MENCKEN

MULTITUDE

The angry buzz of a multitude is one of the bloodiest noises in the world.

LORD HALIFAX

To succeed in chaining the multitude, you must seem to wear the same fetters.

VOLTAIRE

See also **Crowd.**

MURDER

When we execute a murderer, it may be that we fall into the same mistake as the child that strikes a chair it has collided with.

G. C. LICHTENBERG

If once a man indulges himself in murder, very soon he comes to think very little of robbing; and from robbing he comes next to drinking and Sabbath breaking, and from that to incivility and pro-

crastination. Once begin upon this downward path, you never know where you are to stop. Many a man has dated his ruin from some murder or other that perhaps he thought little of at the time.

THOMAS DE QUINCEY

Everything in the world has two handles. Murder, for instance, may be laid hold of by its moral handle (as it generally is in the pulpit, and at the Old Bailey); and *that*, I confess, is its weak side; or it may also be treated *aesthetically*, as the Germans call it, that is, in relation to good taste. THOMAS DE QUINCEY

If the desire to kill and the opportunity to kill came always together, who would escape hanging?

MARK TWAIN

We welcome almost any break in the monotony of things, and a man has only to murder a series of wives in a new way to become known to millions of people who have never heard of Homer. ROBERT LYND

See also **Crime.**

MUSIC

Virtue is the strong stem of man's nature, and music is the blossoming of virtue. CONFUCIUS

Music produces a kind of pleasure which human nature cannot do without. CONFUCIUS

There can be no mischief sure where there is music. CERVANTES

Nevertheless, the passions, whether violent or not, should never be so expressed as to reach the point of causing disgust; and music, even in situations of the greatest horror, *should never be painful to the ear but should flatter and charm it, and thereby always remain music.* MOZART

Listen to music religiously, as if it were the last strain you might hear.
HENRY DAVID THOREAU

The best sort of music is what it should be—sacred; the next best, the military, has fallen to the lot of the devil.
SAMUEL TAYLOR COLERIDGE

Music is the sound of universal laws promulgated.
HENRY DAVID THOREAU

When I hear music I fear no danger, I am invulnerable, I see no foe. I am related to the earliest times, and to the latest.
HENRY DAVID THOREAU

Music fathoms the sky.
CHARLES BAUDELAIRE

To know whether you are enjoying a piece of music or not you must see whether you find yourself looking at the advertisements of Pears' soap at the end of the libretto.
SAMUEL BUTLER

The best music should be played as the best men and women should be dressed—neither so well nor so ill as to attract attention to itself.
SAMUEL BUTLER

We often feel sad in the presence of music without words; and often more than that in the presence of music without music.
MARK TWAIN

And the minute the words were out of his mouth somebody over in the crowd struck up the doxolojer, and everybody joined in with all their might, and it just warmed you up and made you feel as good as church letting out. Music *is* a good thing; and after all that soul-butter and hogwash I never see it freshen up things so, and sound so honest and bully.
MARK TWAIN

When people hear good music, it makes them homesick for something they never had, and never will have.
E. W. HOWE

After playing Chopin, I feel as if I had been weeping over sins that I had never committed, and mourning over tragedies that were not my own. Music always seems to me to produce that effect. It creates for one a past of which one has been ignorant and fills one with a sense of sorrows that have been hidden from one's tears.
OSCAR WILDE

I am highly susceptible to the force of all truly religious music, especially to the music of my own church, the church of Shelley, Michelangelo, and Beethoven.
GEORGE BERNARD SHAW

Music comes before religion, as emotion comes before thought, and sound before sense. What is the first thing you hear when you go into a church? The organ playing.
ALFRED NORTH WHITEHEAD

Classic music is the kind that we keep thinking will turn into a tune.
KIN HUBBARD

After silence that which comes nearest to expressing the inexpressible is music.
ALDOUS HUXLEY

See also **Bruckner, Fiddle, Mozart, Opera, Oratorio.**

MUST

I have great trouble getting beyond the first paragraph of articles which begin 'The time is coming, if indeed it is not already here, when the American people must . . .' From my experience I am able to make the following generalisations,

sometimes known as Morton's Law: 1. The American people must do no such thing, or 2. They have already done it or decided not to do it, a circumstance to which the author is not privy.
CHARLES W. MORTON

MUTABILITY

Naught may endure but Mutability.
SHELLEY

See also **Change.**

MYSTERIOUS

The most beautiful experience we can have is the mysterious. It is the fundamental emotion which stands at the cradle of true art and true science. ALBERT EINSTEIN

MYSTERY

The world of the living contains enough marvels and mysteries as it is; marvels and mysteries acting upon our emotions and intelligence in ways so inexplicable that it would almost justify the conception of life as an enchanted state.
JOSEPH CONRAD

India! What mysteries does the very mention of its name not bring to mind? (Answer: Mysteries of the Deep, Mysteries of the Arctic Wastes, the Lizzie Borden Mystery, and Sweet Mystery of Life.)
ROBERT BENCHLEY

MYSTICISM

Mysticism has not the patience to wait for God's revelation.
SÖREN KIERKEGAARD

It is not worldly ecclesiastics that kindle the fires of persecution, but mystics who think they hear the voice of God. GEORGE SANTAYANA

The simplest rudiment of mystical experience would seem to be that deepened sense of the significance of a maxim or formula which occasionally sweeps over one.
WILLIAM JAMES

The union of scepticism and yearning begets mysticism.
FRIEDRICH NIETZSCHE

Mysticism is not a religion but a religious disease.
GEORGE SANTAYANA

Mysticism is usually an incurable disease. GEORGE SANTAYANA

Mysticism, the hyphen between paganism and Christianity.
CHARLES BAUDELAIRE

Mysticism keeps men sane.
G. K. CHESTERTON

There is a hard clear rationality about Quakers—and, indeed, all mysticism, which, once experienced, makes other ways appear indirect, childish, and crude.
JESSAMYN WEST

See also **Religion.**

MYTH

You cannot really understand any myths till you have found out that one of them is not a myth.
G. K. CHESTERTON

N

NAME

A man that should call everything by its right name, would hardly pass the streets without being knocked down as a common enemy.
LORD HALIFAX

'Of course they answer to their names?' the Gnat remarked carelessly. 'I never knew them to do it.' 'What's the use of their having names,' the Gnat said, 'if they won't answer to them?' LEWIS CARROLL

Some men complain about the queerest things. W. T. Hawley, of this neighbourhood, does not like to be called Will; he says it sounds effeminate. Nor does he like to be called Bill. He says it sounds too rough. E. W. HOWE

Sam Johnson is hardly a name for a great writer.
GEORGE BERNARD SHAW

Our names are labels, plainly printed on the bottled essence of our past behaviour.
LOGAN PEARSALL SMITH

An evil name—a drawback at first —sheds lustre on old age.
LOGAN PEARSALL SMITH

When a woman says, 'I don't wish to mention any names,' it ain't necessary. KIN HUBBARD

God created things by naming them; the artist recreates them by taking their name off or giving them a new one. MARCEL PROUST

When Rotary began to spread over the world, taking the great boons and usufructs of American *Kultur* with it, the given-name habit went along, and no doubt it was as influential as any other Rotarian idea in preventing World War II.
H. L. MENCKEN

The first Rotarian was the first man to call John the Baptist Jack.
H. L. MENCKEN

We were named by a certain Professor Waldseemüller, who got all mixed up in his facts and thought the credit belonged to Amerigo Vespucci, which it didn't at all. So Professor Waldseemüller gave the name of America to the New World in a geography that he published in 1507, and from that day to this nobody has ever had time to fix it. Isn't that the way things go in this world? WILL CUPPY

People who specialize in knowing the names of birds and flowers are always in a ferment, because they are always running up against some variety which stumps them.
ROBERT BENCHLEY
See also **Title.**

NAP

The pleasure of an afternoon nap is double that of sleep at night.
LIWENG

I never take a nap after dinner but when I have had a bad night, and then the nap takes me.
SAMUEL JOHNSON

There is more refreshment and stimulation in a nap, even of the briefest, than in all the alcohol ever distilled. E. V. LUCAS
See also **Dozing, Sleep.**

NAPOLEON

God was bored by him.
VICTOR HUGO

Bonaparte was a lion in the field only. In civil life, a cold-blooded, calculating, unprincipled usurper, without a virtue; no statesman, knowing nothing of commerce, political economy, or civil government, and supplying ignorance by bold presumption.
THOMAS JEFFERSON

Napoleon had himself the illusions which he gave to the people. This was his strength and his weakness, this was his beauty.
ANATOLE FRANCE

The Napoleonic legend is the triumph of vulgarity.

ANATOLE FRANCE

A galley-slave has a happier life than Napoleon. He worked everywhere and always; at table, at the theatre, in his carriage, in his bath. He hardly slept three hours at night. He wore everyone out. He was not a man, but a machine.

ANATOLE FRANCE

This dark little archaic personage, hard, compact, capable, unscrupulous, imitative, and neatly vulgar.

H. G. WELLS

NATION

We do not know a nation until we know its pleasures of life, just as we do not know a man until we know how he spends his leisure.

LIN YUTANG

NATIONAL

Altogether, national hatred is something peculiar. You will always find it strongest and most violent where there is the lowest degree of culture.   GOETHE

NATIONALISM

Nationalism in every country requires a strong admixture of internationalism to prevent its becoming a stupefying drug.

G. W. RUSSELL (Æ)

The technical advances which are common to all nations strip them more and more of their national characteristics. Therefore they become nationalist. Modern nationalism is a defensive movement against the crude encroachments of civilization.   FRANZ KAFKA

NATURAL

Make for the shortest path, which is that of nature; in other words, healthiness in every speech and action. For a man with this aim in life is free from all doubt and vexation, all thought of ways and means and all pretence.

MARCUS AURELIUS

Being natural is simply a pose, and the most irritating pose I know.

OSCAR WILDE

NATURAL LAW

People make the mistake of talking about 'natural laws.' There *are* no natural laws. There are only temporary habits of nature.

ALFRED NORTH WHITEHEAD

It helps to remind oneself very often that over everything that exists there are laws which never fail to operate, which come rushing, rather, to manifest and prove themselves upon every stone and upon every feather we let fall. So all erring consists simply in the failure to recognize the natural laws to which we are subject in the given instance, and every solution begins with our alertness and concentration, which gently draw us into the chain of events and restore to our will its balancing counterweights.   RAINER MARIA RILKE

See also **Law, Nature.**

NATURE

We cannot fail in following nature.

MONTAIGNE

I always think of nature as a great spectacle, somewhat resembling the opera.

BERNARD DE FONTENELLE

A blade of grass is always a blade of grass. Men and women are *my* subjects of inquiry.

SAMUEL JOHNSON

Nature is visible thought.

HEINRICH HEINE

The love of nature is the only love that does not deceive human hopes.

HONORÉ DE BALZAC

The permanent interest of every man is, never to be in a false position, but to have the weight of nature to back him in all he does.

RALPH WALDO EMERSON

One day when Cézanne was picnicking in the country with some friends and a collector, the latter suddenly realized that he had dropped his overcoat somewhere on the way. Cézanne raked the landscape with his gaze, then exclaimed: 'I'll swear that black over there doesn't belong to nature!' Sure enough it was the overcoat.

ANDRÉ MALRAUX

'I only assisted natur', ma'am, as the doctor said to the boy's mother, arter he'd bled him to death.'

CHARLES DICKENS

He approaches the study of mankind with great advantages who is accustomed to the study of nature.

HENRY DAVID THOREAU

There is no other door to knowledge than the door nature opens; there is no truth except the truths we discover in nature.

LUTHER BURBANK

See also **Country, Human Nature, Natural, Natural Law, Scenery, Tree.**

NECESSARY

The vast majority of our words and deeds are unnecessary. Eliminate them, and how much toil and trouble will vanish with them! Therefore, on every occasion, let's ask ourselves, 'Is this necessary?'

MARCUS AURELIUS

In so far as we understand, we can desire nothing save that which is necessary.

SPINOZA

All that is necessary, providential, in short, *unimputable*, I could bear, I think, with some strength of mind. But responsibility mortally envenoms grief; and as an act is essentially voluntary, therefore I act as little as possible.

FRÉDÉRIC AMIEL

It is no use saying 'We are doing our best.' You have got to succeed in doing what is necessary.

WINSTON S. CHURCHILL

See also **Luxury.**

NECESSITY

Necessity is a better pain-killer than thinking. VAUVENARGUES

If you would have your actions in accordance with what is right, allow yourself to fall in with the dictates of necessity. CHUANG-TSE

A wise man will see to it that his acts always seem voluntary and not done by compulsion, however much he may be compelled by necessity. MACHIAVELLI

To try to kick against natural necessity is to repeat the folly of Ctesiphon, who undertook to outkick his mule. MONTAIGNE

Necessity frees us from the embarrassment of choice.

VAUVENARGUES

Great necessity elevates man, petty necessity casts him down.

GOETHE

A man's power is hooped in by necessity, which, by many experiments, he touches on every side, until he learns its arc.

RALPH WALDO EMERSON

Necessity is the mother of 'taking chances.' MARK TWAIN

Even the most winged spirit cannot escape physical necessity.

KAHLIL GIBRAN

Necessity is God's veil.

SIMONE WEIL

See also **Inevitable.**

NEEDLE

No needle is sharp at both ends.

CHINESE PROVERB

NEGRO

Some Negroes who believe the resurrection, think that they shall rise white. SIR THOMAS BROWNE

The Negro, thanks to his temperament, appears to make the greatest amount of happiness out of the smallest capital.

RALPH WALDO EMERSON

'. . . We blowed out a cylinder head.' 'Good gracious! Anybody hurt?' 'No'm. Killed a nigger.' 'Well, it's lucky; because sometimes people do get hurt.'

MARK TWAIN

NEIGHBOUR

Everyone in this world has as much as they can do in caring for themselves, and few have leisure really to think of their neighbour's distresses, however they may delight their tongues with talking of them.

SAMUEL JOHNSON

With all humility, I think 'Whatsoever thy hand findeth to do, do it with thy might' infinitely more important than the vain attempt to love one's neighbour as one's self.

OLIVER WENDELL HOLMES, JR.

The love of humanity as such is mitigated by violent dislike of the next-door neighbour.

ALFRED NORTH WHITEHEAD

We make our friends; we make our enemies; but God makes our next-door neighbour. G. K. CHESTERTON

There is more pleasure in being shocked by the sin of one's neighbour or one's neighbour's wife than in eating cream buns.

ROBERT LYND

NERO

Nero renamed the month of April after himself, calling it Neroneus, but the idea never caught on because April is not Neroneus and there is no use pretending that it is.

WILL CUPPY

NEUROSIS

Everything great in the world comes from neurotics. They alone have founded our religions and composed our masterpieces.

MARCEL PROUST

The true believer is in a high degree protected against the danger of certain neurotic afflictions; by accepting the universal neurosis he is spared the task of forming a personal neurosis. SIGMUND FREUD

The mistake which is commonly made about neurotics is to suppose that they are interesting. It is not interesting to be always unhappy, engrossed with oneself, ungrateful and malignant, and never quite in touch with reality.

CYRIL CONNOLLY

NEW

The glory of novelty is short-lived; after four days respect is gone.

BALTASAR GRACIÁN

When I was young, I thought all the world, as well as myself, was wholly taken up in discoursing upon the last new play.
  JONATHAN SWIFT

Few moments are more pleasing than those in which the mind is concerting measures for a new undertaking. SAMUEL JOHNSON

I hate to read new books.
  WILLIAM HAZLITT

Anybody amuses me for once. A new acquaintance is like a new book. I prefer it, even if bad, to a classic. BENJAMIN DISRAELI

How people love an old saying! They are always quoting 'There is nothing new under the sun,' yet there is something new every day.
  E. W. HOWE

There is nothing new in the world except the history you do not know.
  HARRY S. TRUMAN

To the old, the new is usually bad news. ERIC HOFFER

See also **Innovation, New Idea, Novice, Old.**

NEW IDEA

Sorrow is a kind of rust of the soul, which every new idea contributes in its passage to scour away.
  SAMUEL JOHNSON

One of the greatest pains to human nature is the pain of a new idea.
  WALTER BAGEHOT

Every new idea has something of the pain and peril of childbirth about it. SAMUEL BUTLER

The man with a new idea is a crank until the idea succeeds.
  MARK TWAIN

A new untruth is better than an old truth.
  OLIVER WENDELL HOLMES, JR.

First a new theory is attacked as absurd; then it is admitted to be true, but obvious and insignificant; finally it is seen to be so important that its adversaries claim that they themselves discovered it.
  WILLIAM JAMES

Almost all really new ideas have a certain aspect of foolishness when they are first produced.
  ALFRED NORTH WHITEHEAD

New and stirring things are belittled, because if they are not belittled the humiliating question arises, 'Why then are you not taking part in them?'
  H. G. WELLS

New ideas cannot be administered successfully by men with old ideas, for the first essential of doing a job well is the wish to see the job done at all. FRANKLIN D. ROOSEVELT

See also **Innovation.**

NEW YORK

Many a New Yorker spends a lifetime within the confines of an area smaller than a country village. Let him walk two blocks from his corner and he is in a strange land and will feel uneasy till he gets back. E. B. WHITE

NEWS

Wait for the second or even the third edition of news.
  BALTASAR GRACIÁN

The dull period in the life of an event is when it ceases to be news and has not begun to be history.
  THOMAS HARDY

Nobody knows what news is important until a hundred years afterwards.   FRIEDRICH NIETZSCHE

There ain't any news in being good. You might write the doings of all the convents of the world on the back of a postage stamp, and have room to spare.
FINLEY PETER DUNNE

Listening four or five times a day to broadcasters and commentators, reading the morning papers and all the weeklies and monthlies—nowadays this is described as 'taking an intelligent interest in politics.' St. John of the Cross would have called it indulgence in idle curiosity and the cultivation of disquietude for disquietude's sake. ALDOUS HUXLEY

NEWSPAPERS

Newspapers always excite curiosity. No one ever lays one down without a feeling of disappointment.
CHARLES LAMB

Nation: A group of men who speak one language and read the same newspapers.
FRIEDRICH NIETZSCHE

I have no time to read newspapers.
HENRY DAVID THOREAU

Amid the vast unimportance of all things, how beyond all calculation important we find it each morning to have at hand, as we sit facing Time and Eternity, an adequate supply of thin paper!
LOGAN PEARSALL SMITH

See also **Press.**

NIAGARA FALLS

Niagara Falls is simply a vast unnecessary amount of water going the wrong way and then falling over unnecessary rocks.
OSCAR WILDE

NIGHT

Observe how much our so-called civilization dulls natural feeling. Hector says to Ajax, Book VII, as he leaves the combat: 'The night is already advanced, and we must all obey night, which sets a limit for the works of men.'
EUGÈNE DELACROIX

Man drinks in light along with the atmosphere. That is why people are right in saying that night air is unhealthy for work.
CHARLES BAUDELAIRE

'Undress,' as George Herbert says, 'your soul at night,' not by self-examination, but by shedding, as you do your garments, the daily sins whether of omission or commission, and you will wake a free man, with a new life.
SIR WILLIAM OSLER

The worst sensation I know of is getting up at night and stepping on a toy train of cars.   KIN HUBBARD

NO

Say, Not so, and you will outcircle the philosophers.
HENRY DAVID THOREAU

If you can't say no, you can't expect to live within your income.
WILLIAM FEATHER

See also **Denial, Refuse, Yes and No.**

NOISE

Two pieces of coin in a bag make more noise than a hundred.
TALMUD

True happiness is of a retired nature, and an enemy to pomp and noise.   JOSEPH ADDISON

Everybody has their taste in noises as well as in other matters.

JANE AUSTEN

Noise proves nothing. Often a hen who has merely laid an egg cackles as if she had laid an asteroid.

MARK TWAIN

Noise: A stench in the ear. Undomesticated music. The chief product and authenticating sign of civilization.　AMBROSE BIERCE

NONSENSE

There are thousands who can see that a statement is nonsense and yet are quite unable to disprove it formally.　G. C. LICHTENBERG

Everything has another side to it, like the moon, the patroness of nonsense. Viewed from that other side, a bird is a blossom broken loose from its chain of stalk, a man a quadruped begging on its hind legs, a house a gigantesque hat to cover a man from the sun, a chair an apparatus of four wooden legs for a cripple with only two. This is the side of things which tends most truly to spiritual wonder.

G. K. CHESTERTON

Good nonsense is good sense in disguise.　JOSH BILLINGS

There is no greater mistake in the world than the looking upon every sort of nonsense as want of sense.

LEIGH HUNT

The wisest thing to do with a fool is to encourage him to hire a hall and discourse to his fellow citizens. Nothing chills nonsense like exposure to the air.

WOODROW WILSON

Nonsense is an assertion of man's spiritual freedom in spite of all the oppression of circumstance.

ALDOUS HUXLEY

NON-SMOKER

Smokers and non-smokers cannot be equally free in the same railway carriage.　GEORGE BERNARD SHAW

It was a non-smoker who committed the first sin and brought death into the world and all our woe. Nero was a non-smoker. Lady Macbeth was a non-smoker. Decidedly, the record of the non-smokers leaves them little to be proud of.　ROBERT LYND

See also **Smoking.**

NON-VIOLENCE

Non-violence is no good unless it is effective.　SIMONE WEIL

NORMAL

What is normal is at once most convenient, most honest, and most wholesome.　FRÉDÉRIC AMIEL

One of the greatest fallacies of near-science and of amateurs in Nature's school is the belief that only from the normal can we get our best development and results.

LUTHER BURBANK

The normal is what you find but rarely.　W. SOMERSET MAUGHAM

The artist is the only one who has normal vision.

GEORGE BERNARD SHAW

See also **Average, Mediocre, Ordinary.**

NOT GOING

One of the delights known to age and beyond the grasp of youth is that of *Not Going*.

J. B. PRIESTLEY

See also **Going, Leaving.**

NOT KNOWING

Shall I teach you what knowledge is? When you know a thing, to hold that you know it; and when you don't know a thing, to allow that you don't know it. This is knowledge. CONFUCIUS

Teach thy tongue to say, 'I do not know.' TALMUD

I do not know much, but if I knew a good deal less than that little I should be much more powerful. SAMUEL BUTLER

I was nearly forty before I felt how stupid it was to pretend to know things I did not know, and I still often catch myself doing so. Not one of my schoolmasters taught me this, but otherwise. SAMUEL BUTLER

I was gratified to be able to answer promptly and I did. I said I didn't know. MARK TWAIN

The average value of conversations could be enormously improved by the constant use of four simple words: 'I do not know,' or of Louis XIV's favourite remark: 'I shall see.' ANDRÉ MAUROIS

Unhappiness is in not knowing what we want and killing ourselves to get it. DON HEROLD

I have no knowledge whatever of the sciences, in which I once received a thorough if rudimentary instruction. . . . I once knew German and read Goethe and Heine. Now I doubt if I could ask for a bed or a cigar in that tongue. I have forgotten nearly all the history and philosophy I once knew (and I made these subjects my special study at one time). . . . I never knew anything about Nature, flowers and birds and trees and so forth, and if I lived to be a thousand I could never become one of those persons who can tell you what anything is at a glance. J. B. PRIESTLEY

See also **Ignorance, Knowing.**

NOT UNDERSTANDING

Sometimes it proves the highest understanding not to understand. BALTASAR GRACIÁN

Lack of understanding is a great power. Sometimes it enables men to conquer the world. ANATOLE FRANCE

See also **Incomprehensible, Misunderstanding, Understanding.**

NOTHING

Great things can be reduced to small things, and small things can be reduced to nothing. CHINESE PROVERB

He has all that makes nothing of what is nothing to him. BALTASAR GRACIÁN

Almost everything comes from almost nothing. FRÉDÉRIC AMIEL

It is extraordinary to what an expense of time and money people will go in order to get something for nothing. ROBERT LYND

Nothing matters to a man who says nothing matters. LIN YUTANG

People seem to me to be happiest when they are working for nothing and can afford to do so. ROBERT LYND

See also **Doing Nothing.**

NOTION

Notions will hurt none but those that have them.

OLIVER CROMWELL

See also **Idea, Opinion.**

NOTORIETY

Men often mistake notoriety for fame, and would rather be remarked for their vices and follies than not to be noticed at all!

HARRY S. TRUMAN

See also **Fame.**

NOVEL

In writing novels and plays the cardinal rule is to treat one's characters as if they were chessmen, and not to try to win the game by altering the rules—for example, by moving the knight as if he were a pawn.   G. C. LICHTENBERG

The best part of our lives we pass in counting on what is to come; or in fancying what may have happened in real or fictitious story to others. I have had more pleasure in reading the adventures of a novel than I ever had in my own.

WILLIAM HAZLITT

There is but one standard English novel, like the one orthodox sermon.   RALPH WALDO EMERSON

Much pessimism is caused by ascribing to others the feelings you would feel if you were in their place. It is this (among much else) that makes novels so false.

W. SOMERSET MAUGHAM

We read a good novel not in order to know more people, but in order to know fewer.

G. K. CHESTERTON

See also **Books, Books and Reading, Literature, Reading.**

NOVICE

When a person excels at something he should do something else in which he is a novice because that brings him down to earth.

GEORGE BERNARD SHAW

See also **New.**

NOW

It is *now* and in *this world* that we must live.   ANDRÉ GIDE

I think it truth that a life uncommanded now is uncommanded; a life unenjoyed now is unenjoyed; a life not lived wisely now is not lived wisely: for the past is gone and no one knows the future.

DAVID GRAYSON

It is good for one to appreciate that life is now. Whatever it offers, little or much, life is now—this day— this hour—and is probably the only experience of the kind one is to have. As the doctor said to the woman who complained that she did not like the night air: 'Madam, during certain hours of the twenty-four, night air is the only air there is."   CHARLES MACOMB FLANDRAU

We are here and it is now: further than that all human knowledge is moonshine.   H. L. MENCKEN

See also **Minute, Moment, Present.**

O

OATH

Oaths are the fossils of piety.

GEORGE SANTAYANA

Oath: In law, a solemn appeal to the deity, made binding upon the conscience by a penalty for perjury.

AMBROSE BIERCE

Take not God's name in vain; select a time when it will have effect.
AMBROSE BIERCE

See also **Profanity.**

OBEDIENCE

Whoever strives to withdraw from obedience, withdraws from grace.
THOMAS À KEMPIS

He who is born to obey will obey even on a throne. VAUVENARGUES

There is real greatness in knowing how to obey and admire.
HONORÉ DE BALZAC

Of obedience, faith, adhesiveness;
As I stand aloof and look, there is to me something profoundly affecting in large masses of men, following the lead of those who do not believe in men.
WALT WHITMAN

The distinguishing mark of religion is not so much liberty as obedience, and its value is measured by the sacrifices which it can extract from the individual. FRÉDÉRIC AMIEL

See also **Command.**

OBLIGATION

Benefits oblige and obligation is thraldom. THOMAS HOBBES

Too great a hurry to discharge an obligation is a kind of ingratitude.
LA ROCHEFOUCAULD

When some men discharge an obligation, you can hear the report for miles around. MARK TWAIN

To serve God is not to pass our lives on our knees in prayer; it is to discharge on earth those obligations which our duty requires.
ROUSSEAU

OBSCURITY (BEING UNKNOWN)

Only the perfect man can go about in the modern world without attracting attention to himself.
CHUANG-TSE

It is better to live in obscurity and to seek the salvation of his soul, than to neglect this even to work miracles. THOMAS À KEMPIS

If I could I would always work in silence and obscurity, and let my efforts be known by their results.
EMILY BRONTË

Obscurity and a competence—that is the life that is best worth living.
MARK TWAIN

See also **Unknown.**

OBSCURITY (LACK OF CLARITY)

Obscurity is the realm of error.
VAUVENARGUES

If only we could train our children so that whatever is obscure would be quite unintelligible to them!
G. C. LICHTENBERG

Before you blame an author for his obscurity, look into your own mind to see whether it is quite clear. The plainest writing becomes illegible in the dusk. GOETHE

Many things have to be said obscurely before they can be said clearly. HENRY JAMES

See also **Clear.**

OBSERVATION

Observation is an old man's memory. JONATHAN SWIFT

'Before turning to those moral or mental aspects of the matter which present the greatest difficulties, let the inquirer begin by mastering more elementary problems. Let him, on meeting a fellow-mortal, learn at a glance to distinguish the history of the man, and the trade or profession to which he belongs. Puerile as such an exercise may seem, it sharpens the faculties of observation and teaches one where to look and what to look for. By a man's fingernails, by his coat-sleeve, by his boots, by his trouser-knees, by the callosities of his fore-finger and thumb, by his expression, by his shirt-cuffs—by each of these things a man's calling is plainly revealed. That all united should fail to enlighten the competent inquirer in any case is almost inconceivable.'

ARTHUR CONAN DOYLE

OBVIOUS

No question is so difficult to answer as that to which the answer is obvious. GEORGE BERNARD SHAW

It requires a very unusual mind to undertake the analysis of the obvious. ALFRED NORTH WHITEHEAD

The obvious is usually what is most thoroughly forgotten and most rarely done.

CHRISTIAN MORGENSTERN

The obvious is that which is never seen until someone expresses it simply. KAHLIL GIBRAN

The course of every intellectual, if he pursues his journey long and un-flinchingly enough, ends in the obvious, from which the non-intellectuals have never stirred.

ALDOUS HUXLEY

To spell out the obvious is often to call it in question. ERIC HOFFER

ODD

The extreme oddness of existence is what reconciles me to it.

LOGAN PEARSALL SMITH

OFFEND

Take care how thou offendest men raised from low condition.

DR. THOMAS FULLER

OFFICE

He that holds public office is no more or less than a public slave.

BALTASAR GRACIÁN

Public employment contributes neither to advantage nor to happiness. It is but honourable exile from one's family and affairs.

THOMAS JEFFERSON

A friend of mine says that every man who takes office in Washington either grows or swells, and when I give a man an office, I watch him carefully to see whether he is swelling or growing.

WOODROW WILSON

OFFICIAL

Nothing, nothing, nothing, no error, no crime is so absolutely repugnant to God as everything which is official; and why? because the official is impersonal and therefore the deepest insult which can be offered to a personality.

SÖREN KIERKEGAARD

OLD

Old friends are best, King James used to call for his old shoes; they were easiest for his feet.

JOHN SELDEN

All the mischief in the world may be put down very plausibly to old laws, old customs, and old religions.

G. C. LICHTENBERG

Let us not be too particular; it is better to have old second-hand diamonds than none at all.

MARK TWAIN

I love the old, I like to have books in my library that were on shelves before America was discovered.

OLIVER WENDELL HOLMES, JR.

Don't cling to the old because it made you glad once: go on to the next, the next region, the next experience.

ALFRED NORTH WHITEHEAD

See also **New.**

OLD AGE

There is nothing more remarkable in the life of Socrates than that he found time in his old age to learn to dance and play on instruments, and thought it was time well spent.

MONTAIGNE

What they tell of Cato, among other things, that in his extreme old age he began to learn Greek with a greedy appetite, as if to quench a long-standing thirst, does not appear to me very greatly to his honour. It is properly speaking what we should call falling into second childhood. MONTAIGNE

Old men delight in giving good advice as a consolation for the fact that they can no longer set bad examples. LA ROCHEFOUCAULD

Few know how to be old.

LA ROCHEFOUCAULD

An old man concludeth from his knowing mankind, that they know him too, and that maketh him very wary. LORD HALIFAX

To Old Age. I see in you the estuary that enlarges and spreads itself grandly as it pours in the Great Sea. WALT WHITMAN

An old man in a house is a good sign. BENJAMIN FRANKLIN

There is a wicked inclination in most people to suppose an old man decayed in his intellect. If a young or middle-aged man, when leaving a company, does not recollect where he laid his hat, it is nothing; but if the same inattention is discovered in an old man, people will shrug up their shoulders, and say, 'His memory is going.'

SAMUEL JOHNSON

In the decline of life, shame and grief are of short duration.

SAMUEL JOHNSON

It is a man's own fault, it is from want of use, if his mind grows torpid in old age. SAMUEL JOHNSON

One evil in old age is, that as your time is come, you think every little illness is the beginning of the end. When a man expects to be arrested, every knock at the door is an alarm. We are, at the close of life, only hurried away from stomach aches, pains in the joints, from sleepless nights and unamusing days, from weakness, ugliness and nervous tremors. SYDNEY SMITH

Few envy the consideration enjoyed by the oldest inhabitant.

RALPH WALDO EMERSON

One capital advantage of old age is the absolute insignificance of a success more or less. I went to town and read a lecture yesterday. Thirty years ago it had really been a matter of importance to me whether it was good and effective. Now it is of none in relation to me. It is long already fixed what I can do and what I cannot do.

RALPH WALDO EMERSON

The evening of life brings with it its lamp. JOSEPH JOUBERT

Old age brings along with its ugliness the comfort that you will soon be out of it. . . . To be out of the war, out of debt, out of the drouth, out of the blues, out of the dentist's hands, out of the second thoughts, mortifications, and remorses that inflict such twinges and shooting pains,—out of the next winter, and the high prices, and the company below your ambition—
RALPH WALDO EMERSON

Old age is a good advertisement.
RALPH WALDO EMERSON

We can't reach old age by another man's road. MARK TWAIN

The tragedy of old age is not that one is old, but that one is young.
OSCAR WILDE

There is more felicity on the far side of baldness than young men can possibly imagine.
LOGAN PEARSALL SMITH

It has seemed to me sometimes as though I could see men hardening before my eyes, drawing in a feeler here, walling up an opening there. Naming things! Objects fall into categories for them and wear little sure channels in the brain. A mountain is a mountain, a tree a tree to them, a field forever a field. Life solidifies itself in words. And finally how everything wearies them and that is old age!
DAVID GRAYSON

When I was young I was amazed at Plutarch's statement that the elder Cato began at the age of eighty to learn Greek. I am amazed no longer. Old age is ready to undertake tasks that youth shirked because they would take too long.
W. SOMERSET MAUGHAM

The greatest compensation of old age is its freedom of spirit. . . . Another compensation is that it liberates you from envy, hatred, and malice.
W. SOMERSET MAUGHAM

Bedridden ladies of advanced age seldom bubble over with fun and *joie de vivre.* P. G. WODEHOUSE

There is nothing more beautiful in this world than a healthy wise old man. LIN YUTANG

See also **Age, Growing Old, Young and Old.**

OLD TESTAMENT

The Old Testament is responsible for more atheism, agnosticism, disbelief—call it what you will—than any book ever written; it has emptied more churches than all the counter-attractions of cinema, motor-bicycle and golf course.
A. A. MILNE

See also **Bible.**

OMEN

Omen: A sign that something will happen if nothing happens.
AMBROSE BIERCE

OMNISCIENCE

SYDNEY SMITH was reported to have said of Dr. Whewell, of Cambridge, whose universality in authorship was one of the marvels of the time, that omniscience was his forte, and science his foible.

ONE

You can't clap hands with one palm. CHINESE PROVERB

Do not depend on one thing or trust to only one resource, however pre-eminent BALTASAR GRACIÁN

I heard a sensible man say he should like to do some one thing better than all the rest of the world, and in everything else to be like all the rest of the world. Why should a man do more than his part? The rest is vanity and vexation of spirit.
WILLIAM HAZLITT

Every man is dangerous who only cares for one thing.
G. K. CHESTERTON

Do not expect too much from any one thing.   ROBERT LYND

The public will go for anything that's limited one to a customer. If polygamy were the law of the land, few persons would bother to marry at all.   SYDNEY HARRIS

ONE-HUNDRED-AND-TEN

I have never known a person to live to 110, or more, and then die, to be remarkable for anything else.
JOSH BILLINGS

OPEN MIND

An open mind is all very well in its way, but it ought not to be so open that there is no keeping anything in or out of it. It should be capable of shutting its doors sometimes, or it may be found a little draughty.
SAMUEL BUTLER

See also **Tolerance.**

OPERA

I have sat through an Italian opera, till, for sheer pain, and inexplicable anguish, I have rushed out into the noisiest places of the crowded streets, to solace myself with sounds, which I was not obliged to follow, and get rid of the distracting torment of endless, fruitless barren attention!   CHARLES LAMB

The lady came home from the opera *and yet* quarrelled with her maid.   PETER ALTENBERG

OPERATION

There is a fashion in operations, as there is in sleeves and skirts.
GEORGE BERNARD SHAW

See also **Medicine.**

OPINION

The superior man does not set his mind either for anything or against anything.   CONFUCIUS

Obstinacy and heat in sticking to one's opinions is the surest proof of stupidity. Is there anything so cocksure, so immovable, so disdainful, so contemplative, so solemn and serious as an ass?
MONTAIGNE

When a man talks on any subject, he rather expresses the opinions of his garb or his fraternity, than his own, and will change them as often as he changes his situation and circumstances.   ROUSSEAU

We always formulate opinions at a time when our judgment is at its weakest.   G. C. LICHTENBERG

How do we spend our old age? In defending opinions, not because we believe them to be true, but simply because we once said that we thought they were.
G. C. LICHTENBERG

Nothing contributes more to peace of mind than to have no opinions whatever.   G. C. LICHTENBERG

To have entertained a number of opinions gives the mind a great deal of flexibility, and strengthens it in its preferences.
JOSEPH JOUBERT

It is always considered a piece of impertinence in England if a man of less than two or three thousand a year has any opinions at all upon important subjects. SYDNEY SMITH

'I never offered an opinion till I was sixty,' said the old Turk; 'and then it was one which had been in our family for a century.'
BENJAMIN DISRAELI

There are two kinds of fools: those who can't change their opinions and those who won't.
JOSH BILLINGS

In all matters of opinion, our adversaries are insane. MARK TWAIN

Absurdity: A statement or belief manifestly inconsistent with one's own opinion. AMBROSE BIERCE

A man who is very busy seldom changes his opinions.
FRIEDRICH NIETZSCHE

How appalling is the ignorance which is the inevitable result of the fatal habit of imparting opinions!
OSCAR WILDE

People are usually more firmly convinced that their opinions are precious than that they are true.
GEORGE SANTAYANA

Few people are capable of expressing with equanimity opinions which differ from the prejudices of their social environment. Most people are even incapable of forming such opinions. ALBERT EINSTEIN

The difficult part in an argument is not to defend one's opinion but rather to know it.
ANDRÉ MAUROIS

See also **Conviction, Notion, Public Opinion, Prejudice, Taking Sides.**

OPPORTUNITY

O what a tremendous advantage is opportunity! Should anyone ask me what is the first advantage in love, I should reply that it is to be able to make one's opportunity; likewise the second, and the third as well. There you have the key to everything. MONTAIGNE

The greatest achievement of the human spirit is to live up to one's opportunities and make the most of one's resources. VAUVENARGUES

OPPOSITE

To do exactly the opposite is also a form of imitation.
G. C. LICHTENBERG

Every word that is uttered evokes the idea of its opposite. GOETHE

Almost every wise saying has an opposite one, no less wise, to balance it. GEORGE SANTAYANA

If there is anything that especially distinguishes us from the angels, it is, I fancy, that the contest of opposites means so much more to us than it does to them.
ROBERT LYND

There are some things one can only achieve by a deliberate leap in the opposite direction. One has to go abroad in order to find the home one has lost. FRANZ KAFKA

OPTIMISM

Animal optimism is a great renovator and disinfectant in the world.
GEORGE SANTAYANA

Being optimistic after you've got everything you want don't count.
KIN HUBBARD

An optimist is always broke.
KIN HUBBARD

An optimist is a fellow who believes what's going to be will be postponed. KIN HUBBARD

An optimist is a guy who has never had much experience.
DON MARQUIS

ORATORIO
Nothing can be more disgusting than an oratorio. How absurd, to see five hundred people fiddling like madmen about the Israelites in the Red Sea! SYDNEY SMITH

ORDERLINESS
Habitual orderliness of ideas is your sole road to happiness, and to reach it, orderliness in all else, even the most casual things, is needed.
EUGÈNE DELACROIX

Have a place for everything and keep the thing somewhere else; this is not advice, it is merely custom. MARK TWAIN

See also **Disorderly.**

ORDINARY
Ordinary men commonly condemn what is beyond them.
LA ROCHEFOUCAULD

All men are ordinary men: the extraordinary men are those who know it. G. K. CHESTERTON

The great man is too often all of a piece; it is the little man that is a bundle of contradictory elements. He is inexhaustible. You never come to the end of the surprises he has in store for you. For my part I would much sooner spend a month on a desert island with a veterinary surgeon than with a Prime Minister. W. SOMERSET MAUGHAM

See also **Average, Everyday, Mediocre.**

ORIGINAL
The greater intellect one has, the more originality one finds in men. Ordinary persons find no difference between men. PASCAL

About the most originality that any writer can hope to achieve honestly is to steal with good judgment.
JOSH BILLINGS

Our Lord never thought of being original. GEORGE MACDONALD

People know nothing. That is why plays are popular and the old, old story can be dished up again and again. It is original thought to which they all object.
GEORGE BERNARD SHAW

What is originality? Undetected plagiarism. W. R. INGE

No one can be original by trying.
W. SOMERSET MAUGHAM

ORTHODOX
Orthodoxy is the grave of intelligence. BERTRAND RUSSELL

See also **Heretic.**

OTHER WORLD
We thank God for having created this world, and praise Him for having made another, quite different one, where the wrongs of this one are corrected. ANATOLE FRANCE

One real world is enough.
GEORGE SANTAYANA

See also **Immortality.**

OTHERS
He who has no faith in others shall find no faith in them. LAO-TSE

Whatever profits one man profits others as well as himself.
MARCUS AURELIUS

He who does not live in some degree for others, hardly lives for himself. MONTAIGNE

No man deals out his money to others; every man deals out his time and his life. MONTAIGNE

We all have strength enough to endure the misfortunes of others. LA ROCHEFOUCAULD

The most useful part of wisdom is for a man to give a good guess what others think of him. It is a dangerous thing to guess partially, and a melancholy thing to guess right. LORD HALIFAX

More men hurt others they do not know why than for any reason. LORD HALIFAX

How happy many people would be if they cared about other people's affairs as little as about their own. G. C. LICHTENBERG

We are cold to others only when we are dull in ourselves. WILLIAM HAZLITT

Those who are at war with others are not at peace with themselves. WILLIAM HAZLITT

We grow tired of everything but turning others into ridicule, and congratulating ourselves on their defects. WILLIAM HAZLITT

Don't do for others what you wouldn't think of asking them to do for you. JOSH BILLINGS

We are franker towards others than towards ourselves. FRIEDRICH NIETZSCHE

Do not do unto others as you would that they should do unto you. Their tastes may not be the same. GEORGE BERNARD SHAW

There is something infinitely mean about other people's tragedies. OSCAR WILDE

See also **Golden Rule, Neighbour, People, Self.**

OUTLINE

Nature has no outline, but imagination has. WILLIAM BLAKE
See also **Line.**

OVER

'It's over, and can't be helped, and that's one consolation, as they always says in Turkey, ven they cuts the wrong man's head off.' CHARLES DICKENS
See also **Done.**

OVERDONE

On the Continent you can't get a rare beef steak—everything is as overdone as a martyr. MARK TWAIN

OVERLOOK

We should often investigate what people usually forget or overlook, or consider so well-known that it isn't worth investigating. G. C. LICHTENBERG

The art of being wise is the art of knowing what to overlook. WILLIAM JAMES

Things that I longed for in vain and things that I got—let them pass. Let me but truly possess the things that I ever spurned and overlooked. RABINDRANATH TAGORE

See also **Attention, Inattention, Unnoticed.**

OWN

A man loves to review his own mind. SAMUEL JOHNSON

Make not thy own person, family relations or affairs the frequent subject of thy tattle. . . . Say not, 'In truth, I cannot allow of such a thing. My manner and custom is to do thus. I neither eat nor drink in a morning. I am apt to be troubled with corns. My child said such a witty thing last night.'
DR. THOMAS FULLER

You can't get rid of what is part of you, even if you throw it away.
GOETHE

No bird soars too high, if he soars with his own wings.
WILLIAM BLAKE

One man's way may be as good as another's, but we all like our own best.
JANE AUSTEN

He who draws upon his own resources, easily comes to an end of his wealth.
WILLIAM HAZLITT

'If everybody minded their own business,' the Duchess said, in a hoarse growl, 'the world would go round a deal faster than it does.'
LEWIS CARROLL

It is at least something to know that one is thrown on one's own resources. One learns then to use them properly.
SIGMUND FREUD

The worst jolt most of us ever get is when we fall back on our own resources.
KIN HUBBARD

See also **Man and Himself, Mine, Self.**

P
PACIFISM

The absolute pacifist is a bad citizen; times come when force must be used to uphold right, justice and ideals.
ALFRED NORTH WHITEHEAD

See also **Peace.**

PAIN

It is easy to stand a pain but difficult to stand an itch.
CHINESE PROVERB

Those who do not feel pain seldom think that it is felt.
SAMUEL JOHNSON

The least pain in our little finger gives us more concern and uneasiness than the destruction of millions of our fellow-beings.
WILLIAM HAZLITT

There are people who have an appetite for grief, pleasure is not strong enough and they crave pain.
RALPH WALDO EMERSON

Every step forward is made at the cost of mental and physical pain to someone.
FRIEDRICH NIETZSCHE

Your pain is the breaking of the shell that encloses your understanding.
KAHLIL GIBRAN

Man is powerless against small pains. He can feel a kind of pride in having broken his leg, but he can feel none in breaking a fingernail.
KAREL ČAPEK

PAINTER

A conceited painter of the name of Edwards went with Romney to Rome; and when they got into the Sistine Chapel, turning round to him, said, 'Egad! George, we're bit!'
JAMES NORTHCOTE

There are painters who transform the sun into a yellow spot, but there are others who, thanks to their art and intelligence, transform a yellow spot into the sun.
PABLO PICASSO

See also **Artist, Painting.**

PAINTING

What has reasoning to do with the art of painting?
WILLIAM BLAKE

If one criticizes painting by its verisimilitude, one's understanding is similar to that of a child.

SU TUNG-P'O

Painting is the intermediate somewhat between a thought and a thing. SYDNEY SMITH

Landscape painting is the obvious resource of misanthropy.

WILLIAM HAZLITT

There is pictorial licence in the same way as there is poetic licence.

EUGÈNE DELACROIX

I swore to die painting.

PAUL CÉZANNE

I have spent my life amusing myself by putting colours on canvas.

AUGUSTE RENOIR

Good painting is like good cooking —it can be tasted, but not explained. MAURICE DE VLAMINCK

What I say to an artist is, *When you can't paint—paint*. JOYCE CARY

See also **Art, Artist, Painter, Painting and Sculpture, Picture, Raphael.**

PAINTING AND SCULPTURE

By sculpture I mean the sort that is executed by cutting away from the block: the sort that is executed by building up resembles painting.

MICHELANGELO

Every art purporting to represent involves a process of *reduction*. The painter reduces form to the two dimensions of his canvas; the sculptor reduces every movement, potential or portrayed, to immobility. ANDRÉ MALRAUX

See also **Sculpture.**

PALACE

A man can live well even in a palace. MARCUS AURELIUS

PAMPHLET

He was one of those men who think that the world can be saved by writing a pamphlet.

BENJAMIN DISRAELI

PARADOX

The truest sayings are paradoxical.

LAO-TSE

If you would contract, you must first expand. If you would weaken, you must first strengthen. If you would overthrow, you must first raise up. If you would take, you must first give. LAO-TSE

The greatest wisdom is like stupidity; the greatest eloquence is like stuttering. LAO-TSE

The paradox is the source of the thinker's passion, and the thinker without a paradox is like a lover without feeling: a paltry mediocrity. SÖREN KIERKEGAARD

Truth is always paradoxical.

HENRY DAVID THOREAU

It is by teaching that we teach ourselves, by relating that we observe, by affirming that we examine, by showing that we look, by writing that we think, by pumping that we draw water into the well.

FRÉDÉRIC AMIEL

The more a man looks at a thing, the less he can see it, and the more a man learns a thing the less he knows it. G. K. CHESTERTON

A paradox arises when premature insight clashes with prevailing nonsense. KARL KRAUS

Man is most comforted by paradoxes. G. K. CHESTERTON

PARENTS

Love is presently out of breath
when it is to go up hill, from the
children to the parents.
LORD HALIFAX

Children and subjects are much
seldomer in the wrong than parents
and kings. LORD CHESTERFIELD

Few parents act in such a manner
as much to enforce their maxims by
the credit of their lives.
SAMUEL JOHNSON

To bring up a child in the way he
should go, travel that way yourself
once in a while. JOSH BILLINGS

A parent must respect the spiritual
person of his child, and approach it
with reverence.
GEORGE MACDONALD

I don't know who are the best
people to educate the young; but
this I am certain, the parents are the
very worst. WILLIAM MORRIS

Some people seem compelled by
unkind fate to parental servitude
for life. There is no form of penal
servitude much worse than this.
SAMUEL BUTLER

Children begin by loving their
parents. After a time they judge
them. Rarely, if ever, do they forgive them. OSCAR WILDE

Speaking personally, I have found
the happiness of parenthood greater
than any other that I have experienced. BERTRAND RUSSELL

The only people who seem to have
nothing to do with the education of
the children are the parents
G. K. CHESTERTON

There are times when parenthood
seems nothing but feeding the
mouth that bites you.
PETER DE VRIES

See also **Children, Father, Mother.**

PARLIAMENT

A parliament is nothing less than a
big meeting of more or less idle
people. WALTER BAGEHOT

See also **Congress.**

PARSON

Merriment of parsons is mighty
offensive. SAMUEL JOHNSON

PARTY

The best party is but a kind of con-
spiracy against the rest of the
nation. LORD HALIFAX

Ignorance makes most men go
into a party, and shame keeps them
from getting out of it.
LORD HALIFAX

If I could not go to heaven but
with a party, I would not go there
at all. THOMAS JEFFERSON

When great questions end, little
parties begin. WALTER BAGEHOT

He calls it loyalty to his party: but
it's only laziness; he doesn't want
to get out of this bed.
FRIEDRICH NIETZSCHE

Any party which takes credit for
the rain must not be surprised if its
opponents blame it for the drought.
DWIGHT W. MORROW

See also **Membership.**

PASSION

If we conquer our passions it is
more from their weakness than
from our strength.
LA ROCHEFOUCAULD

Wise people may say what they
will, but one passion is never cured
by another. LORD CHESTERFIELD

When you have found out the pre-vailing passion of any man, re-member never to trust him where that passion is concerned.
LORD CHESTERFIELD

What our age lacks is not reflection but passion. SÖREN KIERKEGAARD

The conclusions of passion are the only reliable ones.
SÖREN KIERKEGAARD

It is said that passion makes one think in a circle. OSCAR WILDE

See also **Emotion, Feeling.**

PASSIVITY

Passivity is an essential feature of the highest form of leisure.
SALVADOR DE MADARIAGA

See also **Doing Nothing.**

PAST

The best way to suppose what may come is to remember what is past.
LORD HALIFAX

Events in the past may be roughly divided into those which probably never happened and those which do not matter. W. R. INGE

Those who cannot remember the past are condemned to repeat it.
GEORGE SANTAYANA

We cannot say the past is past without surrendering the future.
WINSTON S. CHURCHILL

If everybody remembered the past, nobody would ever forgive any-body. ROBERT LYND

See also **Future, Past and Future, Present.**

PAST AND FUTURE

I like the dreams of the future better than the history of the past.
THOMAS JEFFERSON

The future influences the present just as much as the past.
FRIEDRICH NIETZSCHE

We are made wise not by the re-collections of our past, but by the responsibilities of our future.
GEORGE BERNARD SHAW

We must welcome the future, remembering that soon it will be the past; and we must respect the past, remembering that once it was all that was humanly possible.
GEORGE SANTAYANA

A European who goes to New York and Chicago sees the future; when he goes to Asia, he sees the past.
BERTRAND RUSSELL

See also **Future, Past.**

PATIENCE

To be patient is sometimes better than to have much wealth.
TALMUD

The man who lacks patience also lacks philosophy. SADI

Patience serves as a protection against wrongs as clothes do against cold. For if you put on more clothes as the cold increases it will have no power to hurt you. So in like manner you must grow in patience when you meet with great wrongs, and they will then be powerless to vex your mind.
LEONARDO DA VINCI

Of all the qualities of an excellent character patience is enough for us.
MONTAIGNE

Patience, and shuffle the cards.
CERVANTES

Have patience with all things, but chiefly have patience with yourself. Do not lose courage in considering

your own imperfections, but instantly set about remedying them—every day begin the task anew.
ST. FRANCIS DE SALES

A man who is master of patience is master of everything else.
LORD HALIFAX

He that can have patience can have what he will. BENJAMIN FRANKLIN

Patience is the art of hoping.
VAUVENARGUES

One is a master only when one brings to things the patience to which they are entitled.
EUGÈNE DELACROIX

Adopt the pace of nature: her secret is patience.
RALPH WALDO EMERSON

The principal part of faith is patience. GEORGE MACDONALD

The most useful virtue is patience.
JOHN DEWEY

Lack of pep is often mistaken for patience. KIN HUBBARD

Every day I learn, with pains, for which I am grateful: Patience is everything! RAINER MARIA RILKE

See also **Waiting.**

PATIENTS

Doctors think a lot of patients are cured who have simply quit in disgust. DON HEROLD

See also **Doctor.**

PATRIOTISM

To me, it seems a dreadful indignity to have a soul controlled by geography. GEORGE SANTAYANA

In Dr. Johnson's famous dictionary patriotism is defined as the last resort of a scoundrel. With all due respect to an enlightened but inferior lexicographer I beg to submit that it is the first. AMBROSE BIERCE

Patriotism is the virtue of the vicious. OSCAR WILDE

'My country, right or wrong,' is a thing that no patriot would think of saying except in a desperate case. It is like saying, 'My mother, drunk or sober.' G. K. CHESTERTON

What is patriotism but love of the good things we ate in our childhood? LIN YUTANG

See also **Fatherland.**

PATRON SAINT

It is a pity that current thought and sentiment offer nothing corresponding to the old conception of patron saints. If they did, there would be a patron saint of plumbers, and this would alone be a revolution, for it would force the individual craftsman to believe that there was once a perfect being who did actually plumb.
G. K. CHESTERTON

PAUSE

The first proof of a well-ordered mind is to be able to pause and linger within itself. SENECA

The pause—that impressive silence, that eloquent silence, that geometrically progressive silence which often achieves a desired effect where no combination of words howsoever felicitous could accomplish it. MARK TWAIN

See also **Silence.**

PAY

I cannot bear to pay for articles I used to get for nothing. When Adam laid out his first penny upon nonpareils at some stall in Mesopotamia, I think it went hard with him, reflecting upon his old goodly orchard where he had so many for nothing. CHARLES LAMB

If you fail, pay your helpers double.
FRIEDRICH NIETZSCHE

I think some folks are foolish to pay what it costs to live.
KIN HUBBARD

See also **Wages.**

PEACE

It is better to be a dog in peaceful times than to be a man in times of unrest.
CHINESE PROVERB

Peace is not absence of war, it is a virtue, a state of mind, a disposition for benevolence, confidence, justice.
SPINOZA

'My friends,' says Mr. Chadband, 'Peace be on this house! On the master thereof, on the mistress thereof, on the young maidens, and on the young men! My friends, why do I wish for peace? What is peace? Is it war? No. Is it strife? No. Is it lovely, and gentle, and beautiful, and pleasant, and serene, and joyful? Oh yes! Therefore, my friends, I wish for peace, upon you and upon yours.'
CHARLES DICKENS

See also **Pacifism.**

PEACE OF MIND

From his cradle to his grave a man never does a single thing which has any first and foremost object save one—to secure peace of mind, spiritual comfort, for himself.
MARK TWAIN

When we do not find peace of mind in ourselves it is useless to look for it elsewhere. LA ROCHEFOUCAULD

How furious it makes people to tell them of the things which belong to their peace!
LOGAN PEARSALL SMITH

Peace of mind is that mental condition in which you have accepted the worst. LIN YUTANG

PEDANTRY

He who is not in some measure a pedant, though he may be a wise, cannot be a very happy man.
WILLIAM HAZLITT

There is nothing so pedantic as pretending not to be pedantic.
WILLIAM HAZLITT

PEDESTRIANS

Pedestrians should be loved.
Pedestrians make up the greater part of humanity. More than that— its best part. Pedestrians have created the world. It was they who built cities, reared many-storied buildings, put through canalization and the water system, paved the streets and lighted them with electric lamps. It was they who spread culture throughout the world, devised printing, invented gunpowder, flung bridges across rivers, deciphered Egyptian hiero-glyphics, introduced the safety razor into common usage, des-troyed the slave trade, and deter-mined that one hundred palatable, nourishing dishes may be prepared out of soya beans.
And when everything was ready, when our native planet assumed a comparatively well-ordered ap-pearance, motorists appeared.
ILYA ILF AND EUGENE PETROV

PENSIONER

Pensioner: A kept patriot.
H. L. MENCKEN

PEOPLE

It is flattering some men to endure them. LORD HALIFAX

People who are much older than they look seldom have much intelligence.   G. C. LICHTENBERG

We don't get to know people when they come to us; we must go to them to find out what they are like.
GOETHE

There may be said to be two classes of people in the world, which remain forever distinct: those who consider things in the abstract, or with a reference to truth, and those who consider them only with a reference to themselves, or to the *main chance*.   WILLIAM HAZLITT

Intercourse with decent or bad people is the good or bad education which goes on throughout one's life.   EUGÈNE DELACROIX

The people are to be taken in very small doses.
RALPH WALDO EMERSON

There are three kinds of people—commonplace men, remarkable men, and lunatics.   MARK TWAIN

It is absurd to divide people into good and bad. People are either charming or tedious.
OSCAR WILDE

One of the astutest men I know has achieved a large measure of his prosperity and general contentment by behaving always as though all men were alike. Because, although of course they are not alike, the differences are too trifling to matter.   E. V. LUCAS

If a man is worth knowing at all, he is worth knowing well.
ALEXANDER SMITH

I do not think I am any better or any worse than most people, but I know that if I sat down every action in my life and every thought that has crossed my mind, the world would consider me a monster of depravity.
W. SOMERSET MAUGHAM

One must be fond of people and trust them if one is not to make a mess of life.   E. M. FORSTER

Just when you're beginning to think pretty well of people, you run across somebody who puts sugar on sliced tomatoes.
WILL CUPPY

See also **Human Nature, Men, Women.**

PERFECTION

In all our resolves we must decide which is the line of conduct that presents the fewest drawbacks and then follow it out as being the best one, because one never finds anything perfectly pure and unmixed, or exempt from danger.
MACHIAVELLI

When a thing bores you, do not do it. Do not pursue a fruitless perfection.   EUGÈNE DELACROIX

The artists who seek perfection in everything are those who can attain it in nothing.   EUGÈNE DELACROIX

The editor of an English magazine having received a letter pointing out the erroneous nature of his views and style, and signed 'Perfection,' promptly wrote at the foot of the letter: 'I don't agree with you,' and mailed it to Matthew Arnold.   AMBROSE BIERCE

The perfection of art is the destruction of art.   WILLIAM HAZLITT

Perfect things teach hope.
FRIEDRICH NIETZSCHE

Perfection just precedes a change, and signifies the approaching end of an epoch.
ALFRED NORTH WHITEHEAD

The indefatigable pursuit of an unattainable perfection, even though it consists in nothing more than in the pounding of an old piano, is what alone gives a meaning to our life on this unavailing star.
LOGAN PEARSALL SMITH

After all, a little taste does no harm, and the fever of perfection is not catching.
LOGAN PEARSALL SMITH

PERIOD

It was the best of times, it was the worst of times, it was the age of wisdom, it was the age of foolishness, it was the epoch of belief, it was the epoch of incredulity, it was the season of Light, it was the season of Darkness, it was the spring of hope, it was the winter of despair, we had everything before us, we had nothing before us, we were all going direct to Heaven, we were all going direct the other way—in short, the period was so far alike the present period, that some of its noisiest authorities insisted on its being received, for good or for evil, in the superlative degree of comparison only.
CHARLES DICKENS

PERPLEXITY

In all perplexity there is a portion of fear, which predisposes the mind to anger.
SAMUEL TAYLOR COLERIDGE

It is something to be capable of perplexity.   HENRY S. HASKINS

Inability to pay decides for many of us perplexing questions that worry the well-to-do. WILLIAM FEATHER

PERSECUTION

Persecution is a bad and indirect way to plant religion.
SIR THOMAS BROWNE

PERSEVERANCE

There are but two roads that lead to an important goal and to the doing of great things: strength and perseverance. Strength is the lot of but a few privileged men; but austere perseverance, harsh and continuous, may be employed by the smallest of us and rarely fails of its purpose, *for its silent power grows irresistibly greater with time.*
GOETHE

By perseverance the snail reached the Ark.   C. H. SPURGEON

PESSIMISM

Pessimism is essentially a religious disease.   WILLIAM JAMES

Show me a person with plenty of worries and troubles and I will show you a person who, whatever he is, is not a pessimist.
G. K. CHESTERTON

Pessimists as a rule live to a ripe old age. It is questionable if a despairing view of the universe even impairs the digestion as much as a single slice of new bread.
ROBERT LYND

See also **Despair, Optimism.**

PHILANTHROPY

Philanthropist: A rich (and usually bald) old gentleman who has trained himself to grin while his conscience is picking his pocket.
AMBROSE BIERCE

See also **Alms, Benevolence, Charity, Giving.**

PHILISTINE

Lowbrows are not Philistines. One has to know enough about the arts to argue about them with highbrows to be a Philistine.

RUSSELL LYNES

See also **Highbrow.**

PHILOSOPHER

I never knew what my theories of life were until it was nearly over and done. I am of a new school—an unpremeditated philosopher.

MONTAIGNE

I generally find the morals and the language of the peasants more in accordance with the teachings of the true philosophy than those of our philosophers.   MONTAIGNE

To make light of philosophy is to be a true philosopher.   PASCAL

Your philosopher will not believe what he sees, and is always speculating about what he sees not—which is a life, I think, not much to be envied.

BERNARD DE FONTENELLE

I believe that there never was a creator of a philosophical system who did not confess at the end of his life that he had wasted his time. It must be admitted that the inventors of the mechanical arts have been much more useful to men than the inventors of syllogisms. He who imagined a ship towers considerably above him who imagined innate ideas.

VOLTAIRE

A philosopher's duty is not to pity the unhappy—it is to be of use to them.   VOLTAIRE

The philosophers have only *interpreted* the world. The point, however, is to *change* it.   KARL MARX

A philosopher should have made many mistakes and been saved often by the skin of his teeth: for the skin of one's teeth is the most teaching thing about one.

SAMUEL BUTLER

Any two philosophers can tell each other all they know in two hours.

OLIVER WENDELL HOLMES, JR.

I always think of a remark of Brooks Adams that the philosophers were hired by the comfortable class to prove that everything is all right. I think it *is* all right, but on very different grounds.

OLIVER WENDELL HOLMES, JR.

All are lunatics, but he who can analyze his delusions is called a philosopher.   AMBROSE BIERCE

There is only one thing that a philosopher can be relied on to do, and that is, to contradict other philosophers.   WILLIAM JAMES

I care for a philosopher only to the extent that he is able to be an example.   FRIEDRICH NIETZSCHE

No one would be angry with a man for unintentionally making a mistake about a matter of fact; but if he perversely insists on spoiling your story in the telling of it, you want to kick him; and this is the reason why every philosopher and theologian is justly vexed with every other.   GEORGE SANTAYANA

Philosophy consists largely of one philosopher arguing that all others are jackasses. He usually proves it, and I should add that he also usually proves that he is one himself.   H. L. MENCKEN

See also **Aristotle, Dewey, Marcus Aurelius, Plato, Socrates, Spinoza.**

PHILOSOPHY

Vain is the word of a philosopher that does not heal any suffering of man. For just as there is no profit in medicine if it does not expel the diseases of the body, so there is no profit in philosophy either if it does not expel the suffering of the mind. EPICURUS

I think if an angel could tell us about his philosophy, some sentences would sound like two times two makes thirteen.
G. C. LICHTENBERG

The flour is the important thing, not the mill; the fruits of philosophy, not the philosophy itself. When we ask what time it is we don't want to know how watches are constructed.
G. C. LICHTENBERG

Language originated before philosophy, and that's what is the matter with philosophy.
G. C. LICHTENBERG

Music is a higher revelation than philosophy.
LUDWIG VAN BEETHOVEN

Philosophy is at bottom homesickness—the longing to be at home everywhere. NOVALIS

So far as I can see, philosophy is invariably an attempt to deny, circumvent or otherwise escape from the way in which the roots of things interlace with one another.
SAMUEL BUTLER

Philosophy as a general rule is like stirring mud or not letting a sleeping dog lie. SAMUEL BUTLER

Viewed from a sufficient distance, all systems of philosophy are seen to be personal, temperamental, accidental, and premature.
GEORGE SANTAYANA

The systems disappear, the insights remain; but probably the great body of insights that we have, touching life and the world, comes in large part from an unknown multitude, not mentioned in the histories of philosophy.
OLIVER WENDELL HOLMES, JR.

The whole function of philosophy ought to be to find out what definite difference it will make to you and me, at definite instants of our life, if this world-formula or that world-formula be the true one.
WILLIAM JAMES

Philosophy is common sense. If it isn't common sense, it isn't philosophy. E. W. HOWE

The object of studying philosophy is to know one's own mind, not other people's. W. R. INGE

The chief error in philosophy is overstatement.
ALFRED NORTH WHITEHEAD

Philosophy asks the simple question: What is it all about?
ALFRED NORTH WHITEHEAD

All philosophies, if you ride them home, are nonsense.
SAMUEL BUTLER

I was of the opinion of the Scottish metaphysician that it is more important that a philosophy should be reasoned than that it should be true. JOHN BUCHAN

I recall walking home with Professor (William) James after one of his lectures and at the end of our talk confessing my inclination toward philosophical studies. He turned on me seriously and remarked, 'Don't do it. You will be filling your belly with east wind.'
WALTER B. CANNON

It is a great advantage for a system of philosophy to be substantially true. GEORGE SANTAYANA

A great philosophy is not one that passes final judgments and establishes ultimate truth. It is one that causes uneasiness and starts commotion. CHARLES PÉGUY

Philosophies are interesting to the majority of people only while they are novelties. ROBERT LYND

Philosophy? Philosophy? I am a Christian and a Democrat—that's all. FRANKLIN DELANO ROOSEVELT

Philosophies are devices for making it possible to do, coolly, continuously, and with a good conscience, things which otherwise one could do only in the heat of passion, spasmodically, and under the threat of subsequent remorse.
ALDOUS HUXLEY

See also **Metaphysics, Philosopher, Stoic.**

PHOTOGRAPH

Nothing can be so deceiving as a photograph. FRANZ KAFKA

PHYSICIAN

He that sinneth before his Maker, let him fall into the hands of a physician. ECCLESIASTICUS 38

The wise physician, if he has failed to cure, looks out for someone who, under the name of consultation, may help him carry out the corpse. BALTASAR GRACIÁN

He had had much experience of physicians, and said 'the only way to keep your health is to eat what you don't want, drink what you don't like, and do what you druther not.' MARK TWAIN

A physician who treats himself has a fool for a patient.
SIR WILLIAM OSLER

Taking a lady's hand gives her confidence in her physician.
SIR WILLIAM OSLER

See also **Doctor, Medicine.**

PICTURE

The first picture was nothing but a line which surrounded the shadow of a man by the sun upon a wall.
LEONARDO DA VINCI

Pictures must not be too picturesque. RALPH WALDO EMERSON

If you try hard enough to seem to like pictures, you will like them in the end. LOGAN PEARSALL SMITH

Modern pictures are not objects intended to be hung on a drawing-room wall to ornament it—even if we do hang them there.
ANDRÉ MALRAUX

See also **Gallery, Painting.**

PIETY

Experience makes us see an enormous difference between piety and goodness. PASCAL

A wicked fellow is the most pious when he takes to it. He'll beat you all in piety. SAMUEL JOHNSON

Piety, stretched beyond a certain point, is the parent of impiety.
SYDNEY SMITH

See also **Impiety.**

PIONEER

Never be a pioneer. It's the Early Christian that gets the fattest lion.
SAKI

PIPE

The pipe draws wisdom from the lips of the philosopher, and shuts up the mouths of the foolish; it generates a style of conversation contemplative, thoughtful, benevolent, and unaffected.
WILLIAM MAKEPEACE THACKERAY

See also **Smoking.**

PIRATE

The ordinary man would rather read the life of the cruellest pirate that ever lived than of the wisest philosopher.   ROBERT LYND

PITY

Heaven arms with pity those whom it would not see destroyed.
LAO-TSE

Pity is often a reflection of our own evils in the ills of others. It is a delicate foresight of the troubles into which we may fall.
LA ROCHEFOUCAULD

We pity in others only those evils that we have ourselves experienced.
ROUSSEAU

When you feel pity, you don't ask other people first whether you ought to.   G. C. LICHTENBERG

It is through pity that we remain truly a man.   ANATOLE FRANCE

Pity is the very basis of genius.
ANATOLE FRANCE

See also **Compassion, Irony and Pity, Sympathy.**

PLACE

There is no place in the whole world so unhealthy and miserable that people, tempted by some advantage, wouldn't pick it as their place to live.   GIACOMO LEOPARDI

One does not love a place the less for having suffered in it.
JANE AUSTEN

PLAIN

The right way if we have something to say is to say it plainly—not for conversion, but for such as may be waiting for our voice.   FREYA STARK

See also **Clear.**

PLATITUDE

Platitude: All that is mortal of a departed truth.   AMBROSE BIERCE

She plunged into a sea of platitudes and with the powerful breast stroke of a channel swimmer made her confident way towards the white cliffs of the obvious.
W. SOMERSET MAUGHAM

See also **Commonplace, Truism.**

PLATO

Plato's *Republic* does not begin, as some of the modern writers would have it, with some such sentence as, 'Human civilization, as seen through its successive stages of development, is a dynamic movement from heterogeneity to homogeneity,' or some other equally incomprehensible rot. It begins rather with the genial sentence: 'I went down to the Peiraeus yesterday with Glaucon, Ariston's son, to pay my devotion to the goddess, and at the same time I wanted to see how they would manage the festival, as this was the first time they held it.'
LIN YUTANG

In my opinion, even the *Dialogues* of Plato drag. They are overwritten, and I regret that a man who had many better things to say wasted so much time in long and needless preliminary conversations.
MONTAIGNE

We can only think of Plato and Aristotle in grand academic robes. They were honest men, like others, laughing with their friends, and when they diverted themselves with writing their *Laws* and the *Politics*, they did it as an amusement. That part of their life was the least philosophic and the least serious; the most philosophic was to live simply and quietly. PASCAL

Plato raises all fundamental questions without answering them.
ALFRED NORTH WHITEHEAD

PLAY

What, then, is the right way of living? Life must be lived as a play, playing certain games, making sacrifices, singing and dancing, and then a man will be able to propitiate the gods, and defend himself against his enemies, and win in the contest. PLATO

Playing as children mean playing is the most serious thing in the world.
G. K. CHESTERTON

Play is one of the main bases of civilization. JOHAN HUIZINGA

See also **Card Playing, Games.**

PLAYWRITING

The secret of playwriting can be given in two maxims: stick to the point and whenever you can, cut.
W. SOMERSET MAUGHAM

PLEASING

If you will please people, you must please them in their own way.
LORD CHESTERFIELD

Men may be convinced, but they cannot be pleased, against their will. SAMUEL JOHNSON

A man will please more on the whole by negative qualities than by positive; by never offending, than by giving a great deal of delight. In the first place, men hate more steadily than they love; and if I have said something to hurt a man once, I shall not get the better of this, by saying many things to please him. SAMUEL JOHNSON

Everything which is written is meant either to please or to instruct. The second object it is difficult to effect, without attending to the first.
SYDNEY SMITH

The art of pleasing consists in being pleased. WILLIAM HAZLITT

It seems to me to be a duty which we owe to society, to feel pleased with ourselves. FRANK SWINNERTON

See also **Agreeable.**

PLEASURE

One should be just as careful in choosing one's pleasures as in avoiding calamities.
CHINESE PROVERB

The truly wise man must be as intelligent and expert in the use of natural pleasures as in all the other functions of life. So the sages lived, gently yielding to the laws of our human lot, to Venus and to Bacchus. MONTAIGNE

We must tooth and nail retain the use of this life's pleasures, which our years snatch from us one after another. MONTAIGNE

'Tis a wrong way to proportion other men's pleasures to ourselves; 'tis like a child's using a little bird, O poor bird thou shalt sleep with me; so lays it in his bosom and stifles it with his hot breath; the bird had rather be in the cold air.
JOHN SELDEN

The race of delight is short, and pleasures have mutable faces.

SIR THOMAS BROWNE

One forsakes pleasures only for greater ones.   PASCAL

It is the part of a wise man to feed himself with moderate pleasant food and drink, and to take pleasure with perfumes, with the beauty of growing plants, dress, music, sports, and theatres and other places of this kind which a man may use without any hurt to his fellows.   SPINOZA

Pleasure is very seldom found where it is sought. Our brightest blazes are commonly kindled by unexpected sparks. SAMUEL JOHNSON

Many a man thinks he is buying pleasure, when he is really selling himself a slave to it.

BENJAMIN FRANKLIN

Fly pleasures and they will follow you.   BENJAMIN FRANKLIN

The secret of the smallest natural pleasures defies understanding.

VAUVENARGUES

'Business first, pleasure arterwards, as King Richard the Third said, when he stabbed t'other king in the Tower, afore he smothered the babbies.'   CHARLES DICKENS

The essence of pleasure does not lie in the thing enjoyed, but in the accompanying consciousness. If I had a humble spirit in my service, who, when I asked for a glass of water, brought me the world's costliest wines blended in a chalice, I should dismiss him, in order to teach him that pleasure consists not in what I enjoy, but in having my own way.

SÖREN KIERKEGAARD

The soul's greatest perfection is capacity for pleasure.

VAUVENARGUES

I have betrayed no woman. Wine has brought me to no sorrow. It has been the companionship of smoking that I have loved, rather than the habit. I have never desired to win money, and I have lost none. To enjoy the excitement of pleasure, but to be free from its vices and ill effects—to have the sweet, and leave the bitter untasted —that has been my study. The preachers tell us that this is impossible. It seems to me that hitherto I have succeeded fairly well.

ANTHONY TROLLOPE

That man is richest whose pleasures are the cheapest.

HENRY DAVID THOREAU

Pleasure, on knowing what gives us. It is idle to say that this is easily known—it is the highest and most neglected of all arts and branches of education.

SAMUEL BUTLER

Pleasure is nature's test, her sign of approval.   OSCAR WILDE

The chief secret of comfort lies in not suffering trifles to vex one, and in prudently cultivating an undergrowth of small pleasures, since very few great ones, alas! are let on long leases.   WILLIAM SHARP

Every perfect action is accompanied by pleasure. By that you can tell that you ought to do it.

ANDRÉ GIDE

Pleasure is more trouble than trouble.   DON HEROLD

See also **Amusement, Enjoyment, Frolic, Fun, Joy.**

PLUCK

Pluck is not so common nowadays as genius.   OSCAR WILDE

See also **Courage.**

PLUMBING

When you consider how indifferent Americans are to the quality and cooking of the food they put into their insides, it cannot but strike you as peculiar that they should take such pride in the mechanical appliances they use for its excretion.   W. SOMERSET MAUGHAM

POCKET

In the ordinary affairs of life the man who knows in which pocket his money is, is in a vastly superior position to the man who does not know in which pocket his money is, and yet, in relation to pickpockets, the man who does not know in which pocket his money is, is the more fortunate. For, if a man himself does not know where his money is, how can a passing stranger know?   ROBERT LYND

POET

To tell of disappointment and misery, to thicken the darkness of futurity, and perplex the labyrinth of uncertainty, has been always a delicious employment of the poets.   SAMUEL JOHNSON

A poet can survive anything but a misprint.   OSCAR WILDE

It is the business of reviewers to watch poets, not of poets to watch reviewers.   WILLIAM HAZLITT

The poet's habit of living should be set on a key so low that the common influences should delight him.   RALPH WALDO EMERSON

The poet is a man who lives at last by watching his moods. An old poet comes at last to watch his moods as narrowly as a cat does a mouse.   HENRY DAVID THOREAU

Knowledge of the subject is to the poet what durable materials are to the architect.   SAMUEL JOHNSON

I think if some of the great poets had lived in our time they might have been not poets but scientists. Shelley, for example; I think it quite possible that he could have been a chemist or physicist.
ALFRED NORTH WHITEHEAD

My quarrel with poets is not that they are unclear but that they are too diligent.   E. B. WHITE

See also **Artist, Byron, Tennyson.**

POETRY

It is easier to write an indifferent poem than to understand a good one.   MONTAIGNE

'Tis a fine thing for children to learn to make verse; but when they come to be men, they must speak like other men, or else they will be laughed at.   JOHN SELDEN

Verses which do not teach men new and moving truths do not deserve to be read.   VOLTAIRE

Thomson had a true poetical genius, the power of viewing everything in a poetical light. His fault is such a cloud of words sometimes, that the sense can hardly peep through. Shiels, who compiled *Cibber's Lives of the Poets*, was one day sitting with me. I took down Thomson and read aloud a large portion of him, and then asked, 'Is not this fine?' Shiels having expressed the highest admiration, 'Well, sir,' said I, 'I have omitted every other line.'
SAMUEL JOHNSON

Poetry is nothing but healthy speech. HENRY DAVID THOREAU

All my poems are 'occasional' poems—occasioned by reality and grounded in it. Poems that come out of thin air are good for nothing.
GOETHE

I consider poetry very subordinate to moral and political science.
SHELLEY

Formerly, people believed that the sugar cane alone yielded sugar; nowadays it is extracted from almost anything. It is the same with poetry. Let us draw it, no matter whence, for it lies everywhere, and in all things. GUSTAVE FLAUBERT

'Poetry,' said Emilia, 'seems like talking on tiptoe.'
GEORGE MEREDITH

If I read a book and it makes my whole body so cold no fire can ever warm me, I know that it is poetry. If I feel physically as if the top of my head were taken off, I know it is poetry. These are the only ways I know it. Is there any other way? EMILY DICKINSON

She warn't particular: she could write about anything you choose to give her to write about just so it was sadful. Every time a man died, or a woman died, or a child died, she would be on hand with her 'tribute' before he was cold. She called them tributes. The neighbours said it was the doctor first, then Emmeline, then the undertaker—the undertaker never got in ahead of Emmeline but once, and then she hung fire on a rhyme for the dead person's name, which was Whistler. She warn't ever the same after that; she never complained, but she kinder pined away and did not live long. MARK TWAIN

All that is worth remembering of life is the poetry of it.
WILLIAM HAZLITT

A poem is no place for an idea.
E. W. HOWE

A man can live three days without water but not one without poetry.
OSCAR WILDE

I am always asked how it is that my opinions have changed so little since my youth. It is because I got to them by poetry. As I always say, the aesthetic is the most convincing and permanent.
GEORGE BERNARD SHAW

Experience has taught me, when I am shaving of a morning, to keep watch over my thoughts, because, if a line of poetry strays into my memory, my skin bristles so that the razor ceases to act.
A. E. HOUSMAN

Take away from modern poetry what appeals to primitive man— the jingle and pathetic fallacy—and the residue, if any, would be better expressed in prose.
NORMAN DOUGLAS

I have always had a sneaking sympathy with George Crabbe who read the poems of Byron, Walter Scott, Keats and Shelley, and thought them all stuff and nonsense. After all, he might have been right. W. SOMERSET MAUGHAM

Indifference to poetry is one of the most conspicuous characteristics of the human race. ROBERT LYND

Almost all the contents of the 'advanced' reviews are just 'Mary had a little lamb' translated into Hebrew and written in cipher. Re-Englished and decoded, they astonish the reader by their silliness.
ALDOUS HUXLEY

See also **Literature, Poet.**

POLITENESS

There is a politeness of the heart. It is akin to love.　GOETHE

True politeness is only hope and trust in men.
HENRY DAVID THOREAU

If we treat people too long with that pretended liking called politeness, we shall find it hard not to like them in the end.
LOGAN PEARSALL SMITH

Some folks are too polite to be up to any good.　KIN HUBBARD

See also **Courtesy, Manners, Rude**

POLITICS

We must free ourselves from the prison of affairs and politics.
EPICURUS

State business is a cruel trade; good nature is a bungler in it.
LORD HALIFAX

Politics is the greatest of all sciences.　VAUVENARGUES

In politics as on the sickbed people toss from one side to the other, thinking they will be more comfortable.　GOETHE

Politics are but the cigar smoke of a man.　HENRY DAVID THOREAU

A politician divides mankind into two classes: tools and enemies. That means that he knows only one class: enemies.
FRIEDRICH NIETZSCHE

Politics makes strange postmasters.
KIN HUBBARD

Politics is the art of government.
HARRY S. TRUMAN

See also **Government.**

POOR

Remember the poor—it costs nothing.　JOSH BILLINGS

Talking with pleasure with my poor wife, how she used to make coal fires, and wash my foul clothes with her own hand for me, poor wretch! in our little room at my Lord Sandwich's; for which I ought forever to love and admire her, and do.　SAMUEL PEPYS

There is no doubt that if the poor should reason, 'We'll be the poor no longer, we'll make the rich take their turn,' they could easily do it, were it not that they can't agree.
SAMUEL JOHNSON

What the poor are to the poor, is little known, excepting to themselves and God. CHARLES DICKENS

And the mistake of the best men through generation after generation, has been the great one of thinking to help the poor by almsgiving, and by preaching of patience or of hope, and by every other means, emollient or consolatory, except the one thing which God orders for them, justice.
JOHN RUSKIN

I thank fate for having made me born poor. Poverty taught me the true value of the gifts useful to life.
ANATOLE FRANCE

I hate the poor and look forward eagerly to their extermination.
GEORGE BERNARD SHAW

Sometimes the poor are praised for their being thrifty. But to recommend thrift to the poor is both grotesque and insulting. It is like advising a man who is starving to eat less.　OSCAR WILDE

The common argument that crime is caused by poverty is a kind of slander on the poor.
H. L. MENCKEN

One of the strangest things about life is that the poor, who need money the most, are the very ones that never have it.

FINLEY PETER DUNNE

If you've ever really been poor you remain poor at heart all your life. I've often walked when I could very well afford to take a taxi because I simply couldn't bring myself to waste the shilling it would cost. ARNOLD BENNETT

It's no disgrace to be poor, but it might as well be. KIN HUBBARD

For the poor, the economic is the spiritual. GANDHI

'No one has ever said it,' observed Lady Caroline, 'but how painfully true it is that the poor have us always with them!' SAKI

Most of our realists and sociologists talk about a poor man as if he were an octopus or an alligator.

G. K. CHESTERTON

The poor on the borderline of starvation live purposeful lives. To be snagged in a desperate struggle for food and shelter is to be wholly free from a sense of futility. ERIC HOFFER

See also **Poverty, Rich and Poor.**

POPE, ALEXANDER

There are two ways of disliking poetry, one way is to dislike it, the other is to read Pope.

OSCAR WILDE

POPERY

Defoe says that there were a hundred thousand stout country-fellows in his time ready to fight to the death against popery, without knowing whether popery was a man or a horse.

WILLIAM HAZLITT

POPULAR

Popularity is a crime from the moment it is sought; it is only a virtue where men have it whether they will or no. LORD HALIFAX

God does not sympathize with the popular movements.

HENRY DAVID THOREAU

See also **Public Opinion.**

POSITIVE

The most positive men are the most credulous. ALEXANDER POPE

Positive: Mistaken at the top of one's voice. AMBROSE BIERCE

POSSESSION

Possession not alone hinders enjoyment: it increases annoyance whether you lend or keep.

BALTASAR GRACIÁN

What we don't understand we don't possess. GOETHE

Most of the happiness in this world consists in possessing what others can't get. JOSH BILLINGS

Happily for our blessedness, the joy of possession soon palls.

GEORGE MACDONALD

The more a man possesses over and above what he uses, the more careworn he becomes.

GEORGE BERNARD SHAW

If we would possess we must not claim. KAHLIL GIBRAN

We only possess what we renounce.

SIMONE WEIL

See also **Property.**

POSSIBILITY

It is very dangerous to go into eternity with possibilities which one has oneself prevented from becoming realities. A possibility is a hint from God. One must follow it. In every man there is latent the highest possibility; one must follow it. If God does not wish it, then let Him prevent it, but one must not hinder oneself. Trusting to God I have dared, but I was not successful; in that is to be found peace, calm, a confidence in God. I have not dared; that is a woeful thought, a torment in eternity.

SÖREN KIERKEGAARD

POST-CHAISE

If I had no duties, and no reference to futurity, I would spend my life in driving briskly in a post-chaise with a pretty woman; but she should be one who could understand me, and would add something to the conversation.

SAMUEL JOHNSON

POVERTY

Poverty, when measured by the natural purpose of life, is great wealth, but unlimited wealth is great poverty.   EPICURUS

Poverty is your treasure. Do not exchange it for an easy life.

ZEN-GETSU

Sir, all the arguments which are brought to represent poverty as no evil show it to be evidently a great evil. You never find people labouring to convince you that you may live very happily upon a plentiful fortune.

SAMUEL JOHNSON

Cultivate poverty like sage, like a garden herb. Do not trouble yourself to get new things, whether clothes or friends. That is dissipation. Turn to the old; return to them. Things do not change; we change.   HENRY DAVID THOREAU

Poverty humiliates people until they blush for their virtues.

VAUVENARGUES

Poverty is the strenuous life—without brass bands, or uniforms, or hysteric popular applause, or lies, or circumlocutions.

WILLIAM JAMES

The prevalent fear of poverty among the educated classes is the worst moral disease from which our civilization suffers.

WILLIAM JAMES

I can recall the moment when I shed poverty like an infected cloak. I had a speaking engagement and as usual dashed after a bus only to see it go off. I began to walk to save money and suddenly stopped short. I realized that I did not need to save twopence. I could now afford half a crown for a taxi. I jumped into a taxi and arrived in style.   GEORGE BERNARD SHAW

The evil to be attacked is not sin, suffering, greed, priestcraft, kingcraft, demagogy, monopoly, ignorance, drink, war, pestilence, nor any of the other scapegoats which reformers sacrifice, but simply poverty.

GEORGE BERNARD SHAW

Poverty does not produce unhappiness: it produces degradation.

GEORGE BERNARD SHAW

If your everyday life seems poor to you, do not accuse it; accuse yourself, tell yourself you are not poet enough to summon up its riches; since for the Creator there is no poverty and no poor or unimportant place.

RAINER MARIA RILKE

Poverty is a great radiance from within.   RAINER MARIA RILKE

See also **Poor, Rich and Poor.**

POWER

Exercise yourself in what lies in your power. EPICTETUS

He is the best of men who dislikes power. MOHAMMED

Let not thy will roar, when thy power can but whisper.
DR. THOMAS FULLER

Power is always gradually stealing away from the many to the few, because the few are more vigilant and consistent. SAMUEL JOHNSON

Consciousness of our powers increases them. VAUVENARGUES

If the arrangement of society is bad and a small number of people have power over the majority and oppress it, every victory over nature will inevitably serve only to increase that power and that oppression. That is what is actually happening. LEO TOLSTOY

Power does not corrupt men; fools, however, if they get into a position of power, corrupt power.
GEORGE BERNARD SHAW

Human nature is much the same in government as in the dry-goods trade. Power and strict accountability for its use are the essential constituents of good government.
WOODROW WILSON

See also **Government.**

PRACTICAL

A practical man is a man who practices the errors of his forefathers. BENJAMIN DISRAELI

PRAISE

Great tranquillity of heart is his who cares for neither praise nor blame. THOMAS À KEMPIS

We refuse praise from a desire to be praised twice.
LA ROCHEFOUCAULD

To praise princes for virtues they do not possess is but to reproach them with impunity.
LA ROCHEFOUCAULD

The highest panegyric that private virtue can receive is the praise of servants. SAMUEL JOHNSON

When you praise someone you call yourself his equal. GOETHE

Woe unto me when all men praise me! GEORGE BERNARD SHAW

When I was young I had an elderly friend who used often to ask me to stay with him in the country. He was a religious man and he read prayers to the assembled household every morning. But he had crossed out in pencil all the passages in the Book of Common Prayer that praised God. He said that there was nothing so vulgar as to praise people to their faces and, himself a gentleman, he could not believe that God was so ungentlemanly as to like it.
W. SOMERSET MAUGHAM

See also **Flattery.**

PRAYER

Rewards for prayers said by people assembled together are twice those said at home. MOHAMMED

There were some mathematicians that could with one fetch of the pen make an exact circle, and with the next touch point out the centre; is it therefore reasonable to banish all use of the compasses? Set forms are a pair of compasses.
JOHN SELDEN

There are few men who dare publish to the world the prayers they make to Almighty God.

MONTAIGNE

He prays well who is so absorbed with God that he does not know he is praying. ST. FRANCIS DE SALES

A memory of yesterday's pleasures, a fear of tomorrow's dangers, a straw under my knees, a noise in my ear, a light in my eye, an anything, a nothing, a fancy, a chimera in my brain, troubles me in my prayer. JOHN DONNE

ST. IGNATIUS LOYOLA was once asked what his feelings would be if the Pope were to suppress the Company of Jesus. 'A quarter of an hour of prayer.' he answered, 'and I should think no more about it.'

Prayer should be short, without giving God Almighty reasons why He should grant this or that; He knows best what is good for us. If your boy should ask you a suit of clothes, and give you reasons 'otherwise he cannot wait upon you, he cannot go abroad but he will discredit you,' would you endure it? You know it better than he; let him ask a suit of clothes.

JOHN SELDEN

The best prayers have often more groans than words. JOHN BUNYAN

I did this night promise to my wife never to go to bed without calling upon God upon my knees by prayer, and begun this night, and hope I shall never forget to do the like all my life; for I do find that it is much the best for my soul and body to live pleasing to God and my poor wife, and will ease me of much care as well as much expense.

SAMUEL PEPYS

We ought to act with God in the greatest simplicity, speaking to Him frankly and plainly, and imploring His assistance in our affairs, just as they happen.

BROTHER LAWRENCE

Serving God is doing good to man, but praying is thought an easier service and therefore more generally chosen. BENJAMIN FRANKLIN

Those who always pray are necessary to those who never pray.

VICTOR HUGO

Prayer does not change God, but changes him who prays.

SÖREN KIERKEGAARD

A man of settled views, whose thoughts are few and hardened like his bones, is truly mortal, and his only resource is to say his prayers. HENRY DAVID THOREAU

The man who says his prayers in the evening is a captain posting his sentries. After that, he can sleep.

CHARLES BAUDELAIRE

Do not lose the habit of praying to the unseen Divinity. Prayer for worldly goods is worse than fruitless, but prayer for strength of soul is that passion of the soul which catches the gift it seeks.

GEORGE MEREDITH

Pray: To ask the laws of the universe to be annulled on behalf of a single petitioner confessedly unworthy. AMBROSE BIERCE

God is like the sun; we come from Him and we shall go to Him; we owe Him all things, but there is no use in praying to Him.

SAMUEL BUTLER

She told me to pray every day, and whatever I asked for I would get it. But it warn't so. I tried it. Once I got a fishline, but no hooks. It warn't any good to me without hooks. I tried for the hooks three or four times, but somehow I couldn't make it work.

MARK TWAIN

Nataly heard the snuffle of hypocrisy in her prayer. She had to cease to pray. GEORGE MEREDITH

I don't know of a single foreign product that enters this country untaxed except the answer to prayer. MARK TWAIN

It is best to read the weather forecasts before we pray for rain.

MARK TWAIN

Indigestion: A disease which the patient and his friends frequently mistake for deep religious conviction and concern for the salvation of mankind. As the simple Red Man of the Western Wild put it, with, it must be confessed, a certain force: 'Plenty well, no pray; big bellyache, heap God.'

AMBROSE BIERCE

If you want to make a man very angry, get someone to pray for him. E. W. HOWE

When the gods wish to punish us they answer our prayers.

OSCAR WILDE

Prayer must never be answered: if it is, it cease to be prayer and becomes correspondence. OSCAR WILDE

A life spent in prayer and almsgiving is really as insane as a life spent in cursing and picking pockets; the effect of everybody doing it would be equally disastrous.

GEORGE BERNARD SHAW

There is nothing more impressive than spontaneous prayer, because it involves long and arduous preparation.

GEORGE BERNARD SHAW

No unsophisticated man prays to have that done for him which he knows how to do for himself.

GEORGE SANTAYANA

A pious Frenchman visiting Westminster Abbey knelt down to pray. The verger, who had never seen such a thing before, promptly handed him over to the police and charged him with brawling. Fortunately the magistrate had compassion on the foreigner's ignorance and even went the length of asking why he should not be allowed to pray in church. The reply of the verger was simple. 'If we allowed that,' he said, 'we should have people praying all over the place.'

GEORGE BERNARD SHAW

Prayer is the very soul and essence of religion and therefore prayer must be the very core of the life of man, for no man can live without religion. GANDHI

The using up of strength is in a certain sense still an increase of strength; for fundamentally it is only a matter of a wide circle; all the strength we give away comes back to us again, experienced and transformed. It is so in prayer. And what is there that, truly done, would not be prayer?

RAINER MARIA RILKE

The ivory tower was an aesthete's creation; others are modelled on ethic principles. Their inhabitants don't fiddle while Rome burns, they pray. ARTHUR KOESTLER

The person who asks the gods for special protection is a racketeer by nature. HENRY S. HASKINS

Her definition of prayer was characteristic. 'I set every ounce of will power to calling up all my strength and endurance. It was wonderful how I felt it rise, when I called,' she said gravely.

DOROTHY CANFIELD FISHER

When you pray you rise to meet in the air those who are praying at that very hour.   KAHLIL GIBRAN

God listens not to your words save when He Himself utters them through your lips.

KAHLIL GIBRAN

Leave your prayers to themselves, and they will come home dragging your objectives behind them.

HENRY S. HASKINS

See also **Lord's Prayer, Prayers (Quoted), Worship.**

PRAYERS (QUOTED)

Beloved Pan, and all ye other gods who haunt this place, give me beauty in the inward soul; and may the outward and inward man be one. May I reckon the wise to be the wealthy, and may I have such quantity of gold as a temperate man and he only can bear and carry.

SOCRATES (Plato, *Phaedrus*)

There was a prayer of the Athenians that ran: 'Rain, rain, O beloved Zeus, on the cornfields and plains of Attica.' If we are to pray at all, let's pray like this, simply and freely.

MARCUS AURELIUS

Lord, I know not what to ask of thee. Thou only knowest what I need. Thou lovest me better than I know how to love myself. Father, give to thy child that which he himself knows not how to ask. Smite or heal, depress me or raise me up: I adore all thy purposes without knowing them. I am silent; I offer myself up in sacrifice; I yield myself to thee; I would have no other desire than to accomplish thy will. Teach me to pray. Pray Thyself in me.

FRANÇOIS DE FÉNELON

Grant, we beseech thee, merciful Lord, to thy faithful people pardon and peace, that they may be cleansed from all their sins, and serve thee with a quiet mind; through Jesus Christ our Lord. *Amen.*

BOOK OF COMMON PRAYER. (Collect. The 21st Sunday after Trinity)

I have read of a wise bishop who, on touring his diocese, met an old woman whose sole prayer consisted of the exclamation 'O!' 'Good mother,' said he, 'go on praying like that always. Your prayer is better than ours.'   ROUSSEAU

Help us, God, and give us light so that we don't stand in our own way; let us do from morning till night what should be done, and give us clear ideas of the consequences of our actions.   GOETHE

The day returns and brings us the petty round of irritating concerns and duties. Help us to play the man, help us to perform them with laughter and kind faces; let cheerfulness abound with industry. Give us to go blithely on our business all this day, bring us to our resting beds weary and content and undishonoured, and grant us in the end the gift of sleep.

ROBERT LOUIS STEVENSON

He was an airman. He was talking of his experiences. 'I never believed in religion before,' he said, 'but when I was in a jam I prayed. "O God," I said, "let me live till to-morrow." I just said it over and over again.'

W. SOMERSET MAUGHAM

I was thinking of an old idea of self-discipline—an old proverb of a Chinese Christian. He prayed every day—he had been taught to pray to our kind of God—and his prayer was, 'Lord, reform Thy world, beginning with me.'

FRANKLIN DELANO ROOSEVELT

Unbeliever's Prayer

Almighty God
forgive me for my agnosticism;
For I shall try to keep it gentle, not
    cynical,
nor a bad influence.

And O!
if Thou art truly in the heavens,
accept my gratitude
for all Thy gifts
and I shall try
to fight the good fight. Amen.

JOHN GUNTHER, JR.

See also **Prayer, Worship.**

PREACHING

To go preaching to the first passer-by, to be schoolmaster to the ignorance and stupidity of any chance person, is a thing I greatly dislike.

MONTAIGNE

A woman's preaching is like a dog's walking on his hind legs. It is not done well; but you are surprised to find it done at all. SAMUEL JOHNSON

Of Dean C., SYDNEY SMITH said his only adequate punishment would be to be preached to death by wild curates.

There is not the least use in preaching to anyone unless you chance to catch them ill. SYDNEY SMITH

Coleridge once asked CHARLES LAMB: 'Pray, Mr. Lamb, did you ever hear me preach?' 'Damme,' said Lamb, 'I never heard you do anything else.'

Whoever would preach Christ in these times must say nothing about him. RALPH WALDO EMERSON

Ballard heard a Methodist preacher as follows: 'And what, I wonder, must have been Joab's feelings on receiving the letter from David telling him to put Uriah the Hittite in the front of the battle. Why, he must have said to himself, "Dear, dear, dear me, whatever can my old uncle be thinking about? Such beautiful psalms as he used to write too."' SAMUEL BUTLER

I once heard a preacher who was powerful good. I decided to give him every cent I had with me. But he kept at it too long. Ten minutes later I decided to keep the bills and just give him my loose change. Another ten minutes and I was darned if I'd give him anything at all. Then when he finally stopped, and the plate came around, I was so exhausted, I extracted two dollars out of sheer spite. MARK TWAIN

That we should practice what we preach is generally admitted; but anyone who preaches what he and his hearers practice must incur the gravest moral disapprobation.

LOGAN PEARSALL SMITH

The best sermon is preached by the minister who has a sermon to preach and not by the man who has to preach a sermon.

WILLIAM FEATHER

See also **Sermon.**

PRECEPT

No precepts will profit a fool.

BEN JONSON

Four precepts: to break off customs; to shake off spirits ill-disposed; to meditate on youth; to do nothing against's one's genius.

NATHANIEL HAWTHORNE

See also **Maxim, Rules of Life.**

PREHISTORIC

In prehistoric times women resembled men, and men resembled beasts. ANATOLE FRANCE

PREJUDICE

Our prejudices are our mistresses; reason is at best our wife, very often needed, but seldom minded.

LORD CHESTERFIELD

Prejudice is never easy unless it can pass itself off for reason.

WILLIAM HAZLITT

Without the aid of prejudice and custom, I should not be able to find my way across the room.

WILLIAM HAZLITT

The very ink with which all history is written is merely fluid prejudice.

MARK TWAIN

Prejudice: A vagrant opinion without visible means of support.

AMBROSE BIERCE

I never approve or disapprove of anything now. It is an absurd attitude to take towards life. We are not sent into the world to air our moral prejudices. OSCAR WILDE

I don't like principles. I prefer prejudices. OSCAR WILDE

There are people who are too stupid to have prejudices.

EGON FRIEDELL

See also **Conviction, Opinion.**

PREMATURE

God screens men from premature ideas. RALPH WALDO EMERSON

To be premature is to be perfect.

OSCAR WILDE

PRESENT

He who has looked on the things of the present has seen all things— both what has been from time eternal and what shall be during the infinite ages to come.

MARCUS AURELIUS

In rivers, the water that you touch is the last of what has passed and the first of that which comes: so with time present.

LEONARDO DA VINCI

Let each one examine his thoughts, and he will find them all occupied with the past and the future. . . . The present is never our end. The past and the present are our means; the future alone is our end. So we never live, but we hope to live; and, as we are always preparing to be happy, it is inevitable that we should never be so. PASCAL

Very few men, properly speaking, live at present, but are providing to live another time.

JONATHAN SWIFT

Always hold fast to the present hour. Every state of duration, every second, is of infinite value. . . . I have staked on the present as one stakes a large sum on one card, and I have sought without exaggerating to make it as high as possible.

GOETHE

Above all, we cannot afford not to live in the present. He is blessed over all mortals who loses no moment of the passing life in remembering the past.

HENRY DAVID THOREAU

Our latest moment is always our supreme moment. Five minutes delay in dinner now is more important than a great sorrow ten years gone. SAMUEL BUTLER

See also **Future, Now, Past.**

PRESENTS

The art of giving men presents is to give them something which they cannot buy for themselves; something which, without your co-operation, they would never be able to possess.　　A. A. MILNE

Presents are the reverse of treats. Presents stand for the expenditure of money, rather than of love.
　　　　　　　　FRANK SWINNERTON

See also **Giving**.

PRESS

The most important service rendered by the press and the magazines is that of educating people to approach printed matter with distrust.
　　　　　　　　SAMUEL BUTLER

See also **Newspaper**.

PRETENSION

Pretensions are a source of pain, and the happy time of life begins as soon as we give them up.
　　　　　　　　NICOLAS CHAMFORT

To give up pretensions is as blessed a relief as to get them gratified.
　　　　　　　　WILLIAM JAMES

See also **Affectation, Insincere**.

PRETTY

It is not easy to be a pretty woman without causing mischief.
　　　　　　　　ANATOLE FRANCE

PRICE

The height of ability consists in knowing the price of things.
　　　　　　　　LA ROCHEFOUCAULD

Nowadays people know the price of everything and the value of nothing.　　　　OSCAR WILDE

PRIDE

Pride may be allowed to this or that degree, else a man cannot keep up his dignity. In gluttony there must be eating, in drunkenness there must be drinking; 'tis not the eating, nor 'tis not the drinking that is to be blamed, but the excess. So with pride.　　　　JOHN SELDEN

Pride is as loud a beggar as want, and a great deal more saucy.
　　　　　　　　LORD HALIFAX

The pride of the peacock is the glory of God.　　WILLIAM BLAKE

PRIEST

My opinion is that there would never have been an infidel if there had never been a priest.
　　　　　　　　THOMAS JEFFERSON

It was Archimedes who said he could move the earth if he had a place to fix his levers on: the priests have always found this *purchase* in the skies.　　JAMES NORTHCOTE

Priests and rituals are only crutches for the crippled life of the soul.
　　　　　　　　FRANZ KAFKA

The priest is always fascinating to an adulterous generation because they think he knows more ways of committing adultery than anybody else. It's logical. He deals in sin as much as a dustman deals in garbage.
　　　　　　　　AUBREY MENEN

See also **Clergyman, Minister, Parson**.

PRIMITIVE

The longing to be primitive is a disease of culture; it is archaism in morals. To be so preoccupied with vitality is a symptom of anemia.
　　　　　　　　GEORGE SANTAYANA

See also **Simple**.

PRINCIPLE

Nobody ever did anything very foolish except from some strong principle. LORD MELBOURNE

It is easier to produce ten volumes of philosophical writing than to put one principle into practice.
LEO TOLSTOY

Prosperity is the best protector of principle. MARK TWAIN

Principles have no real force except when one is well fed. MARK TWAIN

To have doubted one's own first principles is the mark of a civilized man.
OLIVER WENDELL HOLMES, JR.

If we looked too close into first principles, we should never believe at all. ANATOLE FRANCE

I like persons better than principles and I like persons with no principles better than anything else in the world. OSCAR WILDE

A man who prides himself upon acting upon principle is likely to be a man who insists upon having his own way without learning from experience what is the better way.
JOHN DEWEY

When a fellow says, 'It ain't the money, but the principle of the thing,' it's the money.
KIN HUBBARD

PRINTING

Printing broke out in the province of Kansu in A.D. 868. The Early Chinese simply could not let well enough alone. WILL CUPPY

PRISON

The most anxious man in a prison is the governor.
GEORGE BERNARD SHAW

PROBABILITY

Wisdom does not trust to probabilities; it always marches in the midday light of reason.
BALTASAR GRACIÁN

Life is a school of probability.
WALTER BAGEHOT

It is better to be satisfied with probabilities than to demand impossibilities and starve.
F. C. S. SCHILLER

PROBLEM

Most of our problems are test questions. HENRY S. HASKINS

See also **Difficult, Difficulty, Trouble.**

PROCESS

Perhaps the only goal on earth toward which mankind is striving lies in the process of attaining, in other words, in life itself, and not in the thing to be attained.
FEODOR DOSTOEVSKI

The process itself is the actuality.
ALFRED NORTH WHITEHEAD

PRODIGAL

Every reformation must have its victims. You can't expect the fatted calf to share the enthusiasm of the angels over the prodigal's return.
SAKI

Tom was feeling more and more like the Prodigal Son and did not like it, as indeed we daresay the Prodigal Son himself did not like it either. For to have to eat fatted calf when you are thoroughly ashamed of yourself and only want to slink in and not to be noticed must be a severe trial; not to speak of one's Good Brother. ANGELA THIRKELL

PROFANITY

Many a man's profanity has saved him from a nervous breakdown.
HENRY S. HASKINS

See also **Damn.**

PROFESSION

An honest man is not accountable for the vice and folly of his trade, and therefore ought not to refuse the exercise of it. It is the custom of his country, and there is profit in it. We must live by the world, and such as we find it, so make use of it.
MONTAIGNE

It is wonderful when a calculation is made, how little the mind is actually employed in the discharge of any profession.   SAMUEL JOHNSON

PROFESSIONAL

One of the great differences between the amateur and the professional is that the latter has the capacity to progress.
W. SOMERSET MAUGHAM

See also **Amateur.**

PROGRESS

True progress quietly and persistently moves along without notice.
ST. FRANCIS DE SALES

Belief in progress is a lazy man's creed. . . . It is the individual counting on his neighbours to perform his task for him.
CHARLES BAUDELAIRE

All progress is based upon a universal desire on the part of every organism to live beyond its income.
SAMUEL BUTLER

All progress is initiated by challenging current conceptions, and executed by supplanting existing institutions.   GEORGE BERNARD SHAW

Old men hold far too obstinately to their own ideas. That is why the natives of the Fiji Islands kill their parents when they grow old. In this way they assist progress, while we retard its advance by founding Academies.   ANATOLE FRANCE

Few men progress, except as they are pushed along by events.
E. W. HOWE

Evolution is the opposite of progress.   ALAIN

Progress does not consist in looking for a direction in which one can go on indefinitely. True progress consists in looking for a place where we can stop.
G. K. CHESTERTON

Progress is the mother of problems.
G. K. CHESTERTON

I have always considered that the substitution of the internal combustion engine for the horse marked a very gloomy milestone in the progress of mankind.
WINSTON S. CHURCHILL

The religion of inevitable progress —which is, in the last analysis, the hope and faith (in the teeth of all human experience) that one can get something for nothing.
ALDOUS HUXLEY

See also **Civilization.**

PROHIBITION

A prohibitionist is the sort of man one wouldn't care to drink with— even if he drank. H. L. MENCKEN

See also **Drinking.**

PROMISE

A wise man, in trusting another, must not rely upon his *promise* against his *nature*. LORD HALIFAX

Being asked one day what was the surest way of remaining happy in this world, the Emperor SIGISMUND of Germany replied: 'Only do in health what you have promised to do when you were sick.'

Some persons make promises for the pleasure of breaking them.
WILLIAM HAZLITT

Half the promises people say were never kept, were never made.
E. W. HOWE
See also **Agreement.**

PROMISING
Whom the gods wish to destroy they first call promising.
CYRIL CONNOLLY

PROMOTE
One-third of the people in the United States promote, while the other two-thirds provide.
WILL ROGERS
See also **Advertising.**

PROOF
God only knows whether there be any Dulcinea or not in the world. These are things the proof of which must not be pushed to extreme lengths.   CERVANTES

It is always better to say right out what you think without worrying too much about proving your point. After all, our proofs are only variations of our opinions, and the contrary-minded listen neither to one nor the other.   GOETHE

No way of thinking or doing, however ancient, can be trusted without proof.   HENRY DAVID THOREAU
See also **Evidence.**

PROPERTY
It is immoral to use private property to alleviate the horrible evils that result from the institution of private property. It is both immoral and unfair.   OSCAR WILDE

Property is merely the art of democracy. It means that every man should have something that he can shape in his own image.
G. K. CHESTERTON
See also **Possession.**

PROPHECY
Among all forms of mistake, prophecy is the most gratuitous.
GEORGE ELIOT

Don't never prophesy, for if you prophesy wrong, nobody will forget it, and if you prophesy right, nobody will remember it.
JOSH BILLINGS

'History repeats itself' and 'History never repeats itself' are about equally true. . . . We never know enough about the infinitely complex circumstances of any past event to prophesy the future by analogy.   G. M. TREVELYAN

PROPHET
The best qualification of a prophet is to have a good memory.
LORD HALIFAX

The New Jerusalem, when it comes, will probably be found so far to resemble the old as to stone its prophets freely.   SAMUEL BUTLER

It is the sad destiny of a prophet that when, after working twenty years, he convinces his contemporaries, his adversaries also succeed, and he is no longer convinced himself.   FRIEDRICH NIETZSCHE

The well-adjusted make poor prophets.   ERIC HOFFER
See also **Prophecy.**

PROSE

Ropes more than any other subject are a test of a man's power of exposition in prose. If you can describe clearly without a diagram the proper way of making this or that knot, then you are a master of the English tongue. HILAIRE BELLOC

See also **Style, Writing.**

PROSPERITY

No man prospers so suddenly as by others' errors. FRANCIS BACON

Few of us can stand prosperity. Another man's, I mean.
MARK TWAIN

PROTESTANT

A Protestant, if he wants aid or advice on any matter, can only go to his solicitor. BENJAMIN DISRAELI

PROVIDENCE

As luck would have it, Providence was on my side. SAMUEL BUTLER

When good befalls a man he calls it Providence, when evil Fate.
KNUT HAMSUN

See also **Fate, Will of God.**

PRUDENCE

The wise man knows that the very polestar of prudence lies in steering by the wind. BALTASAR GRACIÁN

There is nothing so imprudent or so improvident as over-prudence or over-providence. SAMUEL BUTLER

PSYCHOANALYSIS

Psychoanalysis is the disease it purports to cure. KARL KRAUS

Psychoanalysis is confession without absolution.
G. K. CHESTERTON

PSYCHOLOGY

Popular psychology is a mass of cant, of slush, and of superstition worthy of the most flourishing days of the medicine man.
JOHN DEWEY

Psychology is as unnecessary as directions for using poison.
KARL KRAUS

See also **Emotion, Mind.**

PUBLIC

The public is merely a multiplied 'me'. MARK TWAIN

PUBLIC OPINION

The sage has no decided opinions and feelings, but regards the people's opinions and feelings as his own. LAO-TSE

Do not condemn alone that which pleases all. What all say, is so, or will be so. BALTASAR GRACIÁN

Happy those who are convinced so as to be of the general opinions.
LORD HALIFAX

It requires ages to destroy a popular opinion. VOLTAIRE

The greatest part of mankind have no other reason for their opinions than that they are in fashion.
SAMUEL JOHNSON

About things on which the public thinks long, it commonly attains to think right. SAMUEL JOHNSON

Where an opinion is general, it is usually correct. JANE AUSTEN

The public buys its opinions as it buys its meat, or takes in its milk, on the principle that it is cheaper to do this than to keep a cow. So it is, but the milk is more likely to be watered. SAMUEL BUTLER

See also **Opinion, Popular.**

PULSE

There are worse occupations in this world than feeling a woman's pulse.
LAURENCE STERNE

PUN

Where the common people like puns, and make them, the nation is on a high level of culture.
G. C. LICHTENBERG

A pun is a noble thing *per se*. It fills the mind, it is as perfect as a sonnet; better.
CHARLES LAMB

Puns should be punished unless they be pungent.
SALVADOR DE MADARIAGA

See also **Humour, Joke.**

PUNCTUALITY

Punctuality is the thief of time.
OSCAR WILDE

Punctuality is a form of self-indulgence.
ROBERT LYND

See also **Unpunctuality.**

PUNISHMENT

He who does not punish evil commands it to be done.
LEONARDO DA VINCI

To inflict unnecessary punishment is to encroach upon God's mercy.
VAUVENARGUES

When I was a boy I'd rather be licked twice than postponed once.
JOSH BILLINGS

Distrust all men in whom the impulse to punish is powerful.
FRIEDRICH NIETZSCHE

PURITAN

Cavaliers and Puritans are interesting for their costumes and not for their convictions.
OSCAR WILDE

PURITANISM

Puritanism: The haunting fear that someone, somewhere, may be happy.
H. L. MENCKEN

PURITY

Simplicity reaches out after God; purity discovers and enjoys Him.
THOMAS À KEMPIS

A pure heart is an excellent thing— and so is a clean shirt.
G. C. LICHTENBERG

PURPOSE

Your purpose in life is simply to help on the purpose of the universe.
GEORGE BERNARD SHAW

PURSUIT

Were this world an endless plain, and by sailing eastward we could for ever reach new distances, and discover sights more sweet and strange than any Cyclades or Islands of King Solomon, then there were promise in the voyage. But in pursuit of those far mysteries we dream of, or in tormented chase of that demon phantom that, some time or other, swims before all human hearts; while chasing such over this round globe, they either lead us on in barren mazes or midway leave us whelmed.
HERMAN MELVILLE

There is a joy in the pursuit of anything.
ROBERT HENRI

Every calling is great when greatly pursued.
OLIVER WENDELL HOLMES, JR.

In every passionate pursuit, the pursuit counts more than the object pursued.
ERIC HOFFER

PUT UP

The first great rule of life is to put up with things.
BALTASAR GRACIÁN

See also **Endure.**

PYRAMID

Cheops built the Great Pyramid of Gizeh about 3050 B.C. Then he felt better. WILL CUPPY

Q

QUALITIES

It is not enough to have great qualities, we should also have the management of them.
LA ROCHEFOUCAULD

See also **Talent.**

QUARREL

A quarrel between friends, when made up, adds a new tie to friendship, as experience shows that the callosity formed round a broken bone makes it stronger than before.
ST. FRANCIS DE SALES

Quarrels would not last long if the fault was only on one side.
LA ROCHEFOUCAULD

In any quarrel that person will generally be thought in the wrong, who it was foretold would quarrel.
LORD CHESTERFIELD

God turns His back on those who quarrel among themselves.
GANDHI

The falling of a teacup puts us out of temper for the day; and a quarrel that commenced about the pattern of a gown may end only with our lives. WILLIAM HAZLITT

Literature is for the most part an idealization of quarrels. Cut quarrels out of literature, and you will have very little history or drama or fiction or epic poetry left.
ROBERT LYND

See also **Arguing, Controversy, Dispute.**

QUESTION

Ignorant men raise questions that wise men answered a thousand years ago. GOETHE

Questions are never indiscreet. Answers sometimes are.
OSCAR WILDE

The 'silly question' is the first intimation of some totally new development.
ALFRED NORTH WHITEHEAD

By nature's kindly disposition most questions which it is beyond a man's power to answer do not occur to him at all.
GEORGE SANTAYANA

Socrates asked so many questions that the exasperated Athenians compelled him to drink poison. King Lear subjected his daughters to a questionnaire, and he and his daughters perished tragically as a result. ROBERT LYND

It is better to ask some of the questions than to know all the answers. JAMES THURBER

See also **Answer.**

QUIET

Everything that does us good is so apt to do us hurt too, that it is a strong argument for men to be quiet. LORD HALIFAX

All human unhappiness comes from not knowing how to stay quietly in a room. PASCAL

A man that will enjoy a quiet conscience must lead a quiet life.
LORD CHESTERFIELD

Hospitality consists in a little fire, a little food, and an immense quiet.
RALPH WALDO EMERSON

An inability to stay quiet, an irritable desire to act directly, is one of the most conspicuous failings of mankind. WALTER BAGEHOT

Very often the quiet fellow has said all he knows. KIN HUBBARD

A happy life must be to a great extent a quiet life, for it is only in an atmosphere of quiet that true joy can live. BERTRAND RUSSELL

The majority of people in this big world live as quietly and industriously as mice.
WILLIAM FEATHER

See also **Pause, Silence, Tranquillity.**

QUOTATION
The Baron de Cambronne did not say at Waterloo, 'The Guard dies, but does not surrender.' Cambronne himself, twenty years later, disavowed the saying, and added with great honesty, 'In the first place, we did not die, and in the second place, we did surrender.'
W. R. INGE

I am reminded of the professor who, in his declining hours, was asked by his devoted pupils for his final counsel. He replied, 'Verify your quotations.'
WINSTON S. CHURCHILL

QUOTING
When a thing has been said and well said, have no scruple: take it and copy it. Give references? Why should you? Either your readers know where you have taken the passage and the precaution is needless, or they do not know and you humiliate them.
ANATOLE FRANCE

The surest way to make a monkey of a man is to quote him. That remark in itself wouldn't make any sense if quoted as it stands.
ROBERT BENCHLEY

R
RADICALISM
If a man is right, he can't be too radical; if he is wrong, he can't be too conservative. JOSH BILLINGS

Radicalism: The conservatism of tomorrow injected into the affairs of today. AMBROSE BIERCE

See also **Conservatism.**

RAIN
This thing called rain can make the days seem short and the nights seem long. CHANG CH'AO

RAINBOW
After fifteen minutes nobody looks at a rainbow. GOETHE

RAPHAEL
Raphael was employed to decorate the Vatican not because he was a great painter but because his uncle was architect to the Pope.
LORD MELBOURNE

READING
If I come across any difficulties in my reading, I do not bite my nails over them; after one or two attacks I give them up. MONTAIGNE

At the Day of Judgment we shall not be asked what we have read but what we have done.
THOMAS À KEMPIS

It is twenty years since I have devoted a whole hour at a time to a book. MONTAIGNE

When we read too fast or too slowly, we understand nothing.

PASCAL

Reading books in one's youth is like looking at the moon through a crevice; reading books in middle age is like looking at the moon in one's courtyard; and reading books in old age is like looking at the moon on an open terrace. This is because the depth of benefits of reading varies in proportion to the depth of one's own experience.

CHANG CH'AO

Who knows if Shakespeare might not have thought less, if he had read more? EDWARD YOUNG

Let blockheads read what blockheads wrote. LORD CHESTERFIELD

A man ought to read just as inclination leads him; for what he reads as a task will do him little good. SAMUEL JOHNSON

People in general do not willingly read, if they can have anything else to amuse them. SAMUEL JOHNSON

Too much reading hinders knowledge. We think we know what we have read, and consider ourselves excused from learning it. ROUSSEAU

Some people read only because they are too lazy to think.

G. C. LICHTENBERG

Desultory reading has always been my greatest pleasure.

G. C. LICHTENBERG

(About J. J. Winckelmann:) You don't learn anything when you read him, but you become something. GOETHE

The greatest pleasure in life is that of reading, while we are young.

WILLIAM HAZLITT

If my life had been more full of calamity than it has been, I would live it over again to have read the books I did in my youth.

WILLIAM HAZLITT

It is better to be able neither to read nor write than to be able to do nothing else.

WILLIAM HAZLITT

I suppose every old scholar has had the experience of reading something in a book which was significant to him, but which he could never find again. Sure he is that he read it there; but no one else ever read it, nor can he find it again, though he buy the book, and ransack every page. RALPH WALDO EMERSON

We often read with as much talent as we write.

RALPH WALDO EMERSON

Society is a strong solution of books. It draws its virtue out of what is best worth reading, as hot water draws the strength of tea leaves.

OLIVER WENDELL HOLMES, SR.

A truly great book teaches me better than to read it. I must soon lay it down, and commence living on its hint. . . . What I began by reading, I must finish by acting.

HENRY DAVID THOREAU

A learned fool is one who has read everything and remembered it.

JOSH BILLINGS

Never read anything until not to have read it has bothered you for some time. SAMUEL BUTLER

On the whole, perhaps, it is the great readers rather than the great writers who are entirely to be envied. They pluck the fruits, and are spared the trouble of rearing them. ALEXANDER SMITH

Do not waste the hours of daylight in listening to that which you may read by night. SIR WILLIAM OSLER

Out of a thousand persons who say, 'I have read this,' or 'I have read that,' there is not one perhaps who is able to express any opinion worth hearing about what he has been reading. LAFCADIO HEARN

Every man claims to read both sides, but no man does.
E. W. HOWE

People say that life is the thing, but I prefer reading.
LOGAN PEARSALL SMITH

It is one of the oddest things in the world that you can read a page or more and think of something utterly different.
CHRISTIAN MORGENSTERN

There are people who read too much: the bibliobibuli. I know some who are constantly drunk on books, as other men are drunk on whisky or religion. They wander through this most diverting and stimulating of worlds in a haze, seeing nothing and hearing nothing. H. L. MENCKEN

When we read, we are, we must be, repeating the words to ourselves unconsciously; for how else should we discover, as we have all discovered in our time, that we have been mispronouncing a word which, in fact, we have never spoken? I refer to such words as 'misled', which I, and millions of others when young, supposed to be 'mizzled'. A. A. MILNE

I have sometimes dreamt that when the Day of Judgment dawns and the great conquerors and lawyers and statesmen come to receive their awards—their crowns, their laurels, their names carved indelibly upon imperishable marble— the Almighty will turn to Peter and will say, not without a certain envy when He sees us coming with our books under our arms, 'Look, these need no reward. We have nothing to give them here. They have loved reading.' VIRGINIA WOOLF

The wise man reads both books and life itself. LIN YUTANG

See also **Books, Books and Reading, Literature, Well-Read.**

REALISM

I hate vulgar realism in literature. The man who could call a spade a spade should be compelled to use one. It is the only thing he is fit for.
OSCAR WILDE

REALIST

You may be sure that when a man begins to call himself a 'realist,' he is preparing to do something he is secretly ashamed of doing.
SYDNEY HARRIS

REALITY

A bill of fare with one real raisin on it instead of the word 'raisin', with one real egg instead of the word 'egg', might be an inadequate meal, but it would at least be a commencement of reality.
WILLIAM JAMES

EMERSON said, when he had to go out and look at a load of wood: 'We must see to these things, you know, as if they were real.'

Reality, however, has a sliding floor. RALPH WALDO EMERSON

Mental activity is easy if it doesn't have to conform to reality.
MARCEL PROUST

The great quality of true art is that it rediscovers, grasps, and reveals to us that reality far from which we live, from which we get farther and farther away as the conventional knowledge we substitute for it becomes thicker and more impermeable, the reality that we might die without having known and which is simply our life, real life, life finally discovered and clarified, consequently the only life that has really been lived—that life which in one sense is to be found at any time in all men as well as in artists.   MARCEL PROUST

REASON

I see men ordinarily more eager to discover a reason for things than to find out whether the things are so.   MONTAIGNE

Reason ever goes astray in all matters, but especially when she meddles with divine things.
MONTAIGNE

In giving reasons, men commonly do with us as the woman does with her child; when she goes to market about her business, she tells it she goes to buy it a fine thing, to buy it a cake or some plums. They give us such reasons as they think we will be catched withal, but never let us know the truth.   JOHN SELDEN

A man that does not use his reason is a tame beast; a man that abuses it a wild one.   LORD HALIFAX

Reason misleads us more often than nature.   VAUVENARGUES

Nothing has an uglier look to us than reason, when it is not on our side.   LORD HALIFAX

In an unreasonable age, a man's reason let loose would undo him.
LORD HALIFAX

Perhaps pure reason without heart would never have thought of God.
G. C. LICHTENBERG

It is the instinct of the understanding to counteract the reason.
NOVALIS

To give a reason for anything is to breed a doubt of it.
WILLIAM HAZLITT

Reason is nothing but the analysis of belief.   FRANZ SCHUBERT

All men have a reason, but not all men can give a reason.
JOHN HENRY NEWMAN

Most people reason dramatically, not quantitatively.
OLIVER WENDELL HOLMES, JR.

I can stand brute force but brute reason is quite unbearable. There is something unfair about its use. It is like hitting below the intellect.
OSCAR WILDE

'It stands to reason' is a formula that gives its user the unfair advantage of at once invoking reason and refusing to listen to it.
H. W. FOWLER

Reason, alas, does not remove mountains. It only tries to walk around them, and see what is on the other side.
G. W. RUSSELL (Æ)

See also **Logic, Thinking.**

REASONABLE

I am sick of reasonable people; they see all the reasons for being lazy and doing nothing.
GEORGE BERNARD SHAW

See also **Reason, Unreasonable.**

RECEIVING

We get forwards in the world, not so much by doing services as receiving them: you take a wither-

ing twig, and put it into the ground; and then you water it, because you have planted it.
LAURENCE STERNE

See also **Giving**.

RECOGNITION

Vaccination is undoubtedly a definite recognition of smallpox.
WINSTON S. CHURCHILL

RECOMMEND

To recommend certain things is worse than to practice them.
WILLIAM HAZLITT

The hardest thing is writing a recommendation for someone we know.
KIN HUBBARD

RECURRENCE

If a man has character, he has also his typical experience, which always recurs.
FRIEDRICH NIETZSCHE

Recurrence is sure. What the mind suffered last week, or last year, it does not suffer now; but it will suffer again next week or next year. Happiness is not a matter of events; it depends upon the tides of the mind.
ALICE MEYNELL

REFINEMENT

Barbarism and rusticity may perhaps be instructed, but false refinement is incorrigible.
WILLIAM HAZLITT

She was not quite what you would call refined. She was not quite what you would call unrefined. She was the kind of person who keeps a parrot.
MARK TWAIN

REFLECTION

As rain breaks through an ill-thatched house, passion will break through an unreflecting mind.
DHAMMAPADA

None are more prone to error than those who act only on reflection.
VAUVENARGUES

The man who has learned to reflect has laid by something nice for a wet day.
JOSH BILLINGS

See also **Thinking**.

REFORM

Why waste your time on reforming what is not worth reforming?
YOSHIDA KENKO

You know how happy I am about any reforms that the future may bring. But I deeply abhor anything sudden or violent *because it is not natural*.
GOETHE

Every reform, however necessary, will by weak minds be carried to an excess which will itself need reforming.
SAMUEL TAYLOR COLERIDGE

It is essential to the triumph of reform that it should never succeed.
WILLIAM HAZLITT

I think I am better than the people who are trying to reform me.
E. W. HOWE

Every reform is only a mask under cover of which a more terrible reform, which dares not yet name itself, advances.
RALPH WALDO EMERSON

If anything ail a man so that he does not perform his functions, if he have a pain in his bowels even . . . he forthwith sets about reforming —the world.
HENRY DAVID THOREAU

Is reform needed? Is it through you? The greater the reform needed, the greater the personality you need to accomplish it.
WALT WHITMAN

Almost every reform consists in the clearing away of an old rather than in the making of a new law.

H. T. BUCKLE

Nothing so needs reforming as other people's habits. MARK TWAIN

Every reform was once a private opinion. RALPH WALDO EMERSON

It is a dangerous thing to reform anyone. OSCAR WILDE

We fret ourselves to reform life, in order that posterity may be happy, and posterity will say as usual: 'In the past it used to be better, the present is worse than the past.'

ANTON CHEKHOV

A man who reforms himself has contributed his full share towards the reformation of his neighbour.

NORMAN DOUGLAS

REFORMER

I believe that what so saddens the reformer is not his sympathy with his fellows in distress, but, though he be the holiest son of God, is his private ail. Let this be righted, and he will forsake his generous companions without apology.

HENRY DAVID THOREAU

All reformers, however strict their conscience, live in houses just as big as they can pay for.

LOGAN PEARSALL SMITH

A man that would expect to train lobsters to fly in a year is called a lunatic; but a man that thinks men can be turned into angels by an election is a reformer and remains at large. FINLEY PETER DUNNE

REFUSAL

To know how to refuse is as important as to know how to consent. BALTASAR GRACIÁN

See also **No, Reject.**

REFUTE

After we came out of the church, we stood talking for some time together, of Bishop Berkeley's ingenious sophistry to prove the non-existence of matter, and that everything in the universe is merely ideal. I observe that though we are satisfied his doctrine is not true, it is impossible to refute it. I never shall forget the alacrity with which Johnson answered, striking his foot with mighty force against a large stone, till he rebounded from it, 'I refute it *thus*.'

BOSWELL (*Life of Johnson*)

REGIMEN

What a tiresome disease is that which forces us to preserve our health by a severe regimen!

LA ROCHEFOUCAULD

Regimen is of more service than medicine; every man ought to be his own physician; he ought to assist nature and never force her; but more than all he ought to learn to bear pain, how to grow old, and how to die. VOLTAIRE

The one thing more difficult than following a regimen is keeping from imposing it on others.

MARCEL PROUST

See also **Diet.**

REGRET

To regret deeply is to live afresh.

HENRY DAVID THOREAU

I seldom if ever regret doing anything, even although I may be convinced that it was wrong. Once it is accomplished, I dismiss it from my mind. H. L. MENCKEN

REGULATIONS

If you destroy a free market you create a black market. If you have

ten thousand regulations you destroy all respect for the law.
WINSTON S. CHURCHILL

See also **Law, Rules.**

REJECT

Among men, reject none; among things, reject nothing.   LAO-TSE

See also **No, Refusal.**

RELATIVES

I advise thee to visit thy relations and friends; but I advise thee not to live too near to them.
DR. THOMAS FULLER

Visit your aunt, but not every day; and call at your brother's, but not every night. BENJAMIN FRANKLIN

Wild animals and one's relations: If one would watch them and know what they are driving at, one must keep perfectly still.
SAMUEL BUTLER

See also **Brother-in-Law, Family.**

RELAXATION

It gives me pleasure to see a general before a fortress which he intends soon to attack, giving his whole attention to the chatting of his friends; and also to think of Brutus stealing a few hours from his nocturnal duties to read and abridge Polybius. It is the insignificant people, weighed down by the burden of their affairs, who do not understand how to put it aside and take it up again. MONTAIGNE

Ease and relaxation are profitable to all studies. The mind is like a bow, the stronger by being unbent.
BEN JONSON

See also **Leisure, Rest.**

RELIGION (DEFINITIONS)

Religion is the metaphysics of the people. SCHOPENHAUER

All the religion we have is the ethics of one or another holy person. RALPH WALDO EMERSON

What is religion? That which is never spoken.
HENRY DAVID THOREAU

Religion consists in a set of things which the average man thinks he believes and wishes he was certain.
MARK TWAIN

Religion is a man's total reaction upon life. WILLIAM JAMES

Religion is the fashionable substitute for belief. OSCAR WILDE

Religion is world loyalty.
ALFRED NORTH WHITEHEAD

Religion is what the individual does with its own solitariness.
ALFRED NORTH WHITEHEAD

Religion is not knowledge but a direction of the heart. . . . The Arab's turning to the East at certain hours and casting himself down, that is religion. . . . It is a natural being-set-in-motion inside an existence through which God's wind sweeps three times daily. . . .
RAINER MARIA RILKE

See also **Religion, Religions, Religious.**

RELIGION

We look after religion as the butcher did after his knife, when he had it in his mouth. JOHN SELDEN

Every man, either to his terror or consolation, has some sense of religion. JAMES HARRINGTON

Men despise religion; they hate it, and fear it is true. PASCAL

Most men's anger about religion is as if two men should quarrel for a lady they neither of them care for.
LORD HALIFAX

Since the whole affair had become one of religion, the vanquished were of course exterminated.
VOLTAIRE

To be of no church is dangerous. Religion, of which the rewards are distant, and which is animated by faith and hope, will glide by degrees out of mind unless it be invigorated and reimpressed by external ordinances, by stated calls to worship, and the salutary influence of example. SAMUEL JOHNSON

Few lines have ever been written to compare with some in the Fourth Psalm. How infinitely much there is in these words: 'Commune with your own heart upon your bed, and be still. Offer the sacrifices of righteousness, and put your trust in the Lord.' A whole religion!
G. C. LICHTENBERG

To have a positive religion is not necessary. To be in harmony with yourself and the universe is what counts, and this is possible without positive and specific formulation in words. GOETHE

Religion is the only philosophy which the common mind is able to understand and adopt.
JOSEPH JOUBERT

You must make your own religion, and it is only what you make yourself which will be of any use to you.
MARK RUTHERFORD

You may depend upon it, religion is, in its essence, the most gentlemanly thing in the world. It will

alone gentilize, if unmixed with cant; and I know nothing else that will, *alone*.
SAMUEL TAYLOR COLERIDGE

Things are coming to a pretty pass when religion is allowed to invade private life. LORD MELBOURNE

The religion of one age is the literary entertainment of the next.
RALPH WALDO EMERSON

Even if God did not exist, religion would still be holy and divine.
CHARLES BAUDELAIRE

Religion is the vaccine of the imagination; she preserves it from all dangerous and absurd beliefs.
NAPOLEON I

Common men talk bagfuls of religion but act not a grain of it, while the wise man speaks little, but his whole life is a religion acted out. RAMAKRISHNA

The first common mistake to get rid of is that mankind consists of a great mass of religious people and a few eccentric atheists. It consists of a huge mass of worldly people, and a small percentage of persons deeply interested in religion and concerned about their own souls and other people's; and this section consists mostly of those who are passionately affirming the established religion and those who are passionately attacking it, the genuine philosophers being very few.
GEORGE BERNARD SHAW

Irreligion: The principal one of the great faiths of the world.
AMBROSE BIERCE

Man is kind enough when he is not excited by religion.
MARK TWAIN

Religion makes easy and felicitous what in any case is necessary.
WILLIAM JAMES

Truth, in matters of religion, is simply the opinion that has survived. OSCAR WILDE

That part of a man's religion which is convenient, that he'll never drop. A. A. HORN

What cannot be followed out in day-to-day practice cannot be called religion. GANDHI

There are two branches of religion —high and low, mystical sleep walkers and practical idealists. J. M. KEYNES

See also **Christianity, Piety, Religion (Definitions), Religions, Religious.**

RELIGION AND SCIENCE see SCIENCE AND RELIGION.

RELIGIONS

One religion is as true as another. ROBERT BURTON

Alteration of religion is dangerous, because we know not where it will stay: 'tis like a millstone that lies upon the top of a pair of stairs; 'tis hard to remove it, but if once it be thrust off the first stair, it never stays till it comes to the bottom. JOHN SELDEN

Men say they are of the same religion, for quietness' sake; but if the matter were well examined, you would scarce find three anywhere of the same religion in all points. JOHN SELDEN

The several sorts of religion in the world are little more than so many spiritual monopolies.

LORD HALIFAX

Religion is like the fashion: one man wears his doublet slashed another laced, another plain; but every man has a doublet. So every man has his religion. We differ about trimming. JOHN SELDEN

The religion of one seems madness unto another. SIR THOMAS BROWNE

Men of sense are really all of one religion. But men of sense never tell what it is.

EARL OF SHAFTESBURY

We ought not, without very strong conviction indeed, desert the religion in which we have been educated. That is the religion given you, the religion in which it may be said Providence has placed you. If you live conscientiously in that religion, you may be safe. But error is dangerous indeed, if you err when you choose a religion for yourself. SAMUEL JOHNSON

All the different religions are only so many religious dialects.

G. C. LICHTENBERG

We are for religion against the religions. VICTOR HUGO

There are many faiths, but the spirit is one, in me, in you, and in every man. LEO TOLSTOY

As one can ascend to the top of a house by means of a ladder or a bamboo or a staircase or a rope, so divers are the ways and means to approach God, and every religion in the world shows one of these ways. RAMAKRISHNA

After long study and experience I have come to these conclusions: that (1) all religions are true, (2) all religions have some error in them, (3) all religions are almost as dear to me as my own Hinduism. GANDHI

There is only one religion, though there are a hundred versions of it. GEORGE BERNARD SHAW

Most people make the mistake of thinking that religion is necessarily a good thing and fail to realize that many, if not most, religions are thoroughly bad. W. R. INGE

Static religions are the death of thought. ALFRED NORTH WHITEHEAD

Is there any religion whose members can be pointed to as distinctly more amiable and trustworthy than those of any other? If so, this should be enough. I find the nicest and best people generally profess no religion at all, but are ready to like the best men of all religions. SAMUEL BUTLER

It is striking how avidly people study other people's religion. MARCEL PROUST

I am myself a dissenter from all known religions, and I hope that every kind of religious belief will die out. BERTRAND RUSSELL

It is the test of a good religion whether you can joke about it. G. K. CHESTERTON

See also **Religion (Definitions), Religion, Religious, Sect.**

RELIGIOUS

I can imagine an age to which our religious ideas will seem as strange as the spirit of chivalry to ours. G. C. LICHTENBERG

A man who has never had religion before, no more grows religious when he is sick, than a man who has never learned figures can count when he has need of calculation. SAMUEL JOHNSON

Men never do evil so completely and cheerfully as when they do it from religious conviction. PASCAL

A religious man thinks only of himself. FRIEDRICH NIETZSCHE

My most religious experience was aesthetic, when touched with my own hand Michelangelo's Sibyl in the Sistine Chapel. GEORGE BERNARD SHAW

Religious experience lacks something which is got out of artistic expression: it stirs but it does not soothe. ALFRED NORTH WHITEHEAD

See also **Piety, Religion (Definitions), Religion, Religions.**

REMEDY

The best remedy for disturbances is to let them run their course, for so they quiet down. BALTASAR GRACIÁN

Of all the home remedies, a good wife is the best. KIN HUBBARD

REMEMBER

It isn't so astonishing, the number of things that I can remember, as the number of things I can remember that aren't so. MARK TWAIN

The things we remember best are those better forgotten. BALTASAR GRACIÁN

Almost twenty years since, I heard a profane jest, and still remember it. How many pious passages of a far later date have I forgotten! It seems my soul is like a filthy pond, wherein fish die soon, and frogs live long. THOMAS FULLER

Could we know what men are most apt to remember, we might know what they are most apt to do. LORD HALIFAX

There is no greater pain than, in misery, to remember happy times. DANTE

What we remember of our actions remains unknown to those closest to us; what we have forgotten we ever said, or even never said at all, will make people laugh even on another planet.

MARCEL PROUST

Unless we remember we cannot understand.   E. M. FORSTER

Remembrance is a form of meeting.

KAHLIL GIBRAN

See also **Forgetting, Memory.**

RENEWAL see SELF-RE-NEWAL

REPARTEE

Repartee: Any reply that is so clever that it makes the listener wish he had said it himself.

ELBERT HUBBARD

See also **Answer.**

REPEAT

The phrases men are accustomed to repeat incessantly, end by becoming convictions and ossify the organs of intelligence.   GOETHE

REPENT

Gloomy penitence is only madness turned upside down.

SAMUEL JOHNSON

To many people virtue consists mainly in repenting sins, not avoiding them.   G. C. LICHTENBERG

A wise man will dispense with repentance.

HENRY DAVID THOREAU

The hardest sinner in the whole lot to convert is the one who spends half of his time in sinning and the other half in repentance.

JOSH BILLINGS

The best repentance is to up and act for righteousness, and forget that you ever had relations with sin.   WILLIAM JAMES

See also **Regret.**

REPUTATION

A man is always stronger while he is making a reputation than he is after it is made.   JOSH BILLINGS

See also **Fame.**

RESIGNATION

I have often observed that resignation is never so perfect as when the blessing denied beings to lose somewhat of its value in our eyes.

JANE AUSTEN

I can imagine no more comfortable frame of mind for the conduct of life than a humourous resignation.

W. SOMERSET MAUGHAM

RESOLUTIONS

'Give power to my good resolutions': this request could be part of the Lord's Prayer.

G. C. LICHTENBERG

Good resolutions are simply cheques that men draw on a bank where they have no account.

OSCAR WILDE

When I was younger, I used to make resolutions, which I imagined were virtuous. I was less anxious to be what I was, than to become what I wished to be. Now, I am not far from thinking that in irresolution lies the secret of not growing old.

ANDRÉ GIDE

All our final resolutions are made in a state of mind that is not going to last.   MARCEL PROUST

Just as soon as we make a good resolution, we get into a situation which makes its observance unbearable.   WILLIAM FEATHER

RESPECT

To feed men and not to love them is to treat them as if they were barnyard cattle. To love them and not to respect them is to treat them as if they were household pets.   MENCIUS

RESPECTABLE

I mean to make some maxims, like Rochefoucauld, and to preserve them. My first is this: After having lived half their lives respectable, many men get tired of honesty, and many women of propriety.   SYDNEY SMITH

Virtue has never been as respectable as money.   MARK TWAIN

RESPONSIBLE

The most powerful men are not public men. The public man is responsible, and a responsible man is a slave.   BENJAMIN DISRAELI

There can be no stable and balanced development of the mind, apart from the assumption of responsibility.   JOHN DEWEY

REST

I like to rest, whether sitting or lying down, with my heels as high as my head, or higher.   MONTAIGNE

Men tire themselves in pursuit of rest.   LAURENCE STERNE

See also **Leisure, Relaxation.**

RESULT

Everything we do has a result. But that which is right and prudent does not always lead to good, nor the contrary to what is bad; frequently the reverse takes place.   GOETHE

Work done with anxiety about results is far inferior to work done without such anxiety.   BHAGAVAD-GITA

Results should not be too voluntarily aimed at or too busily thought of. They are *sure* to float up of their own accord, from a long enough daily work on a given matter.   WILLIAM JAMES

RESURRECTION

There is a story of two clergymen asked by mistake to conduct the same funeral. One came first and had got no further than 'I am the Resurrection and the Life,' when the other entered. '*I* am the Resurrection and the Life,' cried the latter.   WILLIAM JAMES

REVELATION

Revelations are seldom beneficent.   GEORGE SANTAYANA

See also **Mysticism.**

REVENGE

Revenge is a kind of wild justice, which the more a man's nature runs to, the more ought law to weed it out.   FRANCIS BACON

See also **Vengeance.**

REVOLUTION

Histories of the downfall of kingdoms, and revolutions of empires, are read with great tranquillity.   SAMUEL JOHNSON

There have been three silent revolutions in England: first, when the professions fell off from the church: secondly, when literature fell off from the professions; and, thirdly, when the press fell off from literature. SAMUEL TAYLOR COLERIDGE

Vanity made the revolution; liberty was only a pretext. NAPOLEON I

A populace never rebels from passion for attack, but from impatience of suffering.
EDMUND BURKE

The generation which commences a revolution rarely completes it.
THOMAS JEFFERSON

Revolutions. In my youth, Spinoza was a hobgoblin; now he is a saint. RALPH WALDO EMERSON

Insurrection: An unsuccessful revolution. AMBROSE BIERCE

Covetousness is not the whole of human nature; it is only a part, like generosity, and that part vanishes only too soon when it is satisfied. Eighteen shillings a week will buy off a revolution.
GEORGE BERNARD SHAW

A violent revolution falls into the hands of narrow-minded fanatics and of tyrannical hypocrites at first. Afterward comes the turn of all the pretentious intellectual failures of the time. Such are the chiefs and the leaders. The scrupulous and the just, the noble, humane and devoted natures; the unselfish and the intelligent may begin a movement—but it passes away from them. They are not the leaders of a revolution. They are its victims.
JOSEPH CONRAD

Few revolutionists would be such if they were heirs to a baronetcy.
GEORGE SANTAYANA

A revolution is legality on vacation. LÉON BLUM

Since 1789 history has had a new perspective, revolution being a successful revolt, and revolt a revolution that has failed.
ANDRÉ MALRAUX

In history there is no Revolution that is not a Restoration.
G. K. CHESTERTON

Every revolution evaporates, and leaves behind only the slime of a new bureaucracy. FRANZ KAFKA

RHETORIC

Rhetoric is either very good, or stark naught; there is no medium in rhetoric. If I am not fully persuaded I laugh at the orator. JOHN SELDEN

See also **Arguments, Eloquence, Speech.**

RHEUMATISM

Much more is known about the stars than about rheumatism.
HENRY S. HASKINS

RICH

It is better for you to be free of fear lying upon a pallet, than to have a golden couch and a rich table and be full of trouble. EPICURUS

To be rich is not the end, but only a change of worries. EPICURUS

The rich man's follies pass for wise sayings, in this world. CERVANTES

A mere madness, to live like a wretch, and die rich.
ROBERT BURTON

Rich people have no passions, except that of hurt vanity.
STENDHAL

The rich should remember that when they reach heaven they will find Lazarus there and have to be polite to him.   JOSH BILLINGS

No man is rich who wants any more than he has got.

JOSH BILLINGS

No man is rich enough to buy back his past.   OSCAR WILDE

To suppose, as we all suppose, that we could be rich and not behave as the rich behave, is like supposing that we could drink all day and stay sober. LOGAN PEARSALL SMITH

If a man is wise, he gets rich, and if he gets rich, he gets foolish, or his wife does.   FINLEY PETER DUNNE

Some men's domestic troubles drive them to drink, others to labour. You read about a man becoming a millionaire and think he done it by his own exertions when it was the fear of coming home empty-handed and dislike of staying around the house all day that made him rich.

FINLEY PETER DUNNE

The rich man and his daughter are soon parted.   KIN HUBBARD

I know a rich man who is under compulsion to change his clothes at least twice a day, and often thrice, to travel at set periods to set places, and to see in rotation each of at least sixty people. He has less freedom than a schoolboy in school, or a corporal in a regiment; indeed, he has no real leisure at all, because so many things are thus necessary to him. HILAIRE BELLOC

The rich never feel so good as when they are speaking of their possessions as responsibilities.

ROBERT LYND

God must love the poor, said Lincoln, or he wouldn't have made so many of them. He must love the rich or he wouldn't divide so much *mazuma* among so few of them.   H. L. MENCKEN

See also **Mammon, Millionaire, Rich and Poor, Riches, Wealth**

RICH AND POOR

The observances of the Church concerning feasts and fasts are tolerably well kept upon the whole, since the rich keep the feasts and the poor the fasts.   SYDNEY SMITH

'I wish the good old times would come again,' she said, 'when we were not quite so rich. I do not mean, that I want to be poor; but there was a middle state in which I am sure we were a great deal happier.'   CHARLES LAMB

Poverty is an anomaly to rich people. It is very difficult to make out why people who want dinner do not ring the bell.

WALTER BAGEHOT

The best condition in life is not to be so rich as to be envied nor so poor as to be damned.

JOSH BILLINGS

Eat with the rich, but go to the play with the poor, who are capable of joy.   LOGAN PEARSALL SMITH

There is only one class in the community that thinks more about money than the rich, and that is the poor. The poor can think of nothing else.   OSCAR WILDE

Short of genius, a rich man cannot imagine poverty.   CHARLES PÉGUY

The petty economies of the rich are just as amazing as the silly extravagances of the poor.

WILLIAM FEATHER

See also **Poor, Rich, Riches, Wealth.**

RICHES

By means of occupations worthy of a beast abundance of riches is heaped up, but a miserable life results. EPICURUS

Riches are chiefly good because they give us time. CHARLES LAMB

See also **Wealth.**

RIDDLE

I have a backward and torpid mind; the least cloud stops its progress. I have never, for example, found a riddle easy enough for me to solve. MONTAIGNE

The riddles of God are more satisfying than the solutions of man. G. K. CHESTERTON

RIDICULE

Ridicule is the test of truth.

WILLIAM HAZLITT

See also **Caricature, Comic, Funny, Laugh.**

RIDICULOUS

We are never made as ridiculous through the qualities we have as through those we pretend to.

LA ROCHEFOUCAULD

If the animals had reason, they would act just as ridiculous as we menfolks do. JOSH BILLINGS

See also **Ridicule.**

RIGHT

If mankind had wished for what is right, they might have had it long ago. WILLIAM HAZLITT

From a worldly point of view, there is no mistake so great as that of always being right.

SAMUEL BUTLER

It's an odd thing about this universe that though we all disagree with each other, we are all of us always in the right.

LOGAN PEARSALL SMITH

Always do right; this will gratify some people and astonish the rest.

MARK TWAIN

See also **Right and Wrong.**

RIGHT AND LEFT

Noel Sullivan dropped in here with a witty line picked out of an editorial in a country newspaper: 'My country right or left.'

LINCOLN STEFFENS

Women have a wonderful sense of right and wrong, but little sense of right and left. DON HEROLD

RIGHT AND WRONG

No one knows what he is doing while he acts right; but of what is wrong we are always conscious.

GOETHE

We are not satisfied to be right, unless we can prove others to be quite wrong. WILLIAM HAZLITT

Those who are fond of setting things to rights, have no great objection to seeing them wrong.

WILLIAM HAZLITT

I do not greatly care whether I have been right or wrong on any point, but I care a good deal about knowing which of the two I have been. SAMUEL BUTLER

A man finds he has been wrong at every preceding stage of his career, only to deduce the astonishing conclusion that he is at last entirely right. ROBERT LOUIS STEVENSON

Any preoccupation with ideas of what is right or wrong in conduct shows an arrested intellectual development. OSCAR WILDE

When a man is old enough to do wrong he should be old enough to do right also. OSCAR WILDE

It is the necessities of life which generate ideas of right and wrong.
W. SOMERSET MAUGHAM

See also **Morality, Right, Wrong.**

RISING

All rising to great place is by a winding stair. FRANCIS BACON

If every man could read the hearts of others, there would be more men anxious to descend than to rise in life. ROUSSEAU

Could we at pleasure change our situation in life, more persons would be found anxious to descend than to ascend in the scale of society. WILLIAM HAZLITT

The social ladder is all very well as long as you can keep on climbing or stick at the top; but it is hard to come down it without stumbling off. SAMUEL BUTLER

See also **Success.**

RISK

Everything is sweetened by risk.
ALEXANDER SMITH

See also **Danger.**

RIVALRY

It almost seems as though the nearer people stand to one another in respect either of money or genius, the more jealous they become of one another. I have seen it said that Thackeray was one day flattening his nose against a grocer's

window and saw two bags o sugar, one marked 10⅔d. and th other 11d. As he left the windo he was heard to say, 'How the must hate one another.'
SAMUEL BUTLE

ROAD

Depart from the highway an transplant thyself in some en closed ground, for it is hard for tree which stands by the waysid to keep her fruit till it be ripe.
ST. JOHN CHRYSOSTON

The road is always better than th inn. CERVANTE

ROGUE

Many a man would have turne rogue if he had known how.
WILLIAM HAZLIT

ROUSSEAU

'Sir, do you think Rousseau as ba a man as Voltaire?' 'Why, sir, it i difficult to settle the proportion o iniquity between them.'
BOSWELL (*Life of Johnson*

ROUTINE

To the right sort of men an women happiness is found in th routine itself, not in departure from it. WILLIAM LYON PHELP

When one wakes up after dayligh one should breakfast; five hour after that, luncheon. Six hours afte luncheon, dinner. Thus one becomes independent of the sun, which otherwise meddles too much in one's affairs and upsets the routine of work. WINSTON S. CHURCHIL

'The love of routine,' a scientifi friend said to me once, 'is nothing to be ashamed of. It is only the love of knowing how to do things

which nature plants in every child,
kitten, and puppy.' JOYCE CARY

See also **Drudgery, Habit, Rut.**

RUDE

It seldoms pays to be rude. It never
pays to be only half rude.
NORMAN DOUGLAS

Rudeness is the weak man's imitation of strength. ERIC HOFFER

See also **Manners, Politeness.**

RULER

Of the best rulers the people only
know that they exist; the next best
they love and praise; the next they
fear; and the next they revile.
LAO-TSE

See also **Government, King.**

RULES

No course of life is so weak and
foolish as that which is carried out
according to rules and discipline.
MONTAIGNE

When I read some of the rules for
speaking and writing the English
language correctly—as that a sentence must never end with a
particle—and perceive how implicitly even the learned obey it,
I think
Any fool can make a rule
And every fool will mind it.
HENRY DAVID THOREAU

To insure peace of mind, ignore the
rules and regulations. GEORGE ADE

There never was a rule that didn't
have to be broken at some time,
and the man who doesn't know
when to break a rule is a fearful
pain in the neck.
WILLIAM FEATHER

See also **Maxim, Precept, Regulations.**

RULES OF LIFE

I have only three rules of life: never
do anything underhand, never get
your feet wet, go to bed at ten.
BISHOP WILLIAM STUBBS

My son, resolve to do the will of
others rather than your own.
Always choose to possess less
rather than more.
Always take the lowest place,
and regard yourself as less than
others.
Desire and pray always that God's
will may be perfectly fulfilled in
you.
A man who observes these rules
shall come to enjoy peace and
tranquillity of soul.
THOMAS À KEMPIS

Those who claim to act according to
rules of life (however beautiful
those rules may be) strike me as
idiots, or at least blunderers, incapable of taking advantage of life
—that is, of learning from life.
ANDRÉ GIDE

For the average man a sufficient
rule of life is to follow his instincts
controlled by the moral standard of
the society in which he lives.
W. SOMERSET MAUGHAM

See also **Art of Living, Golden
Rule, Maxim, Rules.**

RUNNING AWAY

Of all the thirty-six alternatives,
running away is best.
CHINESE PROVERB

RUSSIANS

It's easier for a Russian to become
an atheist than for anyone else in
the world. FEODOR DOSTOEVSKI

RUT

You won't skid if you stay in a rut.
KIN HUBBARD

See also **Habit, Routine.**

S

SAFE

Every place is safe to him who lives with justice.   EPICTETUS

The way to be safe is never to be secure.   BENJAMIN FRANKLIN

Don't play for safety. It's the most dangerous thing in the world.
HUGH WALPOLE

SAINT

Saints in stone have done more in the world than living ones.
G. C. LICHTENBERG

One should be fearful of being wrong in religion when one thinks differently from the saints.
JOSEPH JOUBERT

(Of Alyosha Karamazov:) Here is perhaps the one man in the world whom you might leave alone without a penny, in the centre of an unknown city of a million inhabitants, and he would not come to harm, he would not die of cold and hunger, for he would be fed and sheltered at once; and if he were not, he would find a shelter for himself, and it would cost him no effort of humiliation. And to shelter him would be no burden, but, on the contrary, would probably be looked on as a pleasure.
FEODOR DOSTOEVSKI

Saint: A dead sinner revised and edited.   AMBROSE BIERCE

Every saint has a bee in his halo.
E. V. LUCAS

'It comes to this,' Tarrou said almost casually; 'what interests me is learning how to become a saint.' . . . The doctor answered. 'But, you know, I feel more fellow-ship with the defeated than with the saints. Heroism and sanctity don really appeal to me, I imagine What interests me is being a man 'Yes, we're both after the same thing, but I'm less ambitious.'
ALBERT CAMU

It is easier to make a saint out of libertine than out of a prig.
GEORGE SANTAYAN

Many of the insights of the sain stem from his experience as sinner.   ERIC HOFFE

'I admire the saints because they are such uncompromisingly difficul people to get on with. My brothe always says that it's a happy bishop who hasn't got a saint in hi diocese.'   AUBREY MENEN

See also **Patron Saint, Sinner.**

ST. PAUL

The Epistles of St. Paul are so sub lime that it is often difficult to understand them.   VOLTAIRE

Flop: Suddenly to change one's opinions and go over to another party. The most notable flop on record was that of Saul of Tarsus, who has been severely criticized as a turncoat by some of our partisan journals.   AMBROSE BIERCE

SALVATION

Every one finds his salvation as he can.   ANATOLE FRANCE

SANITY

A sane man knows when something would drive him mad, just as a man standing up knows at what angle he would fall down.
G. K. CHESTERTON

See also **Mad.**

SARONG

A sarong is a simple garment carrying the implicit promise that it will not long stay in place.

E. B. WHITE

SATISFACTION

Every man gets about the same satisfaction out of life.

ALEXANDER SMITH

As long as I have a want, I have a reason for living. Satisfaction is death.   GEORGE BERNARD SHAW

See also **Contentment.**

SAVIOUR

Let no one think that he has been awaited as the Saviour!   GOETHE

SAY

Remember my unalterable maxim, When we love, we have always something to say.

LADY MARY WORTLEY MONTAGU

What people say behind your back is your standing in the community in which you live.   E. W. HOWE

If we disregard what the world says of someone, we live to repent it.

LOGAN PEARSALL SMITH

A man never becomes an orator if he has anything to say.

FINLEY PETER DUNNE

SCANDAL

In the case of scandal, as in that of robbery, the receiver is always thought as bad as the thief.

LORD CHESTERFIELD

Scandal is merely the compassionate allowance which the gay make to the humdrum. Think how many blameless lives are brightened by the blazing indiscretions of other people.   SAKI

See also **Gossip.**

SCARE

A good scare is worth more to a man than good advice.

E. W. HOWE

See also **Fear, Terrified.**

SCENERY

Scenery is fine but human nature is finer.   JOHN KEATS

See also **Country, Nature**

SCEPTICISM

A saint is a sceptic once in twenty-four hours.

RALPH WALDO EMERSON

A real sceptic may come nearer to what I should call religion than most if not all of those who go to church.

OLIVER WENDELL HOLMES, JR.

Sceptics laugh in order not to weep.

ANATOLE FRANCE

There is no one like a sceptic for being always moral and a good citizen.   ANATOLE FRANCE

Scepticism is the beginning of faith.

OSCAR WILDE

Scepticism is the chastity of the intellect.   GEORGE SANTAYANA

A mind enlightened by scepticism and cured of noisy dogma, a mind discounting all reports, and free from all tormenting anxiety about its own fortune or existence, finds in the wilderness of essence a very sweet and marvellous solitude. The ultimate reaches of doubt and renunciation open out for it, by an easy transition, into fields of endless variety and peace, as if through the gorges of death it had passed into a paradise where all things are crystalized into the image of themselves, and have lost their urgency and their venom.

GEORGE SANTAYANA

SCHEME   254   SCIENCE

A sceptic who turns dogmatist has decided it is high time to take it easy.   HENRY S. HASKINS

The only safe sceptic is one who was never exposed to faith in his infancy.   H. L. MENCKEN

See also **Belief, Dogma, Doubt, Faith, Unbeliever.**

SCHEME

Nothing is more hopeless than a scheme of merriment.
SAMUEL JOHNSON

Every man has a scheme that won't work.   E. W. HOWE

In war, as in life, it is often necessary, when some cherished scheme has failed, to take up the best alternative open, and if so, it is folly not to work for it with all your might.
WINSTON S. CHURCHILL

World ain't going to be saved by nobody's scheme. It's fellows with schemes that got us into this mess. Plans get you into things but you got to work your way out.
WILL ROGERS

SCHOOL

There is now less flogging in our great schools than formerly, but then less is learned there; so that what the boys get at one end they lose at the other.
SAMUEL JOHNSON

Wellington is supposed to have said that the Battle of Waterloo was won on the playing fields of Eton. It may be that the historians of the future will say that India was lost in the public schools of England.
W. SOMERSET MAUGHAM

I was happy as a child with my toys in the nursery. I have been happier every year since I became a man.

But this interlude of school makes a sombre grey patch upon the chart of my journey.
WINSTON S. CHURCHILL

See also **Education, Sunday School.**

SCHOOLMASTER

It is when the gods hate a man with uncommon abhorrence that they drive him into the profession of a schoolmaster.   SENECA

See also **Teaching.**

SCIENCE

It seems to me that those sciences which are not born of experience, the mother of all certainty, and which do not end in known experience—that is to say, those sciences whose origin or process or end does not pass through any of the five senses—are vain and full of errors.   LEONARDO DA VINCI

The real and legitimate goal of the sciences is the endowment of human life with new inventions and riches.   FRANCIS BACON

I perceived it to be possible to arrive at a knowledge highly useful in life; and, in place of the speculative philosophy usually taught in the schools, to discover a practical philosophy, by means of which—knowing the force and action of fire, water, air, the stars, the heavens and all the other bodies that surround us, as distinctly as we know the various crafts of our artisans—we might also apply them in the same way to all the uses to which they are adapted, and thus make ourselves the lords and possessors of nature.   DESCARTES

I will say, in the spirit of the wise Locke: Philosophy consists in stopping when the torch of physical science fails us. VOLTAIRE

Galileo died in the same year Newton was born. That is the Christmastide of the modern age. GOETHE

The Germans, and not they alone, have a gift for making science inaccessible. GOETHE

Science always departs from life and returns to it by a detour. GOETHE

Alas! can we ring the bells backward? Can we unlearn the arts that pretend to civilize, and then burn the world? There is a march of science; but who shall beat the drums for its retreat? CHARLES LAMB

In everything that relates to science, I am a whole encyclopaedia behind the rest of the world. CHARLES LAMB

Science increases our power in proportion as it lowers our pride. CLAUDE BERNARD

The greatest and saddest defect is not credulity, but our habitual forgetfulness that our science is ignorance. HENRY DAVID THOREAU

The sciences are beneficent; they prevent man from thinking. ANATOLE FRANCE

If the habits of thought favoured by physical science do but sink deep enough, and no vast calamity come to check mankind in its advance to material contentment, the age of true positivism may arise. Then it will be the common privilege 'rerum cognoscere causas', the word supernatural will have no sense; superstition will be a dimly understood trait of the early race; and where now we perceive an appalling mystery, everything will be lucid and serene as a geometric demonstration. GEORGE GISSING

Science is the literature of truth. JOSH BILLINGS

A science which hesitates to forget its founders is lost. ALFRED NORTH WHITEHEAD

Hitherto a man has been living in a slum, amidst quarrels, revenges, vanities, shames and taints, hot desires and urgent appetites. He has scarcely tasted sweet air yet, and the great freedoms of the world that science has enlarged for him. H. G. WELLS

It is the unscientific who are the materialists, whose intellect is not quickened, and the divinity which is everywhere eludes their stupid gaze. G. W. RUSSELL (Æ)

Science is a collection of successful recipes. PAUL VALÉRY

Although this may seem a paradox, all exact science is dominated by the idea of approximation. BERTRAND RUSSELL

Science, at bottom, is really anti-intellectual. It always distrusts pure reason, and demands the production of objective fact. H. L. MENCKEN

A science which does not bring us nearer to God is worthless. SIMONE WEIL

See also **Art and Science, Atom, Invention, Mathematics, Science and Religion, Scientist.**

SCIENCE AND ART see ART AND SCIENCE

SCIENCE AND RELIGION

He who has science and art has religion too.   GOETHE

There is more religion in men's science, than there is science in their religion.
HENRY DAVID THOREAU

Men of science, if they are worthy of the name, are indeed about God's path and about his bed and spy out all his ways.   SAMUEL BUTLER

Science and Religion. We should endow neither; we should treat them as we treat conservatism and liberalism, encouraging both, so that they may keep watch upon one another, and letting them go in and out of power with the popular vote concerning them.
SAMUEL BUTLER

Religions die when they are proved to be true. Science is the record of dead religions.   OSCAR WILDE

Religion will not regain its old power until it can face change in the same spirit as does science.
ALFRED NORTH WHITEHEAD

Science is only an episode of religion—and an unimportant one at that.   CHRISTIAN MORGENSTERN

Science without religion is lame, religion without science is blind.
ALBERT EINSTEIN

Theology, not religion, is the antithesis to science.
ARNOLD J. TOYNBEE

See also **Religion, Science.**

SCIENTIST

The mind of most scientists is like a glutton with a poor digestion.
VAUVENARGUES

Scientists. There are two classes, those who want to know, and do not care whether others think they know or not, and those who do not much care about knowing, but care very greatly about being reputed as knowing.   SAMUEL BUTLER

When the last Puritan has disappeared from the earth, the man of science will take his place as a killjoy, and we shall be given all the same old advice but for different reasons.   ROBERT LYND

Scientists regard it as a major intellectual virtue, to know what not to think about.   C. P. SNOW

See also **Science.**

SCOTSMEN

Much may be made of a Scotchman if he be *caught* young.
SAMUEL JOHNSON

SCOTT, SIR WALTER

Then comes Sir Walter Scott with his enchantments, and by his single might checks this wave of progress, and even turns it back; sets the world in love with dreams and phantoms; with decayed and swinish forms of religion; with decayed and degraded systems of government; with the silliness and emptiness, sham grandeurs, sham gauds, and sham chivalries of a brainless and worthless long-vanished society. He did measureless harm; more real and lasting harm, perhaps, than any other individual that ever wrote.   MARK TWAIN

SCRUPLES

Scruples certainly make men miserable, and seldom make them good.
SAMUEL JOHNSON

See also **Doubt, Hesitate.**

SCULPTURE

It is only well with me when I have a chisel in my hand.
MICHELANGELO

Painting consumes labour not disproportionate to its effect; but a fellow will hack half a year at a block of marble to make something in stone that hardly resembles a man. The value of statuary is owing to its difficulty. You would not value the finest head cut upon a carrot. SAMUEL JOHNSON

For Rodin what he gazes at and surrounds with gazing is always the only thing, the world in which everything happens; when he fashions a hand, it is alone in space, and there is nothing besides a hand; and in six days God made only a hand and poured out the waters around it and bent the heavens above it; and rested over it when it all was finished, and it was glory and a hand. RAINER MARIA RILKE

See also **Painting and Sculpture, Statue.**

SCULPTURE AND PAINTING see PAINTING AND SCULPTURE

SEA

To sail the sea is an occupation at once repulsive and attractive.
HILAIRE BELLOC

SECRET

When a prince trusteth a man with a dangerous secret, he would not be sorry to hear the bell toll for him.
LORD HALIFAX

There are some occasions in which a man must tell half his secret, in order to conceal the rest; but there is seldom one in which a man should tell it all.
LORD CHESTERFIELD

He that has a secret should not only hide it, but hide that he has it to hide. THOMAS CARLYLE

The vanity of being known to be trusted with a secret is generally one of the chief motives to disclose it. SAMUEL JOHNSON

Those who can keep secrets, have no curiosity. WILLIAM HAZLITT

A secret may be sometimes best kept by keeping the secret of its being a secret. SIR HENRY TAYLOR

Every man has reminiscences which he would not tell to everyone, but only to his friends. He has other matters in his mind which he would not reveal even to his friends, but only to himself, and that in secret. But there are other things which a man is afraid to tell even to himself, and every decent man has a number of such things stored away in his mind. The more decent he is, the greater the number of such things in his mind.
FEODOR DOSTOEVSKI

If you wish to preserve your secret, wrap it up in frankness.
ALEXANDER SMITH

SECT

Sect and error are synonymous.
VOLTAIRE

Different sects like different clocks may be all near the matter, though they don't quite agree.
BENJAMIN FRANKLIN

Sects are stoves, but fire keeps its old properties through them all.

RALPH WALDO EMERSON

See also **Religions.**

SECURE

To believe is very dull. To doubt is intensely engrossing. To be on the alert is to live; to be lulled into security is to die.   OSCAR WILDE

It is a sort of paradox, but it is true: we are never more in danger than when we think ourselves most secure, nor in reality more secure than when we seem to be most in danger.   WILLIAM COWPER

Spiritual life and secure life do not go together. To save oneself one must struggle and take risks.

IGNAZIO SILONE

See also **Safe.**

SEEING

A wise man sees as much as he ought, not as much as he can.

MONTAIGNE

A fool sees not the same tree that a wise man sees.   WILLIAM BLAKE

A mind lively and at ease can do with seeing nothing, and can see nothing that does not answer.

JANE AUSTEN

The art of seeing nature is a thing almost as much to be acquired as the art of reading the Egyptian hieroglyphics.   JOHN CONSTABLE

As singular and unexpected as the spectacles offered to our eyes may be, they never surprise us completely, there is within us an echo which replies to all impressions; either we have seen a given thing at some other place, or else all possible combinations of things are prepared in advance within our brain. When we encounter them in this passing world, we do no more than open a compartment of our brain or of our soul.

EUGÈNE DELACROIX

We shall see but a little way if we require to understand what we see.

HENRY DAVID THOREAU

First of all a man must see, before he can say.

HENRY DAVID THOREAU

A man has not seen a thing who has not felt it.

HENRY DAVID THOREAU

Enveloped in a common mist, we seem to walk in clearness ourselves, and behold only the mist that enshrouds others.   GEORGE ELIOT

Seeing and not believing is the prime virtue of a thinker: appearance is his greatest temptation.

FRIEDRICH NIETZSCHE

My task which I am trying to achieve is, by the power of the written word, to make you hear, to make you feel—it is, before all, to make you *see.* That, and no more, and it is everything.

JOSEPH CONRAD

Self-respecting people do not care to peep at their reflections in unexpected mirrors, or to see themselves as others see them.

LOGAN PEARSALL SMITH

People don't use their eyes. They never see a bird, they see a sparrow. They never see a tree, they see a birch. They see concepts.

JOYCE CARY

St. Bernard of Clairvaux could walk all day by the lake of Geneva and never see the lake.

ERIC HOFFER

See also **Invisible.**

SEEKING

To be a Seeker is to be of the best sect next to a Finder, and such an one shall every faithful, humble Seeker be at the end.

OLIVER CROMWELL

We never seek things for themselves, but for the search. PASCAL

What nobody seeks is rarely found.

PESTALOZZI

No matter how much we seek, we never find anything but ourselves.

ANATOLE FRANCE

What you seek in vain for, half your life, one day you come full upon, all the family at dinner.

HENRY DAVID THOREAU

SELF

To the possession of the self the way is inward.   PLOTINUS

No man would, I think, exchange his existence with any other man, however fortunate. We had as lief not be, as not be ourselves.

WILLIAM HAZLITT

Delight is to him—a far, far upward, and inward delight—who against the proud gods and commodores of this earth, ever stands forth his own inexorable self.

HERMAN MELVILLE

See also **Ego, Egotism, I, Know Thyself, Mine, Others, Own, Self-Balanced, Self-Conscious, Self-Control, Self-Denial, Self-Esteem, Self-Help, Self-Importance, Self-Improvement, Self-Interest, Self-Love, Self-Reliance, Self-Respect, Self-Restraint, Self-Sacrifice, Self-Satisfaction, Self-Surrender, Selfish.**

SELF-BALANCED

O to be self-balanced for contingencies!
O to confront night, storms, hunger, ridicule, accidents, rebuffs, as the trees and animals do.   WALT WHITMAN

SELF-CONSCIOUS

We are wicked because we are frightfully self-conscious.

OKAKURA KAKUZO

SELF-CONTROL

Whatever liberates our spirit without giving us self-control is disastrous.   GOETHE

Self-control is the quality that distinguishes the fittest to survive.

GEORGE BERNARD SHAW

See also **Moderation, Self-Restraint, Temperance.**

SELF-DENIAL

'Tis much the doctrine of the times, that men should not please themselves, but deny themselves everything they take delight in; not look upon beauty, wear no good clothes, eat no good meat, etc., which seems the greatest accusation that can be upon the maker of all good things. If they be not to be used, why did God make them?   JOHN SELDEN

Abstainer: A weak person who yields to the temptation of denying himself a pleasure.

AMBROSE BIERCE

Self-denial is simply a method by which man arrests his progress.

OSCAR WILDE

I should fancy that the real tragedy of the poor is that they can afford nothing but self-denial

OSCAR WILDE

See also **Abstain.**

SELF-ESTEEM

That kind of life is most happy
which affords us most opportunities of gaining our own esteem.
SAMUEL JOHNSON

To do everything he is asked to do,
a man must overestimate himself.
GOETHE

SELF-EVIDENT

'That's what I call a self-evident
proposition, as the dog's-meat man
said, when the housemaid told him
he warn't a gentleman.'
CHARLES DICKENS

Self-evident: Evident to one's self
and to nobody else.
AMBROSE BIERCE

SELF-HELP

It is vain to ask of the gods what a
man is capable of supplying for
himself.   EPICURUS

The fox provides for himself; but
God provides for the lion.
WILLIAM BLAKE

SELF-IMPORTANCE

Every man is of importance to
himself.   SAMUEL JOHNSON

If you think you came into being
for the purpose of taking an important part in the administration
of events, to guard a province of
the moral creation from ruin, and
that its salvation hangs on the
success of your single arm, you
have wholly mistaken your business.
RALPH WALDO EMERSON

See also **Importance.**

SELF-IMPROVEMENT

He who asks of life nothing but the
improvement of his own nature,
and a continuous moral progress
toward inward contentment and
religious submission, is less liable
than anyone else to miss and waste
life.   FRÉDÉRIC AMIEL

JUSTICE OLIVER WENDELL HOLMES
was sitting in his library one day
when Franklin D. Roosevelt called,
a few days after his inauguration in
1933, and found him reading Plato,
at the age of ninety-two. 'Why do
you read Plato, Mr. Justice?' 'To
improve my mind, Mr. President,'
Holmes replied.

See also **Improvement.**

SELF-INTEREST

The best way of saving oneself a lot
of trouble in life is to pay very little
heed to one's own interests.
JOSEPH JOUBERT

Self-interest is but the survival of
the animal in us. Humanity only
begins for a man with self-surrender.   FRÉDÉRIC AMIEL

The world will always be governed
by self-interest: we should not try
and stop this: we should try and
make the self-interest of cads a
little more co-incident with that of
decent people.   SAMUEL BUTLER

See also **Interest.**

SELF-LOVE

Seldom is anyone so spiritual as to
strip himself entirely of self-love.
THOMAS À KEMPIS

See also **Egotism, Selfish.**

SELF-RELIANCE

The individual must be self-reliant
and, in a sense, self-sufficient, or
else he goes down.
LUTHER BURBANK

SELF-RENEWAL

So long as man is capable of self-renewal he is a living being.
FRÉDÉRIC AMIEL

SELF-RESPECT

When people do not respect us we are sharply offended; yet deep down in his private heart no man much respects himself.　MARK TWAIN

See also **Self-Esteem.**

SELF-RESTRAINT

Few are those who err on the side of self-restraint.　CONFUCIUS

In managing human affairs, there is no better rule than self-restraint.
LAO-TSE

See also **Moderation, Self-Control, Temperance.**

SELF-SACRIFICE

It takes a thoroughly selfish age, like our own, to deify self-sacrifice.
OSCAR WILDE

Self-sacrifice enables us to sacrifice other people without blushing.
GEORGE BERNARD SHAW

No one ever feels helpless by the side of the self-helper; whilst the self-sacrificer is always a drag, a responsibility, a reproach, an ever-lasting and unnatural trouble with whom no really strong soul can live. Only those who have helped themselves know how to help others, and to respect their right to help themselves.
GEORGE BERNARD SHAW

As long as you derive inner help and comfort from anything you should keep it. If you were to give it up in a mood of self-sacrifice or out of a stern sense of duty, you would continue to want it back, and that unsatisfied want would make trouble for you. Only give up a thing when you want some other condition so much that the thing no longer has any attraction for you, or when it seems to interfere with that which is more greatly desired.
GANDHI

Only he can understand what a farm is, what a country is, who shall have sacrificed part of himself to his farm or his country, sought to save it, struggled to make it beautiful.
ANTOINE DE SAINT-EXUPÉRY

Self-sacrifice is a thing that should be put down by law. It is so demoralizing to the people for whom one sacrifices oneself.
OSCAR WILDE

SELF-SATISFACTION

Of the five vices, the vice of the mind is the worst. What is the vice of the mind? The vice of the mind is self-satisfaction.　CHUANG-TSE

SELF-SURRENDER

When opportunity for self-surrender arises, seize it.
THOMAS À KEMPIS

See also **Self-Sacrifice.**

SELFISH

Selfishness is one of the qualities apt to inspire love.
NATHANIEL HAWTHORNE

Selfishness is calm, a force of nature: you might say the trees were selfish.
ROBERT LOUIS STEVENSON

Selfishness is not living as one wishes to live, it is asking others to live as one wishes to live.
OSCAR WILDE

See also **Egotism.**

SELLING

Nothing is as irritating as the fellow that chats pleasantly while he's over-charging you. KIN HUBBARD

I remember well the time when a cabbage could sell itself just by being a cabbage. Nowadays it's no good being a cabbage—unless you have an agent and pay him a commission. Nothing is free any more to sell itself or give itself away.
JEAN GIRAUDOUX

See also **Bargain, Buying.**

SENSE

Scholarship is less than sense.
PANCHATANTRA

What grace is to the body good sense is to the mind.
LA ROCHEFOUCAULD

Where sense is wanting, everything is wanting. LORD HALIFAX

If poverty is the mother of crimes, want of sense is the father.
JEAN DE LA BRUYÈRE

There is nobody so irritating as somebody with less intelligence and more sense than we have.
DON HEROLD

See also **Common Sense.**

SENSES

Life must be filled up, and the man who is not capable of intellectual pleasures must content himself with such as his senses can afford.
SAMUEL JOHNSON

I never know whether to pity or congratulate a man on coming to his senses.
WILLIAM MAKEPEACE THACKERAY

Nothing can cure the soul but the senses, just as nothing can cure the senses but the soul. OSCAR WILDE

The man who cannot believe his senses, and the man who cannot believe anything else, are both insane.
G. K. CHESTERTON

SENSIBILITY

Never despise any person's sensibility. His sensibility is his genius.
CHARLES BAUDELAIRE

SENTENCE

The essential structure of the ordinary British sentence is a noble thing. WINSTON S. CHURCHILL

Caress your sentence tenderly: it will end by smiling at you.
ANATOLE FRANCE

You become a good writer just as you become a good joiner: by planing down your sentences.
ANATOLE FRANCE

A man who takes half a page to say what can be said in a sentence will be damned.
OLIVER WENDELL HOLMES, JR.

See also **Style, Writing.**

SENTIMENT

All our reasoning is merely yielding to sentiment. PASCAL

It is as healthy to enjoy sentiment as to enjoy jam.
G. K. CHESTERTON

See also **Emotion, Feeling, Sentimentality.**

SENTIMENTALITY

A sentimentalist is simply one who desires to have the luxury of an emotion without paying for it.
OSCAR WILDE

Sentimentality is only sentiment that rubs you up the wrong way.
W. SOMERSET MAUGHAM

Sentimentality—that's what we call the sentiment we don't share.

GRAHAM GREENE

See also **Emotion, Feeling, Sentiment.**

SERIOUS

I have never yet seen or heard anything serious that was not ridiculous.   HORACE WALPOLE

The one serious conviction that a man should have is that nothing is to be taken seriously.

SAMUEL BUTLER

One must be serious about something if one wants to have any amusement in life.   OSCAR WILDE

Seriousness is the only refuge of the shallow.   OSCAR WILDE

Humanity takes itself too seriously. It is the world's original sin. If the cavemen had known how to laugh, history would have been different.

OSCAR WILDE

It is a curious fact that the worst work is always done with the best intentions, and that people are never so trivial as when they take themselves very seriously.

OSCAR WILDE

My taste for the serious prompts me to find most pleasure in talking with children.   ANDRÉ MAUROIS

See also **Frivolity, Importance, Levity, Light and Heavy, Solemn.**

SERMON

Few sinners are saved after the first twenty minutes of a sermon.

MARK TWAIN

See also **Preaching.**

SERVICE

Men exist for mutual service.

MARCUS AURELIUS

I think there should be an Eleventh Commandment, 'Always make friends with people who do you a service.'

ALFRED NORTH WHITEHEAD

SEVENTY

It wouldn't be worth while to live to the age of seventy if all the wisdom of the world were folly in the sight of God.   GOETHE

SEVENTY-FIVE

My diseases are an asthma and a dropsy and, what is less curable, seventy-five.   SAMUEL JOHNSON

SEX

Rare are they who prefer virtue to the pleasures of sex.   CONFUCIUS

We have no right to boast of despising and combating carnal pleasure, if we cannot feel it, if we know nothing of it, of its charms and power, and its most alluring beauties. I know both, and so have a right to speak.   MONTAIGNE

When a man says he had pleasure with a woman he does not mean conversation.   SAMUEL JOHNSON

The sexes are the first, or are among the first, great experiments in the social subdivision of labour.

SAMUEL BUTLER

Answering questions is a major part of sex education. Two rules cover the ground. First, always give a truthful answer to a question; secondly, regard sex knowledge as exactly like any other knowledge.

BERTRAND RUSSELL

The time will come—it's a great way off—when a joke about sex will be not so much objectionable as unintelligible. . . . To the perfectly enfranchised mind it should be as impossible to joke about sex as about mind or digestion or physiology.   W. N. P. BARBELLION

SHAKESPEARE

To the King's Theatre, where we saw *Midsummer Night's Dream*, which I had never seen before, nor shall ever again, for it is the most insipid ridiculous play that ever I saw in my life.   SAMUEL PEPYS

After dinner to the Duke's house, and there saw *Twelfth Night* acted well, though it be but a silly play, and not related at all to the name or day.   SAMUEL PEPYS

Shakespeare never has six lines together without a fault.
SAMUEL JOHNSON

Let every man recollect, and he will be sensible how small a part of his time is employed in talking or thinking of Shakespeare, Voltaire, or any of the most celebrated men that have ever lived, or are now supposed to occupy the attention and admiration of the world.
SAMUEL JOHNSON

The unquestionable glory of a great genius which Shakespeare enjoys is a great evil, as is every untruth.
LEO TOLSTOY

I suppose that most persons would rather know what Shakespeare was doing on any one day from dawn to sunset . . . than be instructed as to the history of the Congress of Vienna.   MARK RUTHERFORD

With the single exception of Homer, there is no eminent writer, not even Sir Walter Scott, whom I can de-

spise so entirely as I despise Shakespeare, when I measure my mind against his.
GEORGE BERNARD SHAW

To this day I cannot read *King Lear*, having had the advantage of studying it accurately in school.
ALFRED NORTH WHITEHEAD

When I was a boy, many people called Shakespeare 'Shackspere'. This was thought a learned discovery at the time. Like many learned discoveries it is now obsolete.   ROBERT LYND

SHAME

Where there is yet shame, there may in time be virtue.
SAMUEL JOHNSON

SHAW, GEORGE BERNARD

If I were not a gloriously successful person, in England they would have dismissed me as an Irishman and in America as a Socialist.
GEORGE BERNARD SHAW

SHOCKING

When we find it amusing to shock people, we forget how shocking an experience it is.
LOGAN PEARSALL SMITH

SHORT

Short prayer pierceth Heaven.
THE CLOUD OF UNKNOWING

Good things, when short, are twice as good.   BALTASAR GRACIÁN

I have made this letter longer than usual because I lack the time to make it shorter.   PASCAL

Innocence has a very short style.
LORD HALIFAX

Whenever you can shorten a sentence, do. And one always can. The best sentence? The shortest.
ANATOLE FRANCE

One of the finest accomplishments is making a long story short.
KIN HUBBARD

Personally, I like short words and vulgar fractions.
WINSTON S. CHURCHILL

See also **Brief, Cut.**

SHOW

Do not show your wounded finger, for everything will knock up against it.   BALTASAR GRACIÁN

See also **Display.**

SHOW OFF

The silliest of all people are those who do foolish things to show off.
VAUVENARGUES

SICK

It is a cold, which God Almighty in justice did give me while I sat lewdly sporting with Mrs. Lane the other day with the broken window in my neck.   SAMUEL PEPYS

It is so very difficult for a sick man not to be a scoundrel.
SAMUEL JOHNSON

If you start to think about your physical or moral condition, you usually find that you are sick.
GOETHE

To be sick is to enjoy monarchal prerogatives.   CHARLES LAMB

A person seldom falls sick, but the bystanders are animated with a faint hope that he will die.
RALPH WALDO EMERSON

It is dainty to be sick, if you have leisure and convenience for it.
RALPH WALDO EMERSON

See also **Disease, Health.**

SILENCE

No man can safely speak, unless he who would gladly remain silent.
THOMAS À KEMPIS

(Of Macaulay:) His enemies might have said before that he talked rather too much; but now he has occasional flashes of silence, that make his conversation perfectly delightful.   SYDNEY SMITH

It is always observable that silence propagates itself, and that the longer talk has been suspended the more difficult it is to find anything to say.   SAMUEL JOHNSON

A man would rather say evil of himself than say nothing.
LA ROCHEFOUCAULD

Silence is one great art of conversation. He is not a fool who knows when to hold his tongue; and a person may gain credit for sense, eloquence, wit, who merely says nothing to lessen the opinion which others have of these qualities in themselves.   WILLIAM HAZLITT

The most silent people are generally those who think most highly of themselves.   WILLIAM HAZLITT

Silence is the essential condition of happiness.   HEINRICH HEINE

Silence is the universal refuge, the sequel to all dull discourses and all foolish acts, a balm to our every chagrin, as welcome after satiety as after disappointment.
HENRY DAVID THOREAU

It takes a man to make a room silent.   HENRY DAVID THOREAU

Silence is not always tact and it is tact that is golden, not silence.

SAMUEL BUTLER

I believe in the discipline of silence and could talk for hours about it.

GEORGE BERNARD SHAW

It ain't a bad plan to keep still occasionally even when you know what you are talking about.

KIN HUBBARD

Silence is the unbearable repartee.

G. K. CHESTERTON

Men fear silence as they fear solitude, because both give them a glimpse of the terror of life's nothingness. ANDRÉ MAUROIS

See also **Pause, Quiet.**

SILLY

No man is exempt from saying silly things; the mischief is to say them deliberately. MONTAIGNE

See also **Foolish, Stupid.**

SIMPLE

Simple truths are a relief from grand speculations.

VAUVENARGUES

When an idea is too weak to support a simple statement, it is a sign that it should be rejected.

VAUVENARGUES

Everything is simpler than you think and at the same time more complex than you imagine.

GOETHE

Simple style is like white light. It is complex but its complexity is not obvious. ANATOLE FRANCE

Life is not complex. We are complex. Life is simple and the simple thing is the right thing.

OSCAR WILDE

I adore simple pleasures, they are the last refuge of the complex.

OSCAR WILDE

A simple life is its own reward.

GEORGE SANTAYANA

I can conceive the subtlest and profoundest sage desiring nothing better than to retain, ever undiminished, a childlike capacity for simple pleasures.

NORMAN DOUGLAS

It is the essence of genius to make use of the simplest ideas.

CHARLES PÉGUY

All the great things are simple, and many can be expressed in a single word: freedom; justice; honour; duty; mercy; hope.

WINSTON S. CHURCHILL

All the books extolling the simple life are written by men.

WILLIAM FEATHER

See also **Complex, Primitive, Simplicity, Simplify.**

SIMPLICITY

Affected simplicity is refined imposture. LA ROCHEFOUCAULD

The art of art, the glory of expression and the sunshine of the light of letters is simplicity; nothing is better than simplicity.

WALT WHITMAN

The only simplicity for which I would give a straw is that which is on the other side of the complex—not that which never has divined it. OLIVER WENDELL HOLMES, JR.

Seek simplicity and distrust it.

ALFRED NORTH WHITEHEAD

There is more simplicity in the man who eats caviare on impulse than in the man who eats grapenuts on principle.

G. K. CHESTERTON

Out of intense complexities intense simplicities emerge.

WINSTON S. CHURCHILL

See also **Simple, Simplify.**

SIMPLIFY

To be always ready a man must be able to cut a knot, for everything cannot be untied; he must know how to disengage what is essential from the detail in which it is enwrapped, for everything cannot be equally considered; in a word, he must be able to simplify his duties, his business and his life.

FRÉDÉRIC AMIEL

Like the Sermon on the Mount, the doctrine of simplification is a revolution that any man can begin here and now without joining an organization. It is also a revolution that can be won in five minutes or a half hour, and costs less than the morning newspaper.

BROOKS ATKINSON

See also **Simple.**

SIN

He who sins against Heaven has nowhere left for prayer.

CONFUCIUS

Commit a sin twice and it will not seem to thee a crime. TALMUD

Expensive and costly iniquities which make the noise cannot be every man's sins; but the soul may be foully inquinated at a very low rate, and a man may be cheaply vicious to his own perdition.

SIR THOMAS BROWNE

That which we call sin in others, is experiment for us.

RALPH WALDO EMERSON

We cannot well do without our sins; they are the highway of our virtue. HENRY DAVID THOREAU

It is much easier to repent of sins that we have committed than to repent of those we intend to commit. JOSH BILLINGS

Our systems, perhaps, are nothing more than an unconscious apology for our faults—a gigantic scaffolding whose object is to hide from us our favourite sin.

FRÉDÉRIC AMIEL

It would be well if the intelligent classes could forget the word *sin* and think less of being good. We learn how to behave as lawyers, soldiers, merchants or what not by being them. Life, not the parson, teaches conduct.

OLIVER WENDELL HOLMES, JR.

Those who have the most frivolous idea of sin are just those who suppose that there is a fixed gulf between good people and others.

FRÉDÉRIC AMIEL

. . . the 'sense of sin'. The worst blight that ever fell on man.

ALFRED NORTH WHITEHEAD

Sin is geographical.

BERTRAND RUSSELL

We have sinned and grown old and our Father is younger than we.

G. K. CHESTERTON

Do not dwell on your sins. David killed Uriah the Hittite for the sake of stealing his wife, had Solomon by her, and everything went well.

HENRY S. HASKINS

See also **Repent, Sinner.**

SINCERITY

Sincerity in art is not an affair of will, of a moral choice between honesty and dishonesty. It is mainly an affair of talent. ALDOUS HUXLEY

See also **Insincere.**

SINGULARITY

Singularity may be good sense at home, but it must not go much abroad. LORD HALIFAX

SINNER

There are only two kinds of men: the righteous who believe themselves sinners; the rest, sinners, who believe themselves righteous.
PASCAL

Nothing makes one so vain as being told that one is a sinner.
OSCAR WILDE

The church saves sinners, but science seeks to stop their manufacture. ELBERT HUBBARD

Every sinner should be vouchsafed a future, as every saint has had a past.
SARVEPALLI RADHAKRISHNAN

We know we sin; and we're not happy unless there are bigger sinners to point to. AUBREY MENEN
See also **Sin**.

SIXTY

My second fixed idea is the uselessness of men above sixty years of age, and the incalculable benefit it would be in commercial, political, and in professional life if, as a matter of course, men stopped work at this age. SIR WILLIAM OSLER

I will tell you what, about this custom of enforced retirement; it is idiotic, because, although a man may not think of anything new after he is sixty, he often finds new ways to use what he already knows.
ALFRED NORTH WHITEHEAD

A man of sixty has spent twenty years in bed and over three years in eating. ARNOLD BENNETT

SKY

Deep sky is, of all visual impressions, the nearest akin to feeling.
SAMUEL TAYLOR COLERIDGE

The sky is the daily bread of the eyes. RALPH WALDO EMERSON

SLEEP

The waking have one common world, but the sleeping turn aside each into a world of his own.
HERACLITUS

I used to enjoy being disturbed in my sleep in order to get a glimpse of it, and not allow it so senselessly to slip away. MONTAIGNE

May blessings light upon him who first invented sleep! It is food for the hungry, drink for the thirsty, heat for the cold, and cold for the hot. It is the coin that buys all things, and the balance that makes the king even with the shepherd, and the fool with the wise.
CERVANTES

He that sleeps feels not the toothache.
SHAKESPEARE (*Cymbeline*, V, iv)

And so away to Stevenage, and staid till a shower was over, and so rode easily to Welling, where we supped well, and had two beds in the room and so lay single, and still remember it that of all the nights that ever I slept in my life I never did pass a night with more epicurism of sleep; there being now and then a noise of people stirring that waked me, and it was a very rainy night, and then I was a little weary, that what between waking and then sleeping again, one after another, I never had so much content in all my life, and so my wife says it was with her. SAMUEL PEPYS

I said to Mme. de Châtelet: 'You go without sleep to study philosophy; on the contrary, you ought to study philosophy to learn how to sleep.' MONTESQUIEU

NAPOLEON said that different ideas were put up in his head as in a closet. 'When I wish to interrupt an affair,' he said, 'I close the drawer which contains it, and open that which contains another. They do not mix together, and do not fatigue me nor inconvenience me.' He had never been kept awake, he said, by an involuntary preoccupation of the mind. 'If I wish to sleep, I shut up all the drawers, and I am asleep.'

There is, perhaps, no solitary sensation so exquisite as that of slumbering on the grass or hay, shaded from the hot sun by a tree, with the consciousness of a fresh light air running through the wide atmosphere, and the sky stretching far overhead upon all sides.
 LEIGH HUNT

A sleeping child gives me the impression of a traveller in a very far country. RALPH WALDO EMERSON

You cannot, with your best deliberation and heed, come so close to any question as your spontaneous glance shall bring you while you rise from your bed or walk abroad in the morning after meditating the matter before sleep on the previous night.
 RALPH WALDO EMERSON

Sleep falls like silence on the earth, it fills the hearts of ninety million men, it moves like magic in the mountains, and walks like night and darkness across the plains and rivers of the earth, until low upon lowlands, and high upon hills, flows gently sleep, smooth-sliding sleep—oh, sleep—sleep—sleep!
 THOMAS WOLFE

See also **Bed, Dozing, Dream, Early Rising, Insomnia, Nap.**

SLIP

The fiery thought of a social slip which makes us feel hot all over, will mellow into a glow to warm our aging bones.
 LOGAN PEARSALL SMITH

See also **Blunder, Mistake.**

SLIPPERS

Fame lies in being able to do what I like. . . . The Académie Française and the renown of being a great writer—this great crown, so to speak—permits me to wear, in season and out of season and wherever I choose, my old grey felt hat. If I wanted, I could go to the opera in slippers.
 ANATOLE FRANCE

SLUGGARD

'Sluggard'—why, it is a calling and vocation, it is a career.
 FEODOR DOSTOEVSKI

See also **Idle, Lazy, Loafing.**

SMALL

A man who cannot tolerate small ills can never accomplish great things. CHINESE PROVERB

The tiniest hair casts a shadow.
 GOETHE

Life is too short to be small.
 BENJAMIN DISRAELI

A multitude of small delights constitute happiness.
 CHARLES BAUDELAIRE

Animal and vegetable organisms do not change by large and few convulsions but by small ones and many of them. So for the most part do states and men's opinions.
SAMUEL BUTLER

It is quite certain that in a general way the small nations are now happier than the great nations.
G. K. CHESTERTON

See also **Large and Small, Little.**

SMELL

The sense of smell is especially effective in arousing memories.
SCHOPENHAUER

The flavour of frying bacon beats orange blossoms.   E. W. HOWE

Perfume: Any smell that is used to drown a worse one.
ELBERT HUBBARD
See also **Stink.**

SMILE

Better is he who shows a smiling countenance than he who offers milk to drink.   TALMUD

SMOKING

The scatterbrain, tobacco. Yet a man of no conversation should smoke.   RALPH WALDO EMERSON

It has always been my rule never to smoke when asleep, and never to refrain when awake.   MARK TWAIN

Wives can be trained to tolerate their husbands' smoking in bed. That is the surest sign of a happy and successful marriage.
LIN YUTANG

See also **Cigar, Cigarette, Non-Smoker, Pipe, Tobacco.**

SNEEZE

The autocrat of Russia possesses more power than any other man in the earth, but he cannot stop a sneeze.   MARK TWAIN

SNOBBERY

He who meanly admires mean things is a snob.
WILLIAM MAKEPEACE THACKERAY

Everybody knows that manners, family, habits, clothes, and like irrelevancies down to the smallest details of toothpick and napkin management are the chief bonds or barriers between men and between nations; that snobbery in one form or another is eternal and omnipotent, and bigger then humanity itself.   FRANK MOORE COLBY

If it were not for the intellectual snobs who pay—in solid cash—the tribute which philistinism owes to culture, the arts would perish with their starving practitioners. Let us thank heaven for hypocrisy.
ALDOUS HUXLEY

Religious snobs talk about God as though nobody had even heard of Him before.   RUSSELL LYNES

SNORING

There ain't no way to find out why a snorer can't hear himself snore.
MARK TWAIN

SNOW

Snow is faked cleanliness.
GOETHE

SOCIAL JUSTICE

In times of conspiratorial and secret struggle the Lord is obliged to hide Himself and assume pseudonyms. . . . Might not the ideal of social justice that animates the

masses today be one of the pseudonyms the Lord is using to free
Himself from the control of the
churches and the banks?

IGNAZIO SILONE

See also **Justice.**

SOCIAL QUESTION

The social question!—If I had encountered that great trap at the
beginning of my career, I should
never have written anything worth
while.   ANDRÉ GIDE

SOCIALISM

There is subconscious agreement
among the vast majority of Americans that the United States is not
evolving *toward* socialism, but *past*
socialism.

FREDERICK LEWIS ALLEN

Socialism will be of value simply
because it will lead to individualism.

OSCAR WILDE

For my part, I look back to the time
when I was a Socialist with something like regret.

ROBERT LOUIS STEVENSON

See also **Communism.**

SOCRATES

Socrates was famed for wisdom not
because he was omniscient but because he realised at the age of
seventy that he still knew nothing.

ROBERT LYND

Socrates went around barefoot
asking people to define their terms.
He taught that the good life consists in being good and that virtue
is knowledge and knowledge is
virtue.   WILL CUPPY

SOLDIER

The soldiers fight and the kings
are heroes.   TALMUD

The most advantageous position in
life and society is that of an
educated soldier.   GOETHE

You can always tell an old soldier
by the inside of his holsters and
cartridge boxes. The young ones
carry pistols and cartridges; the
old ones, grub.

GEORGE BERNARD SHAW

It is the man who is afraid of the
enemy's General Staff that is a
coward; the man who is afraid of
his own is merely an old soldier.

AUBREY MENEN

See also **War.**

SOLEMN

Solemnity is a device of the body
to hide the faults of the mind.

LA ROCHEFOUCAULD

Some people think that whatever is
done solemnly must make sense.

G. C. LICHTENBERG

I no longer regard solemnity as a
means of attaining truth; observation of life shows one that solemn
people are generally humbugs.

BERTRAND RUSSELL

See also **Serious.**

SOLIDARITY

Everywhere in these days men have,
in their mockery, ceased to understand that the true security is to
be found in social solidarity rather
than in isolated individual effort.

FEODOR DOSTOEVSK

SOLITUDE

As there is both good and bad
society, there is also both good and
bad solitude.

ST. FRANCIS DE SALES

He that can live alone resembles the
brute beast in nothing, the sage in
much and God in everything.

BALTASAR GRACIÁN

There are some solitary wretches, who seem to have left the rest of mankind only as Eve left Adam, to meet the devil in private.
ALEXANDER POPE

Remember that the solitary mortal is certainly luxurious, probably superstitious, and possibly mad.
SAMUEL JOHNSON

Solitude is dangerous to reason without being favourable to virtue.
SAMUEL JOHNSON

Study requires solitude, and solitude is a state dangerous to those who are too much accustomed to sink into themselves.
SAMUEL JOHNSON

The happiest of all lives is a busy solitude. VOLTAIRE

The life of a solitary man will be certainly miserable, but not certainly devout. SAMUEL JOHNSON

Solitude is to the mind what fasting is to the body, fatal if it is too prolonged, and yet necessary.
VAUVENARGUES

Solitude is fine when you are at peace with yourself and have something definite to do.
GOETHE

There are wounds, which an imperfect solitude cannot heal. By imperfect I mean that which a man enjoyeth by himself
CHARLES LAMB

Solitude is a good place to visit but a poor place to stay.
JOSH BILLINGS

Solitude makes us tougher toward ourselves and tenderer toward others: in both ways it improves our character. FRIEDRICH NIETZSCHE

Love and friendship are there for the purpose of continually providing the opportunity for solitude.
RAINER MARIA RILKE

See also **Alone, Loneliness.**

SOLUTION
To gain one's way is no escape from the responsibility for an inferior solution. WINSTON S. CHURCHILL

SOLVENT
I want to be thoroughly used before I die, and I want to die gloriously solvent, intellectually, morally, and financially.
GEORGE BERNARD SHAW

Solvency is entirely a matter of temperament.
LOGAN PEARSALL SMITH

SOPHISTICATION
The spirit's foe in man has not been simplicity, but sophistication.
GEORGE SANTAYANA

See also **Simplicity.**

SORROW
The busy bee has no time for sorrow. WILLIAM BLAKE

See also **Grief.**

SOUL
A man's soul is sometimes wont to bring him tidings, more than seven watchmen that sit on high on a watchtower. ECCLESIASTICUS 37

There is no light in souls in which there is no warmth.
JOSEPH JOUBERT

Be careless in your dress if you must, but keep a tidy soul.
MARK TWAIN

I take it, no fool ever made a bargain for his soul with the devil: the fool is too much of a fool, or the devil too much of a devil— I don't know which.

JOSEPH CONRAD

My soul would have been quite different if I had not stammered or if I had been four or five inches taller; I am slightly prognathous; in my childhood they did not know that this could be remedied by a gold band worn while the jaw is still malleable; if they had, my countenance would have borne a different cast, the reaction toward me of my fellows would have been different and therefore my disposition, my attitude toward them, would have been different too. But what sort of thing is this soul that can be modified by a dental apparatus?

W. SOMERSET MAUGHAM

The soul, too, has her virginity and must bleed a little before bearing fruit. GEORGE SANTAYANA

Most people sell their souls, and live with a good conscience on the proceeds. LOGAN PEARSALL SMITH

The situation of no one in the world is such that it could not be of peculiar use to his soul.

RAINER MARIA RILKE

See also **Body and Soul, Salvation, Spirit.**

SOUND

Sound is more than sense.

LOGAN PEARSALL SMITH

SPEAKER

Of all the substitutes, a substitute speaker is the worst.

KIN HUBBARD

SPEAKING

He who knows does not speak; he who speaks does not know.

LAO-TSE

But when they deliver you up, take no thought how or what ye shall speak: for it shall be given you in that same hour what ye shall speak.

ST. MATTHEW 10:19

There are some who speak well and write badly. For the place and the audience warm them, and draw from their minds more than they think of without that warmth.

PASCAL

There are not many situations more incessantly uneasy than that in which the man is placed who is watching an opportunity to speak, without courage to take it.

SAMUEL JOHNSON

Always be ready to speak your mind, and a base man will avoid you. WILLIAM BLAKE

See also **Say, Speech, Talk.**

SPECIALIST

No man can be a pure specialist without being in the strict sense an idiot. GEORGE BERNARD SHAW

See also **Scientist.**

SPECTATOR

For though the most be players, some must be spectators.

BEN JONSON

I am not an actor, I am a spectator only. My sole occupation is sightseeing. In a certain imperial idleness, I amuse myself with the world.

ALEXANDER SMITH

The spectator's judgment is sure to miss the root of the matter, and to possess no truth.

WILLIAM JAMES

To become a spectator of one's own life is to escape the suffering of life. OSCAR WILDE

Everywhere there are spectators—people who are interested in something they are not interested in at all. PETER ALTENBERG

See also **Detachment, Looking.**

SPECULATE

There are two times in a man's life when he should not speculate: when he can't afford it and when he can. MARK TWAIN

See also **Gamble.**

SPECULATION

The busy part of mankind will furnish the contemplative with the materials of speculation to the end of time. SAMUEL JOHNSON

If the world were good for nothing else, it is a fine subject for speculation. WILLIAM HAZLITT

See also **Reflection.**

SPEECH

Be sparing of speech, and things will come right of themselves.
LAO-TSE

Even though a speech be a thousand words, but made up of senseless talk, one word of sense is better, which if a man hears, he becomes quiet. DHAMMAPADA

I would as soon make an insignificant speech as make it evident that I have primed myself with a good one. MONTAIGNE

The habit of common and continuous speech is a symptom of mental deficiency. It proceeds from not knowing what is going on in other people's minds.
WALTER BAGEHOT

It usually takes more than three weeks to prepare a good impromptu speech. MARK TWAIN

You know very well that after a certain age a man has only one speech. GEORGE BERNARD SHAW

See also **Eloquence, Rhetoric, Speaking, Talk.**

SPEED

I foresee the time when human beings, having ceased to regard speed as a novelty, will lose much of their taste for it. ROBERT LYND

Turtles can tell more about the roads than hares. KAHLIL GIBRAN

Speed, it seems to me, provides the one genuinely modern pleasure.
ALDOUS HUXLEY

SPELLING

A man occupied with public or other important business cannot, and need not, attend to spelling.
NAPOLEON I

The spelling of words is subordinate. Morbidness for nice spelling and tenacity for or against some one letter or so means dandyism and impotence in literature.
WALT WHITMAN

See also **English Language, Grammar, Language.**

SPENDING

The sinner who spends and gives away is better than the devotee who begs and lays by. SADI

Once you have decided to keep a certain pile, it is no longer yours; for you can't spend it. MONTAIGNE

Riches are for spending.
FRANCIS BACON

Though I am much against too much spending, yet I do think it best to enjoy some degree of pleasure now that we have health, money, and opportunity, rather than to leave pleasures to old age and poverty, when we cannot have them so properly. SAMUEL PEPYS

A man cannot make a bad use of his money, so far as regards society, if he do not hoard it; for if he either spends it or lends it out society has the benefit. It is in general better to spend money than to give it away; for industry is more promoted by spending money than by giving it away.
SAMUEL JOHNSON

A man who spends money is sure he is doing good with it: he is not sure when he gives it away. A man who spends ten thousand a year will do more good than a man who spends two thousand and gives away eight. SAMUEL JOHNSON

Almost any man knows how to earn money, but not one in a million knows how to spend it.
HENRY DAVID THOREAU

The advantage of keeping family accounts is clear. If you do not keep them you are uneasily aware of the fact that you are spending more than you are earning. If you do keep them, you *know* it.
ROBERT BENCHLEY

SPINOZA

Spinoza lived amongst people, Roman Catholic and Protestant, who worshipped sorrow. Sorrow was the divinely decreed law of life and joy was merely a permitted exception. He reversed this order and his claim to be considered in this respect as one of the greatest revolutionary religious and modern reformers has not been sufficiently recognized. MARK RUTHERFORD

SPIRIT

He that hath no rule over his own spirit is like a city that is broken down, and without walls.
BOOK OF PROVERBS

When my spirit soars, my body falls on its knees. G. C. LICHTENBERG

Lamb said of an old acquaintance of his, that when he was young, he wanted to be a tailor, but had no spirit! WILLIAM HAZLITT

Every act has its spiritual, economic, and social implications. The spirit is not separate. It cannot be.
GANDHI

The life of the spirit, the veritable life, is intermittent and only the life of the mind is constant.
ANTOINE DE SAINT-EXUPÉRY

See also **Mind, Soul, Spiritual.**

SPIRITUAL

The trees reflected in the river—they are unconscious of a spiritual world so near them. So are we.
NATHANIEL HAWTHORNE

Any work of sculpture or music that elevates and purifies your feelings must correspond to some spiritual reality. MARCEL PROUST

SPIRITUALISM

It is undecided whether or not there has ever been an instance of the spirit of any person appearing after death. All argument is against it; but all belief is for it.
SAMUEL JOHNSON

The grossest materialists I know are the spiritualists.
JOHN BURROUGHS

My biggest argument that the whole thing (radio) is a fake is the quality of the stuff that comes out of the air. It is the same thing which makes me distrust spiritualism—the quality of the material offered us from the spirit world.
ROBERT BENCHLEY

See also **Ghost, Supernatural.**

SPLIT INFINITIVE

Word has somehow got around that the split infinitive is always wrong. This is of a piece with the outworn notion that it is always wrong to strike a lady.
JAMES THURBER

See also **Grammar.**

SPORT

Racing and hunting excite man's heart to madness.
LAO-TSE

Of common sports he once pleasantly remarked to me, 'How wonderfully well he continued to be idle without them.'
BOSWELL (*Life of Johnson*)

When a man wantonly destroys one of the works of man we call him a vandal. When he wantonly destroys one of the works of God we call him a sportsman.
JOSEPH WOOD KRUTCH

See also **Baseball, Exercise, Fishing, Football, Games, Golf.**

STAMP

Consider the postage stamp: its usefulness consists in the ability to stick to one thing till it gets there.
JOSH BILLINGS

See also **Perseverance.**

START

In conversation, listen to what is being said; in starting an activity, watch what is being done.
MARCUS AURELIUS

A man must stoop sometimes to his ill start, but he must never lie down to it.
LORD HALIFAX

STATE

To educate the wise man, the state exists; and with the appearance of the wise man, the state expires.
RALPH WALDO EMERSON

If science could operate unchecked it would soon produce a single world state.
BERTRAND RUSSELL

See also **Government.**

STATESMAN

A constitutional statesman is in general a man of common opinions and uncommon abilities.
WALTER BAGEHOT

A great statesman, like a good housekeeper, knows that cleaning has to be done every morning.
ANDRÉ MAUROIS

The less a statesman amounts to, the more he loves the flag.
KIN HUBBARD

STATUES

To see the frock-coat of the drawing room done in bronze, or the double waistcoat perpetuated in marble, adds a new horror to death.
OSCAR WILDE

See also **Sculpture.**

STATURE

Neglect nothing that can increase your stature.
STENDHAL

STEP

The tree which needs two arms to span its girth sprang from the tiniest shoot. Yon tower, nine stories high, rose from a little mount of earth. A journey of a thousand miles began with a single step.　　　　　LAO-TSE

What saves a man is to take a step. Then another step. It is always the same step, but you have to take it.
ANTOINE DE SAINT-EXUPÉRY

STILL

The very best and utmost of attainment in this life is to remain still and let God act and speak in thee.
MEISTER ECKHART

A genius never can be quite still.
SAMUEL JOHNSON

Some men are born great, some achieve greatness, and others just keep still.　　　KIN HUBBARD

Shutting away is not essential to stillness. The supreme stillness is achieved in the open. We suffer and enjoy; we fight and love, win and lose; but, in the midst of it all, are still.　　CHARLES MORGAN

Expect poison from the standing water.　　　WILLIAM BLAKE

. . . the stilling of the soul within the activities of the mind and body so that it might be still as the axis of a revolving wheel is still.
CHARLES MORGAN
See also **Quiet.**

STINK.

A stink is still worse for the stirring.
CERVANTES
See also **Smell.**

STOIC

It is harder for an artist to be a stoic than for anybody else.
LUDWIG VAN BEETHOVEN

STOMACH

A well-filled stomach is indeed a great thing: all else is luxury of life.
CHINESE SAYING

Happiness is made by the stomach.
VOLTAIRE

One's stomach is one's internal environment.　　SAMUEL BUTLER
See also **Digestion, Eating, Indigestion.**

STOP

He who knows when to stop runs into no danger.　　　LAO-TSE

The hardest thing to stop is a temporary chairman.
KIN HUBBARD

The art of public life consists to a great extent of knowing exactly where to stop and going a bit further.　　　　　SAKI

It is much easier to stop than to do.
WINSTON S. CHURCHILL

STORY

When one is relating anything, interrupt him not, unless there be great reason for it: Don't say, 'No, it was thus, but I'll tell you. You leave out the best part of it, etc.'
DR. THOMAS FULLER

Story-telling is not an art, but what we call a 'knack.'
SIR RICHARD STEELE

Patience is a most necessary qualification for business; many a man would rather you heard his story than granted his request.
LORD CHESTERFIELD

I knew a man who had a story about a gun, which he thought a good one and that he told it very well. He tried all means in the world to turn the conversation upon guns; but, if he failed in his attempt, he started in his chair, and said he heard a gun fired; but when the company assured him they heard no such thing, he answered, perhaps then I was mistaken; but however, since we are talking of guns—and then told his story, to the great indignation of the company. LORD CHESTERFIELD

Seldom any splendid story is wholly true.   SAMUEL JOHNSON

My gift, which God gave me, is a vivid description of all things I know about, large and small, truth and fiction, etc. As soon as I join a circle, they all become gay and happy while I tell my stories. . . . One thing more: always look cheerful, that makes people feel good and doesn't cost anything.
                    GOETHE'S MOTHER

We may be willing to tell a story twice, never to hear more than once.   WILLIAM HAZLITT

The best tales are told at a certain hour—no one ever told a story well standing up, or fasting.
                    HONORÉ DE BALZAC

It is no easy thing to tell a story plainly and distinctly by mouth; but to tell one on paper is difficult indeed, so many snares lie in the way. People are afraid to put down what is common on paper, they seek to embellish their narratives, as they think, by philosophic speculations and reflections; they are anxious to shine, and people who are anxious to shine can never tell a plain story. GEORGE BORROW

If you wish to lower yourself in a person's favour, one good way is to tell his story over again, the way you heard it.   MARK TWAIN

It is now a convention that all speakers at banquets must begin with a funny story. I am quite sure that if the Archbishop of Canterbury were invited to address the Episcopal Church of America, the senior bishop would introduce him with a story about an old darky, and the Archbishop would rise to reply with a story about a commercial traveller.
                    STEPHEN LEACOCK

There should be tellers of funny stories to visit the sick. A good funny story is an elixir of life.
                    CHRISTIAN MORGENSTERN

In a story as in a play, you must make up your mind what your point is and stick to it like grim death.   W. SOMERSET MAUGHAM

See also **Anecdote, Joke.**

STRATEGY

I have often tried to set down the strategic truths I have comprehended in the form of simple anecdotes and they rank this way in my mind. One of them is the celebrated tale of the man who gave the powder to the bear. He mixed the power with the greatest care, making sure that not only the ingredients but the proportions were absolutely correct. He rolled it up in a large paper spill, and was about to blow it down the bear's throat. But the bear blew first.
                    WINSTON S. CHURCHILL

STUBBORN

Stubborn audacity is the last refuge of guilt.   SAMUEL JOHNSON

A man will do more for his stubbornness than for his religion or his country.   E. W. HOWE

STUDY

Just as eating contrary to the inclination is injurious to the health, so study without desire spoils the memory, and it retains nothing that it takes in.
LEONARDO DA VINCI

Hard students are commonly troubled with gowts, catarrhes, rheums, *cachexia*, *bradypepsia*, bad eyes, stone, and collick, crudities, oppilations, *vertigo*, winds, consumptions, and all such diseases as come by overmuch sitting; they are most part lean, dry, ill-coloured; spend their fortunes, lose their wits, and many times their lives; and all through immoderate pains and extraordinary studies.
ROBERT BURTON

One of the wisest rules than can be observed in study, is to eschew those subjects which afford no footing to the mind.
JAMES A. ST. JOHN

Avoid studies of which the result dies with the worker.
LEONARDO DA VINCI
See also **Learning.**

STUPID

There are people whose only merit consists in saying and doing stupid things at the right time, and who ruin all if they change their manners.   LA ROCHEFOUCAULD

Ordinarily he was insane, but he had lucid moments when he was merely stupid.   HEINRICH HEINE

The stupid you have always with you.   HENRY DAVID THOREAU

It is better to be stupid like everybody than clever like none.
ANATOLE FRANCE

The only thing that ever consoles a man for the stupid things he does is the praise he always gives himself for doing them. OSCAR WILDE

There is no sin except stupidity.
OSCAR WILDE

See also **Foolish, Muddle-Headed, Silly.**

STYLE

When we see a natural style, we are astonished and delighted; for we expected to see an author, and we find a man.   PASCAL

All styles are good that are not tiresome.   VOLTAIRE

Read over your compositions, and when you meet with a passage which you think is particularly fine, strike it out. SAMUEL JOHNSON

Whatever is translatable into other and simpler words of the same language, without loss of sense or dignity, is bad.
SAMUEL TAYLOR COLERIDGE

In composing, as a general rule, run your pen through every other word you have written; you have no idea what vigour it will give your style.   SYDNEY SMITH

Style is the physiognomy of the mind, and a safer index to character than the face.   SCHOPENHAUER

As for style of writing, if one has anything to say, it drops from him simply and directly, as a stone falls to the ground.
HENRY DAVID THOREAU

Effectiveness of assertion is the alpha and omega of style. He who has nothing to assert has no style and can have none.

GEORGE BERNARD SHAW

People think I can teach them style. What stuff it all is! Have something to say, and say it as clearly as you can. That is the only secret of style.

MATTHEW ARNOLD

Say that which has to be said in such language that you can stand cross-examination on each word.

T. H. HUXLEY

Style: A noble manner in an easy manner. GEORGE MEREDITH

A man's style in any art should be like his dress—it should attract as little attention as possible.

SAMUEL BUTLER

I should like to put it on record that I never took the smallest pains with my style, have never thought about it, and do not know or want to know whether it is a style at all or whether it is not, as I believe and hope, just common, simple straightforwardness. I cannot conceive how any man can take thought for his style without loss to himself and his readers.

SAMUEL BUTLER

The great men often write very badly, and so much the better for them. It is not to them that we must go for the art of form, but to the second bests. GUSTAVE FLAUBERT

An elaborate style has perils like those of an elaborate house. It commits the author, by habit and the expectation of others, to a special and costly way of living, which will become a burden when he loses the wish or the power to keep it up.

CHARLES HORTON COOLEY

This bombastic style has marked all English official utterance for many years. . . . Some of its masterpieces are famous—for example, the sign reading 'The basins are for casual ablutions only,' formerly hanging in the men's washroom of the British Museum. H. L. MENCKEN

If I were going to cultivate a style of writing, I would try to make it as simple as possible and straightforward, and state the facts as they are. That was Cicero's way. He stated his case, and then he argued it and that is all there was to it.

HARRY S. TRUMAN

It may have been all right for Stevenson to 'play the sedulous ape' and consciously imitate the style of Hazlitt, Lamb, Montaigne and the rest, but if the rest of us were to try it there would result a terrible plague of insufferably artificial and affected authors, all playing the sedulous ape and all looking the part. ROBERT BENCHLEY

See also **Adjective, Clear, Clichés, Description, Obscurity, Sentence Writing.**

SUBMIT

It is extremely silly to submit to ill fortune.

LADY MARY WORTLEY MONTAGU

If one has to submit, it is wasteful not to do so with the best grace possible. WINSTON S. CHURCHILL

SUBORDINATE

Always mistrust a subordinate who never finds fault with his superior.

JOHN CHURTON COLLINS

SUBTLE

The most subtle folly grows out of the most subtle wisdom.

LA ROCHEFOUCAULD

If something very subtle is to be made evident, it must be coloured.
JOSEPH JOUBERT

SUCCESS

Most people judge men only by success or by fortune.
LA ROCHEFOUCAULD

In this world there are only two ways of getting on—either by one's own industry or by the imbecility of others.   JEAN DE LA BRUYÈRE

Success generally depends upon knowing how long it takes to succeed.   MONTESQUIEU

Success has ruined many a man.
BENJAMIN FRANKLIN

I saw that a humble man, with the blessing of the Lord, might live on a little; and that where the heart was set on greatness, success in business did not satisfy the craving; but that commonly, with an increase of wealth, the desire of wealth increased.   JOHN WOOLMAN

Half the things that people do not succeed in, are through fear of making the attempt.
JAMES NORTHCOTE

Success in your work, in finding a better method, the better understanding that insures the better performing is hat and coat, is food and wine, is fire and horse and health and holiday. At least, I find that any success in my work has the effect on my spirits of all these.
RALPH WALDO EMERSON

Nothing makes a man so cross as success, or so soon turns a pleasant friend into a captious acquaintance.
ANTHONY TROLLOPE

Success is the necessary misfortune of life, but it is only to the very unfortunate that it comes early.
ANTHONY TROLLOPE

Success is a poison that should only be taken late in life and then only in small doses.
ANTHONY TROLLOPE

It is provided in the essence of things that from any fruition of success, no matter what, shall come forth something to make a greater struggle necessary.
WALT WHITMAN

There is always something about your success that displeases even your best friends.   OSCAR WILDE

The moral flabbiness born of the exclusive worship of the bitch-goddess Success.   WILLIAM JAMES

The secret of success in life is known only to those who have not succeeded.
JOHN CHURTON COLLINS

How can they say my life is not a success? Have I not for more than sixty years got enough to eat and escaped being eaten?
LOGAN PEARSALL SMITH

A successful man cannot realize how hard an unsuccessful man finds life.   E. W. HOWE

I dread success. To have succeeded is to have finished one's business on earth, like the male spider, who is killed by the female the moment he has succeeded in his courtship.
GEORGE BERNARD SHAW

The flavour of social success is delicious, though gravely scorned by those to whose lips the cup has not been proffered.
LOGAN PEARSALL SMITH

If at first you do succeed, don't take any more chances.
KIN HUBBARD

There is an old motto that runs, 'If at first you don't succeed, try, try again.' This is nonsense. It ought to read, 'If at first you don't succeed, quit, quit at once.'
STEPHEN LEACOCK

Men, on the average, will be kindly or hostile in their feelings toward each other in proportion as they feel their lives unsuccessful or successful. BERTRAND RUSSELL

There is nothing that fails like success. G. K. CHESTERTON

The common idea that success spoils people by making them vain, egotistic, and self-complacent is erroneous; on the contrary it makes them, for the most part, humble, tolerant, and kind. Failure makes people bitter and cruel.
W. SOMERSET MAUGHAM

The essence of success is that it is never necessary to think of a new idea oneself. It is far better to wait until somebody else does it, and then to copy him in every detail, except his mistakes.
AUBREY MENEN

A successful man is he who receives a great deal from his fellow-men, usually incomparably more than corresponds to his service to them.
ALBERT EINSTEIN

Of all the enemies of literature, success is the most insidious.
CYRIL CONNOLLY

See also **Achievement, Attain, Failure, Prosperity, Rising, Success and Failure.**

SUCCESS AND FAILURE

Failure is the foundation of success, and the means by which it is achieved. Success is the lurking-place of failure; but who can tell when the turning point will come?
LAO-TSE

Our business in this world is not to succeed, but to continue to fail, in good spirits.
ROBERT LOUIS STEVENSON

Success makes us intolerant of failure, and failure makes us intolerant of success.
WILLIAM FEATHER

From the Taoist point of view, an educated man is one who believes he has not succeeded when he has, but is not so sure he has failed when he fails. LIN YUTANG

See also **Failure, Success.**

SUFFERING

Never to suffer would have been never to have been blessed.
EDGAR ALLAN POE

Suffering! . . . We owe to it all that is good in us, all that gives value to life; we owe to it pity, we owe to it courage, we owe to it all the virtues. ANATOLE FRANCE

Suffering is the sole origin of consciousness. FEODOR DOSTOEVSKI

The more a man loves, the more he suffers. The sum of possible grief for each soul is in proportion to its degree of perfection.
FRÉDÉRIC AMIEL

You should not be oppressed by the frightful sum of human suffering. There is no sum. Poverty and pain are not cumulative, and you must not let your spirit be crushed by the fancy that it is.
GEORGE BERNARD SHAW

How much further suffering goes in psychology than psychology!
MARCEL PROUST

We shall draw from the heart of suffering itself the means of inspiration and survival.
WINSTON S. CHURCHILL

It is a glorious thing to be indifferent to suffering, but only to one's own suffering. ROBERT LYND

Experience is valuable only when it has brought suffering and when the suffering has left its mark upon both body and mind.
ANDRÉ MAUROIS

If there were no suffering in this world we might think we were in paradise. SIMONE WEIL

Suffering is also one of the ways of knowing you're alive.
JESSAMYN WEST

See also **Pain.**

SUICIDE

Not even those who commit suicide regard it as a light matter, and are as much alarmed as the rest of the world if death meets them in a different way than the one they have selected.
LA ROCHEFOUCAULD

I take it that no man is educated who has never dallied with the thought of suicide.
WILLIAM JAMES

Nowadays not even a suicide kills himself in desperation. Before taking the step he deliberates so long and so carefully that he literally chokes with thought. It is even questionable whether he ought to be called a suicide, since it is really thought which takes his life. He does not die *with* deliberation, but *from* deliberation.
SÖREN KIERKEGAARD

Mental diseases can be fatal and cause suicide. G. C. LICHTENBERG

It is always consoling to think of suicide: in that way one gets through many a bad night.
FRIEDRICH NIETZSCHE

To be busy with material affairs is the best preservative against reflection, fears, doubts—all these things which stand in the way of achievement. I suppose a fellow proposing to cut his throat would experience a sort of relief while occupied in stropping his razor carefully. JOSEPH CONRAD

SUN

The sun will set without thy assistance. TALMUD

SUNDAY

Everything has its weekday side and its Sunday side.
G. C. LICHTENBERG

SUNDAY SCHOOL

A Sunday school is a prison in which children do penance for the evil conscience of their parents.
H. L. MENCKEN

SUPERFICIAL

It is only the superficial qualities that last. Man's deeper nature is soon found out. OSCAR WILDE

SUPERFLUOUS

The superfluous is the most necessary. VOLTAIRE

We dare more when striving for superfluities than for necessities.
ERIC HOFFER

See also **Luxury, Necessary.**

SUPERIORITY

If you are always offending others by your superiority, you will probably come to grief.

CHUANG-TSE

Superiority is always detested.

BALTASAR GRACIÁN

Such is the delight of mental superiority, that none on whom nature or study have conferred it, would purchase the gifts of fortune by its loss.   SAMUEL JOHNSON

Sir, there is nothing by which a man exasperates most people more, than by displaying a superior ability or brilliancy in conversation. They seem pleased at the time; but their envy makes them curse him in their hearts.   SAMUEL JOHNSON

There is no defence against someone else's superiority except love.

GOETHE

It is a notorious fact that patients in a madhouse are all of them suffering from the idea, developed beyond the normal, of their own superiority.   CHARLES BAUDELAIRE

See also **Inferior.**

SUPERNATURAL

At bottom, this is the only courage we are called upon to have: the courage to face the strangest, the most mysterious and the most incomprehensible we may encounter. Cowardice in this sense has done immeasurable harm to life; our daily resistance has pushed visions, death, the supernatural, all those things that are so close to us, so far out of life, that the senses have been stunted by which we could experience them.

RAINER MARIA RILKE

The Master would not discuss prodigies, prowess, lawlessness, or the superantural.

SAYINGS OF CONFUCIUS

See also **Ghost, Other World, Spiritualism.**

SUPERSTITION

There is a superstition in avoiding superstition, when men think to do best if they go furthest from the superstition formerly received.

FRANCIS BACON

To carry piety as far as superstition is to destroy it.   PASCAL

Most men of education are more superstitious than they admit— nay, than they think.

G. C. LICHTENBERG

Superstition is the poetry of life.

GOETHE

The unbelieving epochs are the cradles of new superstitions.

FRÉDÉRIC AMIEL

Let me make the superstitions of a nation and I care not who makes its laws, or its songs either.

MARK TWAIN

SURE

I am sure of very few things in this world. . . . I should be tempted to put very large question marks after all that I write, all that I say, and all that I think.   ANATOLE FRANCE

When we are not sure, we are alive.

GRAHAM GREENE

Discretion consists in a natural tendency to the most rational course, combined with a liking for the surest.   BALTASAR GRACIÁN

See also **Certain.**

SURPRISE

The real artist's work is a surprise to himself.   ROBERT HENRI

A work of art always surprises us; it has worked its effect before we have become conscious of its presence.   HERBERT READ

See also **Expect, Unexpected.**

SUSPICION

There is nothing makes a man suspect much, more than to know little.   FRANCIS BACON

Suspicion is rather a virtue than a fault, as long as it does like a dog that *watches* and does not *bite*.
          LORD HALIFAX

I know of no rule which holds so true as that we are always paid for our suspicion by finding what we suspect.   HENRY DAVID THOREAU

Mankind had rather suspect something than to know it.
          JOSH BILLINGS

When we say we are certain so-and-so can't possibly have done it, what we mean is that we think he very likely did.
          LOGAN PEARSALL SMITH

Nothing can happen but the suspicous man believes that somebody did it on purpose.   ROBERT LYND

SYMPATHIZER

A sympathizer is a fellow that's for you as long as it doesn't cost anything.   KIN HUBBARD

SYMPATHY

Nobody welcomes sympathy for his errors.   VAUVENARGUES

A sympathetic person is placed in the dilemma of a swimmer among drowning men, who all catch at him, and if he give so much as a log or finger, they will drown him.
          RALPH WALDO EMERSON

If all the people in the world should agree to sympathize with a certain man at a certain hour, they could not cure his headache.
          E. W. HOWE

See also **Compassion, Pity.**

SYSTEM

The most ingenious way of becoming foolish is by a system.
          EARL OF SHAFTESBURY

A system-grinder hates the truth.
          RALPH WALDO EMERSON

In relation to their systems most systematizers are like a man who builds an enormous castle and lives in a shack close by; they do not live in their own enormous systematic buildings. But spiritually that is a decisive objection. Spiritually speaking a man's thought must be the building in which he lives—otherwise everything is topsy-turvy.
          SÖREN KIERKEGAARD

A system like that of Kant or Hegel does not differ essentially from those combinations of cards with which women foretell fortunes, and so cheat the monotony of their lives.   ANATOLE FRANCE

Every system should allow loopholes and exceptions, for if it does not it will in the end crush all that is best in man.
          BERTRAND RUSSELL

What's the use of inventing a better system as long as there just aren't enough folks with sense to go around!

DOROTHY CANFIELD FISHER

See also **Scheme.**

T

TAKING SIDES

One should never take sides in anything. Taking sides is the beginning of sincerity and earnestness follows shortly afterwards and the human being becomes a bore.

OSCAR WILDE

See also **Opinion.**

TALENT

Talent is often a defect of character.

KARL KRAUS

See also **Genius and Talent, Qualities.**

TALK

No man would listen to you talk if he didn't know it was his turn next.

E. W. HOWE

A dog is not considered a good dog because he is a good barker. A man is not considered a good man because he is a good talker.

CHUANG-TSE

Sir, people may come to do anything almost, by talking of it.

SAMUEL JOHNSON

The more you are talked about, the less powerful you are.

BENJAMIN DISRAELI

Talk, to me, is only spading up the ground for crops of thought. I can't answer for what will turn up. If I could, I wouldn't be talking, but 'speaking my piece'.

OLIVER WENDELL HOLMES, SR.

Walk through life and talk to anybody.

PERSIAN PROVERB

Look out for the fellow who lets you do all the talking.

KIN HUBBARD

Everything is worth talking about.

NORMAN DOUGLAS

To every man alive, one must hope, it has in some manner happened that he has talked with his more fascinating friends round a table on some night when all the numerous personalities unfolded themselves like great tropical flowers.

G. K. CHESTERTON

You talk when you cease to be at peace with your thoughts. And in much of talking, thinking is half murdered.

KAHLIL GIBRAN

Great talkers are so constituted that they do not know their own thoughts until, on the tide of their particular gift, they hear them issuing from their mouths.

THORNTON WILDER

See also **Discussion.**

TAOISM

Acting without design, occupying oneself without making a business of it, finding the great in what is small and the many in the few, repaying injury with kindness, effecting difficult things while they are easy, and managing great things in their beginnings: this is the method of Tao.

LAO-TSE

TASTE

When our integrity declines, our taste does also.

LA ROCHEFOUCAULD

A true taste is never a half taste.

JOHN CONSTABLE

Men lose their tempers in defending their taste.

RALPH WALDO EMERSON

People care more about being thought to have taste than about being thought either good, clever, or amiable. SAMUEL BUTLER

TATTOOING

Painting and tattooing of the body is a return to the animal in us.

GOETHE

TAUGHT

Most men are unwilling to be taught. SAMUEL JOHNSON

To please, one must make up his mind to be taught many things which he already knows, by people who do not know them.

NICOLAS CHAMFORT

The human mind is full of curiosity but it don't love to be taught.

JOSH BILLINGS

Personally I am always ready to learn, although I do not always like being taught.

WINSTON S. CHURCHILL

See also **Education, Learning, Teaching.**

TAXES

Taxes are the price we pay for civilized society.

OLIVER WENDELL HOLMES, JR.

See also **Income Tax.**

TEACHING

In teaching there should be no class distinctions. CONFUCIUS

That scholarship which consists in the memorization of facts does not qualify one to be a teacher.

CONFUCIUS

The vanity of teaching often tempts a man to forget he is a blockhead.

LORD HALIFAX

To teach is to learn twice.

JOSEPH JOUBERT

We talked of the education of children; and I asked him what he thought was best to teach them first. Johnson: 'Sir, it is no matter what you teach them first, any more than what leg you shall put into your breeches first. Sir, you may stand disputing which is best to put in first, but in the meantime your breech is bare. Sir, while you are considering which of two things you should teach your child first, another boy has learnt them both.'

BOSWELL (*Life of Johnson*)

All teaching depends on a certain presentiment and preparation in the taught; we can only teach others profitably what they already virtually know; we can only give them what they had already.

FRÉDÉRIC AMIEL

To be good is noble, but to teach others how to be good is nobler— and less trouble. MARK TWAIN

Everybody who is incapable of learning has taken to teaching— that is really what our enthusiasm for education has come to.

OSCAR WILDE

It is said that if you wash a cat it will never again wash itself. This may or may not be true: what is certain is that if you teach a man anything he will never learn it; and if you cure him of a disease he will be unable to cure himself the next time it attacks him.

GEORGE BERNARD SHAW

He who can, does. He who cannot, teaches. GEORGE BERNARD SHAW

Everybody is now so busy teaching that nobody has any time to learn.
AGNES REPPLIER

The object of teaching a child is to enable him to get along without his teacher. ELBERT HUBBARD

Teaching must be determinedly slow in pace. ALAIN

A teacher who is not dogmatic is simply a teacher who is not teaching. G. K. CHESTERTON

See also **Education, Learning, Schoolmaster, Taught, Training.**

TEDIOUS

You cannot give me an instance of any man who is permitted to lay out his own time, contriving not to have tedious hours.
SAMUEL JOHNSON

TEETOTALISM

Habitual teetotallers. There should be asylums for such people. But they would probably relapse into teetotalism as soon as they came out. SAMUEL BUTLER

TELEPHONE

We can hardly realize now the blissful quietude of the pre-telephone epoch. NORMAN DOUGLAS

The telephone is the greatest nuisance among conveniences, the greatest convenience among nuisances. ROBERT LYND

There is something about saying 'O.K.' and hanging up the receiver with a bang that kids a man into feeling that he has just pulled off a big deal, even if he has only called up central to find out the correct time. ROBERT BENCHLEY

TELLING THE TRUTH

I tell the truth, not as much as I would but as much as I dare—and I dare more and more as I grow older. MONTAIGNE

It is better to remain silent than to speak the truth ill-humouredly, and so spoil an excellent dish by covering it with a bad sauce.
ST. FRANCIS DE SALES

The only way to speak the truth is to speak lovingly.
HENRY DAVID THOREAU

Often, the surest way to convey misinformation is to tell the strict truth. MARK TWAIN

If you tell the truth, you don't have to remember anything.
MARK TWAIN

The most awful thing that one can do is to tell the truth. It's all right in my case because I am not taken seriously.
GEORGE BERNARD SHAW

If one tells the truth, one is sure, sooner or later, to be found out.
OSCAR WILDE

See also **Sincerity, Truth, Truth and Lying.**

TEMPERANCE

Temperate temperance is best. Intemperate temperance injures the cause of temperance.
MARK TWAIN

Temperance? I would call it the exercise of our faculties and organs in such a manner as to combine the maximum of pleasure with the minimum of pain.
NORMAN DOUGLAS

See also **Moderation.**

TEMPTATION

You know, humanly speaking, there is a certain degree of temptation which will overcome any virtue.   SAMUEL JOHNSON

I can resist everything except temptation.   OSCAR WILDE

Though it be false and mischievous to speak of hereditary vice, it is most true and wise to observe the mysterious fact of hereditary temptation.   WALTER BAGEHOT

It is good to be without vices, but it is not good to be without temptations.   WALTER BAGEHOT

There are several good protections against temptation but the surest is cowardice.   MARK TWAIN

The man who has never been tempted don't know how dishonest he is.   JOSH BILLINGS

Men and women being what they are, it is only by reducing the number and intensity of temptations that human societies can be, in some measure at least, delivered from evil.   ALDOUS HUXLEY

TEN COMMANDMENTS

Decalogue: A series of commandments, ten in number,—just enough to permit an intelligent selection for observance, but not enough to embarrass the choice.
AMBROSE BIERCE

TENNYSON

Tennyson is a beautiful half of a poet.   RALPH WALDO EMERSON

TERRIFIED

We are terrified by the idea of being terrified.   FRIEDRICH NIETZSCHE

See also **Fear, Scare.**

TESTAMENT   see   LAST WILL

TEXAS

I like the story, doubtless antique, that I heard near San Antonio. A child asks a stranger where he comes from, whereupon his father rebukes him gently, 'Never do that, son. If a man's from Texas, he'll tell you. If he's not, why embarrass him by asking?'   JOHN GUNTHER

THEOLOGY

I have only a small flickering light to guide me in the darkness of a thick forest. Up comes a theologian and blows it out.   DIDEROT

The thelogical problems of original sin, origin of evil, predestination and the like are the soul's mumps, and measles, and whooping-coughs.   RALPH WALDO EMERSON

Theology is anthropology.
LUDWIG FEUERBACH

I consider Christian theology to be one of the great disasters of the human race.
ALFRED NORTH WHITEHEAD

Is not Darwin the chief modern theologian, since he made the largest and most fruitful study of how God works?
CHARLES HORTON COOLEY

Theology is the effort to explain the unknowable in terms of the not worth knowing.   H. L. MENCKEN

Christian theology is not only opposed to the scientific spirit; it is opposed to every other form of rational thinking.   H. L. MENCKEN

THEORY

I know the people you mean: they are all brains and theory and can't sew on a button.

          G. C. LICHTENBERG

Grey is all theory, green life's golden tree.   GOETHE

Goethe could not explain and so he said theory was grey.

      OLIVER WENDELL HOLMES, JR.

A favourite theory is a possession for life.   WILLIAM HAZLITT

Almost every person, if you will believe himself, holds a quite different theory of life from the one on which he is patently acting.

      ROBERT LOUIS STEVENSON

It is no paradox to say that in our most theoretical moods we may be nearest to our most practical applications.

      ALFRED NORTH WHITEHEAD

I got up with stoic fortitude of mind in the cold this morning; but afterwards, in my hot bath, I joined the school of Epicurus. I was a materialist at breakfast; after it an idealist, as I smoked my first cigarette and turned the world to transcendental vapour. But when I began to read *The Times* I had no doubt of the existence of an external world.

So all the morning and all the afternoon opinions kept flowing into and out of the receptacle of my mind; till by the time the enormous day was over, it had been filled by most of the widely-known theories of existence, and emptied of them.

      LOGAN PEARSALL SMITH

A work of art that contains theories is like an object on which the price tag has been left.

      MARCEL PROUST

See also **Doctrine, System.**

THIEF

The thief. Once committed beyond a certain point he should not worry himself too much about not being a thief any more. Thieving is God's message to him. Let him try and be a good thief.   SAMUEL BUTLER

Kleptomaniac: A rich thief.

      AMBROSE BIERCE

Many a man is saved from being a thief by finding everything locked up.   E. W. HOWE

A thief believes everybody steals.

      E. W. HOWE

See also **Crime.**

THINGS

The more we understand individual things, the more we understand God.   SPINOZA

There are many things that we would throw away, if we were not afraid that others might pick them up.   OSCAR WILDE

All greatness in style begins, I imagine, with such respect, deep and passionate enough to produce a humility which will not assert itself at the expense even of inanimate things: out of which submissiveness a desire to serve is born, in disinterested accuracy toward the object, whatever it may be.   FREYA STARK

THINKING

There is no expedient to which man will not resort to avoid the real labour of thinking.

      SIR JOSHUA REYNOLDS

Thinking without learning makes one flighty, and learning without thinking is a disaster. CONFUCIUS

No occupation is at once idler and more fruitful than entertaining one's own thoughts. MONTAIGNE

God is a thing that thinks. SPINOZA

Great men, by teaching weak minds to think, have put them on the road to error. VAUVENARGUES

All that we are is the result of what we have thought. DHAMMAPADA

Thinking is more interesting than knowing, but less interesting than looking. GOETHE

All good ideas have already been thought; the point is to try and think them again. GOETHE

I never could find any man who could think for two minutes together. SYDNEY SMITH

In a million people there are a thousand thinkers, and in a thousand thinkers there is one self-thinker. LUDWIG BÖRNE

A man thinks as well through his legs and arms as his brain. HENRY DAVID THOREAU

'Really, now you ask me,' said Alice, very much confused, 'I don't think—' 'Then you shouldn't talk,' said the Hatter. LEWIS CARROLL

We think as we do, mainly because other people think so. SAMUEL BUTLER

A polyp would be a conceptual thinker if a feeling of 'Hollo! thingumbob again!' ever flitted through his mind. WILLIAM JAMES

The mania of thinking renders one unfit for every activity. ANATOLE FRANCE

If you think before you speak, the other fellow gets in his joke first. E. W. HOWE

We cannot think first and act afterwards. From the moment of birth we are immersed in action, and can only fitfully guide it by taking thought. ALFRED NORTH WHITEHEAD

You must always let yourself think about everything. And you must think about everything as it is, not as it is talked about. GEORGE BERNARD SHAW

A 'new thinker', when studied closely, is merely a man who does not know what other people have thought. FRANK MOORE COLBY

A child, asked how he happened to think of something, said, 'I got a kick in the mind and it said itself.' LINCOLN STEFFENS

It is not much good thinking of a thing unless you think it out. H. G. WELLS

'A man becomes what he thinks,' says an Upanishad mantra. Experience of wise men testifies to the truth of the aphorism. The world will thus become what its wise men think. GANDHI

I think and think, for months, for years, ninety-nine times the conclusion is false. The hundredth time I am right. ALBERT EINSTEIN

The old lady in the anecdote was accused by her nieces of being illogical. For some time she could not be brought to understand what logic was, and when she grasped its true nature she was not so much angry as contemptuous. 'Logic! Good gracious! What rubbish!' she exclaimed. 'How can I tell what I think till I see what I say?' E. M. FORSTER

Often one must forget what he happens to wish before he can become susceptible to what the situation itself requires. . . . This transition is one of the great moments in many genuine thought processes. . . . Real thinkers forget about themselves in thinking.
MAX WERTHEIMER

If I ever felt inclined to blush it would not be at the crooked behaviour of men, but at their crooked intellectual processes.
NORMAN DOUGLAS

The psychologists and metaphysicians wrangle endlessly over the nature of the thinking process in man, but no matter how violently they differ otherwise they all agree that it has little to do with logic and it is not much conditioned by overt facts.
H. L. MENCKEN

See also **Analysis, Brooding, Logic, Meditation, Reflection, Speculation, Thought.**

THIRTY-NINE

Thirty-nine. It is a good age. One begins to appreciate things at their true value.
NORMAN DOUGLAS

THOUGHT

A man may dwell so long upon a thought that it may take him prisoner.
LORD HALIFAX

All motion in this world has its origin in something that is not motion. Why, then, shouldn't the universal force be the cause of my thoughts just as it is the cause of fermentation?
G. C. LICHTENBERG

One thought fills immensity.
WILLIAM BLAKE

A thought must tell at once, or not at all.
WILLIAM HAZLITT

Oh, for a life of sensations rather than of thoughts!
JOHN KEATS

A fine life is a thought conceived in youth and realized in maturity.
ALFRED DE VIGNY

All the thoughts of a turtle are turtle.
RALPH WALDO EMERSON

In every work of genius we recognize our own rejected thoughts; they come back to us with a certain alienated majesty.
RALPH WALDO EMERSON

A rush of thought is the only conceivable prosperity that can come to us.
RALPH WALDO EMERSON

Thought breeds thought. It grows under your hands.
HENRY DAVID THOREAU

Thought pure and simple is as near to God as we can get, it is through this that we are linked with God.
SAMUEL BUTLER

Our thoughts are our feelings gone to seed.
JOHN BURROUGHS

A thought is only a sign, just as a word is only a sign of a thought.
FRIEDRICH NIETZSCHE

An attack upon systematic thought is treason to civilization.
ALFRED NORTH WHITEHEAD

Every situation in life provides us ready-made with the outfit of thoughts and ways of behaving which perfectly fit it.
LOGAN PEARSALL SMITH

Thoughts left unsaid are never wasted.
HENRY S. HASKINS

See also **Idea, Thinking, Thought and Action.**

THOUGHT AND ACTION

Thinking and doing has been compared to Rachel and Leah: one was prettier, the other more productive.
GOETHE

Thinking is easy, acting is difficult, and to put one's thoughts into action is the most difficult thing in the world.
GOETHE

If men would think more they would act less.   LORD HALIFAX

See also **Action, Doing.**

THRONE

Perched on the loftiest throne in the world, we are still sitting on our own behind.   MONTAIGNE

TICKET OFFICE

'O, for an axe!' my soul cries out in railway stations, 'to hew limb from limb all the fiends and Jezebels between me and the ticket-office!'
LOGAN PEARSALL SMITH

TIME

Time is the greatest innovator.
FRANCIS BACON

He spoke a great word who said, 'Time and I against any two.'
BALTASAR GRACIÁN

Nothing really belongs to us but time, which even he has who has nothing else.   BALTASAR GRACIÁN

In order to see famous hills and rivers, one must have also predestined luck; unless the appointed time has come, one has no time to see them even though they are situated within a dozen miles.
CHANG CH'AO

You are not born for fame if you don't know the value of time.
VAUVENARGUES

Eternity is in love with the productions of time.   WILLIAM BLAKE

That is the only true time, which a man can properly call his own—that which he has all to himself; the rest, though in some sense he may be said to live it, is other people's time, not his.   CHARLES LAMB

Time itself is an element.
GOETHE

I have never had a watch nor any other mode of keeping time in my possession, nor ever wish to learn how time goes.   WILLIAM HAZLITT

We work not only to produce but to give value to time.
EUGÈNE DELACROIX

God had infinite time to give us; but how did He give it? In one immense tract of a lazy millenium? No, but He cut it up into a neat succession of new mornings, and, with each, therefore, a new idea, new inventions, and new applications.   RALPH WALDO EMERSON

A man is wise with the wisdom of his time only, and ignorant with its ignorance.
HENRY DAVID THOREAU

As if we could kill time without injuring eternity!
HENRY DAVID THOREAU

Let a man take time enough for the most trivial deed, though it be but the paring of his nails.
HENRY DAVID THOREAU

There is nothing good in this world which time does not improve.
ALEXANDER SMITH

Time is the only true purgatory.
SAMUEL BUTLER

I despise making the most of one's time. Half of the pleasures of life consist of the opportunities one has neglected.

OLIVER WENDELL HOLMES, JR.

Whoever has not two-thirds of his time to himself is a slave.

FRIEDRICH NIETZSCHE

Time is money—says the vulgarest saw known to any age or people. Turn it round about and you get a precious truth—money is time.

GEORGE GISSING

In the dark, time feels different than when it is light.

FRIEDRICH NIETZSCHE

Time preserves nothing that you make without its help.

ANATOLE FRANCE

Time is waste of money.

OSCAR WILDE

There is no difference between time and any of the three dimensions of space except that our consciousness moves along it. H. G. WELLS

One can always trust to time. Insert a wedge of time, and nearly everything straightens itself out.

NORMAN DOUGLAS

A loafer always has the correct time. KIN HUBBARD

Our judgments about things vary according to the time left us to live —that we think is left us to live.

ANDRÉ GIDE

There are optical illusions in time as well as in space.

MARCEL PROUST

Theoretically we know that the earth revolves, though in fact we are not aware of this; the ground we walk on does not seem to move and our minds are undisturbed. The same may be said of time.

MARCEL PROUST

In general, when we are looking forward to something, the shorter the time is the longer it seems to us— because we measure it in shorter units or simply because we think of measuring it. MARCEL PROUST

We can see more clearly across the mists of time how Hannibal conquered at Cannae than why Joffre won at the Marne.

WINSTON S. CHURCHILL

A good holiday is one spent among people whose notions of time are vaguer than yours.

J. B. PRIESTLEY

We all find time to do what we really want to do.

WILLIAM FEATHER

To us, the moment 8.17 A.M. means something—something very important, if it happens to be the starting time of our daily train. To our ancestors, such an odd eccentric instant was without significance— did not even exist. In inventing the locomotive, Watt and Stevenson were part inventors of time.

ALDOUS HUXLEY

See also **Future, Minute, Moment, Now, Past, Present, Time and Space, Timing, Today, Tomorrow, Waiting.**

TIME AND SPACE

Nothing puzzles me more than time and space; and yet nothing puzzles me less, for I never think about them. CHARLES LAMB

TIMING

Timing is the chief ingredient in judgment. WILLIAM FEATHER

TINFOIL

I have never yet met anyone who did not think it was an agreeable sensation to cut tinfoil with scissors.
G. C. LICHTENBERG

TITLE

Books with striking and ingenious titles are seldom worth reading.
G. C. LICHTENBERG

The *Ancient Mariner* would not have taken so well if it had been called 'The Old Sailor.'   SAMUEL BUTLER

See also **Name.**

TOBACCO

Tobacco was not known in the golden age. So much the worse for the golden age.   WILLIAM COWPER

Tobacco, divine, rare, superexcellent tobacco, which goes far beyond all the panaceas, potable gold, and philosophers' stones, a sovereign remedy for all diseases. A good vomit, I confess, a virtuous herb, if it be well qualified, opportunely taken, and medicinally used; but as it is commonly abused by most men, which take it as tinkers do ale, 'tis a plague, a mischief, a violent purger of goods, lands, health, hellish, devilish, and damned tobacco, the ruin and overthrow of body and soul.   ROBERT BURTON

The believing we do something when we do nothing is the first illusion of tobacco.
RALPH WALDO EMERSON

See also **Smoking.**

TODAY

The obscurest epoch is today.
ROBERT LOUIS STEVENSON

See also **Now, Present.**

TOLERANCE

If you are desirous to prevent the overrunning of a state by any sect, show it toleration.   VOLTAIRE

There is a limit at which forbearance ceases to be a virtue.
EDMUND BURKE

One has only to grow older to become more tolerant. I see no wrong that I might not have committed myself.   GOETHE

To tolerate is to insult.   GOETHE

I have seen gross intolerance shown in support of toleration.
SAMUEL TAYLOR COLERIDGE

We are none of us tolerant in what concerns us deeply and entirely.
SAMUEL TAYLOR COLERIDGE

So much blood has been shed by the Church because of an omission from the Gospel: 'You shall be *indifferent* as to what your neighbour's religion is.' Not merely tolerant of it, but indifferent to it.
MARK TWAIN

This duty of toleration has been summed up in the words, 'Let both grow together until the harvest.'
ALFRED NORTH WHITEHEAD

See also **Intolerance, Open Mind.**

TOLSTOY

I consign my own artistic productions to the category of bad art, excepting the story *God Sees the Truth*, and *The Prisoner of the Caucasus*.   LEO TOLSTOY

Tolstoy had no business to be born in Europe. He should have been an Indian sage, and then his exit to meditate in the wilderness would have been quite in the regular course and troubled nobody.
OLIVER WENDELL HOLMES, JR.

I recently saw an old gentleman working conscientiously—so I thought—through Tolstoy's *War and Peace*. He sighed a little when he spoke to me, and held up the book for inspection. 'My daughter-in-law sent it to me,' he explained resignedly, 'and said I must be sure and read it. But,'—this with a sudden sense of gratitude and deliverance—'thank Heaven! one volume was lost on the way.'

AGNES REPPLIER

TOMORROW

He that is down today may be up tomorrow, unless he has a mind to lie abed. CERVANTES

Tomorrow is an old deceiver, and his cheat never goes stale.

SAMUEL JOHNSON

Never put off till tomorrow what you can do the day after tomorrow just as well. MARK TWAIN

TOWN

There isn't much to be seen in a little town, but what you hear makes up for it. KIN HUBBARD

TOWN AND COUNTRY

I am in love with this green earth; the face of town and country; the unspeakable rural solitudes, and the sweet security of the streets.

CHARLES LAMB

TRADE

A man is obliged to teach his son a trade, and whoever does not teach his son a trade teaches him to become a robber. The person who has a trade in his hand is like a vineyard which is fenced in, so that cattle and beasts cannot get in, or passers-by eat of it. TALMUD

A merchant may, perhaps, be a man of an enlarged mind, but there is nothing in trade connected with an enlarged mind.

SAMUEL JOHNSON

We rail at trade, but the historian of the world will see that it was the principle of liberty; that it settled America, and destroyed feudalism, and made peace and keeps peace; that it will abolish slavery.

RALPH WALDO EMERSON

See also **Business.**

TRAINING

Training is everything. The peach was once a bitter almond; cauliflower is but cabbage with a college education. MARK TWAIN

See also **Teaching.**

TRANQUILLITY

Periods of tranquillity are seldom prolific of creative achievement. Mankind has to be stirred up.

ALFRED NORTH WHITEHEAD

See also **Quiet.**

TRANSGRESSOR

The reason the way of the transgressor is hard is because it's so crowded. KIN HUBBARD

See also **Sin, Sinner.**

TRANSITION

When our first parents were driven out of Paradise, Adam is believed to have remarked to Eve: 'My dear, we live in an age of transition.'

W. R. INGE

TRANSLATION

Translation from one language to another is like viewing a piece of tapestry on the wrong side where though the figures are distinguishable yet there are so many ends and threads that the beauty and exactness of the work is obscured.

CERVANTES

When a book is not of such character that even a bad translation can't spoil it for an intelligent reader, then it is certainly not a book written for posterity.

G. C. LICHTENBERG

TRAVEL

The world is a country which nobody ever yet knew by description; one must travel through it one's self to be acquainted with it.

LORD CHESTERFIELD

Travel and society polish one, but a rolling stone gathers no moss, and a little moss is a good thing on a man.   JOHN BURROUGHS

We only need travel enough to give our intellects an airing.

HENRY DAVID THOREAU

I hold that it is the duty of a man to see other lands but love his own.

E. V. LUCAS

The whole object of travel is not to set foot on foreign land; it is at last to set foot on one's own country as a foreign land.

G. K. CHESTERTON

The traveller sees what he sees; the tripper sees what he has come to see.   G. K. CHESTERTON

In American there are two classes of travel—first class, and with children.   ROBERT BENCHLEY

My father had a theory that, as the child in the womb goes through the various stages of the created animal world, so in early years it continues its progress through the primitive history of man: and it is therefore most necessary, he would say, that children should travel, at the time when in their epitome of history they are nomads by nature.

FREYA STARK

A good traveller is one who does not know where he is going to, and a perfect traveller does not know where he came from.

LIN YUTANG

See also **Abroad, Foreign, Journey.**

TREE, SIR HERBERT BEERBOHM

(On his *Hamlet*:) Funny without being vulgar.   OSCAR WILDE

TREES

What I know of the divine sciences and Holy Scripture, I learnt in woods and fields. I have had no other masters than the beeches and the oaks.

ST. BERNARD OF CLAIRVAUX

A visitor strolling through the noble woods of Ferney complimented VOLTAIRE on the splendid growth of his trees. 'Ay,' he replied, 'they have nothing else to do,' and walked on without another word.

Were I a rich man, I would propagate all kinds of trees that will grow in the open air. A green-house is childish. I would introduce foreign animals into the country: for instance, the reindeer.

SAMUEL JOHNSON

The tree which moves some to tears of joy is in the eyes of others only a green thing that stands in the way.

WILLIAM BLAKE

See also **Country, Nature, Scenery.**

TRIAL

In trials of skill, at first all is friendliness; but at last it is all antagonism. CHUANG-TSE

Our trials increase with the years.
GOETHE

To court trial is to tempt God.
FRÉDÉRIC AMIEL

See also **Difficulties, Problem, Trouble.**

TRIANGLE

If the triangles made a god, they would give him three sides.
MONTESQUIEU

TRIFLE

God requires a faithful fulfilment of the merest trifle given us to do, rather than the most ardent aspiration to things to which we are not called. ST. FRANCIS DE SALES

A mere trifle consoles us, for a mere trifle distresses us. PASCAL

Trifles make up the happiness or the misery of mortal life. The majority of men slip into their graves without having encountered on their way thither any signal catastrophe or exaltation of fortune or feeling. ALEXANDER SMITH

See also **Little, Small.**

TROJAN WAR

It is conceivable that the wise man, while accepting the sensational as an essential part of nature, would turn from it with profounder interest to quieter and more beneficent streams of events. Such a man might have taken more interest in the Greeks and the Trojans, if on the first day of the landing, the leaders on both sides had shaken each other by the hand and the Greeks had gone home with an invitation to return the following summer with their wives and children. ROBERT LYND

TROUBLE

Trouble that is easily recognized is half-cured. ST. FRANCIS DE SALES

Some troubles, like a protested note of a solvent debtor, bear interest.
HONORÉ DE BALZAC

'Trouble has done it, Bilgewater, trouble has done it; trouble has brung these grey hairs and this premature balditude.' MARK TWAIN

Trouble creates a capacity to handle it. OLIVER WENDELL HOLMES, JR.

The way out of trouble is never as simple as the way in. E. W. HOWE

Nobody ever grew despondent looking for trouble.
KIN HUBBARD

See also **Cross, Difficulties, Hot Water, Problem, Trial.**

TRUE

Everything that is true is God's word, whoever may have said it.
ULRICH ZWINGLI

All the principles of sceptics, stoics, atheists, etc., are true. But their conclusions are false, because the opposite principles are also true.
PASCAL

What is true by lamplight is not always true in the sunshine.
JOSEPH JOUBERT

How awful to reflect that what people say of us is true!
LOGAN PEARSALL SMITH

'Tell me a story,' said the Baroness, staring out desperately at the rain. 'What sort of story?' asked Clovis. 'One just true enough to be interesting and not true enough to be tiresome,' said the Baroness.   SAKI

True experiences take place in the unexpressed and the inexpressible. What can be expressed can never be quite true. Clothe an idea in words, and it loses its freedom of movement.   EGON FRIEDELL

See also **Telling the Truth, Truth.**

TRUISM

There is only one thing that requires real courage to say, and that is a truism.   G. K. CHESTERTON

See also **Commonplace, Obvious, Platitude.**

TRUST

Never trust a man who speaks well of everybody.
JOHN CHURTON COLLINS

Woe to the man whose heart has not learned while young to hope, to love—and to put its trust in life!
JOSEPH CONRAD

We used to trust in God. I think it was in 1863 that some genius suggested that it be put upon the gold and silver coins which circulated among the rich. They didn't put it on the nickels and coppers because they didn't think the poor folks had any trust in God.   MARK TWAIN

See also **Faith.**

TRUTH

Truth does not depart from human nature. If what is regarded as truth departs from human nature, it may not be regarded as truth.
CONFUCIUS

It is not truth that makes man great, but man that makes truth great.   CONFUCIUS

If a man hear the truth in the morning, he may die in the evening without regret.   CONFUCIUS

Truth does not do as much good in the world as its counterfeits do evil.
LA ROCHEFOUCAULD

Men who never take back their words love themselves more than truth.   JOSEPH JOUBERT

Some people do not know what to do with truth when it is offered to them.   CHARLES LAMB

No man speaks the truth or lives a true life for two minutes together.
RALPH WALDO EMERSON

Truth should not be absolutely lost sight of but it should not be talked about.   SAMUEL BUTLER

There is but one sure road of access to truth—the road of patient, cooperative inquiry operating by means of observation, experiment, record, and controlled reflection.
JOHN DEWEY

Truth is that which seems true to the best and most competent men of any given age and place where truth is sought. It is what these men can acquiesce in with the least discomfort.   SAMUEL BUTLER

Truth is the most valuable thing we have. Let us economize it.
MARK TWAIN

I don't believe or know anything about absolute truth.
OLIVER WENDELL HOLMES, JR.

All I mean by truth is the road I can't help travelling.
OLIVER WENDELL HOLMES, JR.

The possession of truth is not frightful but dull—like all possessions. FRIEDRICH NIETZSCHE

I overheard the other day a scrap of conversation, which I take the liberty to reproduce. 'What I advance is true,' said one. 'But not the whole truth,' answered the other. 'Sir,' returned the first (and it seemed to me there was a smack of Dr. Johnson in the speech), 'Sir, there is no such thing as the whole truth!' ROBERT LOUIS STEVENSON

Truth is like the use of words, it depends greatly on custom. SAMUEL BUTLER

We have to change the truth a little in order to remember it. GEORGE SANTAYANA

Truth is a jewel which should not be painted over; but it may be set to advantage and shown in good light. GEORGE SANTAYANA

The truth would become more popular if it were not always stating ugly facts. HENRY S. HASKINS

But men do not seek the truth. It is the truth that pursues men who run away and will not look around. LINCOLN STEFFENS

To love the truth is to refuse to let oneself be saddened by it. ANDRÉ GIDE

'My dear Mr. Greech,' said Lady Caroline, 'we all know that Prime Ministers are wedded to the truth, but like other wedded couples they sometimes live apart.' SAKI

Philosophy should be piecemeal and provisional like science; final truth belongs to heaven, not to this world. BERTRAND RUSSELL

He who does not bellow the truth when he knows the truth makes himself the accomplice of liars and forgers. CHARLES PÉGUY

If you are out to describe the truth, leave elegance to the tailor. ALBERT EINSTEIN

See also **Error, Fact, Telling the Truth, True, Truism, Truth and Error, Truth and Fiction, Truth and Lying, Truth and Untruth, Truths.**

TRUTH AND ERROR

When we do not know the truth of a matter, it is well that there should be a common error to fix the spirits of men. PASCAL

The most dangerous of all falsehoods is a slightly distorted truth. G. C. LICHTENBERG

Error has the advantage that you can talk about it forever; truth must be put to use right away, or it disappears. GOETHE

Nothing hurts a new truth more than an old error. GOETHE

Error is to truth as sleep is to waking. Refreshed, we return from error to truth. GOETHE

Truth is a good thing; but beware of barking too close to the heels of an error, lest you get your brains kicked out. SAMUEL TAYLOR COLERIDGE

There is no such source of error as the pursuit of absolute truth. SAMUEL BUTLER

Man approaches the unattainable truth through a succession of errors. ALDOUS HUXLEY

See also **Error, Truth, Truth and Untruth.**

TRUTH AND FICTION

Truth is stranger than fiction, but it is because fiction is obliged to stick to possibilities; truth isn't.
MARK TWAIN

Truth must necessarily be stranger than fiction; for fiction is the creation of the human mind and therefore congenial to it.
G. K. CHESTERTON

Fiction reveals truths that reality obscures.   JESSAMYN WEST

TRUTH AND LYING

Accustom your children constantly to this: if a thing happened at one window, and they, when relating it, say it happened at another, do not let it pass, but instantly check them; you do not know where deviation from truth will end. . . . It is more from carelessness about truth than from intentional lying that there is so much falsehood in the world.   SAMUEL JOHNSON

A man had rather have a hundred lies told about him, than one truth which he does not wish should be told.   SAMUEL JOHNSON

Half a truth is often a great lie.
BENJAMIN FRANKLIN

All men are born truthful, and die liars.   VAUVENARGUES

Lying is the strongest acknowledgement of the force of truth.
WILLIAM HAZLITT

Truth is beautiful. Without doubt; and so are lies.
RALPH WALDO EMERSON

Truth does not consist in never lying but in knowing when to lie and when not to do so.
SAMUEL BUTLER

Some men love truth so much that they seem in continual fear lest she should catch cold on over-exposure.
SAMUEL BUTLER

If you want to be thought a liar, always tell the truth.
LOGAN PEARSALL SMITH

Lies are essential to humanity. They are perhaps as important as the pursuit of pleasure and moreover are necessary to that pursuit.
MARCEL PROUST

It is hard to believe that a man is telling the truth when you know that you would lie if you were in his place.   H. L. MENCKEN

If one cannot invent a really convincing lie, it is often better to stick to the truth.   ANGELA THIRKELL

See also **Lying, Sincerity, Telling the Truth, Veracity.**

TRUTH AND UNTRUTH

Every truth is true only up to a point. Beyond that, by way of counterpoint, it becomes untruth.
SÖREN KIERKEGAARD

A new untruth is better than an old truth.
OLIVER WENDELL HOLMES, JR.

Truth blends well with untruth.
NORMAN DOUGLAS

See also **Truth, Truth and Error, Truth and Lying.**

TRUTHS

It is said, I know, that truth is *one*; but to this I cannot subscribe, for it appears to me that truth is *many*. There are as many truths as there are things and causes of action and contradictory principles at work in society.   WILLIAM HAZLITT

A higher truth, though only dimly hinted at, thrills us more than a lower expressed.
HENRY DAVID THOREAU

I am convinced that the desire to formulate truths is a virulent disease. WILLIAM JAMES

There are no whole truths; all truths are half-truths. It is trying to treat them as whole truths that plays the devil. ALFRED NORTH WHITEHEAD

The mind celebrates a little triumph whenever it can formulate a truth.
GEORGE SANTAYANA

Large contemplative truths never keep one awake nights nor make his heart beat too fast.
CHARLES HORTON COOLEY

There were eternal truths, I decided, but not very many, and even these required frequent spring-cleanings. JOHN BUCHAN

Say not, 'I have found the truth,' but rather, 'I have found a truth.'
KAHLIL GIBRAN
See also **Truth.**

TRY

He always reminds me of the too celebrated amateur who being asked could he play the violin, replied that he had no doubt he could if he tried.
GEORGE BERNARD SHAW

TUBER

A potato is a tuber, but the fact should be left in the decent obscurity of agricultural textbooks.
H. W. FOWLER

TUNNEL

I always feel an optimist when I emerge from a tunnel.
ROBERT LYND

TURKISH BATH

A man seldom thinks of taking Turkish baths until it is too late.
ROBERT BENCHLEY

TWENTY-SEVEN

The thing to do is to make so much money that you don't have to work after the age of twenty-seven. In case this is impracticable, stop work at the earliest possible moment, even if it is at a quarter past eleven on the morning of the day when you find you do have enough money. ROBERT BENCHLEY

TWICE

Chi Wen Tzu used to think thrice before acting. The Master hearing of it said: 'Twice would do.'
SAYINGS OF CONFUCIUS

'No, my Lord,' he (LORD MELBOURNE) replied to the disconcerted Archbishop of York, who had invited him to attend the evening service, 'once is orthodox, twice is puritanical.'

TWO

When speculation has done its worst, two and two still make four.
SAMUEL JOHNSON

There are two things in this life for which we are never fully prepared, and that is twins.
JOSH BILLINGS

I admit that twice two makes four is an excellent thing, but if we are to give everything its due, twice two makes five is sometimes a very charming thing too.
FEODOR DOSTOEVSKI

There are two words for everything. E. V. LUCAS

Mediocrity adds two and two, and gets only four. HENRY S. HASKINS

Two can live as cheap as one, but it costs them twice as much.
FRANK SULLIVAN

U

UMBRELLA

Don't put up your umbrella until it begins to rain. LORD SAMUEL

UNBELIEVER

'My dear Archdeacon,' Lady Caroline said, 'no one can be an unbeliever nowadays. The Christian apologists have left one nothing to disbelieve.' SAKI

See also **Believing, Faith, Scepticism.**

UNCERTAIN

To learn truly what each thing is, is a matter of uncertainty.
DEMOCRITUS

As to us—we are uncertain people, who are chased by the spirits of our destiny from purpose to purpose, like clouds by the wind.
SHELLEY

See also **Certain, Doubt, Sure.**

UNCLUBBABLE

Sir John Hawkins once refused point-blank to pay his share of the supper bill, whereupon DR. JOHNSON observed: 'Sir John, sir, is a very *unclubbable* man.'

UNCONSCIOUS

The unconsciousness of man is the consciousness of God.
HENRY DAVID THOREAU

UNDERSTANDING

Care should be taken, not that the reader may understand if he will; but that he must understand, if he will or not. QUINTILIAN

Were the works of God readily understandable by human reason, they would be neither wonderful nor unspeakable.
THOMAS À KEMPIS

There are three things I have always loved and never understood—painting, music, and women.
BERNARD DE FONTENELLE

Some people will never learn anything, for this reason, because they understand everything too soon. ALEXANDER POPE

Nothing cheers me up like having understood something difficult to understand. I should try it more often. G. C. LICHTENBERG

Everyone hears only what he understands. GOETHE

You don't have to travel around the world to understand that the sky is blue everywhere. GOETHE

It was at the age of seventy-three that I almost understood the form and the true nature of birds, of fish and of plants. HOKUSAI

We see nothing truly until we understand it. JOHN CONSTABLE

Those who have the largest hearts have the soundest understandings; and he is the truest philosopher who can forget himself.
WILLIAM HAZLITT

A man only understands what is akin to something already existing in himself. FRÉDÉRIC AMIEL

One gets tired of everything, except understanding. ANATOLE FRANCE

Our dignity is not in what we do, but what we understand. The whole world is doing things.
GEORGE SANTAYANA

We hear in retrospect when we have understood. MARCEL PROUST

There is a great difference between knowing a thing and understanding it. You can know a lot about something and not really understand it. CHARLES F. KETTERING

A doctrine that is understood is shorn of its strength.
ERIC HOFFER

See also **Comprehension, Misunderstanding, Not Understanding.**

UNDERTAKER

At least one *mortician* has promoted himself to the estate and dignity of a *mortuary consultant*, and another has become a *funeral counsellor*, but so far I have heard of none who calls himself a *mortuary*, *obituary*, or *obsequial engineer*. No doubt it will come.
H. L. MENCKEN

UNEDUCATED

I derived my education from the uneducated.
GEORGE BERNARD SHAW

Uneducated clever women, who have seen much of the world, are in middle life so much the most cultured part of the community. They have been saved from this horrible burden of inert ideas.
ALFRED NORTH WHITEHEAD

See also **Educated.**

UNEXPECTED

Unless the unexpected was sprung upon us continually to enliven us, we should pass life as it were in sleep. SAMUEL BUTLER

Our brightest blazes of gladness are commonly kindled by unexpected sparks. SAMUEL JOHNSON

See also **Expect, Surprise.**

UNFINISHED

The unfinished is nothing.
FRÉDÉRIC AMIEL

See also **Complete.**

UNHAPPY

Men who are unhappy, like men who sleep badly, are always proud of the fact. BERTRAND RUSSELL

See also **Happiness, Happy.**

UNIVERSAL

You must see the infinite, *i.e.* the universal, in your particular or it is only gossip.
OLIVER WENDELL HOLMES, JR.

Do not scorn particulars; they are universals made easy.
HENRY S. HASKINS

See also **Generality.**

UNIVERSE

The man who doesn't know what the universe is doesn't know where he lives. MARCUS AURELIUS

The universe is a single life comprising one substance and one soul.
MARCUS AURELIUS

He who lives in harmony with his own self, his daemon, lives in harmony with the universe; for both the universal order and the personal order are nothing but different expressions and manifestations of a common underlying principle. MARCUS AURELIUS

The universe is becoming a bore.
LOKAN PEARSALL SMITH

Man is not born to solve the problems of the universe, but to find out where the problems begin, and then to take his stand within the limits of the intelligible.
GOETHE

The good writer seems to be writing about himself, but has his eye always on that thread of the universe which runs through himself, and all things.
RALPH WALDO EMERSON

I like my universe as immense, grim, icy and pitiless as possible.
LOGAN PEARSALL SMITH

The universe is true for all of us and different for each of us.
MARCUS PROUST

UNIVERSITY
You will hear more good things on the outside of a stagecoach from London to Oxford than if you were to pass a twelvemonth with the undergraduates, or heads of colleges, of that famous university.
WILLIAM HAZLITT

UNKNOWABLE
Where there is an unknowable there is a promise.
THORNTON WILDER

UNKNOWN
He who can live unknown and not fret, is not he a gentleman?
CONFUCIUS

The pleasantest condition of life is in *incognito*. What a brave privilege is it to be free from all contentions, from all envying, or being envied, from receiving or paying all kind of ceremonies! ABRAHAM COWLEY

If you desire to know or learn anything to your advantage, then take delight in being unknown and unregarded.
THOMAS À KEMPIS

Live unknown. EPICURUS

Not a day passes over the earth, but men and women of no note do great deeds, speak great words and suffer noble sorrows.
CHARLES READE

See also **Obscurity.**

UNNOTICED
Most things must be left unnoticed among relatives and friends, and even among enemies.
BALTASAR GRACIÁN

See also **Attention, Inattention, Overlook.**

UNPREDICTABLE
Unpredictability, too, can become monotonous. ERIC HOFFER

UNPUNCTUALITY
Unpunctuality is a vile habit.
WINSTON S. CHURCHILL

See also **Punctuality.**

UNREASONABLE
The reasonable man adapts himself to the world: the unreasonable one persists in trying to adapt the world to himself. Therefore all progress depends on the unreasonable man.
GEORGE BERNARD SHAW

See also **Reasonable.**

UNSETTLED
People wish to be settled; only as far as they are unsettled, is there any hope for them.
RALPH WALDO EMERSON

USE

It is a great misfortune to be of use to nobody; scarcely less to be of use to everybody.
BALTASAR GRACIÁN

My only anxiety is: How can I be of use in the world, how can I serve some purpose and be of any good, how can I learn more and study profoundly certain subjects?
VINCENT VAN GOGH

See also **Useful, Useless.**

USED

This is the true joy in life, the being used for a purpose recognized by yourself as a mighty one; the being thoroughly worn out before you are thrown on the scrap heap; the being a force of nature instead of a feverish little clod of ailments and grievances complaining that the world will not devote itself to making you happy. GEORGE BERNARD SHAW

USED TO

Nothing is wonderful when you get used to it. E. W. HOWE

Learn to get used to it. Eels get used to skinning.
WINSTON S. CHURCHILL

See also **Habit.**

USEFUL

The sure way of knowing nothing about life is to try to make oneself useful. OSCAR WILDE

See also **Use, Used, Useless.**

USELESS

There is nothing useless in nature; not even uselessness itself.
MONTAIGNE

Words are like money. There is nothing so useless in themselves, unless when in actual use.
SAMUEL BUTLER

A friend who is very near and dear may in time become as useless as a relative. GEORGE ADE

'Depend upon it, there comes a time when for every addition of knowledge you forget something that you knew before. It is of the highest importance, therefore, not to have useless facts elbowing out the useful ones.' 'But the solar system!' I protested. 'What the deuce is it to me?' he interrupted, impatiently; 'you say that we go round the sun. If we went round the moon it would not make a pennyworth of difference to me or to my work.'
ARTHUR CONAN DOYLE

Music is essentially useless, as life is.
GEORGE SANTAYANA

See also **Use, Used, Useful.**

UTTERANCE

All unuttered truths become poisonous. FRIEDRICH NIETZSCHE

It is healthful to every sane man to utter the art within him; it is essential to every sane man to get rid of the art within him at all costs.
G. K. CHESTERTON

V

VANITY

When not prompted by vanity we say little. LA ROCHEFOUCAULD

The world is nothing but vanity cut out into several shapes.
LORD HALIFAX

To this principle of vanity, which philosophers call a mean one, and which I do not, I owe a great part of the figure which I have made in life. LORD CHESTERFIELD

Their vanity was in such good order, that they seemed to be quite free from it, and gave themselves no airs. JANE AUSTEN

We have an old saying in Japan that a woman cannot love a man who is truly vain, for there is no crevice in his heart for love to enter and fill up.
OKAKURA KAKUZO

See also **Conceit.**

VEDAS

To the illumined seer, the Vedas are all superfluous.
BHAGAVAD-GITA

VEGETARIANISM

Most vegetarians I ever see looked enough like their food to be classed as cannibals.
FINLEY PETER DUNNE

It is nearly fifty years since I was assured by a conclave of doctors that if I did not eat meat I should die of starvation.
GEORGE BERNARD SHAW

See also **Diet.**

VENGEANCE

Nothing is more costly, nothing is more sterile, than vengeance.
WINSTON S. CHURCHILL

See also **Revenge.**

VERACITY

Veracity is the heart of morality.
T. H. HUXLEY

See also **Sincerity, Telling the Truth.**

VICE

To tell the truth, we do not so much abandon our vices as change them, and, in my opinion, for the worse. MONTAIGNE

There is a division of labour, even in vice. Some persons addict themselves to the speculation only, others to the practice.
WILLIAM HAZLITT

When our vices leave us we flatter ourselves with the idea that we have left them.
LA ROCHEFOUCAULD

The vices are never so well employed as in combating one another. WILLIAM HAZLITT

He hasn't a single redeeming vice.
OSCAR WILDE

Vice is waste of life. Poverty, obedience and celibacy are the canonical vices.
GEORGE BERNARD SHAW

Vice is ever the senses gone astray.
DAVID GRAYSON

No exile at the South Pole or on the summit of Mont Blanc separates us more effectively from others than the practice of a hidden vice.
MARCEL PROUST

See also **Sin, Virtue, Virtue and Vice.**

VICIOUS

Nobody wants to be vicious.
SOCRATES

See also **Vice.**

VICTORY

The good man wins a victory and then stops; he will not go on to acts of violence. LAO-TSE

You can be invincible if you never enter a contest where victory is not in your power. EPICTETUS

Avoid victories over superiors. BALTASAR GRACIÁN

The victor need not explain. BALTASAR GRACIÁN

The way to get the most out of a victory is to follow it up with another which makes it look small. HENRY S. HASKINS

The most dangerous moment comes with victory. NAPOLEON I

See also **Conquer, Conquest.**

VIRTUE

I have three precious things, which I hold fast and prize. The first is gentleness; the second is frugality; the third is humility, which keeps me from putting myself before others. Be gentle and you can be bold; be frugal, and you can be liberal; avoid putting yourself before others, and you can become a leader among men. LAO-TSE

Courtesy is near to propriety. Economy is near to humanity. Good faith is near to the truth of things. If these virtues are practised with respect and humility, one may fall into errors, but they will not be very great. CONFUCIUS

There is no greater injury to one's character than practising virtue with motivation. CHUANG-TSE

You are a man, not God; you are human, not an angel. How can you expect to remain always in a constant state of virtue, when this was not possible even for an angel of Heaven, nor for the first man in the Garden? THOMAS À KEMPIS

My virtue is more innocence than virtue; or, better said, it is the product of chance. If I had been born with a more lawless nature, I would have made poor work of it. MONTAIGNE

The strength of a man's virtue must not be measured by his efforts, but by his ordinary life. PASCAL

Premeditated virtue doesn't count for much. Feeling or habit is the thing. G. C. LICHTENBERG

Virtue is too often merely local. SAMUEL JOHNSON

If mankind suddenly took to virtue many thousands would inevitably be reduced to starvation. G. C. LICHTENBERG

What is virtue but whatever behaviour fits a given situation? GOETHE

Virtue by calculation is the virtue of vice. JOSEPH JOUBERT

No virtue looks small when it is prominently staged. JOSEPH JOUBERT

Virtue knows that it is impossible to get on without compromise, and tunes herself, as it were, a trifle sharp to allow for an inevitable fall in playing. SAMUEL BUTLER

Each class preaches the importance of those virtues it need not exercise. The rich harp on the value of thrift, the idle grow eloquent over the dignity of labour. OSCAR WILDE

There are only three absolute virtues: objectivity, courage, and a sense of responsibility. ARTHUR SCHNITZLER

A man is an in-dividual; he cannot be divided or taken to pieces; he cannot be expected to possess

virtues incompatible with the rest of his mental equipment, however desirable such virtues may be.
NORMAN DOUGLAS

There is an element of the busybody in our conception of virtue; unless a man makes himself a nuisance to a great many people, we do not think he can be an exceptionally good man. BERTRAND RUSSELL

When you enjoy loving your neighbour it ceases to be a virtue.
KAHLIL GIBRAN
See also **Virtue and Vice, Virtuous.**

VIRTUE AND VICE

Live by old ethics and the classical rules of honesty. Put no new names upon authentic virtues and vices. SIR THOMAS BROWNE

Vices enter into the composition of virtues as poison into that of medicines. LA ROCHEFOUCAULD

We do not sustain ourselves in virtue by our own strength, but by balancing two opposed vices, just as we remain upright amidst two contrary gales. PASCAL

Men wish to be saved from the mischiefs of their virtues, but not from their vices.
RALPH WALDO EMERSON

The virtues of society are vices of the saint.
RALPH WALDO EMERSON

The vice we embrace seems at least a cousin to virtue.
HENRY S. HASKINS

Any of us can achieve virtue, if by virtue we merely mean the avoidance of the vices that do not attract us. ROBERT LYND

Always study the vices of a people, not its virtues. Virtues are always the same wherever you go.
AUBREY MENEN
See also **Vice, Virtue.**

VIRTUOUS

Nothing is more unpleasant than a virtuous person with a mean mind. WALTER BAGEHOT

Be virtuous and you will be eccentric. MARK TWAIN

VITAMINS

All the vitamins needed seem to be found in plebeian dishes.
WILLIAM FEATHER
See also **Diet, Food.**

VOCABULARY

Let the child's vocabulary, therefore, be limited; it is very undesirable that he should have more words than ideas, that he should be able to say more than he thinks. One of the reasons why peasants are generally shrewder than townsfolk is, I think, that their vocabulary is smaller. They have few ideas. but those few are thoroughly grasped. ROUSSEAU

A vocabulary of truth and simplicity will be of service throughout life. WINSTON S. CHURCHILL
See also **Words.**

VOW

Vows begin when hope dies.
LEONARDO DA VINCI

A vow is a horrible thing, it is a snare for sin. SAMUEL JOHNSON

The desert Hindus vow to eat no fish. GOETHE

W

WAGES

Give the labourer his wage before his perspiration be dry.

MOHAMMED

WAITING

True waiting means waiting without anxiety. ST. FRANCIS DE SALES

See also **Patience.**

WALKING

It is good to collect things; it is better to take walks.

ANATOLE FRANCE

It is a fact that not once in all my life have I gone out for a walk.

MAX BEERBOHM

Unhappy businessmen, I am convinced, would increase their happiness more by walking six miles every day than by any conceivable change of philosophy.

BERTRAND RUSSELL

WAR

Where troops have been quartered, brambles and thorns spring up. In the track of great armies there must follow lean years. LAO-TSE

It will be a wonder if, a hundred years hence, it is remembered in a general way that there were civil wars in our time in France.

MONTAIGNE

I hate war, for it spoils conversation. BERNARD DE FONTENELLE

I had left London with so much precipitation, that it never entered my mind that we were at war with France; and had reached Dover, and looked through my ·glass at the hills beyond Boulogne, before the idea presented itself; and with this in its train, that there was no getting there without a passport.

LAURENCE STERNE

Success in war depends so much on quicksightedness, and on seizing the right moment, that the battle of Austerlitz, which was so completely won, would have been lost if I had attacked six hours sooner.

NAPOLEON I

The whole art of war consists in getting at what is on the other side of the hill, or, in other words, in learning what we do not know from what we do.

DUKE OF WELLINGTON

(On the Civil War:) In our youth our hearts were touched with fire. It was given us to learn at the outset that life is a profound and passionate thing.

OLIVER WENDELL HOLMES, JR.

What is human warfare but just this—an effort to make the laws of God and nature take sides with one party.

HENRY DAVID THOREAU

War is little more than a catalogue of mistakes and misfortunes.

WINSTON S. CHURCHILL

When one is comfortable and well off, it is easy to talk high talk. I remember just before the battle of Antietam thinking and perhaps saying to a brother officer that it would be easy after a comfortable breakfast to come down the steps of one's house pulling on one's gloves and smoking a cigar, to get on to a horse and charge a battery up Beacon Street, while the ladies wave handkerchiefs from a balcony. But the reality was to pass a night on the ground in the rain with your bowels out of order and then after no particular breakfast to wade a stream and attack the enemy.

OLIVER WENDELL HOLMES, JR.

It's usual on the eve of every war for the two leaders of the people concerned to meet privately at some innocent village on a terrace in a garden overlooking a lake. And they decide together that war is the world's worst scourge, and as they watch the rippling reflections in the water, with magnolia petals dropping onto their shoulders, they are both of them peace-loving, modest and friendly. . . . And when their meeting is over, they shake hands in a most sincere brotherly fashion, and turn to smile and wave as they drive away. And the next day war breaks out. JEAN GIRAUDOUX

You can't say that civilization don't advance, for in every war they kill you a new way. WILL ROGERS

(August 5, 1862) The war goes on educating us to a trust in the simplicities and to see the bankruptcy of all narrow views.
RALPH WALDO EMERSON

As long as war is looked upon as wicked it will always have its fascination. When it is looked upon as vulgar it will cease to be popular.
OSCAR WILDE

The belief in the possibility of a short decisive war appears to be one of the most ancient and dangerous of human illusions.
ROBERT LYND

See also **Conquest, Soldier, Strategy, Victory, Waterloo.**

WASHING

The classes that wash most are those that work least.
G. K. CHESTERTON

If the father of our country, George Washington, was Tutankhamened tomorrow and, after being aroused from his tomb, was told that the American people today spend two billion dollars yearly on bathing material, he would say, *'What got 'em so dirty?'*
WILL ROGERS

WASTE

It is a basic rule never to waste anything, be it time or scraps of paper. G. C. LICHTENBERG

There is nobody poorer than the rich man who doesn't know how to be wasteful. ARTHUR SCHNITZLER

WATERLOO

If the little cowboy who acted as a guide to Bülow, Blücher's lieutenant, had advised him to debouch from the forest above Frischermont rather than below Plancenoit, the shaping of the nineteenth century would perhaps have been different. Napoleon would have won the battle of Waterloo. By any other road than below Plancenoit, the Prussian army would have brought up at a ravine impassable for artillery, and Bülow would not have arrived.
VICTOR HUGO

The loss of the battle of Waterloo was the salvation of France.
THOMAS JEFFERSON

WE

Only presidents, editors, and people with tapeworm have the right to use the editorial 'we.'
MARK TWAIN

WEAK

The soft overcomes the hard; the weak overcomes the strong.
LAO-TSE

We are oftener treacherous through weakness than through calculation. LA ROCHEFOUCAULD

Weak men are apt to be cruel, because they stick at nothing that may repair the ill effect of their mistakes.   LORD HALIFAX

No man is weak by choice.
            VAUVENARGUES

To be in the weakest camp is to be in the strongest school.
            G. K. CHESTERTON

WEALTH

It takes a kind of genius to make a fortune, and especially a large fortune. It is neither goodness, nor wit, nor talent, nor strength, nor delicacy. I don't know precisely what it is: I am waiting for someone to tell me.
            JEAN DE LA BRUYÈRE

Sir, the insolence of wealth will creep out.   SAMUEL JOHNSON

If you look up a dictionary of quotations you will find few reasons for a sensible man to desire to become wealthy.
            ROBERT LYND

Wealth: Any income that is at least $100 more a year than the income of one's wife's sister's husband.   H. L. MENCKEN

See also **Rich, Riches.**

WEATHER

Whenever people talk to me about the weather, I always feel certain that they mean something else.
            OSCAR WILDE

A change in the weather is enough to renew the world and ourselves.
            MARCEL PROUST

WEDDING

The music at a wedding procession always reminds me of the music of soldiers going into battle.
            HEINRICH HEINE

There are not many men who lie abed too late or oversleep themselves on their wedding morning.
            CHARLES DICKENS

An invitation to a wedding involves more trouble than a summons to a police court.   WILLIAM FEATHER

The smallest piece of silver which can qualify as a wedding gift is a marmalade spoon.
            CHARLES W. MORTON

WELL-BRED

Everybody thinks himself well-bred.   EARL OF SHAFTESBURY

Good breeding consists in concealing how much we think of ourselves and how little we think of the other person. MARK TWAIN

The difference between a well-bred and ill-bred man is this: One immediately attracts your liking, and the other your aversion. You love the one till you find reason to hate him; you hate the other till you find reason to love him.
            SAMUEL JOHNSON

He is not well-bred that cannot bear ill-breeding in others.
            BENJAMIN FRANKLIN

To have been well brought up is a great drawback nowadays. It shuts one out from so much.
            OSCAR WILDE

See also **Gentlemen, Lady.**

WELL-READ

His hearers were frankly incredulous. They pointed out that the friendship between the two artistes had always been a byword or whatever you called it. A well-read Egg summed it up by saying that they were like Thingummy and What's-his-name.
            P. G. WODEHOUSE

See also **Reading.**

WICKED

Man is not born wicked: he becomes so, as he becomes sick.
VOLTAIRE

If it be true that men are miserable because they are wicked, it is likewise true that many are wicked because they are miserable.
SAMUEL TAYLOR COLERIDGE

Flee the wicked, even when they are agreeable, instructive, and charming. EUGÈNE DELACROIX

Wickedness is a myth invented by good people to account for the curious attractiveness of others.
OSCAR WILDE

People are so wicked that their life would be miserable without the consolation of religion.
GEORGE BERNARD SHAW

See also **Bad, Good, Vicious.**

WIDOW

I saw a widow once with a crêpe umbrella. She was what St. Paul calls 'a widow indeed'.
SAMUEL BUTLER

Why don't some of the married women look as pretty as the widows? What's to hinder?
E. W. HOWE

So far as is known, no widow ever eloped. E. W. HOWE

The determination of life-insurance salesmen to succeed has made life pretty soft for widows.
WILLIAM FEATHER

WIFE

Ascend a step to choose a friend, descend a step to choose a wife.
TALMUD

It is perhaps easier to keep clear of the whole sex than to behave entirely as we should in companionship with our wives. MONTAIGNE

'Tis reason, a man that will have a wife should be at the charge of her trinkets, and pay all the scores she sets on him. He that will keep a monkey 'tis fit he should pay for the glasses he breaks.
JOHN SELDEN

A man is in general better pleased when he has a good dinner upon his table, than when his wife talks Greek. SAMUEL JOHNSON

An omnibus conductor has hardly time to love his own wife, let alone other people's. G. K. CHESTERTON

No money is better spent than what is laid out for domestick satisfaction. A man is pleased that his wife is drest as well as other people; and a wife is pleased that she is drest. SAMUEL JOHNSON

Warburg's old friend said to Warburg one day, talking about his wife, who was ill, 'If God were to take one or the other of us, I should go and live in Paris.'
SAMUEL BUTLER

Avoid wine and women—choose a freckle-faced girl for a wife; they are invariably more amiable.
SIR WILLIAM OSLER

When we think we are making a great hit with the world we don't know what our own wives think of us. FINLEY PETER DUNNE

Variability is one of the virtues of a woman. It avoids the crude requirement of polygamy. So long as you have one good wife you are sure to have a spiritual harem.
G. K. CHESTERTON

The true index of a man's character is the health of his wife.
CYRIL CONNOLLY

See also **Husband, Marriage, Married, Woman.**

WILL

You can capture the commander-in-chief of three armies, but you cannot overcome a private man's will. CONFUCIUS

Ask not that events should happen as you will, but let your will be that events should happen as they do, and you shall have peace.
EPICTETUS

Character is a perfectly educated will. NOVALIS

The will is that which has all power; it makes heaven and it makes hell; for there is no hell but where the will of the creature is turned from God, nor any heaven but where the will of the creature worketh with God. WILLIAM LAW

If I repeat 'My will be done,' with the necessary degree of faith and persistency, the chances are that, sooner or later and somehow or other, I shall get what I want. Whether my will coincides with the will of God, and whether in getting what I want I shall get what is spiritually, morally or even materially good for me are questions which I cannot answer in advance.
ALDOUS HUXLEY

See also **Free Will, Last Will, Will of God, Will Power.**

WILL OF GOD

Abide courteously and meekly the will of the Lord and snatch not overhastily as it were a greedy greyhound.
THE CLOUD OF UNKNOWING

We should ask nothing and refuse nothing, but leave ourselves in the arms of divine Providence without wasting time in any desire, except to will what God wills of us.
ST. FRANCIS DE SALES

It is against the will of God to eat delicate food hastily, to pass gorgeous views hurriedly, to express deep sentiments superficially, to pass a beautiful day steeped in food and drink, and to enjoy your wealth steeped in luxuries. CHANG CH'AO

If God wants us to do a thing. He should make His wishes sufficiently clear. Sensible people will wait till he has done this before paying much attention to Him.
SAMUEL BUTLER

See also **God, Providence.**

WILL POWER

Some of the old tomcats at the Players remember the day when Don Marquis came downstairs after a month on the wagon, ambled over to the bar, and announced: 'I've conquered that god damn will power of mine. Gimme a double scotch.'
E. B. WHITE

WIND

The winds men fear most are those that blow open their coats.
MONTAIGNE

WINE

Diogenes was asked what wine he liked best; and he answered as I would have done when he said: 'Somebody else's.' MONTAIGNE

One of the disadvantages of wine is that it makes a man mistake words for thoughts. SAMUEL JOHNSON

I think wealth has lost much of its value, if it have not wine. I abstain from wine only on account of the expense. RALPH WALDO EMERSON

Connoisseur: A specialist who knows everything about something and nothing about anything else.— An old wine-bibber having been smashed in a railway collision,

some wine was poured on his lips
to revive him. 'Pauillac, 1873,' he
murmured and died.

AMBROSE BIERCE

See also **Drinking.**

WINK

There's a time to wink as well as to
see. BENJAMIN FRANKLIN

WISDOM

Wisdom is to the soul what health
is to the body.

LA ROCHEFOUCAULD

Our wisdom is no less at the mercy
of fortune than our goods.

LA ROCHEFOUCAULD

Nothing shows more clearly the
lack of wisdom and philosophy
than the wish to have all of life full
of wisdom and philosophy.

GIACOMO LEOPARDI

See also **Common Sense, Know-
ledge and Wisdom, Wisdom and
Folly, Wisdom and Ignorance,
Wisdom and Learning, Wise.**

WISDOM AND FOLLY

The wise generally die after they
have lost their reason: fools before
they have found it.

BALTASAR GRACIÁN

The wise does at once what the
fool does at last.

BALTASAR GRACIÁN

A fool's paradise is a wise man's
hell. THOMAS FULLER

It is great folly to wish only to be
wise. LA ROCHEFOUCAULD

He who lives without folly is
hardly so wise as he thinks.

LA ROCHEFOUCAULD

Fools and wise men are equally
harmless. It is the half-fools and
the half-wise that are dangerous.

GOETHE

WISDOM AND IGNOR-
ANCE

The greatest wisdom often consists
in ignorance, or the pretense of it.

BALTASAR GRACIÁN

WISDOM AND LEARNING

Those who are wise have no wide
range of learning; those who range
most widely are not wise.

LAO-TSE

No man is the wiser for his learning. JOHN SELDEN

Learning sleeps and snores in
libraries, but wisdom is everywhere, wide awake, on tiptoes.

JOSH BILLINGS

WISE

The wise man is informed in what
is right. The inferior man is informed in what will pay.

CONFUCIUS

The heart of the wise, like a mirror,
should reflect all objects, without
being sullied by any. CONFUCIUS

The truly wise make no plans, and
therefore require no wisdom.

CHUANG-TSE

It is far easier to be wise for others
than to be so for oneself.

LA ROCHEFOUCAULD

He is really wise who is nettled at
nothing. LA ROCHEFOUCAULD

He who is only wise lives a sad
life. VOLTAIRE

The tigers of wrath are wiser than
the horses of instruction.

WILLIAM BLAKE

(Of Daniel Webster:) God Almighty never created a man half as
wise as he looks.

THOMAS CARLYLE

Slowly but surely humanity realizes the dreams of the wise.

ANATOLE FRANCE

See also **Clever, Intelligent, Wisdom.**

WISH

Leave something to wish for, so as not to be miserable from very happiness. BALTASAR GRACIÁN

Most men let their wishes run away with them. They have no mind to stop them in their career, the motion is so pleasing.

LORD HALIFAX

It is well that we know not all our wishes. LA ROCHEFOUCAULD

If a man could have half his wishes, he would double his troubles.

BENJAMIN FRANKLIN

The vanity of human wishes. There is only one thing vainer than this, and that is the having no wishes.

SAMUEL BUTLER

All thinking is wishful, and we cannot think until our wishes or fears or cupidities or curiosities create what we call attention.

GEORGE BERNARD SHAW

See also **Desire.**

WIT

Wit without an employment is a disease. ROBERT BURTON

He that will give himself to all manner of ways to get money, may be rich; so he that lets fly all he knows or thinks, may by chance be satirically witty. Honesty sometimes keeps a man from growing rich, and civility from being witty.

JOHN SELDEN

Many get the repute of being witty, but thereby lose the credit of being sensible. BALTASAR GRACIÁN

If it was not for the company of fools, a witty man would often be greatly at a loss.

LA ROCHEFOUCAULD

Wit consists in knowing the resemblance of things that differ, and the difference of things that are alike. MADAME DE STAËL

Wit is the rarest quality to be met with among people of education, and the most common among the uneducated. WILLIAM HAZLITT

A wise man will live as much within his wit as his income.

LORD CHESTERFIELD

Wit is the clash and reconcilement of incongruities, the meeting of extremes round a corner.

LEIGH HUNT

Wit is the sudden marriage of ideas which before their marriage were not perceived to have any relation.

MARK TWAIN

Wit is the epitaph of an emotion.

FRIEDRICH NIETZSCHE

See also **Comic, Funny, Humour, Joke, Wit and Humour.**

WIT AND HUMOUR

Humour is consistent with pathos, whilst wit is not.

SAMUEL TAYLOR COLERIDGE

Wit and Humour—if any difference it is in duration—lightning and electric light. Same material, apparently; but one is vivid, and can do damage—the other fools along and enjoys elaboration.

MARK TWAIN

See also **Humour, Wit.**

WOMAN

There is no load heavier than a light woman. CERVANTES

Every woman is a science.

JOHN DONNE

A woman may like science, but all sciences are not suitable for her, and the doctrines of certain sciences never become her, and when applied to her are always false.
LA ROCHEFOUCAULD

The nakedness of woman is the work of God. WILLIAM BLAKE

I don't know of anything better than a woman if you want to spend money where it'll show.
KIN HUBBARD

Nature is in earnest when she makes a woman.
OLIVER WENDELL HOLMES, SR.

What, sir, would the people of the earth be without woman? They would be scarce, sir, almighty scarce. MARK TWAIN

A woman who is confuted is never convinced.
JOHN CHURTON COLLINS

A woman never loafs: she shops, entertains, and visits.
E. W. HOWE

The charms of a passing woman are usually in direct relation to the speed of her passing.
MARCEL PROUST

A woman is incapable of feeling love for an automobile.
BERNARD DEVOTO

The only way to understand a woman is to love her—and then it isn't necessary to understand her.
SYDNEY HARRIS

See also **Women.**

WOMEN

Verily the best of women are those who are content with little.
MOHAMMED

There are few good women who do not tire of their role.
LA ROCHEFOUCAULD

Women do not know all their powers of flirtation.
LA ROCHEFOUCAULD

Women who are either indisputably beautiful, or indisputably ugly, are best flattered upon the score of their understandings.
LORD CHESTERFIELD

Women have often more of what is called *good sense* than men. They have fewer pretensions; are less implicated in theories; and judge of objects more from their immediate and involuntary impression on the mind, and, therefore, more truly and naturally. They cannot reason wrong; for they do not reason at all. WILLIAM HAZLITT

Nature has given women so much power that the law has very wisely given them little.
SAMUEL JOHNSON

There are two things I have always loved madly: they are women and celibacy. NICOLAS CHAMFORT

Women are always afraid of things which have to be divided.
HONORÉ DE BALZAC

Female: One of the opposing, or unfair, sex. AMBROSE BIERCE

Women are always on the defensive. JOHN CHURTON COLLINS

Women, as some witty Frenchman once put it, inspire us with the desire to do masterpieces, and always prevent us from carrying them out.
OSCAR WILDE

For my part I distrust *all* generalizations about women, favourable and unfavourable, masculine and feminine, ancient and modern.
BERTRAND RUSSELL

In France a man who has ruined himself for women is generally regarded with sympathy and admiration; there is a feeling that it was worth while, and the man who has done it feels even a certain pride in the fact; in England he will be thought and will think himself a damned fool.

W. SOMERSET MAUGHAM

Few women are dumb enough to listen to reason.

WILLIAM FEATHER

WOMEN AND MEN see MEN AND WOMEN

WONDER

Infinite knowledge can never wonder. All wonder is the effect of novelty upon ignorance.

SAMUEL JOHNSON

Our wisest and best teachers—the Seraphim themselves teach us—that our Maker is most seen in His works—and best adored in our wonder and admiration of them.

JOHN CONSTABLE

We must not wonder things away into nonentity.

GEORGE MACDONALD

As knowledge increases, wonder deepens.   CHARLES MORGAN

The purpose of a contemplative is to develop the faculty of wonder.

CHARLES MORGAN

WORDS

He who does not know the force of words cannot know men.

CONFUCIUS

A bait is used to catch fish. When you have got the fish, you can forget about the bait. Words are used to express meaning; when you understand the meaning, you can forget about the words.

CHUANG-TSE

An unusual word should be shunned as a ship would shun a reef.

JULIUS CAESAR

Words are feminine; deeds are masculine.   BALTASAR GRACIÁN

A man who uses a great many words to express his meaning is like a bad marksman who instead of aiming a single stone at an object takes up a handful and throws at it in hopes he may hit.

SAMUEL JOHNSON

Do not accustom yourself to use big words for little matters.

SAMUEL JOHNSON

She was not a woman of many words; for, unlike people in general, she proportioned them to the number of her ideas.

JANE AUSTEN

It is by the use of familiar words that style affects the reader. People feel that using them is the mark of a man who knows life and its daily concerns, and maintains contact with them.   JOSEPH JOUBERT

Words, like glasses, obscure everything they do not make clear.

JOSEPH JOUBERT

Before using a fine word, make a place for it!   JOSEPH JOUBERT

Words are the only things that last forever.   WILLIAM HAZLITT

The words of some men are thrown forcibly against you and adhere like burrs.

HENRY DAVID THOREAU

She couldn't help saying to herself, as she went, 'of all the unsatisfactory—' (she repeated this aloud, as it was a great comfort to have such a long word to say) 'of all the unsatisfactory people I *ever* met—'

LEWIS CARROLL

Words are an attempt to grip and dissect that which in ultimate essence is as ungrippable as a shadow.   SAMUEL BUTLER

Words are not as satisfactory as we should like them to be, but, like our neighbours, we have got to live with them and must make the best and not the worst of them.
SAMUEL BUTLER

Words are the clothes that thoughts wear—only the clothes.
SAMUEL BUTLER

I love words but I don't like strange ones. You don't understand them, and they don't understand you. Old words is like old friends, you know 'em the minute you see 'em.
WILL ROGERS

An average English word is four letters and a half. By hard, honest labour I've dug all the large words out of my vocabulary and shaved it down till the average is three and a half. . . . I never write *metropolis* for seven cents, because I can get the same price for city. I never write *policeman*, because I can get the same money for *cop*.
MARK TWAIN

The difference between the right word and the almost right word is the difference between lightning and the lightning bug.
MARK TWAIN

The finest words in the world are only vain sounds if you cannot understand them.
ANATOLE FRANCE

With all that we hear of American hustle and hurry, it is rather strange that Americans seem to like more than we do to linger upon long words. . . . They say *elevator* when we say *lift*, just as they say *automobile* when we say *motor* and *stenographer* when we say *typist*.
G. K. CHESTERTON

Short words are best and the old words when short are best of all.
WINSTON S. CHURCHILL

See also **Circumlocution, Dictionary, Language, Meaning, Spelling, Tuber, Vocabulary.**

WORDSWORTH, WILLIAM

In his youth, Wordsworth sympathized with the French Revolution, went to France, wrote good poetry, and had a natural daughter. At this period, he was a 'bad' man. Then he became 'good,' abandoned his daughter, adopted correct principles, and wrote bad poetry.
BERTRAND RUSSELL

Wordsworth went to the lakes, but he never was a lake poet. He found in stones the sermons he had already hidden there.
OSCAR WILDE

WORK

A man's own natural duty, even if it seems imperfectly done, is better than work not naturally his own, even if this is well performed. When a man acts according to the law of his nature, he cannot be sinning. Therefore, no one should give up his natural work, even though he does it imperfectly. For all action is involved in imperfection, like fire in smoke.
BHAGAVAD-GITA

Work makes a callus against grief.
CICERO

Hire yourself out to work which is beneath you rather than become dependent on others.   TALMUD

Greater even than the pious man is he who eats that which is the fruit of his own toil; for Scripture declares him twice-blessed.   TALMUD

An ounce of work is worth many pounds of words.
ST. FRANCIS DE SALES

It is equally unfortunate to waste your precious life in mechanical tasks or in a profusion of important work. BALTASAR GRACIÁN

The labour of the body frees us from the pains of the mind, and thus makes the poor happy.
LA ROCHEFOUCAULD

Do all the work you can: that is the whole philosophy of the good way of life. EUGÈNE DELACROIX

A man who has work that suits him and a wife whom he loves, has squared his accounts with life.
HEGEL

No man loves labour for itself.
SAMUEL JOHNSON

The crowning fortune of a man is to be born to some pursuit which finds him employment and happiness, whether it be to make baskets, or broadswords, or canals, or statues, or songs.
RALPH WALDO EMERSON

'If you've got to make pitch hot, you can't make it too hot, and if you swab a deck you should swab it as if Davy Jones was after you.'
CHARLES DICKENS

Those who work much do not work hard.
HENRY DAVID THOREAU

As a remedy against all ills—poverty, sickness, and melancholy—only one thing is absolutely necessary: *a liking for work*.
CHARLES BAUDELAIRE

One must work, if not from inclination, at least out of despair—since it proves, on close examination, that work is less boring than amusing oneself.
CHARLES BAUDELAIRE

Work! God wills it. That, it seems to me, is clear.
GUSTAVE FLAUBERT

Work with some men is as besetting a sin as idleness. SAMUEL BUTLER

Let us be grateful to Adam our benefactor. He cut us out of the 'blessing' of idleness and won for us the 'curse' of labour.
MARK TWAIN

I do not like work even when another person does it.
MARK TWAIN

One must work, nothing but work. And one must have patience.
RODIN

It's no credit to anyone to work too hard. E. W. HOWE

Work is love made visible.
KAHLIL GIBRAN

The very last thing the ordinary industrial worker wants is to have to think about his work.
GEORGE BERNARD SHAW

Stew Nugent has decided to go to work till he can find something better. KIN HUBBARD

What we call 'creative work' ought not to be called work at all, because it isn't. . . . I imagine that Thomas Edison never did a day's work in his last fifty years.
STEPHEN LEACOCK

Happiness, I have discovered, is nearly always a rebound from hard work. DAVID GRAYSON

I think that there is far too much work done in the world, that immense harm is caused by the belief that work is virtuous, and that what needs to be preached in modern industrial countries is quite different from what always has been preached.   BERTRAND RUSSELL

Work is of two kinds: first, altering the position of matter at or near the earth's surface relatively to other such matter; second, telling other people to do so. The first kind is unpleasant and ill paid; the second is pleasant and highly paid.   BERTRAND RUSSELL

Work is what you do so that some time you won't have to do it any more.   ALFRED POLGAR

There are only two sure means of forgetfulness known to man—work and drink—and, of the two, work is the more economical.   ROBERT LYND

You work that you may keep pace with the earth and the soul of the earth.   KAHLIL GIBRAN

Work is a form of nervousness.   DON HEROLD

'Don't you ever feel like work?' a lazy boy was asked, and he answered: 'Yes, sir, but I do without.'   SALVADOR DE MADARIAGA

Anyone can do any amount of work, provided it isn't the work he is *supposed* to be doing at that moment.   ROBERT BENCHLEY

Like every man of sense and good feeling, I abominate work.   ALDOUS HUXLEY

See also **Drudgery, Employment, Job, Routine.**

WORK OF ART

A man's work whether in music, painting or literature is always a portrait of himself. SAMUEL BUTLER

See also **Art, Masterpiece.**

WORLD

Man draws the nearer to God as he withdraws further from the consolations of this world.   THOMAS À KEMPIS

The world is nothing but an endless seesaw.   MONTAIGNE

Every man's nose will not make a shoehorn. Let us leave the world as it is.   CERVANTES

The world, which took but six days to make, is like to take six thousand years to make out.   SIR THOMAS BROWNE

It is the fools and knaves that make the wheels of the world turn. *They* are the *world*; those few who have sense or honesty sneak up and down single, but never go in herds.   LORD HALIFAX

To understand the world and to like it are two things not easily to be reconciled.   LORD HALIFAX

You should live in the world so as it may hang about you like a loose garment.   LORD HALIFAX

Pretend not thou to scorn the pomp of the world before thou knowest it.   DR. THOMAS FULLER

When I reflect back upon what I have seen, what I have heard, and what I have done myself, I can hardly persuade myself that all that frivolous hurry and bustle, and pleasures of the world, had any reality; but they seem to have been the dreams of restless nights.   LORD CHESTERFIELD

A boy being flogged at school is not so severe as a man having the hiss of the world against him.   SAMUEL JOHNSON

In seventy or eighty years, a man may have a deep gust of the world; know what it is, what it can afford, and what 'tis to have been a man.
SAMUEL TAYLOR COLERIDGE

The world is wide; no two days are alike, nor even two hours; neither was there ever two leaves of a tree alike since the creation of the world; and the genuine productions of art, like those of nature, are all distinct from each other.
JOHN CONSTABLE

Happy those who live in the dream of their own existence, and see all things in the light of their own minds; who walk by faith and hope; to whom the guiding star of their youth still shines from afar, and into whom the spirit of the world has not entered!
WILLIAM HAZLITT

The world will, in the end, follow only those who have despised as well as served it.
SAMUEL BUTLER

The ingenuity of judgment of no one man is equal to that of the world at large, which is the fruit of the experience and ability of all mankind.
WILLIAM HAZLITT

Here is the world, sound as a nut, not the smallest piece of chaos left, never a stitch nor an end, not a mark of haste, or botching, or second thought; but the theory of the world is a thing of shreds and patches.
RALPH WALDO EMERSON

It is not given to the children of men to be philosophers without envy. Lookers-on can hardly bear the spectacle of the great world.
WALTER BAGEHOT

It is no part of God's scheme that any very large number of people in this world should be positively wise, good, and well-to-do. If it had been, He would have taken measures to ensure that such should be the case.
SAMUEL BUTLER

One is happy in the world only when one forgets the world.
ANATOLE FRANCE

We are told that when Jehovah created the world He saw that it was good. What would He say now?
GEORGE BERNARD SHAW

A man's feet should be planted in his country, but his eyes should survey the world.
GEORGE SANTAYANA

The world ain't getting no worse; we've only got better facilities.
KIN HUBBARD

The world was not created once and for all for each of us. In the course of life things that we never even imagined are added to it.
MARCEL PROUST

The world gets better every day—then worse again in the evening.
KIN HUBBARD

The globe-trotter lives in a smaller world than the peasant.
G. K. CHESTERTON

If we were tomorrow morning snowed up in the street in which we live, we should step suddenly into a much larger and much wilder world than we have ever known.
G. K. CHESTERTON

God rules the world not from the outside, not by gravity and chemical affinity, but in the hearts of men: as your soul is, so is the fate of the world you live in and move in. Nothing is outside.
EGON FRIEDELL

The world is whatever is the case.
LUDWIG WITTGENSTEIN

Every day is a miracle. The world gets up in the morning and is fed and goes to work, and in the evening it comes home and is fed again and perhaps has a little amusement and goes to sleep. To make that possible, so much has to be done by so many people that, on the face of it, it is impossible. Well, every day we do it; and every day, come hell, come high water, we're going to have to go on doing it as well as we can.   JAMES GOULD COZZENS

See also **Universe.**

WORM

You can straighten a worm, but the crook is in him and only waiting.
MARK TWAIN

WORRY

We can always get along better by reason and love of truth than by worry of conscience and remorse. Harmful are these and evil, inasmuch as they form a particular kind of sadness; and the disadvantages of sadness I have already proved, and shown that we should strive to keep it from our life.   SPINOZA

Happy is the man who has broken the chains which hurt the mind, and has given up worrying once and for all.   OVID

I looked through the list of diseases and couldn't find worry and melancholy thoughts among them: this is quite wrong.   G. C. LICHTENBERG

The worst thing you can possibly do is worrying and thinking about what you could have done.
G. C. LICHTENBERG

Small worries are worst when we are idle and are often dispersed by motion like a flock of gnats.
CHARLES HORTON COOLEY

As soon as a wife presents her husband with a child, her capacity for worry becomes acuter: she hears more burglars, she smells more things burning, she begins to wonder, at the theatre or the dance, whether her husband left his service revolver in the nursery.
JAMES THURBER

See also **Anxiety, Fret.**

WORSHIP

There is not one command in all the Gospel for public worship. ... The frequent attendance at it is never so much as mentioned in all the New Testament.
WILLIAM LAW

For the Christian who loves God, worship is the daily bread of patience.   HONORÉ DE BALZAC

There is simply no other way of worshipping God than doing your duty and acting according to the rules of reason.
G. C. LICHTENBERG

See also **Prayer.**

WRITER

Even the best writers talk too much.   VAUVENARGUES

The only impeccable writers are those that never wrote.
WILLIAM HAZLITT

Writers, like teeth, are divided into incisors and grinders.
WALTER BAGEHOT

There is no need for the writer to eat a whole sheep to be able to tell you what mutton tastes like. It is enough if he eats a cutlet. But he should do that.
W. SOMERSET MAUGHAM

It is by reading that the foreigner will gain most insight into a strange people, and here writers of the second class will be of more service to him than those of the first. . . . Chekhov will tell you more about the Russians than Dostoyevsky.

W. SOMERSET MAUGHAM

The writer must be willing, above everything else, to take chances, to risk making a fool of himself—or even to risk revealing the fact that he *is* a fool. JESSAMYN WEST

See also **Author, Writing.**

WRITING

The man who writes a good book while sitting in torn breeches should first mend his breeches.

MONTAIGNE

I never set pen on paper except when an overdose of idleness drives me to it. MONTAIGNE

It is the glory and merit of some men to write well, and of others not to write at all.

JEAN DE LA BRUYÈRE

No man but a blockhead ever wrote, except for money.

SAMUEL JOHNSON

When a man writes from his own mind, he writes very rapidly. The greater part of a writer's time is spent in reading, in order to write; a man will turn over half a library to make one book.

SAMUEL JOHNSON

A man may write at any time, if he will set himself doggedly to it.

SAMUEL JOHNSON

The ancients wrote at a time when the great art of writing badly had not yet been invented. In those days to write at all meant to write well.

G. C. LICHTENBERG

There is something in our minds like sunshine and the weather, which is not under our control. When I write, the best things come to me from I know not where.

G. C. LICHTENBERG

The more a man writes, the more he can write. WILLIAM HAZLITT

In the field opposite the window where I write this, there is a country-girl picking stones: in the one next it, there are several poor women weeding the blue and red flowers from the corn: farther on, are two boys, tending a flock of sheep. What do they know or care about what I am writing about them, or ever will?—or what would they be the better for it, if they did? WILLIAM HAZLITT

We cannot write well or truly but what we write with gusto.

HENRY DAVID THOREAU

Whilst writing the *Chartreuse*, in order to acquire the correct tone I read every morning two or three pages of the Civil Code. STENDHAL

The man who writes a book imposes upon himself the obligation of not contradicting himself. . . . The lack of sincerity that any man of good faith will find in all the books or in almost all, comes from this ridiculous desire to get the thought of the moment into harmony with that of the day before.

EUGÈNE DELACROIX

I am a natural reader, and only a writer in the absence of natural writers. In a true time, I should never have written.

RALPH WALDO EMERSON

Good writing is a kind of skating which carries off the performer where he would not go.

RALPH WALDO EMERSON

Write without pay until somebody offers pay. If nobody offers within three years the candidate may look upon this circumstance with the most implicit confidence as the sign that sawing wood is what he was intended for. MARK TWAIN

It is often harder to boil down than to write. SIR WILLIAM OSLER

A man really writes for an audience of about ten persons. Of course if others like it, that is clear gain. But if those ten are satisfied, he is content.
ALFRED NORTH WHITEHEAD

Writing a book was an adventure. To begin with, it was a toy, and amusement; then it became a mistress, and then a master, and then a tyrant. WINSTON S. CHURCHILL

If you require a practical rule of me, I will present you with this: Whenever you feel an impulse to perpetrate a piece of exceptionally fine writing, obey it—whole-heartedly —and delete it before sending your manuscript to press. *Murder your darlings.*
SIR ARTHUR QUILLER-COUCH

Once a lady who had a son of a literary bent asked me what training I should advise if he was to become a writer; and I replied: 'Give him a hundred and fifty a year for five years and tell him to go to the devil.' W. SOMERSET MAUGHAM

The four greatest novelists the world has ever known, Balzac, Dickens, Tolstoy and Dostoyevsky, wrote their respective languages very indifferently. It proves that if you can tell stories, create character, devise incidents, and if you have sincerity and passion, it doesn't matter a damn how you write. W. SOMERSET MAUGHAM

Modern writing at its worst . . . consists in gumming together long strips of words which have already been set in order by someone else, and making the results presentable by sheer humbug. The attraction of this way of writing is that it is easy. It is easier—even quicker, once you have the habit—to say *In my opinion it is not an unjustifiable assumption that* than to say *I think*
GEORGE ORWELL

See also **Description, History Writing, Novel, Playwriting, Prose, Story, Style, Writer, Written.**

WRITTEN

What is written is merely the dregs of experience. ·FRANZ KAFKA

The most intelligible part of language is not the words, but the tone, force, modulation, tempo in which a group of words are spoken —that is, the music behind the words, the emotion behind that music, the person behind that emotion: everything that cannot be written. This is what defeats authorship.
FRIEDRICH NIETZSCHE

There is a sort of magic in the written word. The idea acquires substance by taking on a visible nature, and then stands in the way of its own clarification.
W. SOMERSET MAUGHAM

See also **Books.**

WRONG

I am not more certain that I breathe, than that the assurance of the wrong or error of any action is often the one unconquerable *force* which impels us, and alone impels us to its prosecution.
EDGAR ALLAN POE

It is not a man's duty, as a matter of course, to devote himself to the eradication of any, even the most enormous wrong; he may still properly have other concerns to engage him; but it is his duty, at least, to wash his hands of it, and, if he gives it no thought longer, not to give it practically his support.

HENRY DAVID THOREAU

The fellow that says, 'I may be wrong, but—' does not believe there can be any such possibility.

KIN HUBBARD

There is a moral element in us that makes us like to know that we are doing wrong when we are doing it.

ROBERT LYND

See also **Right and Wrong.**

X

X RAYS

Their moral is this—that a right way of looking at things will see through almost anything.

SAMUEL BUTLER

Y

YES

The tepid yes of a remarkable man is worth more than all the applause of the vulgar.

BALTASAR GRACIÁN

See also **Affirmation, Yes and No.**

YES AND NO

A gilded no is more satisfactory than a dry yes.

BALTASAR GRACIÁN

I like the sayers of no better than the sayers of yes.

RALPH WALDO EMERSON

One half the troubles of this life can be traced to saying yes too quick, and not saying no soon enough.

JOSH BILLINGS

See also **No, Yes.**

YESTERDAY

Procrastination is the art of keeping up with yesterday.

DON MARQUIS

YOUNG

Meek young men grow up in libraries, believing it their duty to accept the views which Cicero, which Locke, which Bacon, have given; forgetful that Cicero, Locke, and Bacon were only young men in libraries when they wrote these books. RALPH WALDO EMERSON

Address yourself to young people; they know everything.

JOSEPH JOUBERT

Most young people think they are natural when they are only boorish and rude. LA ROCHEFOUCAULD

No wise man ever wished to be younger. JONATHAN SWIFT

For God's sake give me the young man who has brains enough to make a fool of himself!

ROBERT LOUIS STEVENSON

One of the hardest things to realize, specially for a young man, is that our forefathers were living men who really knew something.

RUDYARD KIPLING

What is more enchanting than the voices of young people, when you can't hear what they say?

LOGAN PEARSALL SMITH

I love to discuss problems with young people because their problems are so simple and can be solved with a few dollars.

WILLIAM FEATHER

Nobody can be so amusingly arrogant as a young man who has just discovered an old idea and thinks it is his own. SYDNEY HARRIS

See also **Young and Old, Youth.**

YOUNG AND OLD

Old boys have their playthings as well as young ones; the difference is only in the price.

BENJAMIN FRANKLIN

I avoid talking before the youth of the age as I would dancing before them; for if one's tongue don't move in the steps of the day, and thinks to please by its old graces, it is only an object of ridicule.

HORACE WALPOLE

What you long for in youth, you get aplenty in old age. GOETHE

The old know what they want; the young are sad and bewildered.

LOGAN PEARSALL SMITH

We never really feel older than other people but only different, to our advantage or disadvantage, in some particular; whereas we always do feel definitely younger than other people. J. B. PRIESTLEY

See also **Age, Old Age, Young, Youth.**

YOUTH

Youth is a continual intoxication; it is the fever of reason.

LA ROCHEFOUCAULD

'Tis a maxim with me to be young as long as one can: there is nothing can pay one for that invaluable ignorance which is the companion of youth; those sanguine groundless hopes, and that lively vanity, which make all the happiness of life. To my extreme mortification I grow wiser every day.

LADY MARY WORTLEY MONTAGU

If youth is a fault one soon gets rid of it. GOETHE

To get back one's youth, one has merely to repeat one's follies.

OSCAR WILDE

It is absurd to talk of the ignorance of youth. The only people to whose opinions I listen now with any respect are people much younger than myself. They seem in front of me. OSCAR WILDE

I remember my youth and the feeling that will never come back any more—the feeling that I could last forever, outlast the sea, the earth, and all men. JOSEPH CONRAD

See also **Age, Young, Young and Old.**

Z

ZOO

Q. If you find so much that is unworthy of reverence in the United States, then why do you live here? A. Why do men go to zoos?

H. L. MENCKEN

INDEX